MW00996578

I'd like every student to read Darrow Miller's c⌐ to battle dualism and the sacred-secular dichotomy. He brilliantly shows how to live and work before God and why it's so important to grasp the biblical theology of vocation. His summary of the Bible's essential metanarrative is pitch-perfect, and his application of that to cultural pursuits is exactly what those who waver need to hear.

MARVIN OLASKY
PROVOST, THE KING'S COLLEGE, NEW YORK CITY
EDITOR-IN-CHIEF, WORLD

Having worked among the poorest of the poor, Darrow Miller has credibility when he writes about the sources of poverty. With his characteristic thoroughness and gentleness, he builds a case for the worldview basis of work and wealth creation.

NANCY PEARCEY
AUTHOR OF TOTAL TRUTH AND COAUTHOR OF HOW NOW SHALL WE LIVE?

LifeWork provides the essentials for transforming nations. In this book you will discover tools for renewing the culture of your cities and nations. LifeWork contains the fundamentals for the fulfillment of Jesus' prayer for God's kingdom to come and his will to be done on earth.

LUIS BUSH
INTERNATIONAL FACILITATOR, TRANSFORM WORLD CONNECTIONS

Darrow has spent a lifetime trying to help Christians worldwide to rediscover the biblical concept of the kingdom of God. How tragic it is that the central mission of Jesus Christ (Luke 4:43) is so foreign to our thoughts, our affections, and our behaviors. How marvelous it is that Lifework reintroduces us again to the wonder of the kingdom and our role in it. This book is vintage Darrow, full of passion, biblical insight, penetrating analysis, and practical application. It is a must read for every Christian in the twenty-first century.

BRIAN FIKKERT
EXECUTIVE DIRECTOR, CHALMERS CENTER FOR ECONOMIC DEVELOPMENT, COVENANT COLLEGE
COAUTHOR OF WHEN HELPING HURTS

We envision the church joined together in every community around the world effectively living out and proclaiming the good news of Jesus. These allied churches seek transformation, holiness, and justice for individuals, families, communities, peoples, and nations. Such a vision requires a significant shift in the worldview of Christians around the world. Darrow Miller's book LifeWork articulates such a worldview. It will be a great tool in helping shape the minds, hearts, and strategies of our global community.

GEOFF TUNNICLIFFE
INTERNATIONAL DIRECTOR/CEO, WORLD EVANGELICAL ALLIANCE

Finally here is a book that captures the foundational teaching on worldview that Darrow Miller has shared so effectively across the globe with Christian leaders for many years. The fruit of his work can be seen from the foothills of Nepal to the plains of West Africa, where Christians have been enabled to move beyond the church building to impact their communities because of what they learned and then applied.

JANE OVERSTREET
PRESIDENT/CEO, DEVELOPMENT ASSOCIATES INTERNATIONAL

God is clearly speaking to the body of Christ globally regarding the task of discipling our communities and serving God 24/7 in every area of our lives. Of those God has called to be forerunners, few speak with more authority and experience than Darrow Miller. For decades he has sought God and served the tribes and nations with this message. Anyone with a serious interest in the rediscovery process of the biblical message for nations will want to add this book to his or her reading list.

LANDA L. COPE
EXECUTIVE DIRECTOR, THE TEMPLATE INSTITUTE
AUTHOR OF THE OLD TESTAMENT TEMPLATE

Against the narrow, individualistic conception of the gospel that unfortunately gets preached in many evangelical churches, Miller offers the biblically accurate—and exhilarating—description of the gospel of the kingdom. Miller paints a picture of how to connect all of our life and work now to our glorious future on the New Earth. *LifeWork* enlarges vision and passion for taking up our high calling of culture making, joining King Jesus on his mission of healing our broken planet.

AMY L. SHERMAN
DIRECTOR, CENTER ON FAITH IN COMMUNITIES
SENIOR FELLOW, SAGAMORE INSTITUTE FOR POLICY RESEARCH

Darrow's book truly deserves classic status. I hope it becomes the "standard" in the field. No other book integrates the biblical worldview with the topic of work in as much depth, breadth, and balance.

CHRISTIAN OVERMAN
FOUNDING DIRECTOR, WORLDVIEW MATTERS

My teaching colleague Darrow Miller has a gift. That gift is to take a complex problem, define it in comprehendible prose, and then inspire those who read to do their part in their world. *LifeWork* is a call to action for every serious disciple.

BOB MOFFITT
PRESIDENT, THE HARVEST FOUNDATION

Darrow Miller has an exceptionally clear and biblical understanding of God and man, creation and culture, church and society, and how these should all relate to each other in a biblical worldview. He understands that men and women, made in the image of God, are intended to be designers, builders, cultivators, nurturers, administrators, teachers, artists, musicians, and communicators. Christian ministry isn't just in the church—it is in life!

LARRY G. SEARS
U.S. FOREST SERVICE RANGER (RETIRED) AND CONSULTING FORESTER

For too long Christians have constructed and maintained a wall of separation between the secular and the sacred. That mythical divide has resulted in a failure of many to live a life grounded in the reality that we are all in "full-time ministry." The effect of that barrier is the absence of the joy and satisfaction we will experience when we follow the biblical command to "glorify God in all we do." This book takes a jackhammer to that wall.

TOM SHRADER
FOUNDER, PRIORITY LIVING OF ARIZONA
TEACHING PASTOR, EAST VALLEY BIBLE CHURCH

What a book! I am convinced the way our culture is going to encounter the gospel is by individual Christians understanding and living out every aspect of their lives before the face of God as an act of worship. Darrow Miller has created an invaluable resource in helping us understand and apply the gospel to all areas of life.

TYLER JOHNSON
DIRECTOR, SURGE SCHOOL FOR TRANSFORMATIONAL LEADERSHIP

Darrow Miller integrates God's kingdom vision with essential realities and demands of the kingdom like no one else I know. Be forewarned! As you pick this book up and read it, you just might find yourself both convicted and compelled to live accordingly with an authentic, kingdom kind of life. But why would anyone settle for less?

PHIL ARENDT
DIRECTOR OF MINISTRY DEVELOPMENT, PARTNERS INTERNATIONAL

Darrow Miller's work on worldviews is more complete and practical than any I have seen. It deserves serious study and implementation by those desiring to reposition their work and businesses for the purpose of establishing God's kingdom. A helpful reference for pastors and ministry leaders alike, this book will be invaluable in their effort to build up believers to be effective and fruitful . . . wherever they go to work. Beneath the text of Darrow's writing lies a big heart to father many who will help disciple nations. I have the privilege of seeing him at work in both Asia and Africa.

SEELOK TING
CONSULTANT FACILITATOR, GROWING CHANGE AGENTS FOR THE WORKPLACE, MALAYSIA

Darrow Miller speaks a prophetic message. Rather than focusing on the symptoms of unhealthy culture, Darrow takes his readers to the cause. He challenges the assumptions of today and invites us to look deeply at the foundational principles God has given to ensure true wellness in all of life. The invitation is to be fully engaged in all of culture as ambassadors of the Living God.

DAVID COLLINS

Founder, Paradigm Ministries

The wonderful yet critical backdrop to this book is that both the author and the words have been "field tested" over decades. For those seeking keys to applying the gospel of the kingdom to all of life as opposed to within the four walls of a church building, you will be equipped to do so. This book's concepts and applications are indispensable to true followers of Christ.

MARK R. SPENGLER

Executive Director, Center for Law and Social Strategy, Kailua-Kona, Hawaii

LifeWork convicts us of dualistic thinking and behavior yet also encourages us by providing a practical framework to apply correct biblical thinking to all of life, work included. Christian businesspeople of all disciplines can see how their work and Christian lives can be reconnected and lead to more personal fulfillment while helping to advance God's kingdom. Skills and experiences gained in a life of work are part of a *life*work that knits our lives and work as one to fit God's purposes instead of separating them into distinct sacred vs. secular realms. What liberation results when we understand the eternal value our seemingly secular work can contribute to God's plan!

JOHN BOTTIMORE

International Aerospace Sales Executive

The comprehension that work is a vocation to be performed for the glory of God and service of man gave me the strong foundation for my development work among poor communities of Brazil. Personally, it's a freeing experience to understand work as a high calling, based in who God is as a worker, and perform it as an act of worship. On a community level, Darrow's teaching in this area is the base for true and lasting development.

MAURICIO J. CUNHA

Center of Integral Assistance and Development (CADI), Brazil

Darrow Miller explains that Christ will become the Lord of all when all his followers bring all of their lives under his Lordship.

VISHAL MANGALWADI

Author of *Truth and Transformation*

LifeWork is full of compelling truth, touching experiences, and compassionate calling to manifest the kingdom of God in all spheres of living. Reading it throughout or just diving into some chapters is an opportunity to review our work and life agenda with an inspiring biblical perspective, connecting our story to His Story in a practical and redemptive way.

ROBERTO RINALDI JR.
Owner, ProBusiness Consulting Services, Brazil

Darrow's book brings hope to the nations, equipping the church with practical knowledge of how the Bible speaks into every sector of culture and society. As a development practitioner working in Central Asia, I have personally witnessed how teaching, understanding, and implementing the biblical worldview impacted our program activities. It inspired and transformed church leaders and laypeople alike. It empowered the body of believers to move outside the local church to bring hope and healing to their community and nation. I have known Darrow and worked with him in Central Asia over the past decade. This book is the culmination of years of success in catalyzing transformation.

ROBERT C. HEDLUND
President and Founder, Joint Development Associates International, Inc.

LifeWork will challenge your worldview of what we should do on earth till Jesus comes. This book makes you stand up taller and live more purposefully to achieve the maximum potential you can for your spouse, children, parents, societies, and God. *LifeWork* describes faith and action as complementing each other. When they go together, they make you live enthusiastically (*enthuse* from *en-Theos,* or God in you). Get and read this book again and again, and start transforming your society and making changes to this beautiful and abundant world.

ANDY BUDI JANTO SUTEDJA
President Director, PT Success Motivation Institute, Indonesia
Representative, Discipling Nations Alliance, Indonesia

Secular dust storms have badly damaged our spiritual eyes. They have blinded us so that we believe status seeking is compatible with seeking the kingdom of God. We delight in all we own and marginalize what the Lord owns. Many of us maintain we love the Lord while we treat others with contempt. These dust storms have darkened our eyesight so we no longer see biblical moral and ethical standards as radically different than Hollywood's. Darrow Miller's book enables us to have our spiritual cataracts replaced with biblical worldview lenses so we can clearly see the good news of the gospel.

JOHN DEHAAN
Executive Director, Association of Evangelical Relief and Development
Organizations, 1998–2006

LifeWork is a breath of fresh air—a reminder and renewal of the true vision of what Christians are called to do here in this life. . . . This book reflects Darrow's long commitment to the gospel as it guides us in very real and powerful ways to what Jesus meant when he told us to "occupy until I come."

HANK GIESECKE
PRESIDENT, REACH OUT MINISTRIES

Three elements are striking in Darrow Miller: his energy, his passion, and his love for Christ and people. He is a man who practices what he preaches, seizing every opportunity—over lunch or as he walks—to lead others closer to the Redeemer and to inspire them to glorify the Lord in every aspect of their lives. God be praised for raising such a man for a time such as this.

FERNANDO GUARANY JR.
ESL TEACHER AND TRANSLATOR, INSTITUTO DE EDUCAÇÃO CRISTÃ IMAGO DEI, BRAZIL

I have known Darrow since 1998 and have used his materials on worldview and development in my teaching. . . . His book *Discipling Nations* is required reading in my classes. Darrow has that unique gift of discussing and writing about his topics in a way that's challenging, transforming, and life-changing to his listeners and readers. I myself am one of the many who have been influenced and transformed by his writings and speaking. All pastors and Christian leaders, as well as those in the academe, should make sure that they read his books, especially his latest, *LifeWork*.

REYNALDO S. TANIAJURA
FACULTY, INTERNATIONAL GRADUATE SCHOOL OF LEADERSHIP AND ASIAN SCHOOL OF
DEVELOPMENT AND CROSS-CULTURAL STUDIES

God's dream is "global transformation," and it will become reality when the walls of the church collapse and old paradigms are demolished. The day of the saints is coming when all believers are equipped to release the kingdom every day and everywhere. This Ezekiel 37 army will trigger transformation in every aspect of culture. If you want to be part of God's dream, you must read Darrow Miller's *LifeWork*.

DAVE GUSTAVESON
DIRECTOR, YWAM LOS ANGELES AND GLOBAL TARGET NETWORK

*Life*WORK

OTHER BOOKS BY DARROW L. MILLER

Discipling Nations: The Power of Truth to Transform Cultures,
with Stan Guthrie

God's Remarkable Plan for the Nations,
with Scott Allen and Bob Moffitt

God's Unshakable Kingdom,
with Scott Allen and Bob Moffitt

The Worldview of the Kingdom of God,
with Scott Allen and Bob Moffitt

Against All Hope: Hope for Africa,
with Scott Allen and the African Working Group of Samaritan Strategy Africa

On Earth As It Is in Heaven: Making It Happen,
with Bob Moffitt

The Forest in the Seed,
with Scott Allen

Nurturing the Nations: Reclaiming the Dignity of Women
in Building Healthy Cultures,
with Stan Guthrie

A BIBLICAL THEOLOGY FOR
WHAT YOU DO EVERY DAY

*Life*WORK

DARROW L. MILLER

WITH MARIT NEWTON

P.O. BOX 55787 / SEATTLE, WA 98155

YWAM Publishing is the publishing ministry of Youth With A Mission. Youth With A Mission (YWAM) is an international missionary organization of Christians from many denominations dedicated to presenting Jesus Christ to this generation. To this end, YWAM has focused its efforts in three main areas: (1) training and equipping believers for their part in fulfilling the Great Commission (Matthew 28:19), (2) personal evangelism, and (3) mercy ministry (medical and relief work).

For a free catalog of books and materials, call (425) 771-1153 or (800) 922-2143. Visit us online at www.ywampublishing.com.

LifeWork: A Biblical Theology for What You Do Every Day
Copyright © 2009 by Darrow L. Miller

Published by YWAM Publishing
a ministry of Youth With A Mission
P.O. Box 55787, Seattle, WA 98155

14 13 12 11 10 09   1 2 3 4 5

ISBN 978-1-57658-406-4

All rights reserved. No part of this book may be reproduced in any form without permission in writing from the publisher, except in the case of brief quotations in critical articles or reviews.

Unless otherwise noted, Scripture quotations in this book are taken from the HOLY BIBLE, NEW INTERNATIONAL VERSION®. NIV®. Copyright © 1973, 1978, 1984 by International Bible Society. Used by permission of Zondervan. All rights reserved.

Library of Congress Cataloging-in-Publication Data
Miller, Darrow L.
    LifeWork : a biblical theology for what you do every day / Darrow L. Miller with Marit Newton.
        p. cm.
    Includes bibliographical references and indexes.
    ISBN 978-1-57658-406-4
    1. Vocation—Christianity. 2. Vocation—Biblical teaching. I. Newton, Marit, 1976– II. Title. III. Title: Life work.
    BV4740.M52 2009
    248.4—dc22   2008049872

Printed in the United States of America

To Francis Schaeffer and Loren and Darlene Cunningham

Dr. Schaeffer had hoped that God would use L'Abri Fellowship to inspire Christians to take the gospel into every sector of society. His sermon "Occupy Till I Come!" provided the genesis for my reflection on this subject.

Loren and Darlene Cunningham founded Youth With A Mission (YWAM) with a similar vision. Their heart has been to raise up Christians to flood the continents with nation builders.

May this book contribute to their hopes and legacies!

CONTENTS

The parable of the ten minas in <u>Luke 19</u> has been my takeoff point for this book. (This parable is also known as the parable of the talents, or the pounds, or the gold coins, depending on which translation you read.) Jesus used this parable to teach his disciples about the kingdom of God and to correct their mistaken view of it—"that the kingdom of God was going to appear at once" (Luke 19:11)—as they approached Jerusalem. Through it, he conveyed a new way of understanding who he was, who they were, and what their lives and their work were all about in relation to the kingdom of God. And through it he instructs and encourages us, too, to live and work actively in and for God's coming kingdom.

My mentor, the late Francis Schaeffer—evangelist, apologist, prophet to our generation, and founder of L'Abri—drew my attention to the parable of the minas many years ago when I was living and studying at L'Abri Fellowship in Switzerland. It greatly inspired me, and for years my heart's message was expressed in a lecture titled "Occupy Till I Come!"—a phrase from the parable as it is translated in the King James Version, in Luke 19:13. Further, my friends Moses Kim, of YWAM's University of the Nations in Hawaii, and Dr. Robert Osburn, of the MacLaurin Institute at the University of Minnesota, challenged me to develop and write Bible studies on the theme of a biblical theology of vocation. Now, after years of teaching on the subject, the time has come to place those teachings in a book.

Thanks go to Dr. George Grant of King's Meadow Study Center, who at a particularly vulnerable time in the writing of this book offered his team to provide editorial assistance. Without Dr. Grant's encouragement and help, this project would not have come to completion.

To Cindy Benn, Sarah Gammill, Lindsay Lavery, and especially Mandie Miller, who have labored tirelessly on this project in research, data entry, word processing, fact checking, and editing.

To my colaborer and friend Scott Allen, who has dialoged, critiqued, and contributed ideas to the book.

To my editor Marit Newton and publisher Warren Walsh at YWAM Publishing, my great appreciation. Their goal has been to help me communicate this message as clearly and powerfully as possible. They have stood behind my vision and have wanted the book to speak to people so effectively that they become players in making it a reality. The success of this book will largely be a product of their farsightedness, hard work, commitment, and partnership. They have gone "beyond the call of duty" to see that *LifeWork* sees the light of day.

To the hundreds of people over the years who have heard the oral presentation of this material as *LifeWork* and the *Biblical Theology of Vocation* and have encouraged me to write this book. Your belief in the importance of this message has kept me going during the years of working on this project.

To Marilyn, my beloved wife and life partner, who in addition to loving me has spent countless hours editing the book.

To our Creator, who has given our lives purpose and who has set us on this small planet and called us to be creators of culture for his glory!

INTRODUCTION

A number of years ago, a missionary to the Philippines met with some young people who were thinking of joining the Maoist rebels. The missionary asked the leader of the group what he had found so compelling in Maoism that he could not experience in Christianity. The young man's answer proved a profound critique, not of Christ and his claims but of the reality and practice of Christianity today:

> Maoism provides us...with four essential things: (1) a unified and coherent vision of the world, history and reality; (2) a definite goal to work for, live for, and die for; (3) a call to all people for a common fraternity; and (4) a sense of commitment and a mission to spread the good news that there is hope for the hopeless. The fact is that the Christian faith in all its beauty seems to be unable to provide us with such a vision.[1]

Sadly the missionary watched these young and idealistic people turn their backs on what they knew of Christianity and embrace something that would lead to their destruction. But why? They may have heard the good news of the gospel, but they had not *seen* the gospel.

Too often, the church is busy proclaiming the gospel but not demonstrating the gospel. We say the words but do not live the life. Often our lives as Christians are ineffective because we have reduced the gospel to good news for eternity and have forgotten the good news for today. Too often we understand our lives as having two distinct, separate parts: the spiritual part of life and the rest of life, our time in religious activities and our time at school or work. We have reduced Christianity to the personal and private sphere, living everyday lives little different from those of others in our society. We have created a comfortable church but one that is largely disengaged from the realities of everyday life in the marketplace, at home and abroad. Thus we have failed to open the truth and hope of the kingdom of God to the millions needing better answers than those offered by other religions or secularism.

However, there is a stirring among some Christians, who are asking, Should not the gospel influence all of life and even help to shape my nation? Shouldn't the gospel impact the marketplace, my work? Do I have to leave my job and become a missionary in order for my life to count for something in the kingdom of God?

A growing group of pastors is asking, Isn't there supposed to be something more to church than buildings, meetings, and programs? How can we get our people out of the building and into the world, where the needs and the needy are? Should not the church have an influence on society? Why are our families, communities, and societies falling apart when there are so many Christians? Never in history have there been more Christians, more churches, and more large churches than there are today, so why are societies so broken?

While many Christians and churches are happy with their comfortable life and church program, while they are happy in their proclamation of the gospel, at the same time many people—the poor, the skeptics, those with the postmodern mind of the early twenty-first century—are waiting to "hear" with their eyes. Words are not enough! They want to see the truth, beauty, and justice of the gospel lived out before their eyes. And too often, the church is busy proclaiming and not living!

The very things the young Filipinos and much of the rest of the world are looking for—a coherent view of reality, something to live for and die for, a sense of community, and something that would bring hope to the hopeless—are nothing less than what they were made for and what Christ gave himself for: the kingdom of God. The world is waiting to see this kingdom demonstrated through our lives and in our daily work.

THE COMPELLING VISION

You, too, were made for the very thing for which the young Filipinos were longing. All men and women were made to live in the reality that God has made, the reality of the kingdom of God. Vision—compelling vision—is one of the most basic of all human needs. This is affirmed in Scripture: "Where there is no vision, the people perish" (Prov. 29:18 KJV). All of our lives are driven by a vision of some kind. But not all visions are true, nor are they equally fulfilling.

Our vision comes from our *worldview*, how we understand the universe and our relationship to it. Our worldview shapes our values and our decisions, and it tells us what is most important in our lives. Because it determines what we see in our lives and in the world around us and *how* we see it, we often use the term *spectacles* to describe this factor in our existence. It is the "spectacles" through which we look at the world that determine our vision of life—and our vision *for* our lives.

The worldview through which we are to live our lives is nothing less than the compelling vision for which Christ lived and died, the kingdom of God. He described this vision as a fire: "I have come to bring fire on the earth, and how I wish it were already kindled!" (Luke 12:49).

Does Christ's vision drive the church today? E. Stanley Jones (1884–1973), the great missionary statesman to India, sadly stated, "The church has lost it. The church has lost [the biblical vision of] the Kingdom of God."[2] Jones describes this loss of vision as "the sickness of our age."[3]

As the church enters the twenty-first century, she is largely divided into two groups, each with a very different understanding of the kingdom of God. The first understands the kingdom of God as mystical, invisible, heavenly, and in the future. These Christians state that Jesus is Lord of all but his kingdom will affect things here on earth only when Christ returns at the end of history. The second group, in contrast, understands that the kingdom of God is to make a difference here and now. Too often, however, these people focus on social and political concerns and using human means to establish God's kingdom now to the exclusion of evangelism and future aspects of the kingdom. Each of these views is misshapen and incomplete.

Most simply stated, the kingdom of God exists wherever God reigns. That "wherever" has no limit in time, location, or realm. Almighty God, who always was, is, and shall be, is King of both the heavens and the earth. He is Lord of history as well as eternity. He is living and present in both the spiritual and material realms. And very important for our purpose here, it is he who defines by his very nature what is true, good, and beautiful. As was recognized by the earliest modern scientists, though too often forgotten later, even the seemingly impersonal "natural laws" come from the divine mind—the way he made our world to operate.

Unfortunately, in their rebellion, human beings lost the ability to live wholly within that divine framework for which they were created, as related in Genesis 3. The kingdom didn't go away, but in rebelling against its ways, people wound up losing even the ability to see and understand it, to be able to restore themselves within it. Instead they created lives based on an illusion of reality that was in sharp conflict with God's kingdom. So far removed from the truth of existence, this counterfeit kingdom and its patchwork of lies was inevitably a way of death.

God never abandoned his creation to this failure, however. The Bible narrative is one of God reaching out to us, revealing the truth of himself to us, and calling us back into his kingdom and true fullness of life with him. Finally, he does the unimaginable and reaches straight to the heart of our existence with the gift of his Son, who most fully reveals the nature of our God and what life in union with him means, and throws wide the door back into the kingdom. Jesus' opening message in Galilee, and to us, is "The kingdom of God is at hand"—a wonderful *now* message—"repent…and believe the gospel [the good news]" (Mark 1:15 KJV). Overcoming the burden of sin on us and defeating even death itself, God has taken us by the hand and is drawing us, and our societies, home to the kingdom. It is a home for now as well as eternity. Jesus shows us the way; the Holy Spirit gives us the inspiration and the power.

"It is this vision [for] which Jesus lived, labored, suffered, and died. And it is this vision he entrusted to his disciples"[4] and the church. This vision, the vision of the kingdom that is "at hand" now, moving toward a time of full realization in all of creation as the end of history, provides the central theme that runs throughout the Scriptures. It is this vision that provides the "most powerful symbol of hope"[5] in the history of humankind. This vision defines the whole thrust of our lives as believers. Our lives as Christians are about growing as citizens of that kingdom, holding open the door for others and helping them through it, and, by our lives, continuing to resist and overcome the "un-Godness" still in our world that damages lives and obscures the kingdom. The kingdom of God is worthy of working for, living for, and dying for.

ANEMIC VISIONS

Unfortunately, most Christians today are working out their lives not by the sharp, clear, and true vision revealed by the worldview of the kingdom of God but by distorted and anemic visions provided by other worldviews. These lesser visions are provided by the cultures in which we grow up and live.

The worldview through which most of us in the West live out our lives is secularism or atheistic materialism. This is the belief that the universe is void of spiritual reality—that it is only a physical universe—and its corresponding materialistic compulsion to ever greater consumption.

The worldview guiding people in the developing world as they live out their lives and work is often derived from animism. In this belief system the universe is understood as ultimately spiritual—that the objects and phenomena of the natural world themselves have spirits. The corresponding worldview tends to be highly fatalistic, seeing all events as predetermined by fate and therefore inevitable and unalterable. This worldview leaves whole nations morally, spiritually, or materially impoverished, with life having little meaning or purpose.

As the so-called developed world enters the twenty-first century, too often we Westerners find that the secular worldview has reduced work to a career and life to an endless consuming of things. As a result we live without hope and purpose, and both our work and life itself carry little if any meaning. High suicide rates; addictions to alcohol, drugs, pornography, and sex; and divorce and increased loneliness (even in crowded apartment complexes) are all signs of the death of the soul of man. People's lives and work are diminished from what God would have them to be. When we see our worth as determined by the marketplace and the amount of money we make, we often sacrifice what matters the most—family, friends, marriages, Christian fellowship—in pursuit of success, prestige, fame, power, and other goals prized by the world. All too often there is a direct relationship between our escalating material prosperity and our increasing moral and spiritual poverty.

In the developing world, too, both work and life itself are often greatly diminished from God's good intentions by people's approach to them. For instance, in much of the animistic (spiritistic) developing world where I travel teaching, work is viewed as a curse and the course of one's life as simply a matter of fate. Both are deep causes of physical suffering and economic poverty. People in these settings may work very hard, some fourteen to sixteen hours a day, yet they receive little fruit for their labor. Often, too, there is little social esteem for their hard work and the contribution they are making to their society.

For both Westerners and peoples of the developing world, therefore, life and work have been separated from the daily, practical values and intentions of the kingdom of God in the world—those things that give our work true value and meaning.

This separation marks the lives of believers as well. Too many Christians separate work and worship. Life is lived in two different compartments. The first is the religious and spiritual life that takes place in church and on Sunday. In this compartment Christians are largely proactive, consciously engaging in "Christian activities." The second is work and our lives in the community Monday through Saturday. In this part of life, Christians are, at best, reactive. In the worst case, we may be utterly passive, acting on the assumption that Christianity is spiritual and the kingdom is only a future reality, not a present existence. There is no connection between these two parts of life. For too many of us, the Bible speaks to the spiritual part of life, but it is the values of our national culture that govern most of life. Individuals and even entire nations are, as a result, not reaching their God-given potentials.

IMMANUEL IS COMING TO KYRGYZSTAN!

One of the English-speaking world's most beloved Christmas hymns, inspired by Isaiah 7:14, is "O Come, O Come, Immanuel." It acknowledges the coming of the Christ Child, the very presence of God himself, who would rule from the throne of David. Isaiah 9:6–7 adds to this revelation, stating that "the government will be on his shoulders....He will reign on David's throne and over his kingdom, establishing and upholding it with justice and righteousness from that time on and forever." Drawing inspiration from Isaiah 9:6–7, this great Christmas hymn includes the lines

> O Come, Thou Wisdom from on high,
> And order all things, far and nigh;
> To us the path of knowledge show,
> And cause us in her ways to go.

When I was in Kyrgyzstan facilitating a conference for pastors, we found ourselves worshiping one afternoon. During the chorus of one particular hymn, a sensation in the room grew so strong that I had chills running up and down my spine. Because I could not understand Russian, I did not understand what the pastors were singing with such conviction. So I asked a translator, "What are they singing when they are singing the chorus?" He responded, "Immanuel is coming to Kyrgyzstan!" They had caught a glimpse, in the midst of their poverty and circumstances, in the midst of the brokenness of their nation, that Isaiah's prophecy was true. There is a good future for Kyrgyzstan with the coming rule of Immanuel, and these Christian leaders knew that they could contribute to bringing that rule of God's kingdom into their nation.

RECONNECTING OUR LIVES AND WORK TO GOD'S MISSION

The pastors in Kyrgyzstan had seen the often overlooked words in the Lord's Prayer: "your kingdom come, your will be done on earth as it is in heaven" (Matt. 6:10). It's quite amazing to me how we pay such little attention to this part of Jesus' prayer. Nevertheless, Jesus is clearly teaching us to pray, here, for the kingdom of God to come to earth as it is in heaven.

It is nowhere supposed that the process will be an easy one. Yes, the kingdom is "at hand," the door has been opened to us, and Jesus is "the Way." However, as Jesus tells his disciples later, "From the days of John the Baptist until now the kingdom of heaven has suffered violence, and the violent take it by force" (Matt. 11:12 NRSV). The violence isn't necessarily physical now (though for many in the world it is), but the resistance against a spreading kingdom can be all too tough. In fact, it begins within, as we come up against old habits, old ways of thinking and responding to situations, and even our conditioned sense of what is a "smart" or "stupid" course of action. The ingrained patterns of a society give way even less easily, sometimes with much outcry against those who break the mold or challenge the status quo—and almost always only through long and concerted effort by many people, often over a long period of time.

In this sense it is indeed a battle, with new ground taken only in small increments and held, or "occupied," as places where God's kingdom is in operation, only by Spirit-empowered faithfulness. This means that the men and women who seek to transform their lives and those of their societies for the sake of the kingdom must be muscular Christians. This is no undertaking for wimps! The difference between the world's soldiers and those of the kingdom, however, is great. While they rely on physical muscle, tanks, guns, and now the power of modern military technology, the kingdom-advancing Christian relies on the example of the Christlike life, the power of the Holy Spirit, and the "full armor of God...truth...righteousness...the gospel of peace...faith...salvation...and...the word of God" (Eph. 6:13–17). Advancing is not about forcing one's will on others but about leading the way according to the vision of God's kingdom, as Christ has led us, right through whatever the resistance may throw against us.

We carry on that work of Christ as the church, his "body" in our world,[6] and each of us has a role to play in that body and thus in the coming of God's kingdom. The apostle Paul makes this point clearly:

> Now the body is not made up of one part but of many. If the foot should say, "Because I am not a hand, I do not belong to the body," it would not for that reason cease to be part of the body. And if the ear should say, "Because I am not an eye, I do not belong to the body," it would not for that reason cease to be part of the body. If the whole body were an eye, where would the sense of hearing be? If the whole body were an ear, where would the sense of smell be? But in fact God has arranged the parts in the body, every one of them, just as he wanted them to be. If they were all one part, where would the body be? As it is, there are many parts, but one body. (1 Cor. 12:14–20)

The roles that individual Christians play vary greatly, but each is critical to the larger effort of advancing God's kingdom. In fact, as Paul says, each person's role is specifically designed by God for *that* person and for the sake of the body. No person, no work that is ethical, is holier, more blessed, more godly, more essential than any other. Every Christian, not just the Christian pastor or leader or missionary, must begin to recognize the significance of his or her own life and work, which God has designed to be an integral part of the body and without which the body is incomplete. Our work, *your* work, is part of God's mission on earth, and this includes not simply your "career"—although that is an important part of it—but all arenas of life, every occupation and activity you undertake.

The common foundation for all is reconnection of our lives and our work to God's mission, his coming kingdom—becoming truly Christ's body, with the risen Christ as its head. The kingdom for which we work not only will come in all its glory when

Christ returns, but it is a kingdom that is also "at hand" and is coming today in substantial ways through each Christian's life and work.

A TOOL FOR THE INTENTIONAL CHRISTIAN

The purpose of this book is to help Christians begin to reconnect their lives and their work to the advancement of God's kingdom. A key for achieving this is developing a biblical worldview that enables us to understand our work in terms of calling and vocation and thus our lives as more consistently glorifying God. This process then transforms our lives and work into what I call our *life*work—the relationship of one's life and work to God and to the unfolding of his kingdom.

LifeWork is a tool to help Christians, worldwide, achieve such transformation. Then they may begin to "kingdomize"[7] their work, whatever that work may be, and thus influence their cultures and societies.

Among those I especially wish to reach with this book are those who want to be what I would call marketplace Christians but who question the value or faithfulness of such a choice. Millions of Christians, especially in the West, have a sense of "calling" to the marketplace, to work in one of the so-called secular domains of life. The trouble is that many of these Christians have learned to think about work within a Christianity that teaches, or implies, that if you are not in "the ministry," you are a second-class Christian; you are not "spiritual." And so they feel guilty about whatever secular work they may be doing. Others, perhaps some who became Christians after starting their careers, leave their secular work not knowing that it may have been their God-given calling. They are taught to vacate "the world" to pursue work that is deemed to be "more spiritual." In the Bible, this sacred-secular dichotomy does not exist; there is only a consecrated or an unconsecrated life.

The second audience I particularly want to reach is pastors, ministers, nongovernmental organization (NGO) workers, social activists, and missionaries who have been called to labor among the world's poor. One of the greatest causes of poverty in the developing world is the lie that work is meaningless, or even a curse. A major component of the Judeo-Christian worldview, however, is the dignity of labor, and this is one of the key tools for lifting people out of poverty. If you are working among poor people, my hope is that you will come to understand that what these friends and sojourners need more than money to solve their problems is Christ and a biblical way of seeing the world—a biblical worldview.

A clarification needs to be made in this context. Many people who are poor are very hard workers. As I said earlier, many work fourteen to sixteen hours a day. But the cultural mindset about work often leads to two things. First, the fruit of their labor is stolen by others through corruption, thus leaving them poorer or even impoverished. Second, the contribution that their work makes to the community is not recognized as significant; thus those who work are seen as foolish. Either of these leads to their impoverishment.

I remember many years ago when, as a young Christian in college in Southern California, I had the opportunity to travel to Mexico City with a group of other students and a pastor and his wife. The trip from Mexicali to Mexico City took three nights and two days. The farther we went into Mexico, the more poverty we saw. We began to see that poverty was the normal social ethos. I was an American middle-class, beach-boy lifeguard. I had never seen such poverty with my own eyes, so this was terribly disturbing to me.

I'll never forget when the train approached Mexico City. We rumbled along slowly (as trains do near the end of their journeys) through a large, horrendous slum. I had a good view through the window and was shocked to see a multitude of people living among mountains of trash. When I stared more closely, I could tell that they had built their "houses" out of the trash. The windows were made from car tires and the doors from dozens of tin cans hammered flat and connected by string or pieces of wire. I saw the children rummaging through the trash, and I learned that they were seeking items of value to sell on the streets. It was as if someone had taken me to another planet, and it became a turning point in my young life. My heart was broken, and I cried. I hadn't seen the poverty just with my eyes. God had let me see it with my heart. I knew that in the future I wasn't going to be able to turn my back on it. A strong desire began to grow in me that by the time I died I would see less of this in the world rather than more. I didn't know then that I would one day be working for Food for the Hungry International,[8] but I did know that I had to do something about poverty.

The calling upon my own life, therefore, is being worked out not only among Western Christians but also in the developing world, where worldviews daily intersect the very practical considerations of poverty and hunger. I have a great burden both for marketplace Christians and for those who labor among the world's poor. Both are seeking to be consciously, or intentionally, Christian.

The fact that you are reading this book indicates that you want to live life intentionally as a Christian. May this book be an encouragement to you. Unfortunately, as in every generation, many Christians are Christians in confession or name only. But thankfully you are not content to live an unexamined life. You want to ask the tough questions and to seek answers from Scripture. You are intentional about your walk with Christ and want to examine the meaning and place of your life and work within the kingdom of God. You want to think about your faith and to act consciously upon it. This book is meant to be a tool for you.

Intentional Christians, each in his or her own way, live in the radical middle ground. They recognize the biblical teaching that the universe is both moral and open.[9] It is moral, and thus everyone has a responsibility to steward what God has created and to care for the larger community, especially the poor. And because it is "open," resources are to be developed and used for the advancement of the kingdom of God, right now. These Christians also recognize, if only intuitively, that God has called them to do this in the world and that they need much more help and instruction here. In *LifeWork* I seek to offer such help.

I also hope that thoughtful people who are just beginning to ponder these things, or those who have not yet responded affirmatively to the claims of Christ, will benefit from exploring the issues of life and work from a distinctly Christian point of view.

PART 1 : THE FAULTY PARADIGM

CHAPTER 1

WORLDVIEWS AT WORK

Most adults in the Western world spend half of their waking hours at work. In many developing countries, the number of hours spent at work is even higher. Yet for all the time we spend working, we seldom reflect on the questions, What is work? Why do we work? We live largely unexamined lives; we do the things our mothers and fathers have done, in some countries for generations, without explanation. To simply begin to take seriously these questions could create a radical reordering of our lives.

As with all questions, the answers are ultimately determined by one's worldview.[1] Our worldview determines how we see the world, the kinds of lives we live, and the kinds of societies we create. Our worldview shapes how we will answer the metaphysical questions we all face—basic questions about the nature of reality. There is an objective worldview, the worldview of the Bible. All other worldviews, to a greater or lesser extent, are a distortion of the reality that God has made.

THE POWER OF STORY

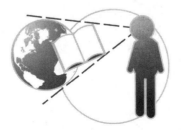

All humans are social beings. We assimilate our mindset, our way of seeing the world, from our culture. We tend to think the way our culture thinks and value what our culture values. This is part of what it means to be human. When we come to Christ, we need to begin to have our minds renewed. The word *repent*—the Greek word *metanoeo*—literally means to change one's mind. To repent is to begin to see the world the way God made the world and then to live and act within that framework. We are to have the mind of Christ; we are to bring every thought captive to Christ; we are no longer to be conformed to the world but are to be transformed by the renewal of our minds.[2] In coming to Christ, we need to begin to think "Christianly." We need to increasingly have the mind of Christ, not the mind we inherit from our culture.

To the extent that the worldviews of our cultures distort reality, they are inadequate to show us the nature of God, the world, and ourselves as they and we really are. Unless we have been intentional about renewing our minds according to the worldview of the kingdom, our cultural worldview will determine, consciously or unconsciously, our concept of work. In addition to biblical theism, there are two major worldviews: secularism, which assumes that reality is only physical, and animism, which assumes that the universe is ultimately spiritual. Sadly, the worldview of much of the evangelical, charismatic, and Pentecostal world today is not biblical theism but rather a subset of the animistic worldview, a Greek dualism that divides reality between the physical and the spiritual and assumes that the spiritual is more important. Each of these worldviews leaves us with an impoverished view of the universe, which in turn impoverishes individuals and whole nations and societies. We see this in both "developed" and "developing" countries, though the trend unfolds in very different directions. How might these worldviews be shaping your own understanding of your life and work?

SECULARISM: THE COST OF CONSUMPTION

Mother Teresa, visiting the city of New York from her home city of Calcutta—perhaps one of the most physically poor cities in the world—said she had never seen such poverty as she faced in New York. She understood the sad truth: Western society has largely exchanged material development for moral and spiritual bankruptcy.

SECULARISM

The concept of work held today in much of the Western world, including Canada and the United States, has been framed by the materialistic or secular paradigm. In this worldview, there is no spiritual reality, only physical reality. From this perspective, what does work do? It gives us access to material things. The purpose of work is to allow us to consume. Man is an animal, a highly evolved animal, but he is basically a consumer. In this paradigm, man has no intrinsic worth. There is no God in whose image we are made, giving our lives value. Instead our value as human beings is determined by what we have. According to this worldview, the more we consume, the better life is. As the modern proverb reads, "Whoever dies with the most toys wins!" Accordingly, success in the workplace means moving higher up the career ladder, accumulating more money or power for the purpose of affording greater consumption.

Falling far short of God's intentions, work in the West is largely utilitarian and self-serving; money, power, leisure, and self-fulfillment are the goals. Hedonism reigns: "Eat, drink and be merry, for tomorrow you die!"

THE COST OF CONSUMPTION

The consequences of this view of life and work are systemic for both individuals and whole societies. Home and community are diminished as work becomes the primary social environment. Because life is reduced to having things, people sacrifice what money can't buy—their spiritual identities, their marriages and children, their friendships and families—for success in the marketplace, doing whatever it takes to get ahead. Truth and virtue give way to pragmatism. Professionalism replaces character as the primary virtue. There is no metaphysical foundation for creativity. The future disappears for present consumption. Service to community is lost in service to self. Stewardship of creation is replaced with a rape of resources for opulent consumption. Ultimately, people miss their purpose in life, spending not only their dearly earned money but also the very days of their lives on what can never satisfy the human soul.

Social critic Os Guinness describes this shift away from a biblical worldview in Western societies as a move from a "calling economy" to a "commercial economy."[3] Since medieval times, however, there has been a broader purpose to education: to enrich and form the inner person in terms of both faith and the ability to think rationally and comprehensively about life and its many elements—to grow in wisdom as well as stature. The very first universities, in Europe, were founded as church schools, in fact, with an intentional, clearly Christian perspective on the gathering of knowledge and study. In earlier America, schools were founded not only to teach the three Rs but also to shape better citizens of God's kingdom. Curricula had frequent reference to biblical information and forthright moral instruction. This extended to higher education as the first American universities were founded by the churches, just as their European predecessors had been. They were places of training for new clergy as well as preparation of young men for other pursuits, most of the same subjects and training of the mind being seen as a good grounding for any worthy direction in life.

By the twentieth century, however, a shift began taking place in our society's understanding of life purpose and the significance of work. Whether or not individuals acknowledged it consciously, the purpose of life was reduced to working so that one could be productive, ensuring that there would be wealth in society for consumption. The marketplace became critical for determining self-worth. People who could make a lot of money were considered more valuable than those who couldn't. So the reason one went to school, even to college or university, was not to learn and grow as a person but to be able to have a job when one graduated.

When our life purpose is stunted in this way and when our worth is based on how much money we make, on how big our paychecks are, we become bankrupt in the ways that truly matter. In this paradigm, work becomes a god, an idol; humankind's good impulse to diligent work is distorted when work is separated from the Creator and from the kingdom of God. Work becomes an escape from the pressures of a broken or meaningless life. People become addicted to work as a means to escape hollow, unexamined, purposeless lives and societies that are morally, intellectually, and spiritually impoverished. But the tragic element of our workaholic society is that because work is separated from God, it becomes equally meaningless. What is promised to give us fulfillment ends up adding to the despair.

As Western Christians we experience the despair and impoverishment of the new commercial economy to varying degrees, depending on how acclimated we are to the surrounding culture. Some of us may be living just like our neighbors to an extent that we don't realize, judging others and ourselves by the affluence of our lifestyles and unconsciously placing undue value on what money can buy. We may place great pressure on ourselves to measure up to others with the prestige of our career or the way we can build a desirable lifestyle or provide amply for our families. We may find ourselves continually dissatisfied, always thinking life will be better—indeed that life will finally *start*—if only we could buy our own home, add the extra room onto the house, move to a better neighborhood, pay off the mortgage, take that dream vacation, or retire early. In short, without realizing it we may be basing our goals, priorities, and plans on a false premise, unmindful of the irreconcilable culture clash between the worldview of Scripture and the worldview of our society.

Alternatively, we may experience a great deal of dissonance, recognizing these cultural tendencies in ourselves and feeling dismayed at the gap between what we believe to be true and how we actually live at this foundational level. We struggle to truly *hear* Jesus saying to us, "I tell you, do not worry about your life, what you will eat or drink; or about your body, what you will wear. Is not life more important than food, and the body more important than clothes?" (Matt. 6:25). We have a good idea of where we ought to be and want to be and are distressed to see the extent to which we are not just in the world but of it. About our own material necessities, Jesus said, "The pagans run after all these things" (Matt. 6:32), and sometimes we find ourselves not much different. In a culture where material expectations run high, we, too, can find our families struggling, our connection to our communities squeezed out, our identities in Christ unsure, our very selves blown here and there. We, too, can find ourselves despairing at the gulf between how we think life is supposed to be and the meaninglessness we sometimes experience, whether deeply or fleetingly, over the repeating mechanics of sustaining the status quo, all the while knowing that so many around us are suffering—that we and the world need something radically different.

It's not just Christians experiencing this dissonance. Many others we know in our communities, universities, workplaces, and children's schools realize that life is more than consumption. They are seeking to live purposeful, intentional lives, according to a set of deeper values. Many are committed to living simply, in a head-on rejection of the materialism of the culture. Many are going green. Many are working to build a healthier community in their own city or across the world. They are volunteers. They are activists. They are concerned. They are zealous. While they do not know that the kingdom of God is what will make sense of their desire and address the brokenness radiating through every aspect of human life, they feel the need acutely.

So many of us experience this dissonance because the need—the lack—is *real*. God created us for a very different kind of life. Life as we experience it, and all we know about ourselves, simply does not fit with the secular materialistic paradigm.

As Christians in the midst of a materialistic culture, we share with many seekers a rampant hunger for the countercultural invitation of the Maker of the universe, who knows how and why he created us. "Come, all you who are thirsty, come to the waters; and you who have no money, come, buy and eat! Come, buy wine and milk without money and without cost. Why spend money on what is not bread, and your labor on what does not satisfy? Listen, listen to me, and eat what is good, and your soul will delight in the richest of fare. Give ear and come to me; hear me, that your soul may live" (Isa. 55:1–3).

ANIMISM: THE CURSE OF FATE

Billions of people in the developing world are also dying to hear this open invitation from the Creator and Savior of the universe. Unaware of their true identity and the true character of God and his creation, they, too, are experiencing the death of the soul of man, and not only that, but also the death of their very bodies.

In many of the countries of the world where people are materially impoverished, some people are lazy, as there are lazy people everywhere. But the vast majority put in long hours of backbreaking work with little return. Even bright young college graduates find stagnant economies with little opportunity for work. Others find jobs in the public sector that do not take advantage of this immense pool of talent.

Much of the blame for these stagnant economies can be laid at the feet of the greedy and corrupt behavior of government officials and those mercantilists and tribal chiefs who control the economy. This behavior is institutionalized in laws and structures that are against freedom and either strip the poor of the fruits of their labor or rob them altogether of the opportunity to work. Autocratic leadership styles squash initiative, innovation, and creativity. Controlled economies and rampant corruption sap economic initiative. Lack of property rights and copyright protections prevent hardworking people and artisans from enjoying their rightful reward.

All this springs from a culture of corruption where bribery is a way of life, where there is no moral or metaphysical challenge. Undergirding such cultures is often a traditional animistic belief system in which spirits animate nature. In such an outlook, moral responsibility is removed from humankind; people are left in the hands of "the fates" or disinterested or even hostile spirits. Seen through this fatalistic lens, reason and efforts to increase understanding and the ability to affect or use natural resources have little apparent value. According to this worldview, work is a curse of fate; work only compounds man's misery. It is drudgery. We work in order to survive.

ANIMISM: THE NEW PAGANISM

ONE

I remember meeting a young man from West Africa after he heard me talk on this subject. He said to me, "I have an illustration for you. In my country all the young people want to go to the university so that after they graduate, they can get a 'tie job.'" They mean a government job where they can work in an air-conditioned office, drive a car that's air-conditioned, and draw a paycheck for not really working. He was serious. In much of the developing world, this is how people see work—as a curse to escape.

THE CURSE OF FATE

In some developing countries you will find men with very long fingernails on their pinky finger as a sign of their disdain for work. Because one cannot do hard physical labor and at the same time grow long fingernails, they are broadcasting to the world that they are above manual labor—that they are elite. When work is a curse, what you want to do is get other people to work for you. In many countries where there is an aristocracy, the aristocrats exist because there is a low view of work. Believing that work is bad, aristocratic people have slaves and servants to do the work for them. This culture of poverty is found in the former Soviet Union. Two Russian proverbs illustrate this: "Labor loves fools" and "Smart people don't work."[4]

I was discussing this with a friend from Venezuela, Xiomara Suarez. She said, "Darrow, I have a song for you," and sang it for me. A year later we were at a conference, and I asked Xiomara to sing this song because it illustrated the attitude toward work in her country. As she began to sing in Spanish, people from four or five other Spanish-speaking countries all immediately joined in. I thought it was just a Venezuelan song, but it is obviously a song known all over the Spanish-speaking world. The song is "The Black Man of the Batei."

> I'm called the black man of the Batei
> Because for me "WORK" *is like an enemy*
> *All work I'll leave it to the ox*
> *Because God made work as a punishment* [italics added].

Now can you imagine if the culture as a whole sings this song all the time? Work is punishment? What is work made for? For the animals, not for man.

I like to dance this merengue music
To dance it with a black good-looking lady
I like to dance it, all night, from side to side
To dance it hugging closely my nice good-looking lady.

I like to dance merengue,
Merengue's better than work
Because having to work
It causes me a great pain [italics added].

Why are some nations poor? When you believe that work is a curse, you avoid work and don't respect the work of others. Work and labor are demeaning. If you have whole nations where the goal is to avoid work and where those with power corruptly live off the efforts of those who are less powerful, what will that tend to produce? It will produce poverty, not productivity. At the root of the poverty is a moral and spiritual impoverishment just as tragic as that of the West, with millions cut off from the true story about themselves and the world.

Even if we live in affluence and think we have no relation to animism, we still can find reflections of ourselves in the animistic worldview. The words to "The Black Man of the Batei" and the crowd's identification with them are really not that shocking to a lot of us. With a different cultural flair, the same sentiments are flying back and forth across the tables of a million restaurants, pubs, and family dining rooms every Friday afternoon. Most everyone knows the familiar acronym TGIF. There's even the restaurant T.G.I. Friday's, where we can duly celebrate the end of the workweek. Like kids released by the school bell, when work lets out we thank God that it's finally Friday, when our time is our own, when "real life" happens. Of course, we can be happy about work well done and happy to rest as God intends us to do. But the sentiment doesn't usually run on that wavelength.

For years the American country-music legend George Jones ushered in every weekend on radio stations all over America with the hit "Finally Friday."[5] Like those of "The Black Man of the Batei," the words of "Finally Friday" are a window on how people think and feel about work. The lyrics contrast the "workin' blues" of a barely survivable workweek with the good times of the free "wild weekend" flush with money and time to burn. While most of us probably don't rush out after work on Fridays to exercise our freedom with booze and women as this song describes, we may be all too familiar with the dread of Mondays…and Tuesdays and Wednesdays and Thursdays. We might identify strongly with the contrast between the working blues and the anticipation and sweetness of freedom. Even though its exact images may be as foreign to some North Americans as those of the Latin folk song, this country classic resonates even in the midst of the workaholic culture of the West. This anthem could be our own: *It's finally Friday; I'm free again.*

In this, too, Christians are not immune from the thought life and emotional landscape of their cultures. Just as we experience a tug-of-war with the self-serving materialistic elevation of work, we may feel a great dissonance between what our Christian faith says about the sacredness of our work and what we may experience as the drudgery of work. Even though we know better, there are times we act as if work is a curse. Even though we may sometimes enjoy our work and on our best days even experience it as a calling, other times we catch ourselves acting or thinking as if we are slaves to it, as if we would abandon it at first chance, as if it has no intrinsic value and no inherent connection to who we really are or what we're really about.

We may know that God didn't institute work as a curse; we may know that God created us in his own image—made us to work as he does with great purpose and reward. But to our disappointment and unease, in our actual experience work is often more about survival than the fulfillment of our destinies. We may work solely to provide the necessities for ourselves and our families, even as we're not sure exactly what *is* necessary, but surely food and shelter and clothing are. We may work simply to get by. On some level we may feel trapped, as a true animist does, at the mercy of forces beyond our control. For the sake of these necessities, because of these hard facts of life, we sacrifice the working hours of our lives—but no more than that. When the weekend comes, or our days off, we greet it with sweet relief.

Sadly, the sweetness often doesn't last. When we've spent all week being dissatisfied and waiting for life to start, we often continue in the same mindset, stuck in a rut. Our days off, and all our hopes pinned on them, are often a disappointment. Our view of work is impossible to separate from our view of life. We find that our expectations for a happy and meaningful life cannot be met in a few days to the exclusion of the others. We run into the truth: rather than a curse, or what we do to get by, work is at the center of our identity and foundational to our purpose.

AN UNBIBLICAL DUALISM: THE PLACE OF SPIRITUAL OUTREACH

The modern evangelical church, instead of providing a worldview that will challenge the tragic impoverishment of the animistic and materialistic paradigms, has largely withdrawn from public life and abandoned the culture and the marketplace. In reaction to the advancement of the secular worldview into modern society, much of the leadership of the church in the early twentieth century abandoned the biblical worldview for a Christian version of an ancient dualistic worldview that divides the universe between the spiritual realm, which is good and holy, and the physical realm, which is evil and profane. (We'll trace how this dualistic thinking infected the church in chapter 2.) The results are familiar to most of us.

EVANGELICAL DUALISM

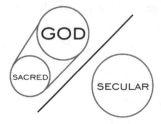

The perceived split between heaven and earth, between the spiritual and the physical worlds, has taken on two forms in Christian thinking about work: the "higher calling" and the "place for spiritual outreach."

The first manifestation of this dualistic thinking among Christians is a desire for a higher calling. According to this mentality, it is best to leave the secular arena and go into the spiritual arena so we can be "full-time Christian workers." Only evangelists, church planters, pastors, missionaries, and theologians are doing full-time Christian work according to this view, because only these kinds of work are spiritual. The "helping professions" (social workers, charity workers, counselors, etc.) rank a close second to "full-time ministry." On the other hand, accounting, carpentry, filmmaking, the arts, farming, and homemaking are secular activities and thus lower activities. They are less spiritual. So Christians will leave the workplace because their desire is to be more spiritual. When Christians don't go out as missionaries but remain in their communities to do the "secular" work they did before they were Christians, they are often made to feel guilty.

A HIGHER CALLING

The second concept holds that the secular workplace is a place for spiritual outreach. The idea is that if we can't be full-time Christian workers, we should do spiritual activity in our workplaces. According to this mindset, having Bible studies and prayer meetings in the workplace justifies our existence as Christians who are not in missions. It allows us to function in this lower realm because we are bringing the higher realm into the lower realm. But this reasoning is still framed by the unbiblical dichotomy, the sense of living in two worlds.

A PLACE FOR
SPIRITUAL OUTREACH

It is not only in the area of profession that Christians struggle with living in two worlds but also in the area of deployment. When we see a division between so-called spiritual and secular work, working overseas becomes the higher deployment. Working at home is the lower deployment. Many Christians feel guilty for not working overseas, because that is the higher calling. Staying home is to be a second-class Christian. But really we can't win. When we accept this unbiblical thinking, going overseas isn't enough. According to some, working in the 10/40 Window or among unreached people groups is the most spiritual, while other cross-cultural missions are only second best.

All of this teaching is a reflection of an unbiblical paradigm that has left individuals mere shadows of what God intends, the church largely disengaged from culture, communities mired in poverty, and nations undiscipled. There have never been more Christians or churches in the world than there are today. Over the past fifty years there has been an unprecedented push on evangelism, church planting, and church growth. In many parts of the world we have been very successful at what we have set out to do: save souls, plant churches, and develop megachurches. But to what end? Material poverty still reigns in developing countries that have been evangelized; meanwhile, moral and spiritual poverty reign in the "Christian" West.

In many parts of the world where the church is growing, the growth is "a mile wide and an inch deep." It has forgotten its function of being salt and light in society, of bringing the kingdom of God to life and light in the everyday street and market-place, and when needed, to be a prophetic voice. In this forgetting, the church has become largely impotent.

We are faced with this dire situation in the moment of unprecedented opportunity. Communism has collapsed around the world. The materialistic paradigm has been found seriously wanting in the West, feeding the body but not the soul, so that amidst all of our relative wealth, even luxury, there are increasing signs of human distress. Meanwhile the church is facing great challenge, even to its existence in places, and Islam is growing around the world. The world is longing for a vibrant Christianity, one that addresses the profound moral, spiritual, social, economic, and political crises facing much of the world.

Why is the church unprepared to respond? Because the Christian's life and work have been separated both from their foundation in the biblical worldview and from the end to which all of life moves—the kingdom of God. Without a transcendent framework that speaks to all areas of life, our life purpose is truncated to dying to go to heaven. We've lost the larger framework in which it is understood that our lives and work are in relationship—in relationship to God through worship, to others through service, and to creation through stewardship. Our lives and work have largely been separated from their mission, and this ultimately stems from a loss of the biblical worldview. When we've succumbed to dualistic thinking, the majority of each of our lives—the supposedly "secular" part—is informed by the impoverishing worldviews of our culture, by elements of the materialism and animism described above, rather than by the truth witnessed to in Scripture.

How has the church of Jesus Christ, and so many of us individually, arrived in this powerless place? In the next chapter we'll trace the roots of dualism in our Christian heritage so that we can move beyond this damaging paradigm once and for all and truly hear God when he says to us and all humankind, "Come to *me*; hear *me*, that your soul may live" (Isa. 55:3; italics added). Life—every aspect, every day of the week, personally and corporately—is found in the God who created and sustains *heaven and earth* and *all* that is in them. Dualism, as we'll see in the next chapters and throughout this book, is antithetical to the Christian faith and untrue to reality.

CHAPTER 2

HOW DID WE GET HERE?

DUALISM THROUGHOUT CHURCH HISTORY

Scripture does not divide existence into separate natural and supernatural, or material and spiritual, realms. The separation that the modern world tends to make is utterly foreign to the biblical world-view. It is doubtful that the people of the Bible could even have wrapped their heads around the way we tend to see our lives and the world now. The Bible reveals that God is Creator of *both* the heavens *and* the earth. He is not only transcendent and eternal but also the God of history, in all its details. God is ruler of the heavens, but he is also Lord of *all* of life—both everyday activities and grand events. He not only created the heavens and the earth and all life within them but also sustains it all as a living and active presence; he is known in the falling of the rain, the fruitful harvest, the birth of a child (all gifts from his hand), as much as in fulfilled prophecy or exceptional divine acts. Worship takes place not just through formal ceremony, however appropriate that may be before a mighty God, but, even more importantly, through the "living sacrifice" of an entire life lived in intimate connection with him.

So how did we move away from this unified understanding of life and relationship with God to the modern separation of life into distinctly different spheres—"spiritual" and "physical," or "religious" and "secular"? Today's dualism, and the values we attach to each realm, is the product of a centuries-long process in which Christianity has incorporated elements of other philosophies and worldviews into its thinking.

Understanding just how we reached this point gives us the opportunity to revisit our own thinking and see where we might be basing some of our own presuppositions and habits on concepts foreign to the biblical worldview. This in turn will free us to begin following Jesus more fully and to be more effective in working with him to bring our world into the kingdom of God until he comes again.

ANCIENT BEGINNINGS

Christianity began, of course, within the traditional Jewish community in the Galilee region of the Holy Land and in the vicinity of Jerusalem. Once Christianity began to spread beyond these boundaries, however, and particularly when it reached the Greek cities in Asia Minor and then Europe itself, it moved into a very different thought world. Though many other religions were present, the realm of ideas in the Greco-Roman world was heavily influenced by Greek philosophy.

The Greek philosopher Plato (c. 428–348 BC) provided the defining inspiration for much thought that was to follow over several centuries. He described the material world as a *shadow* of the spiritual, or real, world. The finite, material world was simply a shadowy projection of the permanent and eternal real world. Plato's allegory of the cave famously pictured his ideas. Here the prisoners in a cave see the shadows of puppets that are cast on the wall of the cave. The prisoners, unable to see the real puppets, think that the shadows of the puppets are the "real puppets." Plato's point is that the things that we observe with our senses are merely shadows of the reality—the universals—that we cannot see.

PLATO'S ALLEGORY OF THE CAVE

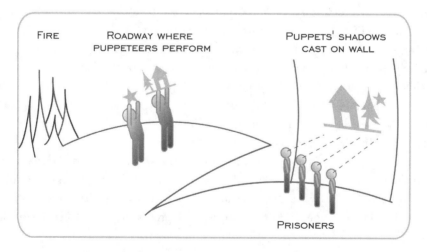

FIRE ROADWAY WHERE PUPPETEERS PERFORM PUPPETS' SHADOWS CAST ON WALL

PRISONERS

Before Plato, another Greek philosopher, Pythagoras (c. 580–c. 500 BC), had already put limits on the value of the physical world. Best known today for the Pythagorean Theorem taught in high-school geometry, Pythagoras taught that the essence of the physical world and even of abstract concepts could be expressed through mathematics. Numbers, not the physical world, represented true or ultimate reality.

Such dualistic concepts, and the schools of thought that developed from them, effectively separated the realm of the good, ideal, and permanent from our physical lives and the world in which we live out our daily existence. Only the mind, participating in the realm of ideas, could connect with the good and the eternal. The material world came to be seen in a negative light. It was temporary and much less valued, and the body was little more than a prison for the truer, valuable element of the self.

Following from this, physical work was seen as having no ultimately good value. In a world where only men of considerable means would have the opportunity for education and the "higher" life of the mind, and in a world where slavery was common and used whenever possible for menial work, physical labor could easily be seen as demeaning. Separation of the physical from the truly "real" further deprived it of value. Physical work was, in effect, an inferior use of a man's time and talents. The Platonic understanding also justified holding women in low status, because they were seen as "physical" beings, made for childbearing (a function of the "lesser," profane, and limiting body) and managing a (material) household.

None of this thought developed in a vacuum, of course. As the borders of empires moved back and forth in the ancient world, ideas spread. Some of the many religions and philosophies with which the Greeks and Romans (as well as Jews and, later, Christians) had contact were also strongly dualistic in their viewpoints. The prevalent Eastern worldview, today present in Hinduism and Buddhism, understood reality as eternal spiritual monism, the absolute spiritual unity of all things. According to this worldview, the spiritual realm is real, while the physical is a nonrational illusion of mystery.

While the Old and New Testament records are utterly wholistic[1] and integrative of the spiritual and natural realms, the ancient Greek dualist worldview had, as we shall see, a profound influence on some of the early church fathers and thus on the church throughout history.

GNOSTICISM

Gnosticism was a widespread and highly varied thought movement that arose before Christianity and continued to develop alongside it. Holding a highly dualistic worldview, the Gnostics believed that the material world was evil and profane. Similar to

Plato, the Gnostics believed that the true self, which was made up of divine elements, was entrapped in the physical body. The word *gnostic* means "secret and mysterious knowledge," and it was by such knowledge, which was given by revelation, that one could escape the material world and progress upward to the eternal, spiritual world.

By the second century, a strain of Gnosticism had mixed with Christianity, becoming a significant element within the church. Among those who embraced Gnostic thought and yet considered themselves Christians was Valentinus (c. 100–c. 155), a leading scholar at that time. Gnostic Christianity was a blending, or syncretism, of Christianity and Greek/Eastern dualistic philosophy.

One of the major disputes between Gnostic Christians and those Christians who held what became orthodox Christian beliefs concerned the nature of Christ. Gnostics held the belief (known as Docetism) that because the material world is evil, Christ, who is pure and divine, only *appeared* to have a real physical body and only *appeared* to have suffered physically. This belief was addressed by the Gospel of John,[2] by Ignatius of Antioch in a letter dated AD 110, and by the Nicene Council in AD 325. Christianity established the doctrine of the incarnation of the Word, affirming both the full deity and full humanity of Christ.

Although Gnosticism faded out as a dominant religion or philosophy, elements of its thought have continued to reappear here and there in later expressions of Christian belief. Today one could describe the dualism—the split between the spiritual and the physical or worldly—that exists within evangelical Protestantism as *evangelical Gnosticism*. This is especially true where we see Christians emphasizing "spiritual" activities (e.g., prayer meetings or Bible studies) or "professional" ministry or missions as the one truly satisfactory way to faithfully live out our Christian lives. Similarly, we are showing a Gnostic orientation whenever we demean things of the physical world or see them as unimportant (e.g., the environment, government, art, justice, or public health), or see work in fields that deal with them as a less-than-full Christian calling.

DISTORTION IN THE EARLY MAINSTREAM OF CHRISTIANITY

Influenced by the culture around it and the philosophies and movements that preceded it, even the mainstream church developed certain dualistic patterns of thought.

One avenue in which dualism was absorbed into the mainstream of Christian thought was through the early development of monasticism. This was at first a solitary lifestyle. In fact, the word *monk* is derived from the Greek for "a solitary person." Although those who chose this life drew on biblical examples, monasticism was more extreme than the temporary withdrawals into the wilderness of biblical figures. The monks' radical rejection of "the world" and their focus on a more perfect union with the holy can best be comprehended in the context of the Greek/Eastern dualistic philosophy described above.

At first monks were all hermits, individuals who would as much as possible forsake all things "of the world" and go off alone (often literally into the wilderness or desert) to pursue "the things of God." Eventually, though, like-minded people joined together, and in 318 the first monastic community was founded. Monasteries and their religious communities quickly became a major element in the church. Though initially places for separated, holy living, monasteries became centers for study, writing, and teaching, as well as the preservation, translation, and duplication of important texts, including Scripture. They also became important centers for missions work. Much of the credit for spreading Christianity to the people of Europe goes to monks who traveled the continent, establishing monasteries as they went. In later centuries religious communities carried the gospel to the world abroad, as when Christianity was brought to the Western Hemisphere.

However, the dualistic philosophy behind early monasticism is demonstrated in the work of various early church writers. One example is Eusebius (c. 260–c. 339), bishop of Caesarea and sometimes called "the father of church history." In *Demonstration of the Gospel,* he wrote that Christ gave "two ways of life" to the church:

> Two ways of life were given by the law of Christ to his Church. The one is above nature, and beyond common human living.... Wholly and permanently separated from the common customary life of mankind, it devotes itself to the service of God alone.... Such then is the perfect form of the Christian life. And the other, more humble, more human, permits men to ... have minds for farming, for trade, and the other more secular interests as well as for religion.... And a kind of secondary grade of piety is attributed to them."[3]

TWO WAYS OF LIFE
EUSEBIUS OF CAESAREA

THE PERFECT LIFE	THE PERMITTED LIFE
VITA CONTEMPLATIVA	VITA ACTIVA
HIGHER, SACRED, CONTEMPLATIVE	LOWER, SECULAR, ACTIVE
THE SOCIALLY, SPIRITUALLY SUPERIOR	THE SOCIALLY, SPIRITUALLY INFERIOR
E.G., PRIESTS, NUNS, MONKS, ARISTOCRATS	E.G., HOMEMAKERS, LABORERS, FARMERS

In this scheme, there were two forms of life, the *perfect* life and the *permitted* life. The perfect life was higher, sacred, and *contemplative*. It was the life of religious workers like priests, nuns, monks, and theologians. These were the social and spiritual "superiors" of the common people or laity. On the other hand, the permitted life was lower, secular, and *active*. This involved manual labor and was the lot of the common man, the farmer, homemaker, cabinetmaker, merchant, and artisan. These were the social and spiritual "inferiors" of the religious class.

Eventually this dualistic contrast would translate into a view in which "the church," in any active sense, actually meant the clergy and perhaps monastics. Throughout the Middle Ages, laypeople—especially those living "in the world," not in a consecrated "religious" life—were seen as having a distinctly passive and inferior role, dependent on "the church" for their relationship with God, the transmission of his grace to them, and their eternal salvation.

THE CLERGY-LAITY DICHOTOMY

CLERGY	SERVING GOD	SPIRITUAL PROFESSIONS HELPING PROFESSIONS
LAITY	SERVING MAMMON	SECULAR PROFESSIONS MANUAL LABOR

That this dualistic way of understanding the Christian life became very imbedded in Christian thinking is suggested even today—despite all the changes that came in later centuries—by the sense that persists among many in the laity that it is the pastor's role, in a sense, to do the Christian living for all. Most dramatically it appears in the elevated view of "full-time" Christian work—a continuing belief in the "perfect" and "permitted" life—and in the lack of integration of faith into the everyday lives of Christians.

THE REFORMATION—*Sixteenth Century*

In Europe, the Protestant Reformation of the sixteenth century responded to the dualism in much of the church and to the man-centered, humanistic thought forms of the European Renaissance (beginning in the fourteenth century) with a reaffirmation and articulation of the biblical worldview. It rekindled the biblical understanding of both living and working consciously and intentionally in the presence of God. Martin Luther (1483–1546), the Roman Catholic monk whom God used to ignite the

Reformation, spoke of all Christians standing "before God" and thus under God's scrutiny. John Calvin (1509–1564), whom God used to bring reform to Geneva and create a light in that city that shone brightly throughout Europe, taught that no area of life is exempt from "business with God."[4]

The mainstream Reformers, like Luther and Calvin and also Ulrich Zwingli (1484–1531), challenged the dualistic worldview that had crept into the church. Recovering a wholistic, biblical worldview, they recognized that there is no sacred-secular dichotomy but only a consecrated or unconsecrated life. What had been considered secular was now understood to be related to the sacred. Notably, this is expressed by the way the Reformers began to popularize the word *call*. Alister McGrath, in his book *Reformation Thought*, writes,

> The Reformation changed such attitudes [of dualism in the workplace], decisively and irreversibly. To illustrate this change in attitude, we may consider the German word *Beruf* ("calling"), as it was used by Martin Luther. In the Middle Ages, the term *Beruf* meant a monastic or clerical calling—in other words, a vocation to a professional ecclesiastical function. Luther began to use the same word to refer to worldly duties. By using the term *Beruf* to refer to activity in the everyday world, Luther applied the religious seriousness of the monastic vocation to activity in the world. One is called by God to serve him in certain specific ways in the world. Here, the modern use and sense of the word "vocation" or "calling" may be seen emerging at the time of the Reformation, through a new approach to work. The languages of every area of Europe affected by the Reformation show a decisive shift in the meaning of the word for work during the sixteenth century: German (*Beruf*), English (*calling*), Dutch (*beroep*), Danish (*kald*), Swedish (*kallelse*) and so forth.[5]

The foundation of Martin Luther's understanding of calling was the doctrine of justification by faith. Christians had come to believe in a hierarchy of vocation: the *vita contemplativa* was higher and more spiritual, while the *vita activa* was common and less spiritual. The work of the priest and the nun, religious workers, was holy, while the farmer's and homemaker's work was "secular." The priests were justified because they were doing holy work. For the common people to be justified, they would have to do "spiritual work," such as attending mass, paying indulgences, and giving alms to the poor. This further enslaved and impoverished those who were already poor. Luther and the Reformers in Northern Europe challenged the idea of "works righteousness" by insisting that no external work, but only the internal act of faith, could make a person righteous or justified before God.

The Reformers restored the concept of work to that of calling. If righteousness is by faith, Luther reasoned, then the contemplative life of the monks and priests is neither higher nor lower than the active life of the faithful farmer, cabinetmaker, or homemaker. Luther, who himself left a monastic order, understood that if we are saved by grace through faith, what matters is not the kind of work one does but the faith with which one works. In other words, what matters is whether one's work is consecrated or not. Suddenly all work, so far as it is morally legitimate (not evil), is sacred. Priest and farmer, nun and homemaker, theologian and laborer, all stand, in faith, before God. Dietrich Bonhoeffer writes of Luther's challenge to man's sense of work:

> Luther's return from the cloister to the world was the worst blow the world had suffered since the days of early Christianity. The renunciation he made when he became a monk was child's play compared with that which he had to make when he returned to the world. Now came the frontal assault. *The only way to follow Jesus was by living in the world.* Hitherto the Christian life had been the achievement of a few choice spirits under the exceptionally favorable conditions of monasticism; now it is a duty laid on every Christian living in the world. The commandment of Jesus must be accorded perfect obedience in one's daily vocation of life [italics added].[6]

The Reformation called the church out of the building and into the world and directly challenged the dualistic mentality of the church in the Middle Ages.

In sum, the Reformers argued two main points. First, all Christians, not just religious workers, have a calling. Second, all work, not just spiritual work, can be considered a calling. The sacred-secular dichotomy is abolished for those who embrace this biblical thinking.

PIETISM—*Seventeenth Century*

By the seventeenth century, the young Protestant church that had turned Europe upside down was fraught with problems. One difficulty was the tendency of some traditions or denominations (e.g., Lutheranism or the Reformed Church) to become excessively concerned with correct theology and doctrine at the expense of a living faith. This was an unfortunate outcome of the theological struggles brought on by the Reformation in the first place.

Another significant problem was the continued close ties between religion and the state. When the Reformation took hold in a particular state or nation, the entire entity, not only individuals or congregations, often became officially Protestant, and new national "established churches" were created. National churches played varying roles in the governance of their states, and for many individuals, being part of a particular church became indistinguishable from their citizenship in a particular state or nation. Additionally, at least in the earlier centuries of the new Protestant states, participation in or support for other churches (such as the Anabaptist) was often suppressed or even punished severely—sometimes quite violently. Actual warfare broke out in various locales as the religious movement combined with political conflicts and social unrest.

The experience with church establishment created a felt need, within just a few generations, for new reform and recovery of spiritual meaning. The movement known as Pietism was one answer to this—one which would have a very wide and long-lasting effect.

The Pietist movement is generally seen as arising within Lutheranism in Germany in the late 1600s. The stirrings of Pietism began with Christian mystics like Jakob Böhme (1575–1624), Johann Arndt (1555–1621), and Heinrich Müller (1631–1675). Müller "described the [baptismal] font, the pulpit, the confessional, and the altar as the four dumb idols of the Lutheran Church."[7]

In general, Pietism stressed religious *experience* over orthodox conviction. This brought a focus on "personal experience." Where earlier reformers had put great emphasis on comprehending, interpreting, and applying Scripture to public and private life—a function of reason as well as spiritual commitment—the newer approach stressed the heart and emotions at the expense of rational thought. On one hand, the emphasis on experience over doctrine led, in part, to later forms of theological liberalism, in which traditional doctrines were modified or abandoned based on an individual's own valuation of them. On the other hand, the focus on personal Christian living brought renewal to the lives of many believers, and for this reason the Pietists led important missionary efforts.

In regard to dualism, Pietism fostered a drive among Christians to focus on the spiritual realm and withdraw from the wider culture. This may be evidenced in the life and teaching of the man known as the father of Pietism, Philipp Spener (1635–1705). Spener began a house-church movement with meetings in his home. He also published a set of proposals for restoration of the church which included, among other things, earnest Bible study in private meetings, a greater role for the laity in the church, reorganization of theological training with more stress on devotional life, and a new preaching style aimed at the heart. Over the years, he stressed the spiritual necessity of a new birth and spoke of the separation of Christians from the world.

Though the Pietist movement itself is considered to have ended in the mid to late 1700s, its influences have been far-reaching. Later in this chapter we will see how its influence came roaring back with the rise of evangelical Gnosticism in the nineteenth and twentieth centuries.

THE ENLIGHTENMENT—*Seventeenth and Eighteenth Centuries*

Also known as the Age of Reason, the Enlightenment was a philosophical movement centered in England, France, and, to some degree, Germany. It was founded on the transitional metaphysic of deism, which assumed, like biblical theism, that the Creator God existed. But unlike the Bible, deism assumed that God was not immanent, or present. In deism, God is Creator but not Savior and Lord. He is a distant God. He created the universe, set it in motion, and left it alone. He does not speak to people and does not answer prayers. His existence explains creation, but because he does not speak, there is no transcendent foundation for truth, goodness, and beauty. Deism laid the foundation for the later rise of secularism (which we've also called atheistic materialism), the metaphysic of modernism.

It was the Enlightenment that ushered in the age of rationalism. Rationalism is reason without revelation. It establishes human reason as the final authority in all things. Under the sway of this worldview, instead of God being the center of the universe and man exploring creation through reason *and* revelation, man is the center of the universe; man is god. The spiritual realm—God, angels, demons, and man as the *imago Dei*—all became premodern ideas.

Contrary to this emerging rationalistic thinking, the founders[8] of modern science were biblical theists who sought to "think God's thoughts after him." They understood that God revealed himself in two "books": Creation and the Bible. They understood that there was no divide between the two revelations. Man was to use his senses and his reason to explore all of God's revelation. Deistic and, later, secular or naturalistic science denied the existence of a transcendent reality. It was assumed that man was alone in the universe. If man was going to understand the universe, he would need to begin from himself and his five senses to discover the origin and meaning of life. Theism's reason and revelation was replaced with philosophic rationalism and naturalistic science.

Without a transcendent metaphysic—without the Infinite-Personal God to establish objectivity—truth, goodness, and beauty became subjective. It was man who determined what was true, good, and beautiful. In the area of morals, the secularist decided that we are born essentially good, or at least with a clean slate, and can fulfill our great potential if provided with the right tools and opportunities. This is a considerable departure from the understanding of human beings as innately sinful, in need of salvation individually as well as corporately. This shift in thinking, as it continued to develop, would have wide implications in all areas of life, eventually including family, education, and public policy.

During this stage of the European Enlightenment, many regular church members and even some clergy held deistic views. The deists attempted to transform traditional Christianity into a religion based on reason. For most, there was still a spiritual realm, but it was rather detached from the physical realm. Some simply came to see spirituality as a figment of the human imagination and irrelevant to our lives. God still existed as Creator, but he no longer was seen as engaged with his creation as the God of history, the Savior and Lord of life. The tendency was to look at the universe in a mechanical way, governed by natural law. These laws flowed from the nature of the Creator, but they were understood to operate without the ongoing personal involvement of the Lawgiver.

The Enlightenment, with its celebration of human reason and tendency to devalue the spiritual realm, marked a transition in the general culture of the Western world. The church responded to the age of Enlightenment with a return to a more orthodox, wholistic faith and practice.

THE GREAT AWAKENING—*Eighteenth and Nineteenth Centuries*

In the early eighteenth century (1730–1750), a Christian revival broke out on both sides of the Atlantic. This revival was a return to biblical faith; it not only had a spiritual component but was wholistic, bringing about one of the great social transformations in modern times. Here we have the birth of what Dr. Ralph Winter, an outstanding missions strategist and the founder of William Carey International University, has identified as *First Inheritance evangelicalism.*[9] First Inheritance evangelicalism had a broad, wholistic understanding of the gospel, encompassing personal salvation, societal transformation, and foreign missions. (This contrasted with what Winter calls *Second Inheritance evangelicalism*, whose focus is primarily on personal salvation, the Rapture, and the soon second coming of Jesus Christ. These later evangelicals have placed little to no emphasis on the ability of the gospel to change society.)

In England the revival was sparked by a First Inheritance evangelical, John Wesley (1703–1791), an Anglican minister who became a fiery evangelist and social reformer and the founder of the Methodist movement. Wesley preached Christ crucified to hundreds of thousands of people, both poor and rich. But he understood that if someone came to Christ in conversion, it was not only to go to heaven. Wesley understood that if a person was saved, his or her life and behavior needed to be transformed, and thus, corporately, there would be a transformation of society.

In America the Great Awakening was sparked by two men, Jonathan Edwards (1703–1758) and George Whitefield (1714–1770). Jonathan Edwards was a Congregational preacher, theologian, and missionary to Native Americans. He is acknowledged as perhaps the finest evangelist and philosophical theologian that America ever produced. The Reformation ideals of John Calvin flowed into early America through his thinking, teaching, and ministry. His preaching, particularly his famous sermon "Sinners in the Hands of an Angry God," led tens of thousands of people to repentance and to the cross of Christ for salvation.

George Whitefield had been a leader in Wesley's Methodist movement in England. In 1738 Whitefield moved to the British colony of Georgia in America and began to preach in a series of revival meetings. Along with Edwards, Whitefield preached Christ and then drew those who were saved into a profound biblical faith and practice.

This awakening, sparked by Wesley in England and by Edwards and Whitefield in the American colonies, was born of a comprehensive biblical worldview, where personal faith led to action in civil society and the marketplace. It understood that God is the God of all of life, not just of the spiritual realm. The Great Awakening produced leaders and citizens, the children and grandchildren of the movement, who set out to change their societies and the world.

In England, God raised up a spiritual son of Wesley, William Wilberforce (1759–1833). Wilberforce was a British parliamentarian, philanthropist, and social reformer. He was the face behind the abolition of slavery in the British Empire and was a force for the civilizing of a coarse English society. He understood that slavery was a moral evil and that the church was to work to bring an end to this institution. Wilberforce understood, because he was working from a biblical worldview, that God was interested in manners and social justice, not simply in personal salvation of the soul. He knew that God was interested in the transformation of society as well as the transformation of the individual human being. So in addition to working for the abolition of slavery, he called the church to fight against rampant alcoholism, drug abuse, sexual promiscuity, what we now call sweatshops, and other injustices and coarse elements of British society.

A group in England known as the Clapham Sect played an important role in the transformation of the nation in their time. These men and women were socially and politically active from 1790 to 1830. Wealthy and influential evangelicals, they had all kinds of vocations—they were scholars, clergy, politicians, bankers, writers, artists, economists, businessmen, and philanthropists. Their common purpose was to provide the political cover and the economic engine to change the culture, and then the laws, of British society. It was this group that created the platform for men and women like Wilberforce to challenge the status quo of British society. God used these men and women and their obedience to him to transform their nation. Among the many accomplishments of this movement was the Slave Trade Act of 1807, which outlawed the slave trade. Then, three nights before Wilberforce died, Parliament passed the Slavery Abolition Act of 1833, emancipating the slaves throughout the British Empire.

Another spiritual son of Wesley's was William Carey (1761–1834). Carey was a poor English shoemaker with an eighth-grade education. When his heart was changed by the revivals sweeping England, he sensed God's call upon his life to become a missionary to India. Carey broke all the patterns for missions work and became known as the "father of modern missions." In 1793 Carey sailed with his young family to India. Carey was a man with a biblical worldview. He preached Christ crucified. People were saved and churches were planted. But Carey longed to see the very roots of culture in the subcontinent of India transformed. His story is well told by Ruth and Vishal Mangalwadi in their book *The Legacy of William Carey: A Model for the Transformation of a Culture.*[10]

Carey not only preached the gospel of salvation and planted churches but also led Indians in the development of many other sectors of their society. For example, he introduced Christians to land stewardship by teaching them new systems of gardening to reclaim wasted land and to replant forests that had been devastated by overharvesting. He also fought for years to establish the dignity of women.

Across the Atlantic, other First Inheritance evangelicals were laying the foundations for the founding of a new nation. Most secular scholars lay the founding of the United States at the feet of deist Enlightenment thinkers like Locke, Voltaire, and Montesquieu. They argue that Jefferson and Franklin, both influenced by deism, were the channels through which the Enlightenment came into American public life. But this is contrary to the historical record.

The American political experiment was founded in biblical faith as a result of the Great Awakening. Christians wanted to form a political culture and a nation based on biblical principles. The National Council on Biblical Curriculum in Public Schools quotes the exhaustive research done by political science professors Charles S. Lutz and Donald S. Hyneman of some fifteen thousand historical documents of published political literature between 1760 and 1805: "Thirty-four percent of the contents of America's founding documents 'were direct quotations from the Bible.'"[11] Prior to the Founding Fathers, the Puritans and the Pilgrims crossed the Atlantic with Bibles in their hands. The Great Awakening called the Founding Fathers back to the Book and the comprehensive worldview of Scripture. *Newsweek* journalists David Gates and Kenneth Woodward have written that "historians are discovering that the Bible, perhaps even more than the Constitution, is our Founding document."[12]

By participating in the Great Awakening's recovery of a wholistic biblical worldview, evangelicals rejoined God's work in the world, transforming the British Empire and founding the United States of America, perhaps the most free, just, and economically prosperous nation in human history. As the church has abandoned her heritage and withdrawn from culture, we have witnessed the rise of modern and postmodern worlds. The question is, will we regain the faith of our First Inheritance forebears?

THE MODERN ERA—*Nineteenth and Twentieth Centuries*

Despite the tangible effect of the Great Awakening, in the modern era, secular materialism has been built on an absolute denial of the spiritual realm. This worldview may be said to have developed as the logical extension of the rationalism of the Enlightenment and was solidified by the publication in 1859 of Charles Darwin's book *On the Origin of*

Species. Darwin's theory of evolution provided a purely natural (as opposed to super-natural) explanation for how life came into existence, paving the way for atheistic materialism.

By definition, the materialistic paradigm, when coupled with atheism, leaves no room for the spiritual and transcendent. *Matter* is the only reality. All things that have their foundation in the reality of God's existence disappear, for God himself does not exist. Miracles cannot happen, prayer can have no effect, there is no heaven. This, in turn, ultimately leads to the death of man, love, justice, truth, morals, grace, and voca-tional call, all things grounded in God's existence. Because there is no God and his kingdom is a figment of man's imagination, work cannot be seen in the light of the kingdom of God; thus it exists for its material rewards alone.

In terms of the sacred-secular dichotomy, materialism does not merely emphasize the secular over the sacred; it recognizes *only* the secular. However, the development of materialism has had an impact on Christianity in ways that are important to recog-nize, so we turn to the church's response to the rise of secularism.

THE CHURCH'S RESPONSE

As atheistic materialism swept through the universities and national cultures of Europe and North America, the foundations of these nations and their churches were challenged.

There were few in the church who stood against the tide of secularism. One who did was Abraham Kuyper (1837–1920). This Dutch pastor and theologian was also a leading journalist and educator and served as Holland's prime minister. In 1898, Kuyper was invited to Princeton Seminary, the elite American theological training institution, to give the prestigious Stone Lectures. His desire was to stem the tide of secularism coming into the church in America and restore her biblical foundations by teaching the reign of Christ over all of life. But as history shows, the church, on the whole, abandoned the biblical worldview.

CHRIST'S SOVEREIGNTY

"THERE IS NOT A SQUARE INCH IN THE WHOLE DOMAIN OF OUR HUMAN EXISTENCE OVER WHICH CHRIST, WHO IS SOVEREIGN OVER ALL, DOES NOT CRY: 'MINE!'"

—ABRAHAM KUYPER
FREE UNIVERSITY'S INAUGURAL CONVOCATION, 1880

In responding to secularism, the church had primarily two problematic responses. The first was to accommodate the new secular paradigm, and the second was to reject it and adopt an ancient Greek paradigm. The church was divided.

THE CHURCH DIVIDED BY SECULARISM

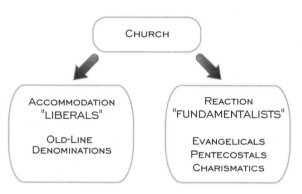

Some branches of the church, often identified today as "liberal," embraced in varying degrees the modern secular paradigm. The concept of absolute truth was replaced with metaphysical relativism. The existence of miracles—God acting outside of the natural realm—was denied. As the teachings from this side of the church became increasingly consistent with the atheistic presupposition, the powerful gospel of the kingdom of God that can lead to the transformation of individual lives and nations (as seen in the Great Awakening) was reduced to mere social activism.

The physical and social needs of the world took precedence over the spiritual needs of the world, and these former needs were met increasingly through secular means, founded on a secular philosophy. Rather than recognizing the transcendent source of justice and healing, the church tried to bring physical justice and societal transformation by its own power and apart from the salvation of the whole person in Christ.

While part of the church embraced the modern secular paradigm, other parts rejected it. The latter reacted to what was seen as an objectionable "modernism" (or "liberalism") that had overtaken the church and threatened orthodox Christianity. These leaders identified themselves as *fundamentalist,* holding to the fundamentals of the faith. But because they, too, abandoned the biblical worldview, they neglected the comprehensive implications of the gospel for the transformation of society. These became what Winter calls the Second Inheritance evangelicals.

The fundamentalists, instead of defending the biblical worldview, adopted the ancient Greek worldview that we talked about earlier in this chapter. The Greeks separated the spiritual and the physical realms. They separated grace and nature. As

Christians adopted this Gnostic-dualistic paradigm, they separated the sacred from the secular, Sunday from Monday. Many became "Sunday Christians" and abandoned the concept of being the church on Monday and bringing the kingdom of God into their *life*work each day of the week, functionally denying that Christ is sovereign over all of life. For the fundamentalists—who were the forerunners of the evangelical, Pentecostal, and charismatic movements—the spiritual realm was deemed sacred while the secular was profane.

THE GREEK DICHOTOMY

SUNDAY	HIGHER MORE IMPORTANT	GRACE	SPIRITUAL (SACRED)	FAITH THEOLOGY ETHICS MISSIONS DEVOTIONAL LIFE GOSPEL
WEEKDAYS	LOWER LESS IMPORTANT	NATURE	PHYSICAL (SECULAR)	REASON SCIENCE BUSINESS/ECONOMICS POLITICS ART/MUSIC PHYSICAL MINISTRY BREAD

Like many Pietists before them, the fundamentalists largely gave up a vigorous Christianity that impacts culture for a personal and private faith, because they placed the spiritual realm above the physical. They became what I have called the evangelical Gnostics.

EVANGELICAL GNOSTICISM

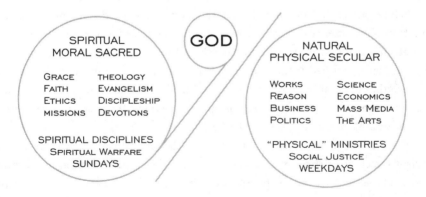

Denying the significance of the secular realm, these Second Inheritance evangelicals—evangelical Gnostics—focused on spiritual things, including an end-times eschatology that featured the Rapture and the immediate return of Jesus Christ. Dwight L. Moody (1837–1899), an American evangelist, publisher, and the founder of the famous Moody Bible Institute, saw the growing tide of secularism and liberalism in the church and concluded that Christ's return was imminent. Another founder of the Second Inheritance evangelical movement was John Nelson Darby (1800–1882), an Anglo-Irish evangelist and the father of the modern dispensational movement, which focuses on, among other things, the immediate return of Jesus Christ, the pretribulation Rapture of the church, and the one-thousand-year reign of Christ on the earth.

From a social and political perspective, the advent of the First and Second World Wars challenged the optimism of the Enlightenment and contributed to a gloomy spirit that led Christians to long to leave this broken world and focus on the world to come. Cultures in Europe and North America became pessimistic. This national psyche reinforced the tendencies of many in the evangelical church to believe that the world was getting worse and worse and that when it finally got bad enough, Christ would return.

Moody and Darby and their followers promoted a last-days dispensational eschatology. Instead of proactively seeking to reform society, this movement proposed that the sinfulness of man and the dire condition of the modern world were an indication that Jesus was surely on the verge of return. Even as they worked hard to bring people to Christ, they adopted a passive stance towards society and *waited* for Christ's return.

In 1970, Hal Lindsey, a dispensational theologian, published the best-selling nonfiction end-times book *The Late Great Planet Earth*. Lindsey's book has been published in fifty-four languages and has sold over thirty-five million copies and is still in print today. This book put the end-times movement into a rapid global acceleration that has profoundly shaped the last three generations of Christians as well as their understanding of the nature of the church, the mission of the church, and the Christian life.

The dynamic of the Great Awakening for transformation of society was lost. The movement of Second Inheritance evangelicals has focused on personal salvation and a privatized faith. It has been marked by an anti-intellectualism ("Don't ask questions—just believe!"), an abandonment of culture, and a withdrawal from the world.

Evangelical Gnostics had returned to a dualistic, pre-Reformation paradigm. Religious work, like that of the pastor, evangelist, missionary, and church planter, was seen as a higher calling than secular employment, as it had been in the Middle Ages. People seeking to be godly would want to go into "full-time Christian service." "Secular" work was often stigmatized by those doing "spiritual" work. So once again, Christians were living in two worlds professionally.

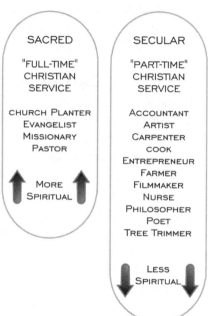

LIVING IN TWO WORLDS
PROFESSION

In terms of missions strategy, instead of recognizing that all Christians are involved in missions, only those who left secular work to dedicate themselves to "spiritual" work full-time were deemed missionaries. Still today, whole missions organizations seek to pull Christians out of the marketplace into what they believe to be the "more significant" missions work.

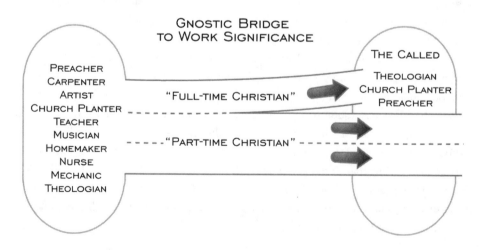

GNOSTIC BRIDGE
TO WORK SIGNIFICANCE

Beyond that, the place of deployment became an issue among spiritual workers. The Great Commission of Matthew 28:18–20 was reinterpreted by the Gnostic paradigm to be for professional religious workers who were willing to work overseas to separate themselves from the "ordinary" local world, to spread the gospel in faraway locations. In this view, being deployed cross-culturally was a higher calling than staying home. I remember that when I shared this at a YWAM North American leadership conference, everyone laughed. When I asked them why they were laughing, they said that if you want to be the *most* spiritual, you must work among unreached people groups.

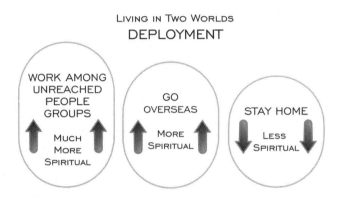

LIVING IN TWO WORLDS
DEPLOYMENT

WORK AMONG UNREACHED PEOPLE GROUPS — MUCH MORE SPIRITUAL

GO OVERSEAS — MORE SPIRITUAL

STAY HOME — LESS SPIRITUAL

For the first time since the Reformation, large numbers of Christians who were not in "full-time Christian service" began living in two worlds—essentially their workdays and their Sundays. By abandoning the biblical worldview and adopting a strongly dualistic worldview, many branches of the church have withdrawn from the marketplace. Within this model, the Christian faith no longer informs the cultural life of many Christians. Sadly, attempts by Christians to reject the secular have resulted in their own lives and the greater life of their communities becoming more godless.

WHERE DO WE GO FROM HERE?

History shows that dualistic thought, manifesting itself in various forms, has long been a problem in the church—indeed, from its beginning. What the Reformation had conceptually and practically eliminated was carried on and perpetuated by later traditions. Today, the sacred-secular dichotomy remains a grave problem. Having charted the history of dualism in the church, we can now, in the next chapter, look at some specific ways in which dualism affects our own thinking. This will help us repudiate this persistent—and false—paradigm and recover a truly biblical view of our lives and work, one in which we consciously live undivided lives, consecrated to God.

CHAPTER 3

THE SACRED-SECULAR DICHOTOMY:

AN ENTIRE WORLDVIEW

Dualism, or the sacred-secular dichotomy, is far more than simply a particular way of looking at faith or what it means to be a disciple in religious terms. It is, by its very nature, an all-encompassing worldview, the lens through which one looks at all that is, and one's place in it—as an individual human being, in all of one's life, and as part of a community of people. As such, it most certainly shapes our basic understanding of our life and work.

FALSE DICHOTOMIES

We've already discussed the false dichotomy that dualism perpetuates between the clergy and the laity, relegating the vast majority of Christians who labor in the "secular" realm to second-class status and making the church as a whole largely irrelevant in the face of the profound cultural crises facing the world. Now, in order to explore the total-life nature of dualism further, let's take a look at how dualism affects our views of several other aspects of existence.

SACRED - SECULAR DUALISM

SPIRIT	BODY
ETERNAL	TEMPORAL
CLERGY	LAITY
HEART	MIND
INDIVIDUAL	COMMUNITY
ENDS	MEANS
THE CROSS	THE CREATION MANDATE

Spirit—Body

To the dualist, the human being is fragmented. He has a body and a soul. The dualist believes that because God is interested in spiritual things, a person's soul has more importance than his or her body. Salvation entails merely saving the soul for heaven. God is not interested in saving the whole human being for time and eternity.

My brothers and sisters in Korea express this dichotomy as it relates to ministering to people's physical and social needs. For years I have traveled to Korea to train young Christians who want to work among the poor in developing countries. Inevitably I am always asked the question, "Darrow, which is more important, bread or gospel?" The hidden question is, "Is man's soul not more important than his body?" For years I tried

BABETTE'S FEAST

Based on a story by Isak Dinesen, the Academy Award–winning film *Babette's Feast* is itself a feast, spreading out before us the bounty and goodness of God and his creation in a beautiful tale that reunites body and spirit, duty and pleasure.

Though heirs of the Protestant Reformation and in fact named after Martin Luther and his friend Philip Melanchthon, the film's two sisters, Martina and Philippa, are thoroughly dualist in their worldview. In a community on the Jutland coast of Denmark, the two lead a small and aging Protestant sect founded by their now-deceased father. Members of this somber group live lives of self-denial. They are suspicious of the "pleasures of the world" and fearful of "too much joy." Though they express longing for their "eternal reward" and seem outwardly pious, their religion has become a set of orthodoxies and abstract principles, rather than a faith lived out in daily life and activity, and the sisters struggle to maintain unity among

its bitter and petty membership. Martina and Philippa themselves, although committed to faithful and dutiful service, also deny themselves any "earthly satisfaction."

But then Babette comes into their lives. When this refugee fleeing war in France arrives at their door and pleads for an opportunity to work, Martina and Philippa consent. Although kind to Babette, the sisters treat her with gentle condescension, not considering that Babette might have something to teach them and wary of allowing themselves to be served. Babette, in fact, had been the celebrated chef of the finest restaurant in Paris but keeps this knowledge to herself and humbly follows the sisters' instructions for preparing their customary plain and tasteless meals. Finally, after serving as their housekeeper for many years, Babette is awarded a sum of money from France and asks for permission to prepare a French meal for the members of the sect in memory of its founder, the sisters' father.

to answer the question in a straightforward manner, only to be asked at the end, "But Darrow, which is more important?" It finally dawned on me that the Gnostic question demanded a dualistic response. If people were ever going to move beyond this dualistic paradigm, the very assumptions of the question need to be challenged. Now whenever I am asked this question, I take the opportunity to expose the nonbiblical paradigm. I respond by saying, "That is not a biblical question! That is a Gnostic question!"

The Bible is wholistic. It brings a whole message: the whole council of God to the whole of each person ("heart…soul…mind and…strength," Mark 12:30), to the whole of humankind ("all nations," Matt. 28:19), for the whole world ("to reconcile to himself all things," Col. 1:20).

Although hesitant to allow it, the sisters consent, mindful of the fact that Babette has never asked them for anything before.

Cartloads of delicacies begin arriving from France—a turtle and a cage of live quail, cows' head, expensive wine and champagne, truffles and caviar, bursting bags of sumptuous fruit—and when the expected guests realize the scope and lavish nature of the feast Babette plans to prepare, they unite in determination to not be undermined in their strict distinction between "heavenly" duty and "worldly" pleasure. Fearing that they have "exposed [themselves] to dangerous and maybe even evil powers," they decide to participate in the upcoming meal out of respect for Babette but proclaim, "We shall use our tongues for prayer," and, "It will be as if we never had the sense of taste." However, as tray after tray of lovingly prepared offerings emerges from the kitchen and the meal progresses, the beginnings of transformation in the group are apparent. Old conflicts seem to be forgotten and there is a visible difference in warmth and unity as the group retires for the evening. One member of the group admits what the others are afraid to: "[Babette] had the ability to transform a dinner into a kind of love affair—a love affair that made no distinction between bodily appetite and spiritual appetite."

In the end, the extent of Babette's sacrifice is revealed: rather than use her money to return home she has given up her career as renowned chef forever and has spent the entire sum of her money on the meal. The sisters are overwhelmed by her love and generosity, but Babette, speaking humbly of her vocation as an artist of cuisine explains, "I was able to make them happy when I gave of my very best." Realizing that Babette's gift to them, lovingly rendered from her deepest passions, was far more representative of God's gracious and generous character than the outwardly pious behavior of the sect or years of dutiful service performed by the sisters, Philippa proclaims, "This is not the end, Babette. In Paradise, you will be the great artist that God meant you to be. Ah, how you will delight the angels."

We find the Scriptures are integrated in regard to the physical-spiritual. God created a universe that had spiritual and physical components. He declared it good. Man, the image of God, has heart, soul, mind, and strength. Jesus Christ, the incarnate Son of God, came in the flesh in space and time to a real earth. Jesus' body was resurrected from the grave and ascended into heaven. Our bodies will be resurrected at the return of Christ. He will come again in the flesh at the end of time with a new heaven and a new earth.[1]

Eternal—Temporal

The Gnostic paradigm diminishes the integration of reality in both space and time. In space, there is a lack of integration between heaven and earth, and in time, between the eternal and the temporal. To the dualist, the eternal is sacred while the temporal is secular. The kingdom of God is in the future beyond history!

In the Gnostic vision, the spiritual realm takes precedence over the physical world, and eternity (transcendent time), over chronological time (clock time). In this dichotomized view of reality, *kairos*[2]—the fullness of time, when eternity breaks through into time—is seldom preserved.

Like much of the animistic world, Gnostic Christians forget that when Christ returns there will be a new heaven and a new earth; instead they see this world as vanishing. Dwight L. Moody, whom we mentioned in the previous chapter, created a dictum that has profoundly shaped the modern church: "Why polish brass on a sinking ship?" For Moody, the world was like a sinking ship. It had no future. Souls were the only things that counted. So save as many souls as you can before the ship sinks. Today this perspective lives on in the great focus for many people on the end times, supported by popular apocalyptic literature. For the many who anticipate the end times as coming very, very shortly, there is little reason to address contemporary issues such as the health of the environment, poverty, or injustice. There is little place for long-term thinking about life on earth. Sometimes their expectations even lead people (especially those assured of the Rapture) to desire the hastening of the end rather than leaving the timing to God, despite the death and destruction their vision would bring.

In this dualistic paradigm, the church focuses on the future aspects of the kingdom at the expense of the present aspects of the kingdom. The Sermon on the Mount is relegated to eternity, not to time and history. The words of the Lord's Prayer "Your kingdom come, your will be done on earth as it is in heaven" are just that—words, spoken by rote on Sunday morning with little present reality for the church in society. As someone has said, "The church is so heavenly minded that she is no earthly good." Too often, the very people whom Christ has died to save sense this attitude from the church.

But Scripture is beautifully balanced. Time and eternity are both real. In those *kairos* moments, eternity breaks through into time. In time, God's people are to be building elements of the kingdom of God. When Christ returns, there will be a great shaking.[3] All that is of the kingdom of God will be left standing; all else will be in a pile of rubble. Similarly there will be a refiner's fire. All that has been built that relates to the kingdom of God will be left by the refiner's fire. All else will be destroyed by the fire.[4] The earth will not disappear when Christ returns! It will be a refined, purified earth, a "re-newed" earth. The kingdom of God is both now and not yet!

Heart—Mind

There have been periods of church history in which the church focused on the Christian mind: orthodox belief, sound theology. This sometimes worked out to be the pursuit of truth at the expense of personal experience. At other times, movements in the church reacted to the deadening quality of a Christian intellectualism with an overemphasis on personal experience—heart religion—giving rise to an anti-intellectualism that can still be found in the modern church. I cannot tell you how many times I have heard Christian leaders and pastors say, "Stop asking questions, just believe!" "Bypass the mind; let God speak straight to your heart!"

In contrast to these two extremes, Scripture stresses a balance. We are to love God with all our heart, soul, and mind.[5] Christians are to have both a warm heart and a thoughtful mind.

Individual—Community

Some cultures order themselves around the concept of the individual; others order themselves around the concept of community. Individualism separates the individual from the community, whereas communalism elevates the community at the expense of undervaluing or ignoring the potential or needs of the individual. The Bible models a fundamental balance in the Trinity, the One-and-Many God—one in being, three in persons. While dualistic thinking gravitates to one extreme or the other, Christian community celebrates both the individual and the communion.

Ends—Means

Dualistic thinking encourages us to believe we can separate ends and means, which in reality are inseparable. The ends of work refer to the purpose to which the work is applied. The means refer to the methodology used to achieve the ends. There are a number of ways to relate ends and means. Some people are pragmatists; they focus on the ends. Good ends justify any means to achieve those ends. If the end result is good enough, you may use immoral, unjust, or illegal means to reach those ends. In many countries where there is a culture of corruption, Christians will bribe officials to get approval or equipment for their ministries, just like unbelievers do. Other people care only about "professionalism"; they focus on the process (the means). Good means are what is important; the ends are not. These people want to "do things right." They can even "do the wrong things right!" This happens in companies or ministries where the focus is on professionalism and quality work. This is good, but to what end is this excellence employed? An international charity may employ excellent methods of distributing aid that ends up creating dependency and greater poverty. Forgotten in either approach is that the means tend to shape the end.

The Bible demands just means to meet just ends worthy of our calling. As Francis Schaeffer was fond of saying, "The Lord's work is to be done in the Lord's way!" Because we live in God's universe—a moral universe—moral processes and moral results must increasingly define our vocation. To use Schaeffer's dictum, we must do the Lord's work in the Lord's way!

MICHAEL BAER'S STORY

Michael Baer's résumé spans the pastorate, entrepreneurship, business consulting, and overseas microbusiness development. As he explains in his book Business as Mission: The Power of Business in the Kingdom of God, *he has come to see all of his work as part of one calling.*

After coming to Christ in college, I spent the first fourteen years of my adult life in the pastoral ministry—youth work, planting two churches, serving a third, and launching a Christian school. The Lord blessed my ministry, and I can truthfully say I enjoyed it and was secure in my call to it. However, over time I began to sense God leading me into a different area. I began to desire to minister "free of charge" and to be out in the business world with lost people. I especially wanted to get away from the constant discounting of the gospel that occurred because people I witnessed to believed that sharing the gospel was my job.

In the early 1980s I began to dabble in business while still in the pastorate. I was testing the waters, so to speak, and seeking to know what God might want me to do. Eventually I left the formal pastorate and spent the next ten years in business—starting several companies (including the one I now own) and leading turnaround endeavors in corporations owned by others. God was pleased to use me in both the pastorate and the corporate world, and I thank him for it. Opportunities abounded to communicate the gospel and to encourage believers I met along the way. It was an exciting time. It was always fun to share how God had led me into the pastorate and then into business—these two apparently distinct parts of my life.

However, just as I sensed a leading from God out of the formal pastorate and into business, I also began to sense that there had to be more in my business life than just being a Christian witness on the job. I began

The Cross—The Creation Mandate

Dualistic thinking is "either-or" thinking. Accordingly, some people limit the power of the cross to only saving souls for eternity. Others focus on our God-given mandate to develop the earth—a mandate we will cover in depth later in the book. The biblical balance stresses that Jesus died to restore *all* things to himself. The cross restores our purpose on earth *as well as* granting us eternal life, reuniting the two as one whole realm of God.

In fact, in each case where we have a divided mind—be it between the cross and the creation mandate, ends and means, individual and community, heart and mind, eternal and temporal, spirit and body—we need to return to Scripture and to the cross of Christ and seek God's help in reuniting the two as one whole realm of his creation and kingship: the all-encompassing kingdom of God.

to pray and ask God to show me how these two apparently distinct parts of my life could actually come together—fourteen years in ministry and ten years in business. Were they separate chapters, or were they, in fact, parts of a greater whole, the "big picture" that God had in store for me?

The answer to my questions came in the strangest of places. In 1993 I was invited to travel to a Muslim area of the former Soviet Union to develop and deliver leadership and management training for medical students. While there, I had what I have come to call the "for this was I born" experience. I finally understood why God had given me seminary training and pastoral experience as well as passion and success in business. His plan was to bring both together in my service for him. Specifically, he desired to use me through business to minister to those I could never reach otherwise. Through my work of business training, relationship and witness opportunities opened that I could never have imagined. God began to bless my work

in powerful ways. For the next four years I returned to the former Soviet Union annually with teams of volunteer Christian business leaders to give business seminars and share the gospel with those who attended.

Even with God's blessing on the volunteer work, I still sensed that the picture was not yet complete. Then, in 1997, I was approached by missionaries working in the same part of the world and asked to develop a program whereby impoverished and disenfranchised Christians could learn to start their own businesses. Their idea was that these persecuted believers could escape unemployment (over 90 percent in the Christian community in one country), provide for their families, support their local church, and even use their new businesses as a basis for church planting in remote areas. We launched this new program in 1998, and today the work that came out of that meeting is operating in more than twenty locations around the world, helping persecuted Christian minorities start businesses to provide economic traction for their own indigenous church-planting movements. At the same time, I left the company I had been working for and started a new consulting company, my current company, for the sole purpose of providing flexible employment for those who wanted to be a part of business missions overseas while remaining involved in business at home.

Today, a strong, for-profit consulting firm and an international microbusiness development agency exist as the result. Staff members and associates who share a commitment to Christ and to kingdom business work together along with hundreds of volunteers from other companies to take their business expertise and align it with church-planting ministries among the unreached.

What I have come to learn through all of this is that there are no "parts" to my life. My story may represent different chapters, but they are all part of one book, a book with one unified story, being written by God. I no longer wonder why God led me out of the pastorate and into business. I no longer think of it as leaving the ministry. Instead, I have begun to see that in God's kingdom all things are equally sanctified by him and unified in him. For Christian business leaders, this leads to what I call "the seamless integration of business and mission." To pursue this seamless integration, we must reject the unbiblical thinking that our lives can be compartmentalized into the sacred and secular or that business and ministry are by definition separate activities. Scripture teaches us rather to embrace the truth that all of Christ's servants have callings that are high and holy and equally pleasing to the Lord. If God has called us into business, our goal is to discover why and to act on that purpose. As we do so, God's creation will be blessed, and he will be glorified.

DISPLACING THE TRUTH

Dualism not only polarizes our understanding of such elements as the eternal and temporal, heart and mind, but also affects the whole of our existence in another important way. By containing our Christian faith to only a part of our existence and the spiritual to a boxed-in realm, a dualistic mindset leaves the larger parts of our lives and reality to be defined according to other worldviews. As we discussed in chapter 1, unless we have consciously renewed our minds according to the worldview of Scripture—the comprehensive, objective worldview of reality as God has made it—then our view of our life and work is largely determined by the worldview of our culture, and for many of us that includes elements of atheistic materialism and animism. Following are just a few of the ways those worldviews fill in the vacuum opened up by the dualistic mindset of believers.

The Nature of the Universe

Biblically, we understand that the universe is creation. We live in reality framed by the infinite Creator, where the universe is a consequence of the Creator's artistry. While God stands outside of creation (transcendent), he is also engaged in creation (immanent). Part of man's role, before and after the Fall, is to care for creation as God's steward—as one entrusted to care for another's property, in this case for the household or estate of God.

The biblical understanding of the universe as creation stands in contrast to the beliefs that arise out of atheistic-materialistic and animistic worldviews. The traditional materialist tends to see nature as existing for man and not for God. It is viewed as a quarry to be mined, a forest to be harvested.

In some forms of animism, this world is actually *maya*—an illusion. In other forms of animism, the natural world lacks importance because it is passing away. Paradoxically, both to animists and to modern-day neopagans in the West, the natural world is a god to be worshiped. Each of these viewpoints creates very different attitudes about our life and work.

The Origin of Humankind

In making humankind, God did not look outside himself for a pattern. Instead he looked at himself. Scripture reveals that we have been created in the image of God. We are united with creation—as one of his creatures. At the same time, we are distinct from creation in that we alone are the image of God and meant to have dominion over the rest of creation. Because we are created by God in his image, each human life is and always will be sacred and significant. Even the smallest, most broken person has dignity because he or she bears the image of God.

This understanding of humankind stands in contrast to the anthropologies created by materialism and animism. In atheistic materialism the human being is merely an animal, an out-of-control consumer of scarce resources. This consumerist mindset flourishes in the West. In contrast, animists tend to see human beings as spirits temporarily inhabiting bodies; physical existence in general is fleeting and thus insignificant. To the animist the material world is of no value and in no need of development. When we allow our understandings to be shaped by either of these false views, our life and work are cut off from the foundational truth that we were made in the image of God.

The Fallen World and the Cross of Christ

Scripture teaches that while we are made in the image of God, we have rejected our Creator and our intended place in his creation, with tragic consequences. While human life has dignity, and each individual is significant, we are also rebels against the

High King of Heaven, sinners against the holy God whose very self defines all that is good. As the prophet Isaiah said, "We all, like sheep, have gone astray, each of us has turned to his own way" (Isa. 53:6). The result can be seen in further words from Isaiah, words like *suffering, infirmities, sorrows, judgment,* and *sin*. We have chosen lies over truth, injustice over justice. We have turned from the way of wholeness and whole-someness and have so harmed ourselves and the rest of creation in the process that we are incapable of turning around on our own. The root problem is *inside* of man; we are, in fact, spiritually dead. Without God's intervention, we are without hope. But we—and this broken world—are not a lost cause. The whole Bible is a witness to God's faithful work of redemption, which culminated in the life, death, and resurrection of Jesus Christ. In Christ, God is reconciling us and *all* things to himself.[6]

The biblical principle of the fallen world and the necessity of the cross of Christ stand in contrast to atheistic materialism, which has no moral framework and yet would argue, irrationally, that man is good. So why are there problems in our world? Why is there suffering and strife? In this view, the root of all problems is not inside of man but *outside* of man, in his environment. Corrupt institutions are the problem. If the structures were improved, man's natural goodness would flourish. According to materialism, there is no Fall, so there is no need for salvation. By education, man and his culture are perfectible.

The events of the past hundred years—the two world wars, the genocides in Cambodia and Rwanda, the ethnic cleansing in the Balkans in the nineties and the planned famines in the Ukraine in the thirties, the inhumanity of Mao and Stalin, apartheid in South Africa, and the deliberate murder of hundreds of millions of preborn babies through abortion—all deny the utopian view of the materialist.

On the other hand, the normalcy of evil and the capriciousness of the gods in animism breed cultures where fatalism, corruption, hopelessness, and despair flourish. You cannot fight evil; you can only hope to appease the gods and avoid disaster. Droughts, floods, disease, and famine are normal. Life, at best, is about surviving these evils.

The pessimism of animism stands in vivid contrast to the utopian visions of secular materialism. The biblical paradigm shouts out a radical position different from either. The Fall is real, but in light of the cross of Christ we are to fight against it. In summary, we are to be realistic idealists, not romantic idealists (as in materialism) or cynical realists (as in animism).

Human Freedom

As Christians, our life and work are shaped by the dance between our dependence and independence, between God's agency and our agency. Scripture holds two truths in tension. First, God is transcendent; we are creatures. God is not dependent on creation, but both we and all of creation are dependent on God. At the same time, humankind is distinct from the rest of creation. As the images of God, we are free moral agents with responsibilities to steward the rest of creation and the ability to make decisions that affect history. In this sense, we are independent.

Approaching the tension from another angle, Scripture witnesses that God is both sovereign over all of creation, including our individual lives, and at the same time, our Father. His sovereignty speaks of his supreme power and absolute authority. In his Fatherhood he has power and authority but also shows his tender mercy, love, fatherly guidance, discipline, and desire for relationship. This understanding of God's nature helps us better understand the nature of our freedom.

Our culture will tell us only part of the story, or none of the story. Materialism sees the universe in a mechanical fashion, supposing the uniformity of natural causes in a closed system. In this worldview, we are autonomous (there is no God) and self-reliant. This worldview leads to two approaches to life and work that are out of sync with reality. On one hand, since we're self-reliant, it's all up to us. If anything is going to happen, we must accomplish it in our own strength and by our own intellect. The assumption is that we are capable of running our lives and the world, of overcoming whatever obstacles there are to perfecting human society and the environment. At the same time, since we have total autonomy, since there is no higher authority and no moral law flowing from the moral Creator, we are not answerable for what we do or leave undone. In this sense, atheistic-materialistic thought leads to seeing humankind as autonomous and powerful but unbound by accountability. On the other hand, since it requires a closed universe driven by natural causes, materialism also leads us finally to the conclusion that our actions and wills are insignificant and futile. In the end, we are just another animal, another part of nature driven solely by genes and chemicals and outside forces, with no real freedom.

Though from a different starting point than atheistic materialism, animism, as we have already seen, leads to fatalism. Moral agency is removed from people and given over to fate and a plethora of spirits who are often capricious. Thus, not only is there no sovereign God working toward a consistent, good end, but also people are powerless. This means that there can never be real meaning to any level of work.

As Christians, we believe in both God's sovereignty and human freedom. It is as unique creatures in God's creation—both dependent and independent—that we find the purpose of our life and work: we are called to serve as God's ambassadors of reconciliation for all the human and natural relationships broken by the Fall, and God has enabled, and expects, us to make sanctified decisions within the framework of the principles that govern his creation.

A GREAT DISCONNECT

We've touched on a handful of biblical teachings about the nature of God, the universe, and humankind to explore this conundrum: as Christians, we assent to foundational biblical truths, yet many of us experience a great disconnect between this knowledge and the life we live in the world most of the time.

Picture a dualist's brain. Instead of a brain divided into the scientific right and left hemispheres and different lobes, envision a brain divided, say 90 percent to 10 percent. Our assent to the foundational truths about reality are contained in the 10 percent lobe, and the nerve pathways to the rest of our body are largely cut off. They transmit unreliably, only when triggered by certain learned cues, perhaps on Sunday mornings when our mindset is challenged or with certain friends who hold us accountable. We haven't developed the pathways that see the connections to all of our actions, to all of our life and work. Instead, the unbiblical ideas that fill up the 90 percent lobe send signals freely, determining what we say and what we do, calling the shots about most everything.

Like the neurological impulses in our body, we don't think consciously about these things most of the time. But here we are with this divided mind, created by our unexamined culture. We see reality as a series of black-and-white dichotomies—soul and body, clergy and laity, eternal and temporal; we see reality falsely divided between the spiritual and the material, the sacred and the secular.

This state of mind blinds us to the true nature of reality, a reality that Jesus expresses as the kingdom of God. In the next chapter we'll hear Jesus himself tell us about his kingdom as we seek to move beyond the false paradigm into the reality that God created us to live in.

CHAPTER 4

ONE LORD, ONE REALM:

A PARABLE

When we see reality from a biblical worldview, we understand that there is one God and one world.

BIBLICAL THEISM

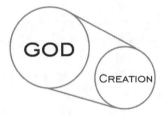

Yet contemporary Christians are not alone among Christ's followers in being blinded to this true nature of the reality that God has made and created us to live in. As was made abundantly clear by our earlier tour of dualism throughout church history, generations before us have misunderstood the nature of God's kingdom and underestimated the scope of God's work in the world. As my coauthors and I wrote in our book *God's Unshakable Kingdom,*

> The concept of the kingdom of God is one of the most confusing, controversial, and misunderstood ideas in the Bible. Some have launched violent revolutions in the name of establishing the kingdom of God on earth. Some have advocated elaborate schemes of social engineering and wealth redistribution in the name of advancing the kingdom of God. Many Christians simply

ignore the concept, associating it with heretical Christian sects. Others think of God's kingdom as heaven or as looking forward to Christ's return, but they are not clear about the kingdom's nature or relevance to their lives on this side of eternity. They would have difficulty explaining it to non-Christians.

Yet it's an indisputable fact that the kingdom of God was the central theme of the teachings of Jesus. The phrase "kingdom of God" or "kingdom of Heaven" appears ninety-eight times in the New Testament!...What was this idea that burned so strongly in the heart of Christ? What was he trying to teach us?[1]

Our difficulty today in trying to grasp Christ's message about the kingdom is not unlike the state of affairs among those who actually walked side by side with Jesus two thousand years ago. Even those closest to Jesus missed what he said about himself and his kingdom, over and over. After three years with him, Jesus' disciples were still in the dark as they accompanied him on his last trip to Jerusalem. Let's join them on the journey and listen in as Jesus tries to correct his own disciples' misunderstanding of the kingdom of God.

THE KINGDOM AT HAND

On their last trip to Jerusalem, Jesus and the twelve traveled in the company of a larger group of followers, people who had followed them from Galilee. The roads were busy, since all the Jewish faithful who were able were on their way to Jerusalem to celebrate Passover. Though the journey was demanding, the mood was happy as people looked forward to worshiping at the great temple at this most special of times, enjoying the city's sights, and, on the way, catching up with people they hadn't seen in a long time.

In addition, for many this was no ordinary Passover pilgrimage; there was an extra current of excitement—and tension. At least some in the crowd believed they were, at long last, about to see the day that the Messiah made himself known in all his glory, defeated the occupying Roman Empire, overthrew the unjust rulers, and established the perfect rule of God on earth. God's people would be free at last, and Zion would realize her scriptural glory. And more than a few around Jesus were sure he was the one, the long-awaited, heaven-sent Messiah—their new king!

The tension was keenly felt by those closest to Jesus. They had heard the threats against him and seen the anger he could elicit, particularly among the ruling elite. Even without that, they knew that the Romans—fearful of Jewish insurgents—would be especially on guard, with tight security, as the crowds pressed into Jerusalem. The

Romans could be expected to respond very harshly to anything or anyone who seemed a threat to public order. At the same time, the twelve disciples were not untouched by the Messianic excitement, even more so because they knew Jesus was full of divine power, and they had heard his preaching about the kingdom being "at hand."

THE PARABLE OF THE MINAS

At one of their last stops on the trip, Jesus tried once again to make clearer to them, and to the gathered crowd, just what kind of kingdom experience he was talking about. Stopping as a guest in the home of Zacchaeus, a tax collector and Roman collaborator, Jesus restated his purpose in coming to earth: "For the Son of Man came to seek and to save what was lost" (Luke 19:10). Then once again, he told them a parable. In relating this parable, the gospel writer Luke makes a point that Jesus is challenging the prevailing misconceptions about the coming of the kingdom: "While they were listening to this, he went on to tell them a parable, because he was near Jerusalem and the people thought that the kingdom of God was going to appear at once" (v. 11). With these words Luke reveals that the people who were anticipating the coming of the Jewish Messiah had a faulty paradigm—just as many of us still do. It is for this reason that Jesus went on to tell the people the parable of the minas:

> A man of noble birth went to a distant country to have himself appointed king and then to return. So he called ten of his servants and gave them ten minas. "Put this money to work," he said, "until I come back."
>
> But his subjects hated him and sent a delegation after him to say, "We don't want this man to be our king."
>
> He was made king, however, and returned home. Then he sent for the servants to whom he had given the money, in order to find out what they had gained with it.
>
> The first one came and said, "Sir, your mina has earned ten more."
>
> "Well done, my good servant!" his master replied. "Because you have been trustworthy in a very small matter, take charge of ten cities."
>
> The second came and said, "Sir, your mina has earned five more."
>
> His master answered, "You take charge of five cities."
>
> Then another servant came and said, "Sir, here is your mina; I have kept it laid away in a piece of cloth. I was afraid of you, because you are a hard man. You take out what you did not put in and reap what you did not sow."
>
> His master replied, "I will judge you by your own words, you wicked servant! You knew, did you, that I am a hard man, taking out what I did not put

in, and reaping what I did not sow? Why then didn't you put my money on deposit, so that when I came back, I could have collected it with interest?"

Then he said to those standing by, "Take his mina away from him and give it to the one who has ten minas."

"Sir," they said, "he already has ten!"

He replied, "I tell you that to everyone who has, more will be given, but as for the one who has nothing, even what he has will be taken away. But those enemies of mine who did not want me to be king over them—bring them here and kill them in front of me." (Luke 19:12–27)

MISCONCEPTIONS OF THE KINGDOM

Jesus told this story to correct his followers' misunderstanding of what kind of kingdom was at hand and what roles he, the King, and they, his servants, had to play. Earlier on the journey, as they had approached the ancient city of Jericho, Jesus told his disciples, for the third time, of his coming death.[2] As Luke goes on to say, however, they "did not understand any of this" (Luke 18:34). The disciples' understanding was blocked by several misconceptions.

First, they believed that when Christ entered Jerusalem he would be made king and would set up a *political* kingdom. The kingdom, they thought, would be present and physical. Their focus was on earthly power and authority, and they wanted "a piece of the action," as we see in Mark 10:35–44. They thought they could get it simply by asking for it.

Second, considering the context of the passage and the words *at once* in Luke 19:11, it is clear that the disciples thought they needed to do nothing more than wait for the kingdom. Jesus would set up the kingdom soon; all a disciple had to do was *wait*.

Despite time passing without the Second Coming, or the Day of the Lord, anticipated by Jesus' first audience, Christians throughout church history have been immobilized by this "theology of waiting." One way this is expressed is in the thought, "I have been saved; now I wait for Christ's return!" Unfortunately this recognizes only the *justification* and *glorification* elements of salvation. For too many in the church, it is as though the *sanctification* element of the Christian life does not exist. They act as though they were saved for heaven only, giving little thought to serving Christ and having a role to play here and now in bringing in the kingdom.

Two false theological trends have developed among Christians that encourage passivity. The first is a fatalism, not very different from that found among animists. Everything that happens in life, these Christians believe, is the will of God. Untimely death? Disease or disablement? These people believe it is God's will. In the face of poverty and hunger or injustice, many believe or act as if "There is nothing I can do!" Many pull out the adage "The poor you will always have with you"[3] to prove their point, looking no further for what call the situation might be making on them. As they accept the inevitability of world hunger, they neglect the One who fed the five thousand and conquered death.

The second trend that breeds passivity in the church is the insidious dualism that we traced in Christian thought from its ancient beginnings. Over time this thinking has led us to see a dichotomy between physical and spiritual reality, with the latter being what is important. In reality, when Christians concern themselves only with narrowly defined "spiritual" concerns, they are unconsciously denying the importance and reality of Christ's teaching about this present world and life, his physical resurrection, and many of his teachings and miracles. Jesus healed the sick and fed the hungry. Rather than following Jesus, Christians influenced by evangelical Gnosticism often become utterly passive. Dualistic thinking keeps them from putting flesh on their faith in their everyday lives, making their faith private and ineffective, as if it has nothing to offer this world and no power or relevance in the present.

A THEOLOGY OF ACTION

In contrast, our Lord, who was about to endure the cross and was acting decisively in history to reverse the results of the Fall, told his listeners a parable that tied the two aspects of reality together and was clearly a contradiction to a theology of waiting. It described the present and future of the kingdom as of one piece, a continuous and ongoing life, with important work for the master's workers throughout. It acknowledged the "not yet" aspect of the kingdom, the time while the master is away before returning after receiving his kingdom, but also presented a theology of action and advancement in the present—in the time of anticipating his return.

Notice the active role of Christ in the parable. Christ, "the nobleman," is going "to a distant country to receive a kingdom for himself, and then return" (Luke 19:12 NASB). Notice also the active role of the disciples, pictured as servants, or slaves, in the parable. "So he called ten of his servants and gave them ten minas. 'Put this money to work,' he said, 'until I come back'" (Luke 19:13).

The ten minas represented the measure of "capital"[4] that Christ invests in each believer's life. In addition to one's natural talents, abilities, interests, and temperament, Christ endows believers with his Spirit, spiritual gifts (1 Cor. 12), and "every spiritual blessing in the heavenly places" (Eph. 1:3 NASB). These are not given to be squandered, hoarded, or used to boost our own egos. They are given as resources to be invested and used in the expansion of his kingdom.

After he gave the "capital," Christ issued a command: in Greek the command is *pragmateuomai*. It means "trade," "do business," or "occupy." The word is used only here in the New Testament. The English word *pragmatic* is related to this Greek word. You can see the pragmatic nature of the word as reflected in many translations: "do business" (NKJV), "put this money to work" (NIV), "trade with these" (RSV), "do business with this" (NASB), and "buy and sell with these" (AMP). The task given by Christ to his disciples is very basic: it is to *pragmatically* use the natural and spiritual capital he has given us to engage our cultures and world for Christ and his kingdom. He has capitalized each of us to make a unique contribution to the present advancement of his kingdom. Our call is to be creative, practical, industrious, energetic, active, and diligent with the "capital" he has given.

THE UNIQUE CONTRIBUTION

In addition to relating our basic call and task as believers, the parable of the minas serves as a reminder of another truth about God's kingdom. The King James Version translates *pragmateuomai* as "occupy," so that Christ's command in Luke 19:13 is translated "occupy till I come." For us today, the word *occupy* carries certain military, but not militaristic, overtones, which accurately places Christ's command and our task in the midst of a historic spiritual conflict. Indeed, there is a cosmic conflict raging. The expansion of the kingdom of God is accomplished in the midst of the ancient spiritual war against the kingdom of darkness.

This spiritual war, however, is manifested here on earth in highly tangible ways; it has consequences for both individuals and cultures. The enemy has taken over the earth, but his reign is temporary. The King has already come and defeated the enemy, and he is returning. He has sent his troops, the church, ahead to establish a beachhead, advance into enemy territory, and then occupy the newly won land for his return. Battles are raging on many fronts. There is a battle for truth, another for the sanctity of life, another for justice, another against hunger, another against poverty, another against ignorance. Servants of the King are to occupy themselves—using their natural gifts, talents, abilities, and spiritual gifts—to fight against the forces of evil and "occupy" enemy territory. In this way, the notion of *occupying* carries for us the double meaning of actively serving God ("being occupied" with God's business) in the midst of real spiritual conflict (in which we must "occupy" territory). This is the unified task our Lord has set before us.

In short, we belong to and serve one Lord and participate in one kingdom, now and forever. The estate of the master in the parable is no less his just because he is away, nor is he surrendering any part of it as unimportant or less valuable. Moreover, the present work of his servants is just as important to him and his final purposes as will be their celebration and service to him upon his return.

Just as he did for his disciples, Jesus wants to open our eyes to the magnitude of God's coming kingdom, which encompasses every aspect of our lives and work. He calls us, we will see, to a new way of living—fully in his presence.

CHAPTER 5

CORAM DEO:

BEFORE THE FACE OF GOD

The parable of the ten minas teaches us that every Christian is called by the Lord to play an important role in manifesting God's kingdom on earth. In contrast to the dualistic or Gnostic paradigm, the Scriptures reveal an integrative, wholistic worldview of the kingdom we're called to advance. God is the Lord of all of life, not just part of life. He is the Lord of faith and missions and church planting, but he is also the Lord of business and science and art. God is Lord of *all*.

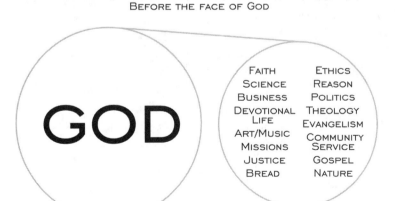

CORAM DEO
BEFORE THE FACE OF GOD

GOD

FAITH	ETHICS
SCIENCE	REASON
BUSINESS	POLITICS
DEVOTIONAL LIFE	THEOLOGY
	EVANGELISM
ART/MUSIC	COMMUNITY
MISSIONS	SERVICE
JUSTICE	GOSPEL
BREAD	NATURE

CREATOR, REDEEMER, SUSTAINER

God's comprehensive Lordship is true on three grounds.

First, God is the *Creator* of the world and *all* that is in it. The book of Genesis reveals that God's artistry was both good and beautiful, in harmony with God and with itself. The physical realm, like the spiritual realm, is sacred. It is all God's creation.

Second, God *sustains all* of his creation today. We see this in Colossians 1:17: "He is before all things, and in him all things hold together," and in Hebrews 1:3: "The Son is the radiance of God's glory and the exact representation of his being, sustaining all things by his powerful word."

Third, in Christ, God is at work *redeeming all* of his creation. The apostle Paul writes, "For God was pleased to have all his fullness dwell in him, and through him to reconcile to himself all things, whether things on earth or things in heaven, by making peace through his blood, shed on the cross" (Col. 1:19–20). God continues his work of reconciliation through Christ until Christ returns at the end of time.[1]

For these three reasons, the Gnostic paradigm is untrue to reality. There is no dichotomy in God's mind. God has made, sustains, and is redeeming one world, not two, and Christians are called to live in one world.

LIVING CORAM DEO

Our forefathers in the faith used the Latin phrase *coram Deo* to describe this way of life. The word *coram* is derived from the Latin *cora*, which means "the pupil of the eye." It is translated "in person," "face-to-face," "in one's presence," "before one's eyes," "in the presence of," "before."[2] The second word, *Deo*, is the Latin word for God. The key idea in the phrase is intimate, personal relationship. In this case, God intimately knows me. Nothing is hidden. And I am to consciously seek to live all of my life in the presence of God—"before the face of God." Some have used the concept of "the audience of one" to describe this lifestyle.

CALLED TO LIVE
CORAM DEO

THIS IS OUR CALL:

WE ARE TO LIVE ALL OF OUR LIFE IN
THE PRESENCE OF GOD, UNDER THE
AUTHORITY OF GOD, AND TO THE
HONOR AND GLORY OF GOD

In Europe, the Protestant Reformation of the sixteenth century rekindled this biblical understanding, as we saw earlier when we charted the history of dualism in the church (chapter 2). Later, the Puritan pastor Cotton Mather (1663–1728) put it this way: "Let every Christian walk with God when he works at his calling, and act in his occupation with an eye to God, act as under the eye of God."[3] Even the great English poet John Milton (1608–1674) captured the sense of living under the gaze of our Heavenly Employer:

> All is, if I have grace to use it so,
> As ever in my great task-Master's eye.[4]

Leland Ryken interprets these two lines from Milton's seventh sonnet as "All that matters is that I have the grace to use my time as though I am always living in my great taskmaster's presence."[5]

MADE FOR GOD'S PRESENCE

What these Christians who walked before us recognized was that humans were made to walk in God's presence. From Genesis to Revelation, God reveals himself as the "Infinite-Personal God," to use Francis Schaeffer's term. In Genesis 1:26, God reveals not only that he is the Personal God but also that he is Community: "Let us make man in our image, in our likeness." Before the creation of the world there was the intimacy of communion and communication between the Persons of the Trinity—the One and Many God.

God made man is his image so that man might have relationship with his own kind (other humans) and also to have communion with his Creator. The intimacy of God's intention is found in Genesis 3:8–9: "Then the man and his wife heard the sound of the LORD God as he was walking in the garden in the cool of the day, and they hid from the LORD God among the trees of the garden. But the LORD God called to the man, 'Where are you?'"

This same sense of communion is found in the wilderness wanderings when God instructs Moses to build a tent for him so the presence of the transcendent God may dwell in the midst of the Hebrew camp. The Hebrews were living in tents, and God so desired to identify with his people that he wanted to "tabernacle"—live in a tent—just like his people. "Then have them make a sanctuary for me, and I will dwell among them. Make this tabernacle and all its furnishings exactly like the pattern I will show you" (Exod. 25:8–9).

Perhaps the most remarkable demonstration that God's intention is to have humans dwell in his presence is that he chose to enter history as a vulnerable baby.

The Incarnation marks the high point of God's communion with man in that the Son of God became the Man, Christ Jesus. *Young's Literal Translation of the Bible* captures the thrill of the intimacy of the Incarnation in John 1:14: "And the Word became flesh, and did tabernacle among us, and we beheld his glory, glory as of an only begotten of a father, full of grace and truth."[6]

The Greek word used for "tabernacle" in Exodus 25:8-9 in the Septuagint (the Greek translation of the Old Testament), *skenoo,* is the same word used in John 1:14. It means "to fix one's tabernacle, have one's tabernacle, abide (or live) in a tabernacle (or tent), tabernacle" or "to dwell."[7] This is a powerful image of God's desire and intentions for us to dwell in his presence, "before the face of God."

God continues to take the initiative and offers to restore intimacy with us through his Son, Jesus Christ. The apostle Paul writes, "Once you were alienated from God and were enemies in your minds because of your evil behavior. But now he has reconciled you by Christ's physical body through death to present you holy in his sight, without blemish and free from accusation—if you continue in your faith, established and firm, not moved from the hope held out in the gospel" (Col. 1:21-23).

In redemption as in creation, we find that God desires for his people to dwell in his presence.

WORK AS WORSHIP

One of the primary themes of the Reformation was that we are justified by faith and we are to live by faith, before the face of God.

The apostle Paul writes of our justification by faith clearly in Ephesians 2:8-9: "For it is by grace you have been saved, through faith—and this not from yourselves, it is the gift of God—not by works, so that no one can boast." When we come to God, we come in faith—with empty hands. Good works will not save us. Rather we stand directly before God only by his grace, through faith in the only intermediary, Jesus Christ.[8]

Just as in salvation we stand before God by faith, Scripture witnesses that we are to live *daily* before God in faith. Once dead, we are now alive *in Christ.* Paul writes of this throughout his letters, perhaps nowhere as clearly as in Galatians: "I have been crucified with Christ and I no longer live, but Christ lives in me. The life I live in the body, I live by faith in the Son of God, who loved me and gave himself for me" (Gal. 2:20). Truly those "who receive God's abundant provision of grace and of the gift of righteousness [will] reign in life through the one man, Jesus Christ" (Rom. 5:17).

For Christians who understand that we are saved by grace through faith, the whole concept of work has been transformed to that of worship. Paul told the Roman believers, "Therefore, I urge you, brothers [and sisters], *in view of God's mercy,* to offer your bodies as living sacrifices, holy and pleasing to God—this is your spiritual act of worship" (Rom. 12:1; italics added).

Scottish historian and social critic Thomas Carlyle (1795–1881) has captured the wonder of what our forefathers understood:

> *Laborare est Orare,* Work is Worship....All true Work is sacred; in all true Work, were it but hand-labour, there is something of divines....No man has work, or can work, except religiously; not even the poor day laborer, the weaver of your coat, the sewer of your shoes.[9]

In 1520 Martin Luther published a short work called *The Babylonian Captivity of the Church.* As this tract began to circulate around Europe, it resulted in a firestorm that transformed entire cultures' thinking on life and work. An anonymous story is told about two priests who read the pamphlet when it reached Holland. The following is part of what they read that so changed their way of thinking:

> The works of monks and priests, however holy and arduous they be, do not differ one whit in the sight of God from the works of the rustic laborer in the field or the woman going about her household tasks, but that all works are measured before God by faith alone....Indeed, the menial housework of a manservant or maidservant is often more acceptable to God than all the fastings and other works of a monk or priest, because the monk or priest lacks faith.[10]

This tract challenged the two priests about the nature of salvation, the nature of the church, and the nature of work. Up to that point, their church had been open to the parish seven days a week. After reading the pamphlet, they announced that the doors of the church building would be opened on Sunday but closed the rest of the week.

That was a shocking change. What could they have been thinking? Through Luther's writings, the priests had come to see that the work their parishioners did six days a week was no less sacred than the work they themselves did, that is, if each worked *in faith.* They understood that people did not need to visit the church building daily to do their "spiritual" service or to add a measure of holiness to their days. Both the clergy and the "laity" were to live every day of the week, every hour of the day, in all they did, *coram Deo,* before the face of God. Both those laboring in the community's church and those laboring in the community's fields, houses, and shops had the potential to worship God in their work. It was not the nature of one's work but the faith with which one worked that mattered.

ANA SANTOS'S STORY

Ana Santos is a Brazilian law student pursuing training in international law with the goal of helping bring justice to women and children around the world. She writes:

Gaining a biblical worldview of *life*work is like having an eruption of ideas that brings to the surface the best of God through us, making it possible to understand what it really means to be made in his image!

It happened to me about fifteen years ago when I first heard the message of "occupy till I come" from Darrow Miller on a ranch in East Texas. That message would make all the difference in the direction my life would take. I realized that we are to connect our abilities and talents to God's kingdom not just to be nice Christians but to take back God's territory in all spheres of society.

It was while working with the government of a Muslim nation that I first started to see and apply the centrality of God to my vocation. I saw that it was so much easier to bring my Christian principles to a whole life system rather than be in a religious box. The environment, the justice system, hygiene and health care—all the things I was facing daily—started to be my own problem too. I quit thinking only of being in heaven walking on streets of gold (which, of course, is a great thing to ponder) and realized that Christianity is much bigger than this dream. I decided to be a steward of my surroundings as a kingdom citizen who has responsibilities, just as a citizen has in any government.

It is impossible to see life as boring after this revelation because there is so much to

SOLI DEO GLORIA

No less now than in the sixteenth century, whatever our occupation, we are called to live twenty-four hours a day, seven days a week, before the face of God and to worship God with all of our life, including our work. God is the beginning and center of all things. Since the time of man's rebellion against God, as recorded in Genesis 3, man has chosen to "be as God." Man has put himself at the center of the universe. There is no greater manifestation of this than the secular materialism of post-Christian Western society. Individually and corporately, in family, church, and civil society, we need to let our lives be framed by the great statement used by the Reformers—*soli Deo gloria,* for the glory of God alone.

What *is* God's glory? What does it mean to live in and for God's glory? And why are we meant to do so? Scriptures across the Old and New Testaments witness to the nature of God's glory.

First, Scripture reveals that God's glory is part and parcel of reality; it is a result of who he is, a fact of his unsurpassable, infinite greatness and goodness. The apostle John expressed God's glory in this way: "God is light; in him there is no darkness at all" be involved with and to bring before the face of God. I discovered my calling in the area of government and justice and decided to study law. In my studies I've found that humanistic universities are one of the biggest challenges anyone can face in our day. If we are not prepared, it can be a failing experience, as the education system has taken God out of everything that he himself created. How can anyone understand law outside of God's justice? How can we understand psychology without the knowledge of the One who created man? Who knows better how a human being functions? How can anyone understand political science without God's government pattern? How can any of it make sense without God?

Our lives in this world only make sense *with God*. When we see Christianity connected with our *life*work, our abilities become a real thing in themselves. They become not only a way to get in somewhere as missionaries but a way to see God's kingdom come in dark places such as a women's prison, because God really does care for the whole person and the whole society, not only for people's souls. This conviction is what has motivated me to share my story here and to believe that God's compassion will touch not only individuals but also the laws of nations.

We have a great challenge before us! Are we going to walk and take back what belongs to the Lord, or are we choosing to play defense? As patriots of God's kingdom, it is our responsibility to break the lies of fatalism and the poor excuse that life should just go along without our intervention. The kingdom is advancing! Something needs to be shaken in order to cement our understanding of what it means to occupy God's territory.

(1 John 1:5). God himself is the light we all see by. This is why John wrote of Jesus, "In him was life, and that life was the light of men. The light shines in the darkness, but the darkness has not understood it" (John 1:4–5). The Old Testament tells us, "The sun will no more be your light by day, nor will the brightness of the moon shine on you, for the LORD will be your everlasting light, and your God will be your glory" (Isa. 60:19). The New Testament affirms this: "The city does not need the sun or the moon to shine on it, for the glory of God gives it light, and the Lamb is its lamp" (Rev. 21:23). God is life and light; outside of God is death and darkness. That's just the truth. God's glory is *our* light.

Second, the whole of Scripture shows that we glorify God by making the truth about God known to others, not from God's point of view so that he can say "I'm great!" or "I'm good!" but so that the whole earth *experiences* his greatness and goodness, so that his whole creation is restored to his original intentions. Where God reigns, there is life and light. Where God reigns, his truth, justice, and beauty are manifest. We work for the day when "the earth will be filled with the knowledge of the glory of the LORD, as the waters cover the sea" (Hab. 2:14).

In a Holy Scripture full of mysteries, we find a God so great, so full of glory, that no human can see him and live.[11] We see a God who inspires people to call out to the mountains and the rocks, "Fall on us and hide us from the face of him who sits on the throne and from the wrath of the Lamb!" (Rev. 6:16). Yet he is a God who for our sakes "made himself nothing, taking the very nature of a servant, being made in human likeness" (Phil. 2:7). With these truths in mind, let's look at more of what Scripture says about the glory of God.

All glory is found in God because all belongs to God.

> Yours, O LORD, is the greatness and the power and the glory and the majesty and the splendor, for everything in heaven and earth is yours. Yours, O LORD, is the kingdom; you are exalted as head over all. (1 Chron. 29:11)

> For from him and through him and to him are all things. To him be the glory forever! Amen. (Rom. 11:36)

God's glory is rooted in his nature and character. From eternity, he, the One and Only God, manifests goodness, love, faithfulness, and wisdom.

> Then Moses said, "Now show me your glory." And the LORD said, "I will cause all my goodness to pass in front of you, and I will proclaim my name, the LORD, in your presence. I will have mercy on whom I will have mercy, and I will have compassion on whom I will have compassion." (Exod. 33:18–19)

> When all the Israelites saw the fire coming down and the glory of the LORD above the temple, they knelt on the pavement with their faces to the ground, and they worshiped and gave thanks to the LORD, saying, "He is good; his love endures forever." (2 Chron. 7:3)

> Not to us, O LORD, not to us but to your name be the glory, because of your love and faithfulness. (Ps. 115:1)

> To the only wise God be glory forever through Jesus Christ! Amen. (Rom. 16:27)

> Now to the King eternal, immortal, invisible, the only God, be honor and glory for ever and ever. Amen. (1 Tim. 1:17)

The nature of God's glory is revealed in his works of creation and redemption.

> The heavens declare the glory of God; the skies proclaim the work of his hands. (Ps. 19:1)

Declare his glory among the nations, his marvelous deeds among all peoples. (Ps. 96:3)

To him who loves us and has freed us from our sins by his blood, and has made us to be a kingdom and priests to serve his God and Father—to him be glory and power for ever and ever! Amen. (Rev. 1:5–6)

What would seem impossible—that the glory of the infinite God be made manifest in human form—became a reality. The life of Jesus Christ perfectly and tangibly represents the glory of the one eternal God.

The Son is the radiance of God's glory and the exact representation of his being. (Heb. 1:3)

The Word became flesh and made his dwelling among us. We have seen his glory, the glory of the One and Only, who came from the Father, full of grace and truth. (John 1:14)

For God, who said, "Let light shine out of darkness," made his light shine in our hearts to give us the light of the knowledge of the glory of God in the face of Christ. (2 Cor. 4:6)

If we want to understand God's glory, we need only look at the face of Christ. As we consider what it means to live constantly in the presence of God and work solely for the glory of God, we can meditate on the Christ who does nothing out of selfish ambition or vain conceit but in humility considers others better than himself.[12] This is the God who longs to dwell with us, who invites us to live intimately in his presence. This is the God who calls us to work with him—*soli Deo gloria.*

BEYOND DUALISM TO CONSECRATION

Paul encourages us, "Whatever you do, work at it with all your heart, as working for the Lord, not for men" (Col. 3:23). *Whatever you do* means just that. Gerard Manley Hopkins said in a sermon, "To lift up the hands in prayer gives God glory, but a man with a dung fork in his hand, a woman with a slop pail, give him glory too. He is so great that all things give him glory if you mean they should."[13] In a slightly different vein, Mother Teresa has been quoted as saying, "We do not do big things; we do only small things with great love."[14] This is the great recovery of the biblical theology of vocation wrought by Martin Luther and the Reformation. This is a discovery that can transform our lives and work today.

CHARLES THAXTON'S STORY

Dr. Charles Thaxton was lying on his bed in our home at Chalet Bethany at L'Abri Fellowship in Huemoz, Switzerland. He had completed his Ph.D. in physical chemistry from Iowa State University and then had come to L'Abri to study under Dr. Francis Schaeffer, well-known Christian evangelist, apologist, and theologian. As I entered his room after lunch one day, I found Charles staring at the ceiling. I asked him if he was okay. He told me that he had taught Bible studies all the way through college and graduate school. He said, "All these years, I had the 'answers,' but have never had the questions." Living and studying at L'Abri, Charles had come to understand that the questions people were asking actually had answers in Scripture.

Like so many Christians in the second half of the twentieth century, we had both been influenced by evangelical Gnosticism. Our work and studies were in the "secular realm" while our Christian faith was in the "spiritual realm." Francis Schaeffer challenged this dichotomy and called the church to return to a biblical worldview. Charles was being confronted with the separation of his Christian faith from his work as a scientist. It was at L'Abri that this "split personality" began to be healed.

Following his time at L'Abri, Dr. Thaxton pursued postdoctorate studies in the history of science at Harvard University and at the molecular biology laboratories of Brandeis University. He later became the academic editor of the 1989 high school biology textbook *Of Pandas and People: The Central Question of Biological Origins,* in which the first significant mention of intelligent design appeared. He is a fellow of the Discovery Institute's Center for Science and Culture, which was birthed to challenge the metaphysical assumptions upon which Darwinian science was founded.

A number of years ago, Charles related in a letter to his friends an experience that he had had while lecturing to a group of science professors in the postcommunist universities of Romania. One professor followed Charles back to his hotel. When the man approached Charles, he said that he had seen a miracle that day. The professor exclaimed, "For the first time in my life, I have seen a Christian and a scientist in the same body!" What a tragedy that this has been so uncommon. Too often Christians who are in the sciences live in two worlds. Perhaps with the work of Dr. Thaxton and his colleagues, the foundations of naturalistic science will crack in the West as they have in the post-Soviet East.

The great Dutch theologian, pastor, educator, and prime minister Abraham Kuyper spoke with passion to the church in the Western world to renew the vision of her call and to return to her first love. Written at the dawn of modern secular materialistic culture, Kuyper's clarion call is just as relevant to us today:

No sphere of human life is conceivable in which religion does not maintain its demands that God shall be praised, that God's ordinances shall be observed, and that every *labora* (work) shall be permeated with its *ora* (prayer/worship) in fervent and ceaseless prayer. Wherever man may stand, whatever he may do, to whatever he may apply his hand, in agriculture, in commerce, and in industry, or his mind, in the world of art, and science, he is in whatsoever it may be, constantly standing before the face of his God, he is employed in the service of his God, he has strictly to obey his God, and above all, he has to aim at the glory of his God."[15]

There are not two worlds to live in, nor two types of lives to live. All of life, including the hours of my work, is to be lived *coram Deo,* for the advancement of God's kingdom, for the glory of the Lord of heaven and earth.

Clearly, living *coram Deo* means that we are not to make a separation between the sacred and the secular. The secular dwells in the presence of the sacred. The secular is infused with the sacred.

LIVING IN ONE WORLD

CONSECRATION	VOCATION	DEPLOYMENT

UNSANCTIFIED	SANCTIFIED		HOME	ACROSS CULTURES
		POET		
		COOK		
		ARTIST		
		CARPENTER		
		EVANGELIST		
		HOMEMAKER		
		ACCOUNTANT		
		PHILOSOPHER		
		TREE TRIMMER		
		CHURCH PLANTER		
		ENTREPRENEUR		
		FILMMAKER		
		MISSIONARY		
		FARMER		
		PASTOR		
		NURSE		

But as the Reformers understood, there is a realm of distinction that we are to make. This distinction is between living a *consecrated* and living an *unconsecrated* life. A consecrated life is the life lived *coram Deo,* in worship, *soli Deo gloria.* A consecrated life is one that glorifies God. It is one that models God's glory as a person lives under the lordship of Christ, who himself represented God's glory on earth. A consecrated life is a life dedicated to God in all its parts. It is sanctified! An unconsecrated life is one where a person functions as a Christian only in the religious part of life or when it is convenient. One person may be a godly auto mechanic while another is an adulterous evangelist. One may be a godly farmer while another is a corrupt pastor.

To be consecrated is to be "devoted or dedicated to the service and worship of God."[16] We worship God in our work as we connect the whole of our lives to his divine purpose, a redemptive purpose expressed throughout Scripture as the kingdom of God. The biblical concept of work is that a person's work is his or her unique contribution to God's kingdom. As we explored in the previous chapter, our occupation is the place where we are deployed to occupy ourselves "occupying territory" for Christ and his kingdom. This is the principal business of the Christian's life.

How our lives and work occupy territory for Christ and his kingdom is one of the questions we'll be exploring in the rest of the book as we set about developing a truly biblical theology of vocation. American president Teddy Roosevelt called forth "the Micah mandate," which can serve as the motto of a Christian's life and work, affirming the means by which we occupy our sphere of influence for Christ:

> He has showed you, O man, what is good.
> And what does the LORD require of you?
> To act justly and to love mercy
> and to walk humbly with your God. (Mic. 6:8)

In the midst of a fallen world, we are to seek to live moral lives. In the midst of injustice and corruption, we are to seek justice. In the midst of cultures that are often brutal and uncaring, we are to love mercy. In the midst of power and arrogance, we are to walk humbly with God. We are, in some small way, to be incarnations of Christ in this broken world. Our place of work is to be where we put flesh on our prayers, "Let your glory be over all the earth" (Ps. 57:5) and "Your kingdom come, your will be done on earth as it is in heaven" (Matt. 6:10). Kingdom life and principles are to be brought to bear in the midst of our life and in the sphere of society where we work.

Leland Ryken captures the radical effects of this biblical view of work in *Redeeming the Time*:

> Obviously this view of work renders every task of intrinsic value and integrates every legitimate vocation or task with a Christian's spiritual life. It makes every job consequential by claiming it as the arena for glorifying God, and it provides a way for workers to serve God not only within their work in the world *but by that work* [italics added].[17]

This is the call each of us needs to hear today: that it is possible to live an integrated life of value and purpose in which we serve God by our work in the world. It is possible to live a life of consecration rather than separation.

Missionary to India E. Stanley Jones has captured the kind of people we are called to be, the kind of people we long to be, in *The Unshakable Kingdom and the Unchanging Person*. He writes that our occupation is framed within the wonder of the kingdom of God:

> That kind of person sees God, not in a vision, but sees God working with him and in him and backing him. He sees God at work everywhere. The universe becomes alive with God—every bush aflame with him, every event full of destiny, life an exciting adventure with God. You see him at work in you, in events, in the universe. He talks with you, guides you. You work in the same *business,* in the same *occupation*—the Kingdom. And it is the most thrilling, exciting business and occupation in the world. All else is tame and inane— dull. Here you are working at the biggest job, on the biggest scale, at the most worthwhile task, at the greatest outcome—the kingdom of God on earth [italics added].[18]

When we understand that all Christians are to live all of life *coram Deo*, we understand that we are all in Christ's mission force. We are all missionaries! In contrast to the graphic of the Gnostic Bridge to Work Significance (at the end of chapter 2), the Bible establishes a bridge where everyone leaves the bridge called into missions, into work significance.

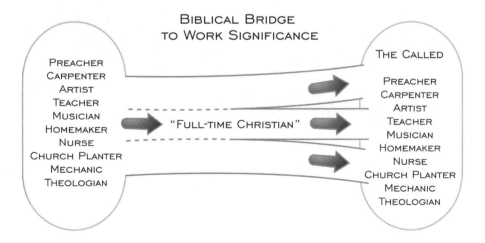

BIBLICAL BRIDGE
TO WORK SIGNIFICANCE

THE CALLED

PREACHER
CARPENTER
ARTIST
TEACHER
MUSICIAN
HOMEMAKER
NURSE
CHURCH PLANTER
MECHANIC
THEOLOGIAN

"FULL-TIME CHRISTIAN"

PREACHER
CARPENTER
ARTIST
TEACHER
MUSICIAN
HOMEMAKER
NURSE
CHURCH PLANTER
MECHANIC
THEOLOGIAN

JOHN BECKETT'S STORY

John Beckett grew up in Elyria, Ohio. Soon after graduating from M.I.T. with a bachelor of science in economics and mechanical engineering, Beckett joined his father in a small family-owned manufacturing business. A few years later, when his father died, Beckett took over the business. Over the years he has grown the company into a global firm with more than six hundred employees. The firm provides global leadership in the sales and manufacture of commercial and residential heating devices.

In 1998 Beckett wrote his first book, *Loving Monday: Succeeding in Business Without Selling Your Soul.* In it he relates his personal life journey. The book opens with Beckett telling about his life in Christ and his desire to grow to be a godly Christian, husband, and father at a time when his life was framed by a Gnostic paradigm. His walk with Christ was impacting his private life but not his business life. It was during this time that his pursuit of godliness led him to the thought that he needed to sell his business to go overseas as a missionary.

Beckett then describes how the life and work of Francis Schaeffer began to influence his own life. Schaeffer challenged his dualistic assumptions that separated faith from work. Schaeffer's words called Beckett to live in one world, before the face of God. Beckett's business was not to be separated from his faith; rather it was to be the place where he lived out his faith. The last part of *Loving Monday* describes how Beckett employed biblical principles of enterprise to change the way he ran his company. John Beckett came to understand that the Lord is Lord of all of life, including business, and that the Bible has much to say about principles for running a godly enterprise.

PART 2 : FIRST STEPS TOWARD A
BIBLICAL THEOLOGY
OF VOCATION

CHAPTER 6

THE NEED FOR
A BIBLICAL THEOLOGY
OF VOCATION

In a speech titled "Why Work?" English author Dorothy Sayers said the following:

> In nothing has the Church so lost her hold on reality as in her failure to understand and respect the secular vocation. She has allowed work and religion to become separate departments, and is astonished to find that, as a result, the secular work of the world is turned to purely selfish and destructive ends, and that the greater part of the world's intelligent workers have become irreligious, or at least, uninterested in religion. But is it astonishing? How can anyone remain interested in a religion which seems to have no concern with nine-tenths of his life?[1]

Sayers made this statement in the 1940s. Sadly, God's church can still see itself—and the world—mirrored in her frank words.

What is the remedy for the division of work and religion that so troubled Sayers and troubles us still today? Flowing from the same Spirit that enlightened the Protestant Reformers, we get a powerful answer from a former pope. In his message for the XXXV World Day of Prayer for Vocations, Pope John Paul II called for Catholic youth to see their unique work within the context of a new culture of vocations:

The Holy Spirit of God writes in the heart and life of every baptized person a project of love and grace, which is the only way to give full meaning to existence, opening the way to the freedom of the children of God and enabling the offering of one's personal and irreplaceable contribution to the progress of humanity on the path of justice and truth. The Spirit does not only help to place oneself sincerely before the great questions of the heart—Where do I come from? Where am I going? Who am I? What is the purpose of life? How should I spend my time?—but opens up the prospect of courageous response. The discovery that each man and woman has his own place in God's heart and in the history of humanity constitutes the point of departure for a new culture of vocations.[2]

Just as Sayers shined the spotlight on the problem we face, this rich vision placed on the heart of John Paul II illuminates the solution. If the tragedy of "a religion which seems to have no concern with nine-tenths of [our] life" and the vision of this "new culture of vocations" resonates with us, what should we do?

EVERYONE'S A THEOLOGIAN

We must accept our role as *theologians* and become good theologians. The call of Pope John Paul II for a new culture of vocations is made in the same spirit as the call of the Reformers of the Protestant Reformation who rallied Christians to live the whole of their lives before the face of God, recovering the biblical theology of vocation we need so desperately to rediscover today.

Someone is surely thinking, *I'm not a theologian.* But the point that cannot be escaped is that everyone is a theologian.

Because God exists and is sovereign, everyone relates to him in one way or another. Some people enter into a direct personal relationship with the living God. Some deny his existence and thus have a hostile relationship with him. But even the atheist who says there is no God is laying down a theological foundation for his or her life. Whether we are atheists or people of faith, we cannot avoid having a theology. The theology may be self-consciously formed or unconsciously formed. It may be good theology or bad theology. But we do have a theology that shapes our lives.

Christians inevitably will live out their true theology with a fair degree of consistency. Some are seeking to live in a consciously Christian manner; that is, they are seeking to intentionally think about and *do* their theology—to live *incarnationally*, by manifesting the living spirit and teachings of Christ in their own lives, in their communities, and in their workplaces.

In contrast, there are people who profess Christ but whose lives, language, and choices reflect that they are practical atheists. They speak the right words about what they believe and may even be active church members, but their lives and practical values are more shaped by the secularized concepts of the contemporary world than by the spirit of the living Christ or the concepts of Scripture.

Like Jesus, his followers are to organize their lives within the framework of a consistent biblical theology, within the framework of the worldview of the kingdom of God. Jesus understood his life and his work within that framework, and he lived his life and conducted his work accordingly, and so should we. To follow Jesus, to understand who we are and what we have been created and called to do, we need both a relationship with the living God and an increasing understanding of the biblical worldview.

LIVING AN EXAMINED LIFE

As philosopher Richard Weaver reminds us, ideas have consequences. The framework through which we look at the universe, our world, and our own lives will shape what we see and what we become and how we live out our lives. As we have seen thus far, the church and our own understanding of Christian life has, in many respects, been shaped by the faulty dualistic worldview, creating the situation described by Dorothy Sayers. What I have called "evangelical Gnosticism" has huge consequences for our own journeys, for the welfare of our society and our churches, and for the building of the kingdom of God in our world.

In order to effectively move out of this faulty worldview, we need to develop a new theology of vocation. This means rediscovering for the contemporary era how to reflect on our lives according to a biblical worldview.

The price of failing to reflect is high. As Dallas Willard says, "Everyone's practical theology vitally affects the course of his or her life....A thoughtless or uninformed theology grips and guides our life with just as great a force as does a thoughtful and informed one."[3]

Yet most of us live unexamined lives. We may rarely, if ever, think about the theology we are living out; we often function routinely, as if by remote control. We seldom think about thinking; we seldom examine why we have been placed here on earth. We may spend 50–75 percent of our waking hours and 60–90 percent of the years of our lives working. Yet how much time is given to answering the questions, What is the purpose in my life? Why do I work? What is the purpose of work?

Not only do we seldom reflect on a personal level, but also the modern church spends little time focusing on the ordinary, spending most of her time focusing on the spectacular, the outrageous, the comforting, or other matters that are comfortably removed from our workaday worlds.

The church has the ability to prepare the mission force—"the body of Christ"—for the workplace, the public square, and the community. A focus on biblical theology of vocation should be part of the regular preaching cycle of the church. Classes need to be established to prepare church members to disciple the marketplace sphere that they occupy during the season of their working life. Yet, when was the last time your pastor taught a series on work? On biblical principles of freedom, enterprise, or business ethics? When was the last time there were small groups or Sunday school classes that focused on the workplace? The absence of this kind of thinking and preaching in the Christian community is a reflection of how the false secular-sacred dichotomy has infected our operative theology.

The principalities and powers, the forces for evil, use work to increase the kingdom of darkness. Concurrently, God uses work to advance the kingdom of light. There are both godly, legitimate means and uses of work and ungodly, illegitimate ones. But it should give us greater reason to pause when we consider that both professed Christians and non-Christians can contribute either to the kingdom of light or to the expanding of the kingdom of darkness. The choice may be made consciously, intuitively, or unwittingly. Non-Christians may actually contribute to the kingdom of light simply because, while the world is fallen, it is intrinsically a moral universe and mankind has been designed for moral activity. On the flip side, sin causes Christians and non-Christians alike to contribute to the kingdom of darkness. While work is part of God's good design for mankind, sin can corrupt both the ends and the means of our work.

If as Christians we do not increasingly act *consciously* on behalf of the kingdom of God, we will likely find ourselves contributing to the kingdom of darkness. Without the awareness of what our personal, functioning theology truly is, we run the risk of waking up too late to realize that we didn't live the life that we wanted to at all, and certainly not the life God has called and enabled us to live. Guided by the distortions of false worldviews and our own sinful nature, without having been transformed by God in our hearts and in our minds, we are unlikely to manifest truth and justice; without living in the presence of God, we are hard-pressed to make him known in our broken world.

A COMPREHENSIVE FRAMEWORK

Both personally and corporately, therefore, there is a need to establish a comprehensive framework for developing a theology of work. Such a framework allows us to build an integrated understanding of our life and work—our *life*work. This will require us to read the Bible in a very different way. Most of us read the Bible as a devotional exercise for our spiritual life. This is a good thing, but we need to see the Scriptures for what they are, God's owner's manual. They speak comprehensively (but not exhaustively) to all of life. We need to read the Bible as a whole, discerning the whole worldview that it presents rather than cobbling together proof texts on a particular subject.

Another way to say this is that the Bible is like a forest. You can study the forest from the inside, examining the individual trees (verses) that make up the Scriptures. But there is a second way to read the Scriptures—from the outside. Here one climbs to the top of the mountain to view the forest from above. This is the worldview perspective of the Scriptures.

There are three concepts that are helpful to understand when approaching the Bible from a worldview perspective: the *breadth* of Scripture, the *depth* of Scripture, and the fact that the Bible is the *owner's manual*.

THE BREADTH AND DEPTH OF SCRIPTURE

THE FLOW OF BIBLICAL HISTORY

BEFORE THE BEGINNING — BREADTH — ETERNITY FUTURE

CREATION: IN THE BEGINNING   FALL   REDEMPTION   CONSUMMATION: CHRIST'S RETURN

THE MEANING OF THE STORY — DEPTH

WHAT IS NATURE?   WHAT IS MAN?   WHERE IS HISTORY GOING?

First, Scripture has breadth. The Bible is a story. It is *HIS*-story. It begins in Genesis and ends with Revelation. There are four main parts to the narrative: the Creation, the Fall, Redemption (the cross of Christ), and the Consummation (the return of Christ and his kingdom).

Second, the Bible has depth. It reveals reality the way God has made it and answers the questions, What is true? What is good? What is beautiful? It answers human beings' basic philosophic questions. There are three primary areas of human questions. There are epistemological questions about *knowledge:* What can I know? How can I know? What is truth? Is there any truth? There are metaphysical questions about the nature of *reality:* What is real? Is there a God? What is man? What is the nature of creation? Where is history going? What is the purpose of my life? And there are *moral* questions: Is there right and wrong? What is right and wrong? If there is a good God, where did evil come from? What is beauty? The depth of Scripture reveals the biblical worldview.

Third, the Bible is the owner's manual. When you buy an appliance or a vehicle, it comes with an owner's manual. Who wrote the manual? The ones who designed and built the item! Why did they write it? So that the owner would know the purpose of the item and how it works. The Bible is the owner's manual that God has written for us. It helps us understand our life's purpose; it reveals the framework for our *life*work.

As we move forward in developing a biblical theology of vocation—and as we seek to discover our own "project of love and grace"—we will be exploring Scripture from these worldview perspectives. We'll look first at the Bible as one story—God's Transforming Story—a narrative that spans from Genesis to Revelation and ultimately extends to encompass our lives and work in time and eternity.

CHAPTER 7

THE ESSENTIAL
METANARRATIVE

Each culture provides the context in which a person's life and work are defined and lived out. This context is derived from the many stories that inform that particular culture. When taken together, those stories form one large story, or *metanarrative,* which provides the framework for how that culture views reality. Individuals, in turn, view their lives in terms of this metanarrative; that is, they derive meaning for their lives and work in terms of how they fit into the "big picture."

As Christians, our metanarrative comes, or should come, not only from our culture but also from our faith. More specifically, our metanarrative comes from the Bible, which shows us how to see all of history in light of God's design for the world, humanity, and the cosmos. This story is powerful and transforming. To the extent that a culture reflects elements of the biblical metanarrative, life is healthier and work has more meaning. To the extent that a culture lacks this framework, the life and work of the people are distorted from God's good intentions for them. Reality, with a capital *R,* as framed by the flow of biblical history, creates a panorama in which our life and work can mature toward God's full intentions. Our life and work are to be played out in the context of biblical history: Creation, Fall, Redemption, Consummation.

History is *HIS*-story! God is at work redeeming the lost and restoring that which is broken, through the work of his Son, Jesus Christ, on the cross. The dominant image used in the Bible to describe God's redemptive purpose in history is the kingdom of

God. It reflects God's original intentions for the earth and all who inhabit it. Human sinfulness interrupted those intentions, but it is God's purpose that his kingdom be reestablished.

The biblical narrative may be called the Transforming Story because it has the ability to change lives, communities, and nations as it reforms our thinking and acting in all areas of life. As the caterpillar is changed into a butterfly, so God has the power to transform darkness into light, death into life, slavery into freedom, corruption into justice, cruelty into compassion, greed into contentment, poverty into bounty. In doing so, he saves individuals, bringing substantial healing to their lives and relationships. The biblical story has the ability to lift communities out of poverty. It has the ability to build nations that are free, just, and compassionate.

The biblical story begins in Genesis and ends in the book of Revelation. It begins in a garden, the Garden of Eden, and ends in a city, the City of God—the New Jerusalem. It begins with the first couple, Adam and Eve, and ends with the wedding of the Lamb. At the end of *HIS*-story, Jesus will return to marry his bride, the church. It is a powerful story, it is *the* Story, and it is truth. It is the Story for which people all over the earth have been made and for which they long.

Let's look at this wonderful narrative.

CREATION—*In the Beginning God!*

The quiet of eternity was broken by the thunderclap of the opening lines of the biblical narrative: In the beginning GOD...created...the heavens and the earth! Every culture has a story, and the opening lines of the story establish what will be the storyline. In Hinduism, the opening line is a de-creation, the breaking of the eternal-one. In secularism, the beginning was a slimy pool of water. God revealed to Moses the opening line of the True Story for all cultures and all times, "In the beginning God created the heavens and the earth."

If there was a "beginning," there must have been, as Francis Schaeffer reminds us, a "before the beginning." If, in the beginning God created, then God existed before that moment. The universe was framed by the nature and character of the Eternal God. An example of this is found in Genesis 1:26: "Then God said, 'Let us make man in our image, in our likeness, and let them rule....'" God reveals himself as the One and Many God. Before the creation there was communion, communication, and community between the members of the Trinity. All of man's longings for community and for significant communication have their grounding in eternity. Likewise, we find these remarkable words from Jesus recorded in John 17:24: "Father, I want those you have given me to be with me where I am, and to see my glory, the glory you have given me because you loved me before the creation of the world." In this text we find that love existed before the creation of the world. All of human longings to love and to be loved are grounded in eternity. The framework for our lives and creation itself has its identity established "before the beginning."

Genesis 1 records that God created the universe out of nothing. He created by speaking words. And after he created each thing, he used words again to name that which he had made. God spoke creation into existence. At the end of each stage of creation,[1] he proclaimed that what he had made was "good" or "pleasant," in the sense of joyful. Similarly, we see God speak a creative command and then read immediately that "it was so," "right," "just," or "true,"[2] in the sense of being firm or stable. After he completed creation by making man, he proclaimed his work was "very [exceedingly] good" (Gen. 1:31). All that God made, both the spiritual and physical realms, is good; it is in harmony with God and with itself. At the time of creation man had an unbroken relationship with his Creator and the rest of creation.

While what God had made was perfect and complete in its germ, it was not finished in its potential. God has made man to develop the potential of creation, as we will explore in depth in Part 3, with exciting ramifications for the importance of our lifework.

FALL—Man Rebels against the High King of Heaven

Man was placed in creation as God's steward, to care for and manage his household— the world. But we find that the serpent—Satan—does what he does well: he distorts the truth and challenges Adam and Eve to sin against the Creator. They choose to believe the lies of Satan rather than the truth of God, rebelling against the High King of Heaven. In this rebellion, the primary relationship between God and man is broken. As a result, all the secondary relationships that were founded upon it were broken as well. All the spiritual and moral dimensions end up reflected in the physical.

Man and self. Man's sin led to death—first spiritual, then physical death. Man's identity was shattered; the image of God in him was distorted, and the anchor of his life's connection to the eternal God was broken. Questions abounded: "Who am I?" "Does my life have any purpose?" "Am I only an animal?" "What happens when I die?"

Man and others. Man's relationship with his fellow man is broken. Because we no longer know who we are, we no longer know who our neighbor is. Now there is hatred, covetousness, greed, and disrespect of others and their property. Racism, trib- alism, male-superiority, and caste systems abound; false hierarchies develop, estab- lished by man to keep men apart, not working together. Murder and war proliferate. There is disrespect for parents. A culture of blame is established in which people do not take responsibility for their own actions but point the finger at others. "Who is my neighbor?" "What responsibility do I have toward others?" "What is a family?" The very anchor for social relationships has been broken.

Man and the physical world. As Genesis 3 records, there will be weeds in the garden and pain in childbirth. In addition to this natural evil, man will act with disrespect toward the creation. Instead of caring for and stewarding creation, man tends to abuse and rape it in his orgy of consumption. Man forgets that, like creation, he too is a creature in the Creator's universe and that he has a responsibility to care for it. "Does this world even exist?" is a question raised in Asia. Other questions raised around the world include, "Where did the universe come from?" "What is the nature of the universe?" "What is my relationship to or responsibility for nature?"

Man and the metaphysical world. In addition to relating to the physical world, man relates to the nonphysical world, to the spiritual realm of the angelic and demonic. Beyond these, man's rebellion has brought distortions in four areas: knowledge, morals, aesthetics, and culture, understood as that aspect of our common life that functions as a bridge between the spiritual realm and the physical realm.

In the realm of knowledge, wisdom is abandoned for folly, truth is exchanged for lies, and the strongholds of the mind are fortified with lies. In the area of morals, good becomes evil and evil good. Corruption replaces justice. Every person does what is right in his or her own eyes. Similarly, in the realm of the aesthetic, beauty is exchanged for utility, loveliness for sterility, splendor for bleakness. Instead of creating culture that reflects truth, justice, and beauty, man creates culture in which lies, corruption, and hideousness flourish. "Is there any truth?" "What is truth?" "Why does the world seem so unfair?" "What is beauty?" These represent some of the metaphysical questions that people labor under since the Fall.

The rebellion against God brought comprehensive and systemic consequences. All of man, all of his relationships, and all of creation were damaged by the Fall. Consequently, if there is any salvation, it must be comprehensive, involving not only the primary relationships but all of the secondary relationships as well. This is exactly the provision of the cross of Christ, the fulfillment and culmination of God's work throughout history in redeeming his creation and establishing his reign in the world.

REDEMPTION—*The Cross*

The effects of the Fall were drastic, but God did not abandon his creation. In Genesis 3, God curses the serpent:

> "Cursed are you above all the livestock
> and all the wild animals!

You will crawl on your belly
 and you will eat dust
 all the days of your life.
And I will put enmity
 between you and the woman,
 and between your offspring and hers;
he will crush your head,
 and you will strike his heel." (Gen. 3:14–15)

Here already we see God's promise of redemption. He declares that he will crush the head of the serpent through Eve's offspring. This offspring, the Christ, will come to the world through the line of a man named Abram. In Genesis 12, God makes a covenant with Abram (who is given the new name Abraham in Genesis 17, when God reiterates this covenant):

The LORD had said to Abram, "Leave your country, your people and your father's household and go to the land I will show you.

"I will make you into a great nation
 and I will bless you;
I will make your name great,
 and you will be a blessing.
I will bless those who bless you,
 and whoever curses you I will curse;
and all peoples on earth
 will be blessed through you." (Gen. 12:1–3)

God's plan to bless *all peoples on earth* began with the call of Abraham, whom God did make into a great nation—the nation of Israel, God's chosen people.

The rest of the Old Testament, from Genesis 12 onward, tells the story of God's people and, together with the New Testament, forms the whole biblical metanarrative. In reality, this is not simply the story about God's people; it is, rather, the Story, the story *of God* and his work in history. God leads his people out of bondage (multiple times), gives them a law to abide by, and speaks to them through the voice of his prophets. God's people, amidst their triumphs and failures, continually look ahead to a time of deliverance, when God will raise up a redeemer. The prophet Isaiah speaks of this time:

A shoot will come up from the stump of Jesse;
 from his roots a Branch will bear fruit.

The Spirit of the LORD will rest on him—
the Spirit of wisdom and of understanding,
the Spirit of counsel and of power,
the Spirit of knowledge and of the fear of the LORD. (Isa. 11:1–2)

Through this servant of Israel, God will redeem all creation, the entire cosmos. The Old Testament ends in eager expectation of this coming redeemer, the Christ, and the New Testament begins with his coming. In the ultimate *kairos* moment—the fullness of time, when eternity breaks through into time—God took on human flesh. The first coming of Christ marked the turning point in the battle for heaven and earth. Fully God and fully human, Jesus Christ lived a perfect life for me. He then died the death that I deserved. He was resurrected on the third day, conquering death, giving me new life. This is the gospel.

The Fall brought cosmic consequences, but so too did the work of Christ. We read in Paul's letter to the Colossians that Christ died to reconcile *all* things to himself.[3] Jesus' death on the cross laid the foundation for man's primary relationship to God to be fully restored and for substantial healing in the secondary relationships between people and the world in which they live. There is to be significant healing within man, in his social relationships, in his relationship to nature and in the metaphysical realm. Man's life and work are placed again within the framework of the kingdom of God. When Christ returns the second time in glory, the process unleashed at Calvary will be consummated.

CONSUMMATION—*The Return in Glory!*

When Jesus returns at the end of time, the process of reconciling all things to himself will be complete. We see a glimpse of this picture through the prophet Isaiah:

The wolf will live with the lamb,
the leopard will lie down with the goat,
the calf and the lion and the yearling together;
and a little child will lead them.
The cow will feed with the bear,
their young will lie down together,
and the lion will eat straw like the ox.
The infant will play near the hole of the cobra,
and the young child put his hand into the viper's nest.
They will neither harm nor destroy

> on all my holy mountain,
> for the earth will be full of the knowledge of the LORD
>   as the waters cover the sea.
>
> In that day the Root of Jesse will stand as a banner for the peoples; the nations will rally to him, and his place of rest will be glorious. (Isa. 11:6–10)

The prophet also says of that day,

> On this mountain the LORD Almighty will prepare
>   a feast of rich food for all peoples,
> a banquet of aged wine—
>   the best of meats and the finest of wines.
> On this mountain he will destroy
>   the shroud that enfolds all peoples,
> the sheet that covers all nations;
>   he will swallow up death forever.
> The Sovereign LORD will wipe away the tears
>   from all faces;
> he will remove the disgrace of his people
>   from all the earth.
> The LORD has spoken. (Isa. 25:6–8)

On that day, the cosmic harmony that existed before the Fall will be restored. The Shalom Peace, that comprehensive peace for which Christ died, will be achieved.

On that day, Christ will return to marry his bride, the church:

> Then I heard what sounded like a great multitude, like the roar of rushing waters and like loud peals of thunder, shouting:
>
> "Hallelujah!
>   For our Lord God Almighty reigns.
> Let us rejoice and be glad
>   and give him glory!
> For the wedding of the Lamb has come,
>   and his bride has made herself ready.
> Fine linen, bright and clean,
>   was given her to wear."
> (Fine linen stands for the righteous acts of the saints.) (Rev. 19:6–8)

On that day he will bring the fullness of his kingdom, the City of God, the New Jerusalem:

> Then I saw a new heaven and a new earth, for the first heaven and the first earth had passed away, and there was no longer any sea. I saw the Holy City, the new Jerusalem, coming down out of heaven from God. (Rev. 21:1–2)

On that day, the kings of the earth will bring the unique glory and splendor of their nations into the City of God:

> The city does not need the sun or the moon to shine on it, for the glory of God gives it light, and the Lamb is its lamp. The nations will walk by its light, and the kings of the earth will bring their splendor into it. On no day will its gates ever be shut, for there will be no night there. The glory and honor of the nations will be brought into it. (Rev. 21:23–26)

On that day he will separate the sheep from the goats—the sheep to eternal life, the goats to eternal death:

> "When the Son of Man comes in his glory, and all the angels with him, he will sit on his throne in heavenly glory. All the nations will be gathered before him, and he will separate the people one from another as a shepherd separates the sheep from the goats. He will put the sheep on his right and the goats on his left.
>
> "Then the King will say to those on his right, 'Come, you who are blessed by my Father; take your inheritance, the kingdom prepared for you since the creation of the world. For I was hungry and you gave me something to eat, I was thirsty and you gave me something to drink, I was a stranger and you invited me in, I needed clothes and you clothed me, I was sick and you looked after me, I was in prison and you came to visit me.'
>
> "Then the righteous will answer him, 'Lord, when did we see you hungry and feed you, or thirsty and give you something to drink? When did we see you a stranger and invite you in, or needing clothes and clothe you? When did we see you sick or in prison and go to visit you?'
>
> "The King will reply, 'I tell you the truth, whatever you did for one of the least of these brothers of mine, you did for me.'
>
> "Then he will say to those on his left, 'Depart from me, you who are cursed, into the eternal fire prepared for the devil and his angels. For I was hungry and you gave me nothing to eat, I was thirsty and you gave me nothing to

drink, I was a stranger and you did not invite me in, I needed clothes and you did not clothe me, I was sick and in prison and you did not look after me.'

"They also will answer, 'Lord, when did we see you hungry or thirsty or a stranger or needing clothes or sick or in prison, and did not help you?'

"He will reply, 'I tell you the truth, whatever you did not do for one of the least of these, you did not do for me.'

"Then they will go away to eternal punishment, but the righteous to eternal life." (Matt. 25:31–46)

THE SIGNIFICANCE OF OUR *Life*WORK

The story line of our lives is drawn from the larger story of God's unfolding kingdom. Secularism and animism, as powerful worldviews, create stories that lead to death, brokenness, and lack of fulfillment. The biblical narrative, with its opening line of "In the beginning God created the heavens and the earth," provides an alternative story line of which we are a part. Paul reveals the significance of our lives intimately in the language of his own letters. In Ephesians 2:10 he calls us poems of Christ,[4] and in 2 Corinthians 3:2–3 we are described as letters from Christ: "You yourselves are our letter, written on our hearts, known and read by everybody. You show that you are a letter from Christ, the result of our ministry, written not with ink but with the Spirit of the living God, not on tablets of stone but on tablets of human hearts."

God is writing his story, and our lives receive their story line when they are connected to the Transforming Story. Os Guinness has said it so well: "Follow the call of Christ despite the uncertainty and chaos of modern circumstances, and you have the story line of your life."[5]

Our *life*work gains significance within the framework of biblical history, specifically occupying time and space between Christ's first coming at the cross and his second coming at the consummation of history at the end of time. Between the Fall and the Second Coming, there are two significant events. The first is Christ's first coming to earth to redeem us. The second is your life!

TWO SIGNIFICANT EVENTS

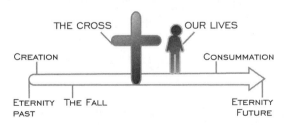

THE CROSS   OUR LIVES

CREATION   CONSUMMATION

ETERNITY THE FALL   ETERNITY
PAST   FUTURE

You have been made, like no other person in history, to take your unique place in the unfolding of the kingdom of God. In God's economy, the words of Mordecai to Esther speak to the uniqueness of each of our lives within the unfolding kingdom: "And who knows but that you have come to royal position for such a time as this?" (Esther 4:14).

What is your place in God's Story? What is your *life*work, the connection of your life and work to God's unfolding kingdom? As we continue to build a biblical theology of vocation, we're going to look closely at key elements of the Transforming Story, starting with God's call to us in creation—a call renewed by the cross of Christ and worthy of the days of our lives and the work of our whole selves: heart, soul, mind, and strength.

PART 3 : THE CULTURAL MANDATE

CHAPTER 8

CULTURE:

WHERE THE PHYSICAL AND SPIRITUAL CONVERGE

When two-year-old Hakani did not walk or talk, the leaders of her tribe ordered her parents to kill her. The leaders' decision reflected a belief common among several Indian tribes in the Amazon that children with physical defects have no soul and should be put down as a deformed or sick animal would be.

Rather than murder their daughter, Hakani's mother and father committed suicide. Hakani's teenage brother inherited the leaders' brutal order and attempted to follow it, knocking his sister out with a machete. But she woke up as she was being buried, and he couldn't bring himself to try again. Hakani's grandfather shot his granddaughter with an arrow, then was so grieved that he tried to kill himself.

Wounded by her grandfather's arrow, Hakani escaped to the jungle, where she lived like an animal for three years, with her brother smuggling her food. Ultimately adopted by Marcia and Edson Suzuki, Hakani still was not safe. Authorities in Brazil wanted to prevent the Suzukis, a Brazilian couple who have worked with the Suruwahá tribe for twenty years, from seeking help for the five-year-old out of "respect" for tribal culture. The official policy of Brazil's health department has been to "respect the culture of the people," meaning that children are allowed to be killed with the full knowledge of the government. Dozens of children in the Amazon are killed each year, children like Hakani as well as twins and triplets, who are believed to be cursed.

Activists like the Suzukis are working to counter not only deadly tribal beliefs but also the deadly views of bureaucrats and academics. Echoing the official government response, one anthropology professor at a university in the Amazon epitomizes the view common among anthropologists: "This is their way of life and we should not judge them on the basis of our values. The difference between the cultures should be respected."[1]

Really? Is culture actually neutral? Is there truly no objective reality against which to measure a culture's beliefs and practices? Are children made in the image of God? If so, we need to stand against cultural relativism; we need to fight a culture and its laws that allow for the taking of innocent human life or the enslavement of a people because of the color of their skin. If culture is relative, then it is power that will determine who lives and who dies. If the powerful want to murder people of color or people who are mentally retarded, what is to prevent them from doing so?

Hakani's mother and father knew better. Hakani's brother and grandfather judged their culture's way of life and came to their own conclusion. To do so they did not have to consult an outside culture's values, and as outsiders we are not meant to judge their people on the basis of *our* values. Rather they and we can make a judgment based on the values that flow from Reality.

CULTURE MAKERS

As we discussed in the previous chapter, there is an objective reality, witnessed to by the metanarrative of Scripture. We discovered that our human identity and the identity of the universe have their roots "before the beginning" in the character and nature of God, their Creator. When we look further into the creation narrative, we come upon a set of truths vital to rightly understanding our nature and ultimate purpose: God made humankind to be *culture* makers, and it matters hugely what kind of culture we create. Whatever our calling and wherever our deployment, as Christians our work is ultimately to create *kingdom culture*—culture that reflects the true nature and character of God.

Our charge as creators of culture has been called the creation mandate or the cultural mandate. It is found in the creation narrative in Genesis 1:26–28:

> Then God said, "Let us make man in our image, in our likeness, and let them rule over the fish of the sea and the birds of the air, over the livestock, over all the earth, and over all the creatures that move along the ground."
>
> So God created man in his own image,
> in the image of God he created him;
> male and female he created them.
>
> God blessed them and said to them, "Be fruitful and increase in number; fill the earth and subdue it. Rule over the fish of the sea and the birds of the air and over every living creature that moves on the ground."

We read here that at the height of his creative activity, God said, "Let us make man in our image." With these words man's identity is established. Man is made *imago Dei*—in the image of God. God also said, "Let them rule." With these words man's purpose is established. Man was made to rule the earth in God's stead, as the steward of God's household.

What God had made was perfect, but it was not finished yet. God is the primary Creator; humankind, to use J. R. R. Tolkien's words, is a "sub-creator."[2] God made primary creation. Humankind is to make a secondary creation—culture—that reveals and glorifies the primary Creator and the primary creation. Human beings were made to be active in creation, as God's stewards. They are to fill the earth with image bearers of God who will, in turn, develop the earth. Like an acorn that is nurtured into a mighty oak tree, creation from the hand of God was perfect and complete in itself, but the potential had to be released by the man and the woman.

One of the most beautiful of the psalms asks the question, "What is man that you are mindful of him?" Then it reveals that human beings, "a little lower than the angels," are to rule in God's stead. Psalm 8:3–8 reads,

> When I consider your heavens,
>   the work of your fingers,
> the moon and the stars,
>   which you have set in place,
> what is man that you are mindful of him,
>   the son of man that you care for him?
> You made him a little lower than the heavenly beings
>   and crowned him with glory and honor.
>
> You made him ruler over the works of your hands;
>   you put everything under his feet:
> all flocks and herds,
>   and the beasts of the field,
> the birds of the air,
>   and the fish of the sea,
>   all that swim the paths of the seas.

Isn't it astounding? God has made humankind "ruler over the works of [his] hands"! How many of us are willing to cede even a little control over something in which we have a huge stake or investment? Yet unlike some of us who rule over much smaller domains, our all-powerful God is not a control freak. God is a master delegator. He invites us lowly interns into the executive boardroom as coworkers. And he does not give assignments that are inconsequential. He has designed and equipped us to bear weight. In making us in his image, in creating us to be creators, God gave each of us an awesome responsibility and opportunity. Indian scholar and writer Vishal Mangalwadi expresses it with appropriate awe: "God speaks and creates the universe. Man speaks and creates culture that shapes the universe."[3]

CULTURE: WORSHIP EXTERNALIZED

Why are the Genesis scriptures referred to as the *cultural* mandate? What is culture anyway? And what does it mean to create culture?

While Hakani's story shows that people don't agree on what culture is and whether it is even "made," in reality *culture* is easy to define. Theologian Henry Van Til states it very clearly and concisely: "Culture is religion externalized."[4]

The closely related words *culture, cultivate,* and *cult* capture this connection. Most of us are familiar with the word *cult* in its many shades of usage, from a religious group gone awry to the obsessive cult followings of celebrities. However, in these cases people have the object of their worship wrong, since at root, *cult* means "worship or reverential homage rendered to a divine being."[5] Like *culture* and *cultivate,* the word *cult* is derived from the Latin *cultus,* the past participle of the verb *colere:* to tend, till, or cultivate. Dictionaries define *cultus*—the root for all three words—as care, adoration, worship, and veneration.

This family of interconnected words reflects the truth that the root of culture is worship. Writing in *Plowing in Hope: Toward a Biblical Theology of Culture,* David B. Hegeman states,

> The term [culture] could also be used in a religious context to mean worship. The idea here seems to be that in the same way the farmer actively fusses over his crops, so the worshiper gives rapt attention to the deity he serves. Thus the term is closely related to the Latin *cultus* meaning adoration or veneration. The English language retains this connection with such terms as *cult, cultic, occult,* etc.[6]

At its heart, a culture is a product of a people's cult, or of their civic religion. It is a reflection of the god they worship.

This stands in contrast to the modern materialist's assumption that culture is somehow merely the sum total of a way of living by specific people groups. George Grant—pastor and educator—has pointed out in his book *The Micah Mandate* the Augustinian understanding of the nature of culture. Grant writes,

According to Augustine, culture is not a reflection of a people's race, ethnicity, folklore, politics, language, or heritage. Rather it is an outworking of a people's creed. In other words, culture is the temporal manifestation of a people's faith. If a culture begins to change, it is not because of fads, fashions, or the passing of time, it is because of a shift in worldview—it is because of a change of faith. Thus, race, ethnicity, folklore, politics, language, or heritage is simply an expression of a deeper paradigm rooted in the covenantal and spiritual matrix of a community's church and the integrity of its witness.

The reason that he spent so much of his life and ministry critiquing the pagan philosophies of the world and exposing the aberrant theologies of the church was that Augustine understood only too well that those things matter not only in the realm of eternity determining the spiritual destiny of masses of humanity but also in the realm of the here and now determining the temporal destiny of whole civilizations.

…Augustine recognized that a people's dominant worldview inevitably shapes the world they have in view.[7]

We can easily see this in our modern-day world. The Taliban in Afghanistan created a society that reflected their worship. Likewise, the USA's popular culture is a reflection of the materialistic ideals of a secular belief system.

The modern concept of anthropology, as derived from materialistic thought, sees culture as neutral. In the materialistic paradigm where there is no God, there is no objective truth; therefore, everything is relative. From this set of assumptions there is no way that one person or culture can critique another. No one culture or aspect of a culture is seen as better than another. As such, all culture is valued for what it is. With this view, how can we distinguish between the death camps of Nazi Germany, the hospitals of Mother Teresa's Sisters of Charity, and the pop culture of contemporary America?

Derived from worship, culture is anything but neutral. Culture stands at the convergence of the spiritual and physical realms. In fact it can be said that the spiritual realm influences the physical realm at the level of culture. Just as ideas have consequences, so does our worship.

The cult leads to the culture. This, in turn, determines the kinds of societies and nations we will build. If people worship a deity who is capricious and can be bribed, as in Eastern animism, then a culture of corruption is established in which bribery is a part of everyday life. This manifests itself in business, economic, government, and judicial systems that are filled with corruption. This, in turn, leads to the material impoverishment of a nation, not to mention spiritual impoverishment.

KATHLEEN NORRIS'S STORY

When the poet Kathleen Norris left the New York art world to move temporarily to South Dakota upon inheriting her grandmother's house, she had no idea what kind of journey she was embarking on. The "temporary" move lasted twenty-five years as she and her husband became a part of the plains community—and a very different culture.

While living in her grandparents' house, Norris became a member of and lay preacher in her grandmother's Presbyterian church, a journey she recounts in her first nonfiction book *Dakota: A Spiritual Geography*. Norris became open to Christianity in part by the monks of a Benedictine monastery. For her, as for many writers, poetry itself was her religion. When she attended literary readings hosted at the monastery, Norris took another step on a profound journey that would be aided by her growing friendships with the monks. Through a long struggle, the poet became a follower of Christ.

At one time convinced that being a Christian and a writer were incompatible, a fear that her writer friends continued to express, Norris has proven otherwise, thriving in her vocation. In addition to her poetry,

she has written several New York Times best-sellers, including *Dakota* and *Amazing Grace: A Vocabulary of Faith*. The latter is a series of essays, each exploring a word important to Christian faith—including many words she says were scary or heavy with baggage when she returned to church as an adult. Norris's intention and achievement in this book is summed up well by the Barclay Agency that represents her: "Her book *Amazing Grace* continues her theme that the spiritual world is rooted in the chaos of daily life. In this book, she sheds light on the very difficult theological concepts such as grace, repentance, dogma, and faith. Her intention is to tell stories about these religious concepts by grounding them in the world in which we live."[1] The *San Francisco Sunday Examiner & Chronicle* calls Norris, very appropriately, "one of the most eloquent yet earthbound spiritual writers of our time."[2]

In an interview, the journal *Homiletics* asked Norris why she had felt for so long that Christianity and writing were irreconcilable:

NORRIS: It was largely my education. I grew up in the '50s and '60s. Psychology

CRITIQUING CULTURE

Clearly, culture is not neutral. Because we live in the universe created by the living God, and because, contrary to postmodernist thought, there is an objective reality, a people's culture can be critiqued and evaluated. Not only can it be, it ought to be. If we are interested in the health of nations, we must distinguish those things that lead to justice from those that breed corruption. We should examine those things that give was a part of it. A lot of writers were very interested in the growth of psychology after World War II and in the Freudian view, religion was infantile and you want to outgrow it. So I think that filtered down into my education and the culture. Religion was something for children and little old ladies, but if you were really sophisticated and really adult, you didn't need it. And you still see this attitude. I didn't have a lot of contemporary writers who I liked who were Christians or expressed Christian ideas in their work. It's changing now. There are a number of writers of my generation and younger who see no problem at all. And I don't see it any more either. But it really was a struggle. I thought that I would have to give up my mind, that my writing would suffer—

HOMILETICS: *That it would be inferior quality.*

NORRIS: Yes, and there were other writers who worried about that and said, "How can you write now?" I remember being at a reading one time, and I had written some poems that were based on biblical themes,

and it was like, "See, I can do this!" And it was fun to bring them together and to say, "These are not polar opposites. One feeds the other. One inspires the other. They work together."[3]

As Norris has discovered, and as she demonstrates so vividly in her work, Christian faith doesn't impede honesty, or creativity, or craft, but calls us to them. Her topics reflect a full life that is not bounded but rather informed by faith; her writing explores diverse experiences, including finding her way in college and the New York art world during the tumultuous 1960s and 1970s, living for months among the Benedictines, interacting with children as a visiting artist in elementary schools across the Dakotas, grappling with her spiritual heritage, wrestling with identity and depression, and struggling and flourishing in her thirty-year marriage. Truly a creator of culture through her work as a writer and her life in the community, Kathleen Norris has engaged herself in creativity and discipline, manifesting for the church and for the broader culture some of God's nature and our nature as people in his creation.

rise to freedom, compassion, and economic well-being in contrast to those that breed enslavement, cruelty, and poverty.

Three major cultural grids can guide us in critiquing culture: kingdom culture, counterfeit culture, and natural culture.[8] These can be found, to differing degrees, in any nation. Every nation will have some kingdom and some counterfeit culture. This grid assumes that there is a God and that he has made a real and objective universe in which there is truth and falsehood, good and evil, beauty and darkness.

ELEMENTS OF CULTURE

Kingdom Culture

Kingdom culture is built on reality, on the reality God made. It is a reflection of the nature and character of the living God. Kingdom culture is produced when people, consciously or unconsciously, obey God's laws, which are a manifestation of his character. Even as God is true, just, and beautiful, so are his creation and the laws that govern it. When Jesus tells his disciples to make disciples of all nations, "teaching them to obey everything I have commanded" (Matt. 28:20), the phrase "everything I have commanded" is bounded by *truth* (which reflects God's metaphysical and physical laws), *justice* (which reflects God's moral laws), and *beauty* (which reflects God's aesthetic laws). Douglas Jones and Douglas Wilson describe this trilogy as "the three faces of culture."[9] These are the foundations of kingdom culture, and they lead to life, health, and development.

KINGDOM CULTURE: BUILT ON REALITY

TRUTH: REFLECTING GOD'S METAPHYSICAL AND PHYSICAL LAWS

JUSTICE: REFLECTING GOD'S MORAL LAWS

BEAUTY: REFLECTING GOD'S AESTHETIC LAWS

Kingdom culture is a manifestation of the kingdom of God. Jesus calls his disciples to have the kingdom of heaven impact the kingdom of earth. The Lord's Prayer[10] recognizes the interplay of the two kingdoms: "Your kingdom come, your will be done on earth as it is in heaven." God's kingdom is any realm where his will is done and where people obey all that he has commanded. The substance of the kingdom is the same in the present and in the future, on the earth and in heaven. The difference is not the substance, but the degree of fulfillment.

Kingdom culture calls each people and nation to come "further up and...further in"[11] to the reign of Jesus. It calls forth the development of the earth, the cultivation of the soil as well as the soul, as an act of worship of the living God. The church is to create culture that manifests the nature and character of the living God to a watching world. This means that we are to bring truth (the biblical metaphysic), justice (the biblical ethic), and beauty (the biblical aesthetic) into *all* of life.

KINGDOM CULTURE LIVED AND PROCLAIMED

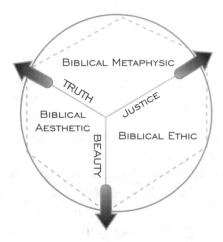

In every nation there will be elements of kingdom culture. Wherever it is found, it is to be nurtured and encouraged.

Counterfeit Culture

Counterfeit culture is the product of believing Satan's lies about what is true, just, and beautiful. Satan lies to both individuals and nations. He lies to nations at the level of culture. Isaiah warns the nation of Israel against the twisting of reality:

> Woe to those who call evil good
>   and good evil,
> who put darkness for light
>   and light for darkness,
> who put bitter for sweet
>   and sweet for bitter. (Isa. 5:20)

It is the believing of these lies that leads to death, enslavement, and impoverishment of entire nations. Every nation has some level of counterfeit culture, such as the Suruwahá tribe's ideas of which babies are fit to live, or the growing American culture that says there is no God, or the sexist culture found in so many parts of the world that insists women are inferior to men. If the nation is to grow with health, it must recognize the destructive elements, root them out, and replace them with kingdom principles.

Natural Culture

The natural elements of a culture fall within the realm of moral neutrality—neither good nor evil. They are the unique colors, textures, sounds, and tastes of a people. While they are morally neutral, they grant savor and life to the people and enjoyment to neighbors from other cultures. The natural elements are to be celebrated and enjoyed.

CULTURE MATTERS

The more a culture manifests, in such things as its music, art, and literature, the primary Creator and the primary creation—reality the way God made it—the more it may be considered good; it promotes a culture of life. The more the culture distorts reality and denies God, the more the culture produces poverty, enslavement, and death for its people. To understand that culture is not a neutral, abstract topic, we need only look at our own lives, at the headlines in our local newspapers, or at the cell phone photos and Internet videos smuggled out of nations oppressed by tyrannical governance. We need only hear a story like Hakani's to see that culture matters.

God created us to be culture makers. As Christians we are called to be intentional about creating *kingdom* culture. In the next chapter we'll look at several key aspects of humankind's consequential calling, the cultural mandate.

CHAPTER 9

ELEMENTS OF
THE CULTURAL MANDATE

As we learned in the previous chapter, the work of a Christian, no matter his or her specific vocation, is ultimately to create *kingdom culture*—culture that reflects the true nature and character of God. The creation narrative provides several key principles to guide us as we live out this calling, filling the earth with the knowledge of God.

TWO PARTS OF THE CULTURAL MANDATE

First, it is important to recognize that there are two major parts to the cultural mandate in Genesis, the societal and the developmental.

The Societal Mandate

After he had created human beings in his image, "God blessed them and said to them, 'Be fruitful and increase in number; fill the earth...'" (Gen. 1:28). Humankind was designed for community. The basic unit of the community is the family. Adam and Eve were to have children, and their children were to have children. They were to be fruitful and to multiply, to fill the earth. But fill the earth with what? The materialist sees the human being as an animal, a consumer of resources, a mouth to be fed—and nothing more. When the command to multiply and fill the earth is kept in a materialist's framework, it means more and more mouths to be fed.

But the biblical model understands that human beings are the image of God. They have minds and hearts that can innovate and create. To "fill the earth" is not to multiply the number of mouths that consume resources but to increase the image bearers who steward and cultivate the earth to bring forth its beauty and bounty.

Culture makers are to be sent to every corner of the world to fill the earth with the knowledge of God.

The Developmental Mandate

The second part of the cultural mandate is developmental. After God made man, he said, "Let them rule over the fish of the sea and the birds of the air, over the livestock, over all the earth, and over all the creatures that move along the ground" (Gen. 1:26). As we discussed in the previous chapter, man was made to rule in God's stead. God made us to be the stewards of his household.

There are two ways humankind can steward—with hands and feet, and with soul and spirit. Genesis 2:15 states, "The LORD God took the man and put him in the Garden of Eden to work it and take care of it." And Genesis 2:19–20 reveals the second aspect of this developmental mandate:

> Now the LORD God had formed out of the ground all the beasts of the field and all the birds of the air. He brought them to the man to see what he would name them; and whatever the man called each living creature, that was its name. So the man gave names to all the livestock, the birds of the air and all the beasts of the field.

We see in these two passages the twin aspects given to man, the culture maker. First, there is the cultivation of the soil, using his hands to work and care for the garden. Second, is the cultivating of the soul, using the mind and heart in the naming of the animals. Here man engages the mind in observation, reason, and categorization and then inflames the heart in creativity and passion.

Interestingly, the intertwined meanings of the words *cultivate* and *culture* testify to these twin aspects of man's work in the cultural mandate. Together *cultivate* and *culture* have two senses: preparing the physical earth for planting and preparing the mind of the individual and society for growth and maturity. Literally, the word *cultivate* means "to improve and prepare (land), as by plowing or fertilizing, for raising crops."[1] From this meaning we've also come to speak of "cultivating the mind," so much so that some dictionaries first define *cultivation* as "refinement" and "culture."

On the flip side, the word *culture* came into the English language meaning a piece of cultivated land. From the sense of cultivation of the soil, this word also took on the sense of cultivation of the mind, faculties, or manners. *Culture* may refer to "the training, development, refinement of mind, tastes and manners; the condition of being thus trained and refined; the intellectual side of civilization."[2] Dictionary definitions capture both the roots and current usage of *culture:* "the cultivation of the soil" and "the totality of socially transmitted behavior patterns, arts, beliefs, institutions, and all other products of human work and thought."[3]

Note that both aspects of our stewardship—the cultivation of the soil and the cultivation of the soul—are accomplished through the use of the body and that there is a balance between action (working and caring for the garden)[4] and reflection (naming the animals).[5] God has given us hands and feet to physically engage with the world. He has given us minds and hearts to think and create. We are not to work mechanically, but we are to think about our work as well.

God established man's dominion over nature by making man a word maker. Part of the image of God in us is our ability to reason, make words, and understand created distinctions. As man follows God in using language, he is separated from the rest of creation as the maker of culture. As guided by worship (cult), Adam and Eve were to create culture by cultivating both soil and soul.

CRITICAL CHARACTERISTICS OF THE CULTURAL MANDATE

Genesis reveals several truths that characterize this work God has created us to do.

A Community Project

First, the cultural mandate is a community project. This mandate and its subordinating societal and developmental elements require both man and woman. Female and male are equally image bearers and equally tasked to steward creation.[6]

The Genesis account reveals that a single man could not complete the task. It took women and men to make community. After he made the man, "The LORD God said, 'It is not good for the man to be alone. I will make a helper suitable for him.'... So the LORD God caused the man to fall into a deep sleep; and while he was sleeping, he took one of the man's ribs and closed up the place with flesh. Then the LORD God made a woman from the rib he had taken out of the man, and he brought her to the man" (Gen. 2:18, 21–22).

Note that the task of culture making is given to both male and female. To carry out the cultural mandate is a social responsibility of the family and the larger community.

Progressing and Conserving

Second, the cultural mandate calls for a progressing *and* a conserving. We see in the words of Genesis 2:15 the balance between "working" and "tending" the garden.

The word for work is *abad*. It is found 290 times in the Old Testament translated to "work" or to "serve."[7] The word for tending is *shamar*. It is found 568 times in the Old Testament and means "to keep," "to guard," "to protect," "to preserve."[8] The former has the sense of stewarding the garden in a way that it grows and increases its yield. The latter has the sense of preserving or protecting from loss. There is, thus, a balance in the assignment between making progress and conserving that which already exists.

John Calvin writes in his commentary on Genesis,

> Moses now adds, that the earth was given to man, with this condition, that he should occupy himself in its cultivation. Whence it follows, that men were created to employ themselves in some work, and not to lie down in inactivity and idleness....Wherefore, nothing is more contrary to the order of nature, than to consume life in eating, drinking, and sleeping, while in the meantime we propose nothing to ourselves to do. Moses adds, that the custody of the garden was given in charge to Adam, to show that we possess the things which God has committed to our hands, on the condition, that being content with a frugal and moderate use of them, we should take care of what shall remain. Let him who possesses a field, so partake of its yearly fruits, that he may not suffer the ground to be injured by his negligence; but let him endeavor to hand it down to posterity as he received it, or even better cultivated. Let him so feed on its fruits, that he neither dissipates it by luxury, nor permits it to be marred or ruined by neglect.[9]

Since the Fall, man has not balanced the twin admonitions to work and to tend. Without a moral and theological framework for stewardship, man tends to either rape nature, to develop it without conserving it, or to underdevelop nature, by conserving without progressing. The former is the tendency of materialistic societies, the latter, of animistic societies.[10]

A Dynamic Process

Third, achieving the potential God has built into creation is a dynamic process, characterized by activity and progress. God's creation is not to be static but stimulated to develop. God turns over the tasks of exploring and of developing and cultivating soil, soul, and culture to man. Resources are to be discovered and created. Godly culture is to be manifested, civilized societies are to be built. Cities are to be established where the arts, science, and enterprise flourish. And the earth is to be filled with the knowledge of the Lord.[11]

There is a theme that ties the Scriptures together. The biblical narrative and all of human history begins in a garden—the Garden of Eden[12]—and ends in a city—the

New Jerusalem.[13] Actually the New Jerusalem, the Holy City, is a garden-city.[14] David Hegeman describes the beauty of the unity of the Scriptures from the beginning of Genesis to the end of Revelation: "There is a profound thread which moves through the course of the entire Bible, from the original garden to the heavenly Jerusalem. The latter place is described both as a garden [*paradeisos*] and a city [*polis*], making the paradigmatic garden-city."[15]

The task given humankind in Genesis as culture makers is to steward creation from a beautiful garden to the glorious city in a park, a garden city. The harmony found in creation before the Fall between man, creation, and God is to be restored and is the goal of the end of time where there is in means and ends a harmony between the man's creation (the city) and God's creation (nature).

From Acorn to Oak

Fourth, as we fulfill the cultural mandate, we follow a progression like that of acorn to oak. Humankind is to unleash the potential built into creation, just as the acorn's potential is to be released into a mighty oak. The small, simple yet complex, beautiful acorn is to be worked and tended in such a way that it becomes a mighty oak. The tree becomes the home for birds and squirrels. It provides shade for the weary traveler and the setting for the lovers' picnic. It becomes the object of the poet's pen and the painter's brush. It produces acorns of its own, manifesting the principle of seeds, creating hundreds of new forests.

God has built into creation the wonder of first principles. The little acorn becomes a mighty oak that has the potential to seed many forests. The DNA of the first dog contains all "dogginess," providing for the incredible variety of dogs that we see around the world today. The DNA in the first wild rose has produced all the roses there are today. From the three primary colors have come all the paintings that have ever been painted or will ever be painted. From the foundations of musical notes and harmonies have come all the symphonies, ballads, and songs of lovers ever written. From the elementary principles of numbers have come mathematics and the unlocking of the scientific truths so far discovered and yet to be discovered. From the first principle of speech have come all the poems, verses, sonnets, and proverbs in every language—even whole worlds, like Middle-earth and Narnia. Indeed, beginning with Adam's work in naming the animals, the vast realms of knowledge at our fingertips continue to multiply daily.

As man builds on first principles, as he discovers the things that are hidden, as he explores the vast reaches of outer and inner space, as he writes, paints, and composes, he does what God intended for him to do. He is stewarding the garden, fulfilling the cultural mandate.

THE LIFE-OR-DEATH QUESTION

Clearly, man was made to make culture. That is his primary task. The question is not, Will man make culture? The question is, Will he make good culture or bad culture? Will culture be built on kingdom principles or counterfeit principles? Will it contribute to truth, justice, and beauty or to ignorance, corruption, and ugliness?

In this chapter we've explored just some of God's rich intentions for us as makers of culture. In the next chapter we'll consider what it means to be culture makers in a fallen world.

CHAPTER 10

THE FALL, THE CROSS, AND CULTURE

While God created man in his own image, giving man the awesome responsibility and joy of being his steward, man rejected both his identity and his purpose. At the Fall, man became a rebel against the High King of Heaven, who himself is the definition of all that is good. Man chose to not participate in God's perfect goodness. Ultimately, the Fall led to human beings creating culture that does not reflect the nature of God. The foundation for perfect culture was destroyed, leaving brokenness in all relationships: God to humankind, person to person, and person to creation. This brokenness includes our relationship with work and our function as makers of culture.

But the story doesn't end with the Fall! God is at work in the world advancing his kingdom. Jesus died on the cross to redeem the lost and to restore that which was broken. Paul reveals that *all* creation is awaiting redemption[1] and that Jesus died to reconcile *all* things to himself.[2] The cross not only restores individual relationship with God but also lays the foundation for substantial healing in all relationships. This means that the cultural mandate found in Genesis 1 and 2 has the capacity to be renewed. Jesus' death restored and affirmed man as God's culture maker.

Dallas Willard, in his marvelous book *The Divine Conspiracy,* says this:

Jesus came among us to show and teach the life for which we were made. He came very gently, opened access to the governance of God with him, and set

afoot a conspiracy of freedom in truth among human beings. Having overcome death he remains among us. By relying on his word and presence we are
enabled to reintegrate the little realm that makes up our life into the infinite
rule of God. And that is the eternal kind of life. Caught up in his active rule,
our deeds become an element in God's eternal history. They are what God
and we do together, making us part of his life and him a part of ours.[3]

Here Willard expresses the mystery of the organic connection between our life and
work and God's life and work. The Fall gave rise to breakaway kingdoms that rejected
the rule of God and resulted in a world of *dis*order and death. But Jesus has overcome
death and has shown us how to *live*. We are enabled by him to work together with God
to repair and reunite the disparate kingdoms spawned by the Fall into the kingdom of
God. The bottom line for Christians considering the cultural mandate is this: The Fall
made our stewardship more difficult. However, following in the footsteps of Christ,
humankind is absolutely able to stand against its consequences.

WORK IN A BENT WORLD

In his masterful work *Out of the Silent Planet*,[4] C. S. Lewis describes the one planet that
is in rebellion against the Creator of the universe as the "silent planet" and the home
of the "bent ones." Since the rebellion of Adam and Eve, we have lived in a fallen world
and we are the bent ones.

There were natural consequences to our rebellion. To deny God's order is to bring
in *dis*order. Moses explains the choice before us to live in God's order, obeying his
ordinances, or to live in disorder and death, the consequences of sin:

> Now what I am commanding you today is not too difficult for you or beyond
> your reach. It is not up in heaven, so that you have to ask, "Who will ascend
> into heaven to get it and proclaim it to us so we may obey it?" Nor is it beyond
> the sea, so that you have to ask, "Who will cross the sea to get it and proclaim
> it to us so we may obey it?" No, the word is very near you; it is in your mouth
> and in your heart so you may obey it.
>
> See, I set before you today life and prosperity, death and destruction. For
> I command you today to love the LORD your God, to walk in his ways, and
> to keep his commands, decrees and laws; then you will live and increase, and
> the LORD your God will bless you in the land you are entering to possess....
>
> This day I call heaven and earth as witnesses against you that I have set
> before you life and death, blessings and curses. Now choose life, so that you

and your children may live and that you may love the LORD your God, listen to his voice, and hold fast to him. For the LORD is your life, and he will give you many years in the land he swore to give to your fathers, Abraham, Isaac and Jacob. (Deut. 30:11–16; 19–20)

E. Stanley Jones, has captured the importance of obedience to God's laws in many of his writings. He explains that as God's laws and ordinances are immutable, they are unbreakable. So when we beings try to break God's laws, it is we who are broken. If we try to break the physical law of gravity by jumping from a high building, we do not break the law, we get broken. If we try to break, for example, the moral law "thou shall not commit adultery," we do not break the law, we break ourselves and our families on the law.

Our sin has made us broken people and has brought a brokenness into creation. Yet in order to rightly understand our work in the world, it is crucial to understand what is broken and what is not broken. In relationship to the issue of work, many Christians argue that work is a curse. But as we have said elsewhere, worked existed before the Fall. It was not work that was cursed, rather it was the ground that was cursed. In addition to the good that it produces, it will now also produce thorns and thistles,[5] and there will be droughts, floods, earthquakes, and famines. There is now evil in the natural realm, or what our forerunners called "natural evil." Man's labor will now be harder (with the "sweat of the brow") but in itself is not evil.

So do we sit passively and let the weeds infest the ground, or do we challenge the weeds? As our forefathers did, we too are to stand actively against natural evil. The great English hymn writer and pastor Isaac Watts (1674–1748) captured the proper mentality for the Christian in his wonderful Christmas carol "Joy to the World." In one stanza we sing of natural evil and our response to it.

No more let sins and sorrows grow,
Nor thorns infest the ground;
He comes to make His blessings flow
Far as the curse is found,
Far as the curse is found,
Far as, far as, the curse is found.

Key to developing a biblical theology of vocation is remembering that work is part of what God declared to be "very good" (Gen. 1:31). Man was made to work as a part of his dignity, as a part of the inherent nature of what it means to be human, to be in the image of the working God. As Pope John Paul II wrote, "Man is made to be in the visible universe an image and likeness of God himself, and he is placed in it in order to subdue the earth. From the beginning therefore he is called to work."[6]

Not only is man's work not cursed, man himself certainly is not. In the decisive battle of the spiritual war, the Son of Eve was destined to crush (defeat) Satan at the same time that Satan wounded Christ on the cross.[7] We human beings are immediately the object of God's redemptive promise, and our work will turn out to be an agent of redemption in the world as we work with God.

Yet the entirety of our life and work, so much part of God's intention for us, will nevertheless feel the strain of sin's corruption. In the difficulties of performing our given roles within the context of sin-induced brokenness, we may experience that work itself is cut off from God and thus from its theological moorings and meaning. Work as stewardship, calling, enterprise, and part of the cultural mandate is challenged, and in this degraded context, we may find it boring, routine, mechanical, repetitive, hard, and even futile.

On a larger scale, the Fall has led to economic systems becoming separated from kingdom principles. Contrary principles lead to systems dominated by greed and corruption. These systems, instead of creating an environment where image bearers of God can flourish in their artistry and abilities, reduce work to no more than the movements of cogs in a machine, as in the communist/materialist worldview, or playing no more of a role than a serf's service at his feudal lord's pleasure, as demonstrated in the mercantilist systems.

Wherever sin has bred systemic evils like these or personal dislocation of our lives and work from God's intentions, God is working to reverse the effects of the Fall, and he calls us to work with him.

REALISM-IDEALISM

Living in a fallen world means that we have a responsibility to fight against both ethical evil and natural evil. There is a war on to redeem all of creation from the effects of the Fall.[8] God continues to work, in common grace, to sustain the universe. Man colabors with God to push back the effects of natural evil through science and technology and the boundaries of poverty through economic enterprise. As the gospel goes forth to transform men's hearts and lives and conform them to Christ's image—the original image of man—the dignity of work is affirmed and man's *life*work is established through connection to the kingdom of God.

We are to have two attitudes toward work in a fallen world: realism and idealism. Realism reminds us to see things as they are: corrupt economic structures, sinful human beings, and natural evil. There is no perfect job or perfect life. Until Christ returns there will be sweat of the brow. We are not to be romantically utopian. As Francis Schaeffer was fond of saying, "If you expect perfection or nothing, you will always get nothing!"

However, in addition to being realistic, we are to be idealistic. We know that Christ, at the cross, won the decisive battle that marked the turning point in the cosmic war over moral and natural evil.[9] We know the ultimate outcome of the conflict. Christ has called us to follow his banner into the midst of the battle. God is at work in the world, redeeming his creation, building his kingdom. We are to have a part in this. Christ's agenda is our agenda. Idealism calls us to see things as they ought to be, reflected in the prayer "Your kingdom come, your will be done on earth as it is in heaven" (Matt. 6:10). We are called to engage in the battle for the advancement of the kingdom and not sit passively on the sidelines. As servants of the King we do this in very tangible ways *here on earth*, employing all the natural and spiritual gifts with which we've been equipped to fight against hunger, poverty, and ignorance and to fight for truth, life, and justice.

In the midst of brokenness, redeemed man is to work to redeem culture and transform nations. David Hegeman summarizes this:

> Thus God seeks to create a community of redeemed men and women who are equipped for every good work. We are redeemed so that we may work! The human race is brought back to a state of righteousness so that we might return to our Edenic calling to develop ("work") the earth into a glorious garden-city and finally take possession of our long-awaited inheritance.[10]

Redeemed man is not simply to go with the flow of existing culture, nor is he to only focus on attacking the negative things in culture. He is to promote a kingdom culture. He is always to be "countercultural" to the world's system. As someone has said, it is not enough to curse the darkness; we are to light a candle in the midst of the darkness.

In short, the Fall is real, but we are to fight against it. Cultures can be transformed and nations reformed. The Abrahamic Covenant[11] to bless all nations is now linked with the Great Commission given us by Christ to disciple nations, "teaching them to obey everything I have commanded" (Matt. 28:20).

This process is progressive and dynamic. The transformation can be substantial, with significant healing in all areas of life. There should be no illusion, however, about our present "perfectibility." Nothing will be perfect this side of Christ's second coming. And the progress will be made in the Spirit, not in the flesh. The process is a dance. Christ is the leader, we are the responders. Christ has his role, and we have ours. Christ will return with his kingdom, while we are to follow his command to "occupy till I come" (Luke 19:13 KJV). The consummation will occur when Christ returns.

THE END OF CULTURE

What is the end of culture? What is the purpose of culture? To what end are we working? When Christ returns at the end of history, he comes to marry his bride, the church.[12] He will return with the Holy City, the New Jerusalem.[13] Then the kings of the earth will come bearing gifts to the wedding feast. We find these remarkable words in Revelation 21:22–26:

> I did not see a temple in the city, because the Lord God Almighty and the Lamb are its temple. The city does not need the sun or the moon to shine on it, for the glory of God gives it light, and the Lamb is its lamp. The nations will walk by its light, and the kings of the earth will bring their splendor into it. On no day will its gates ever be shut, for there will be no night there. The glory and honor of the nations will be brought into it.

What a picture! The kings of the earth will bring the glory and honor of the nations into the City of God.

At the end of time, as a fulfillment of the blessing of the nations and the discipling of the nations, the unique glory of each nation will be revealed in the light of the glory of God. Just as the magi from the East brought gifts of gold, incense, and myrrh[14] to the baby Jesus, so the kings of the earth will bring the glory and splendor of their nations to Christ on his wedding day.

We see the images of Revelation 21 foretold in Psalms 47; 72:10–17; and 117 and in Isaiah 60:1–20; 62:1–3; and 66:18–21. Hegeman points out the four similarities of the two visions:[15] First will be the ingathering of the nations for worship.[16] Second, there will be no more suffering.[17] Third, the gates of the city are never shut.[18] And fourth, the gifts of the nations are given.[19]

Let's look at the gifts that are given as recorded in Isaiah 60:4–14:

> "Lift up your eyes and look about you:
>   All assemble and come to you;
> your sons come from afar,
>   and your daughters are carried on the arm.
> Then you will look and be radiant,
>   your heart will throb and swell with joy;
> the wealth on the seas will be brought to you,
>   to you the riches of the nations will come.
> Herds of camels will cover your land,
>   young camels of Midian and Ephah.

And all from Sheba will come,
    bearing gold and incense
    and proclaiming the praise of the LORD.
All Kedar's flocks will be gathered to you,
    the rams of Nebaioth will serve you;
they will be accepted as offerings on my altar,
    and I will adorn my glorious temple.

"Who are these that fly along like clouds,
    like doves to their nests?
Surely the islands look to me;
    in the lead are the ships of Tarshish,
bringing your sons from afar,
    with their silver and gold,
to the honor of the LORD your God,
    the Holy One of Israel,
    for he has endowed you with splendor.

"Foreigners will rebuild your walls,
    and their kings will serve you.
Though in anger I struck you,
    in favor I will show you compassion.
Your gates will always stand open,
    they will never be shut, day or night,
so that men may bring you the wealth of the nations—
    their kings led in triumphal procession.
For the nation or kingdom that will not serve you will perish;
    it will be utterly ruined.

"The glory of Lebanon will come to you,
    the pine, the fir and the cypress together,
to adorn the place of my sanctuary;
    and I will glorify the place of my feet.
The sons of your oppressors will come bowing before you;
    all who despise you will bow down at your feet
and will call you the City of the LORD,
    Zion of the Holy One of Israel."

In this passage in Isaiah we see foretold the ingathering of the nations to worship the living God and celebrate the wedding of the Lamb. At the end of *HIS*-story, Christ will return with the fullness of his kingdom. Every part of our life and work that brings glory to God will be presented to Christ. We get the sense that unique natural resources of the nations will be part of the gifts. But not only these; the work of people's hands—the crafts, arts, and products from those resources—will be among the gifts given to Christ.

During a trip to Rwanda for a pastors' conference, my good friends Bob Moffitt and John Wood took a gift of choir T-shirts to a church choir in an impoverished part of the capital city of Kigali. After the T-shirts were given, this choir began to sing gospel hymns in the rich, textured rhythms and harmonies of Africa. As my two friends listened to the choir, they felt like they were being swept up to the gates of heaven. In all their worldwide travels, they had never heard anything like this before. As tears flooded their eyes in response to the beauty and worship they were experiencing, they noted to one another that this might be one of the gifts given by the kings of Rwanda to the glorified Christ.

From each nation will come the beauty of its culture—in crafts, music, arts, drama, and dance—and the beauty of its varied natural resources. The unique glory of each nation, which is revealed in the light of the glory of God, may be taken into eternity as a gift to Christ. Theologian Anthony Hoekema (1913–1988), writing in *The Bible and the Future,* contemplates the end of culture:

> The inhabitants of the earth will include people who attained great prominence and exercised great power on the present earth—kings, leaders and the like. One could also say that whatever people have done on this earth which glorified God will be remembered in the life to come (see Revelation 14:13). But more must be said. Is it too much to say that, according to these verses, the unique contributions of each nation to the life of the present earth will enrich the life of the new earth? Shall we then perhaps inherit the best products of culture and art which this earth has produced?[20]

In Revelation 14:13 we find these words: "And I heard a voice from heaven saying unto me, Write, Blessed are the dead which die in the Lord from henceforth: Yea, saith the Spirit, that they may rest from their labours; and their works [*ergon*] do follow them" (KJV). Hegeman muses on Revelation 14:13: "Here we see the works for which man was created (Gen. 2:15) and later redeemed (Eph. 2:10) apparently being taken into eternity!"[21]

G. B. Caird, in his commentary on the book of Revelation, writes concerning the glory and honor of the nations,

> Nothing from the old order which has value in the sight of God is disbarred from entry into the new. John's heaven is no world-denying Nirvana, into

which men may escape from the incurable ills of sublunary existence, but the seal of affirmation on the goodness of God's creation. The treasure that men find laid up in heaven turns out to be the treasures and wealth of the nations, the best they have known and loved on earth redeemed of all imperfections and transfigured by the radiance of God.[22]

C. S. Lewis captures this in his book *The Last Battle*.[23] The fallen world that we currently inhabit, Lewis calls the "Shadowlands," and he refers to "the new heaven and new earth" as "Aslan's country." Aslan, a lion, is the figure of Christ, the King of heaven and earth. When the heroes and heroines of *The Last Battle* pass from the Shadowlands to Aslan's country, Aslan welcomes them with the call "Come further up and come further in."[24] As the children in the story come further up and further in, there is a dawning, a progressive revelation. The further they go, the more they realize that where they are now is free of the Shadowlands; it is the place of their longing, the place they were meant for. Lewis writes, "I have come home at last! This is my real country! I belong here. This is the land I have been looking for all my life, though I never knew it until now." And not only have the English children come home at last, but as they "come further up and further in" they sense that they "have been there before." As they continue their journey, they find they are in England in all her glory. All the dross has been burned off. Only the unique beauty of England is left.[25] In this image, Lewis dramatizes beautifully the truth of the goodness of each culture being redeemed, being purified in the light of the glory of God.

OUR ORIGINAL AND ULTIMATE PURPOSE

What kind of culture are you and others in your community working to create? It matters immensely, for both time and eternity. Man as the image of God is a culture maker. His original purpose by God's command in the cultural mandate is to create godly culture—culture that incarnates the nature and character of God himself in all his truth, beauty, and justice. In defiance and in ignorance we have multiplied brokenness over the earth. But God is working to reconcile all things to himself. It is as a reconciler that he advances his kingdom, and it is as reconcilers that we work with him, manifesting on earth the culture of a kingdom that is truly heavenly.

Dutch Theologian Herman Bavinck (1854–1921) wrote,

Culture in the broadest sense is the purpose for which God created man after His image... [which] includes not only the most ancient callings of...hunting and fishing, agriculture and stock raising, but also trade and commerce and science and art."[26]

Whether doctors, chefs, landscapers, pastors, or software developers, all of us work as culture makers. Understanding our work in the context of the cultural mandate is foundational to building a biblical theology of vocation. As the whole metanarrative of Scripture witnesses from Creation to Consummation, our work is ultimately to see people come to Christ, be drawn into the life of his kingdom, and give their *life*work to the advancement of kingdom culture. It is in this context that we find our callings— the connection of our life and work to the kingdom of God. In the next chapters, we'll search out what it means for each of us to be called to a *life*work as we continue to explore God's Transforming Story.

PART **4** : *Life*WORK

CHAPTER 11

THE CALL: *Life*WORK

Os Guinness writes in *The Call*, "If there is no Caller, there are no callings—only work."[1] And meaningless work at that. If the universe is silent, as the modernist would say, there is no purpose in life, only "outer darkness" and questions with no answers.

But in reality, the universe is not silent. Before the creation of the world, community existed in the Trinity. Relationships are one of the fundamental principles of the universe. God created man to live in deeply personal connection with him. Within the relationship of God and man, God is the Caller and man is the called. Our calling, therefore, is found in community with the Trinity, the Sovereign God who orders all things and has a place in that order specifically for "me."

OUR DOUBLE CALLING

From Adam and Eve in the Garden, to the Patriarchs, to the apostles, to women and men of the present day the world over, we see the God of the universe calling people into a face-to-face relationship with him and calling them to their personal assignment for the advancement of his kingdom.

Our call is first and foremost to salvation. This is the *primary* call to which all believers must respond. But the *secondary* calling, which is unique to each believer, is to one's vocation, or occupation. Each of us in Christ is called to a unique role in advancing the kingdom of God, no less than how God calls each star by name. The Lord's Prayer, "Your kingdom come, your will be done, on earth as it is in heaven" (Matt. 6:10), is to be taken seriously by loyal subjects of the kingdom of God. We are called to enter the kingdom and then to extend that kingdom into the world by bringing truth (the biblical metaphysic), justice (the biblical ethic), and beauty (the biblical aesthetic) into all of life, through our faith and our vocation.

The word *vocation* comes from the Latin *vocatio,* meaning a calling, a summons, or an invitation, as in "a calling from God." In turn, *vocatio* comes from *vocare,* to call. Noah Webster defined *vocation* in the *1828 American Dictionary of the English Language*:

> Among divines, a calling by the will of God; or the bestowment of God's distinguishing grace upon a person or nation, by which that person or nation is put in the way of salvation; 2. Summons; call; inducement. 3. Designation or destination to a particular state or profess. 4. Employment; calling; occupation; trade; a word that includes professions as well as mechanical occupations. Let every divine, every physician, every lawyer, and every mechanic, be faithful and diligent in his vocation."[2]

Webster, the first lexicographer of American English, functioned from a biblical worldview. His definitions are rooted in biblical language and thought. In Webster's dictionary, the biblical understanding of vocation includes the sense of both calling to salvation and calling to one's occupation. While we often use the word *vocation* to refer to our special area of employment, in a larger sense our vocation includes our entire *life*work, our primary occupation but also all service God gives us to do in this world. In other words, the call of God on the believer is a call to Christ and a call for *each* believer to be an instrument of God's kingdom in the world. It is a general call to life, and it is a unique and particular call to work: a *life*work.

GOD'S COMPREHENSIVE CALL

Understanding the whole of our life and work in the context of God's call is essential to developing a biblical theology of vocation. Remember that it was the Reformers who recovered the application of the concept of calling to the larger arena of life, teaching that all Christians have callings to all kinds of legitimate vocations rather than solely to the monastic and clerical ones. This application spread across Europe as Christians touched by Reformation thinking recovered a wholistic biblical worldview.

As the Reformers understood, the call of God is not fragmented; it is wholistic, integrative, and comprehensive. It encompasses the whole of our being and the whole of reality. Unfortunately, the church today is largely presenting a truncated, narrow, spiritually oriented call. It is a call to only the salvation of the soul for eternity. This Greek concept of the call leaves the world longing for something that speaks to all of our existence, both now and in eternity.

In the Introduction, I opened our whole discussion of vocation by relating the story of a group of young Filipinos who were thinking of joining the Maoist rebels. Asked by a missionary what they saw in Maoism that they didn't see in Christianity, their leader said,

> Sir, Maoism provides us young people in our present situation with four essential things: (1) a unified and coherent view of the world, history, and reality; (2) a definite goal to work for, live for, and die for; (3) a call to all people for a common fraternity; and (4) a sense of commitment and a mission to spread the good news that there is hope for the hopeless. The fact is, sir, that the Christian faith in all of its beauty seems to be unable to provide us with such a vision.[3]

Oh, how we should weep. Though the young Filipinos didn't know it, they were looking for nothing other than the King and his kingdom. The soul of man and the soul of cultures are longing for that for which they have been made. In addition to truth, justice, and beauty, the Christian faith provides the "four essentials" that the world is longing for: a coherent view of reality, something to live for and die for, a sense of community, and something that will bring hope to the hopeless. But the church offers only a shadow of the glory that she has received.

As members of Christ's body, we need to be reminded that the call of God involves all of man and all of his relationships. It involves man's heart, mind, soul, and strength. It involves his relationships with God, with his neighbor, and with creation.

As Os Guinness states, "Calling is the premise of Christian existence itself. Calling means that everyone, everywhere and in everything fulfills his or her (secondary) callings in response to God's (primary) calling."[4]

EXPLORING THE WORD *CALL*

In Scripture the Hebrew and Greek words for *call* are used more than seven hundred times.[5] As the word *call* does in English, the Hebrew and Greek words carry a wealth of meanings and shadings of meaning. The Greek word *keleo,* used in the New Testament, means "to call" or "to call by name." It is translated *call* and *bid.* It comes from the root *keleuo,* which is translated "to command" or "to order." A second Greek word, *klesis,* is translated *calling* and *vocation*. It can be used for an invitation as to a feast or a divine invitation to salvation. The Old Testament word is *qara*. It is translated *call* and *cried*. It is used variously to mean to summon, invite, appoint, call for, call and commission, or call and endow.

Again, referring to Webster's 1828 dictionary, we find many of the rich biblical meanings that inform the concept of calling in his definition of the English word *call*:

> the word call [Heb. To hold or restrain.] In a general sense, to drive; to strain or force out sound. Hence, To name; to denominate or give a name. And God called the light day, and the darkness he called night (Gen. 1)....To convoke; to summon; to direct or order to meet; to assemble by order or public notice;...To give notice to come by authority; to command to come; as, call a servant....To appoint or designate, as for an office, duty or employment. (See, I have called by name Bezaleel. Ex. 31. Paul called to be an apostle. Rom. 1.)...To invite or draw into union with Christ; to bring to know, believe and obey the gospel ([Rom.] 8:28)....To call forth, to bring or summon to action; as, to call forth all the faculties of the mind....To call out, to summon to fight; to challenge; also, to summon into service; as, to call out the militia.[6]

To think that God has called us! The very God who called the universe into existence by speaking words and who gave identity to the things created by calling them by name has called us into being and has called us by name. He has invited us and drawn us.

THE CALLER EQUIPS THE CALLED

Not only does God call us, but he also equips us for our calling. We see this in our first parents, Adam and Eve, at the time of the cultural mandate: "God blessed them" (Gen. 1:28–29). In the Old Testament the word *bless* (Hebrew *barak*) is found 330 times. It means to "endue with power for success, prosperity, fecundity, longevity, etc."[7] God blessed Adam and Eve for the purpose for which he had made them and gave them a world in which they were to exercise their vocations. Likewise with Abraham, God blessed Abraham for the task of becoming a model nation from which all the nations of the world would be blessed: "I will bless you" (Gen. 12:2). God called Moses to build the tabernacle. He provisioned him for the task by calling the people to bring their material abundance and their skills.[8] Likewise, in the Great Commission, Jesus called his disciples to disciple the nations.[9] And we find that he equipped them for that task.[10]

What does it mean to equip? In the New Testament, the word *equip* is *katartis-mos*.[11] It is found one time in Ephesians 4:12, in the King James Version, where it is translated "perfecting"; here the apostles, prophets, evangelists, pastors, and teachers are given to the church for the "equipping" or "complete furnishing" for the works of service. This word is derived from the word *katartizo*, which means "to put in order," "to prepare," "to strengthen," "to make one what he ought to be."[12] We find this used in Hebrews 13:20–21: "May the God of peace...equip you with everything good for doing his will."

The common theme in the Old and New Testaments is that God has a purpose for our lives and he equips us for that purpose. On a personal level, we find this revealed in the wonderful words of the psalmist:

> For you created my inmost being;
>   you knit me together in my mother's womb.
> I praise you because I am fearfully and wonderfully made;
>   your works are wonderful,
>   I know that full well.
> My frame was not hidden from you
>   when I was made in the secret place.
> When I was woven together in the depths of the earth,
>   your eyes saw my unformed body.
> All the days ordained for me
>   were written in your book
>   before one of them came to be. (Ps. 139:13–16)

We have been fearfully and wonderfully made for a purpose, and God has designed, equipped, and gifted us for the purpose for which we have been made. The DNA of our genetic code has established our physical endowment. At the same time there is a metaphysical DNA that shapes our own unique calling. There is something that we have been created to do that no one else has been made to do in the way that we do it. Michael Novak, the economic philosopher, says it so eloquently: "What shows each of us to be distinctive is the trajectory of the calling we pursue, like meteorites across the night sky of history."[13]

MADE FOR THE CALLER

God designed man to work with him, shaping the course of history. Each person's words and actions influence the history of other individuals, communities, and nations.

Dr. Francis Schaeffer said that a person is like a pebble that is thrown into a pond and makes ripples, ripples that "go on forever." My good friend, Dr. Bob Moffitt, the founder of The Harvest Foundation, has said, "Everyone has been made to write his or her signature on the universe."

We have longings for purpose, meaning, and fulfillment because there is something for which we have been made. We have been made for the Caller, for the eternal. Os Guinness captures this wonderfully: "The very fact that we humans experience desire is proof that we are creatures. Incomplete in ourselves, we desire whatever we think is beckoning to complete us."[14]

We are like Abraham, who was called, in faith, to leave his home and culture in Ur of the Chaldeans to wander in the desert.[15] He left all that was familiar, all that was comfortable for the journey, for the kingdom of God. What was he looking for in his desert wanderings? He was looking for the City of God.[16] And so, too, were all the saints of old. They wandered in the desert looking for the city. They all died in faith without receiving the things promised.[17] Like Abraham and the great cloud of witnesses, we are "pilgrims on a journey," "strangers in a strange land," longing for the kingdom of God, looking for our place in the universe.

Guinness writes,

> Personally summoned by the Creator of the universe, we are given a meaning in what we do that flames over every second and inch of our lives.... The call is always to the higher, the deeper, and the farther.
>
> Awakened to our deepest gifts and aspirations, we know that consideration of calling always has to precede considerations of career and that we can seek the deepest satisfaction in work only within the perspectives of calling.
>
> ...God has called us, and we are never more ourselves than when we are fully stretched in answering.[18]

We are to leave the familiar and the comfortable of our own Ur of the Chaldeans and wander in the desert, fixing our eyes on that which is just out of reach, "the city with foundations, whose architect and builder is God" (Heb. 11:10).

CALLED TO A *Life*WORK

Our journey to the City of God begins at the point of our conception. We have been called to life. We are born into a family, a community, a people group, and a nation. We are all born into a specific context and web of relationships. The journey continues with the call to salvation; it is here that we join a new family; we are adopted into the family of God. This is a fraternity that spans space and time. It connects to the great cloud of witnesses spoken of in Hebrews 11 and continues to the present. It connects to a family from every tribe and nation.[19] The call is to enter the kingdom of God.

The journey continues with God's call to work and to a place of deployment. Here God equips us for our occupation, for the place where we will do our *life*work. In this place or these places we are to grow and mature until the work that he has called us to is complete.

Whatever our *life*work, it is to be understood in the midst of God's agenda—in the context of *HIS*-story. God is working to advance his kingdom, reconciling all things to himself, and he has called us to work with him.

CHAPTER 12

THE GENERAL CALL:

TO LIFE

The general call to salvation—to enter the kingdom of God—is foundational to our particular call to work—to extend the kingdom. The general call defines, in moral and spiritual terms, the framework for our particular call.

As we seek to respond to God's double call—to connect the whole of our lives and work to the kingdom of God—we stand firmly in reality. This quest is both possible and vital because God's work of reconciliation encompasses *all* things for *all* time. God's call to life—to salvation—is comprehensive.

THE NEED FOR A BIG AGENDA

As we have seen before, prior to man's rebellion against God, all of creation was in harmony. Genesis 1 records that at each stage of creation God examines what he had made and declared it "good" or "excellent"[1] or "just," "right" or "true."[2] These are not arbitrary judgments but the determinations of the divine Creator over what he had made and maintains. In Genesis 1:31, when man, the crown jewel of creation had been made, God declared it "very" ("exceedingly" or "abundantly") good. All of creation was in harmony with God and with itself.

In man's rebellion against God, this harmony was shattered, and the primary relationship between man and God was broken. Because this primary relationship is foundational to all the others, all of humankind's secondary relationships were broken as well. The ripples of the rebellion extended to *all* relationships, to *all* of creation.

Both man's *internal* relationship, or his unique ability to reflect on his own existence, and man's *external* relationships with others and with the rest of creation were affected. With his relationship with God broken, man's own sense of identity is lost. All the questions of identity—Who am I? What is the purpose in my life? Do I have any significance?—begin to raise themselves.

In addition to not knowing who he is, man also does not know what the rest of creation is. In relationship to his fellow man, the most intimate relationships of family are broken. Nowhere is this more apparent than in contemporary America, where marriages and children are sacrificed for the marketplace or personal convenience. In many places in the world, it is forgotten that women are made in the image of God. They are too often treated as slaves in their own homes, as the property of their husbands, or as sex objects. The wonders of the sacredness of marriage are exchanged for adultery and fleeting one-night stands. The beauty of love is replaced with the destruction of hatred and murder. Family fights against family, clan against clan, nation against nation. The marvel of justice is exchanged for the short-term gains of greed and corruption. In relationship to the rest of God's creation, instead of being stewards, people rape and destroy the place that God has given them in which to live and work. They fail to see the value of caring for creation, instead defiling the very location of their *life*work. In his rebellion, man has divorced all that he is and does from its created meaning.

GOD'S COMPREHENSIVE PROVISION

Because the Fall is comprehensive, salvation must be equally comprehensive. In the Old Testament, the word that best describes this salvation is *peace*. In the New Testament the word is *salvation*.

The New Bible Dictionary gives the breadth of understanding of the word *peace* as used in the Old Testament:

> "completeness," "soundness," "well-being"...It is used when one asks of or prays for the welfare of another (Gn. 43:27; Ex. 4:18; Jdg. 19:20), when one is in harmony or concord with another (Jos. 9:15; 1 Ki. 5:12), when one seeks the good of a city or country (Ps. 122:6; Je. 29:7). It may mean material prosperity (Ps. 73:3) or physical safety (Ps. 4:8). But also it may mean spiritual well-being. Such peace is the associate of righteousness and truth, but not of wickedness (Ps. 85:10; Is. 48:18, 22; 57:19–21).[3]

As used in the New Testament, the Greek word for *peace* embraces the full meaning of the Old Testament word "and nearly always carries a spiritual connotation. The breadth of its meaning is especially apparent from its linking with such key words as grace (Rom. 1:7, etc.), life (Rom. 8:6), righteousness (Rom. 14:17), and from its use in benedictions such as 1 Thes. 5:23 and Heb. 13:20."[4]

As used in the Bible, *peace* expresses the fullness of God's redemptive plan, healing all of the relationships broken in the Fall:

> For sinful man there must first be peace with God, the removal of sin's enmity through the sacrifice of Christ (Rom. 5:1; Col. 1:20). Then inward peace can follow (Phil. 4:7), unhindered by the world's strife (Jn. 14:27; 16:33). Peace between man and man is part of the purpose for which Christ died (Eph. 2) and of the Spirit's work (Gal. 5:22); but man must also be active to promote it (Eph. 4:3; Heb. 12:14), not merely as the elimination of discord, but as the harmony and true functioning of the body of Christ (Rom. 14:19; 1 Cor. 14:33).[5]

The biblical concept of God's solution to the problem of sin and its consequences is all encompassing. We find these remarkable words in Paul's letter to the Colossians:

> For God was pleased to have all his fullness dwell in him, and through him to reconcile to himself all things, whether things on earth or things in heaven, by making peace through his blood, shed on the cross. (Col. 1:19–20)

When people are asked, "Why did Christ die on the cross?" the answer given is usually "To save my soul!" or "So that I might go to heaven!" These are true, but they are limiting the effect of the blood of Christ on the cross to matters of individuals' souls only. What God reveals to us in Colossians is that God has a big agenda, and that big agenda is nothing less than reconciling *all* things to himself. This includes the soul of man. It includes the whole of each person. But it is not limited merely to mankind. Because man's rebellion brought consequences to all things, the reconciliation must be for all things. Christ's sacrifice was not just to secure forgiveness of sin but also to restore man's relations to each other and creation.

We see the big agenda of God described in the book of Romans. Paul writes,

> The creation waits in eager expectation for the sons of God to be revealed. For the creation was subjected to frustration, not by its own choice, but by the will of the one who subjected it, in hope that the creation itself will be liberated from its bondage to decay and brought into the glorious freedom of the children of God. We know that the whole creation has been groaning as in the pains of childbirth right up to the present time. (Rom. 8:19–22)

Paul's language plunges to the depth of the impact of sin on creation—"frustration," "bondage to decay," and "groaning as in the pains of childbirth"—and it soars to the heights of the redemption that is to come—"waits in eager expectation," "liberated," and "brought into the glorious freedom." God's big agenda extends to all creation.

SUBSTANTIAL HEALING

This process can be seen as a series of concentric circles. The inner circle represents the restoration of man's primary relationship with the heavenly Father, the new birth. The middle circle represents the substantial healing[6] in the life of the individual because of the healing of the primary internal relationship—physical, psychological, intellectual, and character (moral) development. The third circle represents the substantial healing that takes place in his secondary external relationships in the external world, with his fellow man and with creation.

EXPLORING THE WORD *SAVED*

In Ephesians 2:1–9 Paul describes man's predicament and God's solution to the problem, salvation:

> And you were dead in your trespasses and sins, in which you formerly walked according to the course of this world, according to the prince of the power of the air, of the spirit that is now working in the sons of disobedience....But God, being rich in mercy, because of His great love with which He loved us, even when we were dead in our transgressions, made us alive together with Christ (by grace you have been saved)....For by grace you have been saved through faith; and that not of yourselves, it is the gift of God; not as a result of works, so that no one may boast. (NASB)

Note how Paul describes the condition of unredeemed man: "And you were dead in your transgressions and sins." Entering into this hopeless state, where a "dead man" cannot make himself alive again, come the wonder-filled words, "*But God*, being rich in mercy because of his great love . . . ." While we were spiritually dead and incapable of saving ourselves, God loved us so much that he sent his own Son to die for us and to be resurrected for us. So our salvation is by the finished work of Christ on the cross.

But what does the word *saved* mean?

While the word *saved* is usually used in the classical spiritual sense of saving the souls of individuals, it actually has a much more comprehensive flavor. When used in the New Testament, it has the sense of healing that which has been broken, purifying that which is profane. The Greek word translated *saved* in the verses of Ephesians we just read is used more than one hundred times in the New Testament. Its meaning encompasses keeping someone safe and sound, rescuing someone from danger or destruction, and restoring to health someone suffering from disease. It is also translated as "make whole," "heal," and "be whole."[7] James speaks of the believer who patiently endures trials as becoming "mature and complete, not lacking anything" (1:4). To be saved includes becoming whole (complete) and holy (morally righteous). In justification we are declared to be holy; in sanctification, we are to live holy lives. Salvation, indeed, has broad connotations; we can thus say that salvation is "(w)holistic"—encompassing the whole.

PARSING THE WORD *SAVED*

Not only is the definition of salvation comprehensive, but so is the time frame in the believer's life and in the unfolding of the kingdom. Throughout the New Testament the concept of salvation appears in past, present, and future tenses as it relates to the believer. As Christians we can say, "I was saved!" "I am being saved!" and "I will be saved!" Those whom God has justified, he is sanctifying and he will glorify.

PAST—I was saved! (Justification)

Each Christian can declare, "I was saved!" In theological language this refers to justification. This is the time of repentance, the time in a sinner's life when he or she is "born again." Another way of saying this is that it is a call to the cross! Jesus said, "Just as Moses lifted up the snake in the desert, so the Son of Man must be lifted up, that everyone who believes in him may have eternal life. For God so loved the world that he gave his one and only Son, that whoever believes in him shall not perish but have eternal life" (John 3:14–16).

Just as physical healing came to those Hebrews who, in faith, looked beyond themselves and lifted their eyes to the upraised staff with the snake coiled around it, so standing in the shadow of the cross saves the believer.

HEALING

Justification is a legal term that refers to the fact that the believer is imputed with Christ's righteousness and that Christ bears the penalty of the believer's sin on himself to the cross. We see this stated in 2 Corinthians 5:21: "God made him who had no sin to be sin for us, so that in him we might become the righteousness of God." Jesus, who was sinless, was made sin for us. We, who were sinners by birth and by choice, had the very righteousness of God accredited to us. Having received it, we are declared "not guilty." "There is now no condemnation for those who are in Christ Jesus" (Rom. 8:1). What wonderful news. This is Good News indeed.

PRESENT—I am being saved! (Sanctification)

Just as a believer can say, "I was saved!" he or she can also say, "I am being saved." While justification marks a point in time, *sanctification* is the theological term that describes a lifelong process of becoming in reality what we already are in our position in Christ. Just as there is a moment of conception in a baby's life, and from then on there is a lifelong process of growth, so there is a similar process marked by spiritual birth and growth. While the call of justification is to stand in the shadow of the cross, sanctification is marked by the denial of self and the call to take up your cross daily and follow Jesus.[8]

In justification we are declared holy and just; in sanctification we are becoming what we have been declared to be—holy and just in practice! We see this in Paul's response in Ephesians 2:10 to the preceding verses 1–9. Sanctification is the response to justification: "For we are God's workmanship, created in Christ Jesus to do good works, which God prepared in advance for us to do." We find that we are saved by faith for a purpose. We are saved by faith to do good works that God has prepared for us to do from the foundations of the world. Our works do not justify us, but they are part of the sanctification process that the Holy Spirit works in us.

Likewise, Philippians 2:12–13 reveals the dual agency of our sanctification. While it is the work of God alone that justifies, both God and human beings work in the process of sanctification: "Therefore, my dear friends, as you have always obeyed—not only in my presence, but now much more in my absence—continue to work out your salvation [sanctification] with fear and trembling, for it is God who works in you to will and to act according to his good purpose."

"Salvation" includes the daily Christian life, lived moment by moment. The just shall live by faith.[9] Sanctification is living before the face of God in all of our life and all of our relationships as we are empowered and restored to Christ's image by the work of the Holy Spirit. Too often in the modern church, when we speak of sanctification, we speak of it inwardly and personally. We speak of personal holiness. This is an important part of the process of sanctification, but it is not the whole process.

In addition to moral or character development of personal holiness, there must also be a change of mindset.[10] Not only is natural man born spiritually dead, but also he grows up to have the metaphysic—mindset—of his family and his culture. Every person, through the process of enculturation, develops a way of seeing the world, a worldview that shapes everything about his or her life. While God created us to live in the world of the biblical worldview, our cultures, unless they are worshiping the living God, have "exchanged the truth of God for a lie" (Rom. 1:25). Part of the process of personal sanctification is to put on the mind of Christ, to have a growing understanding of the biblical worldview, the worldview that reflects reality.

The process of sanctification also produces both social and stewardship responsibilities. It is living in the present and bringing substantial healing to all of man's secondary relationships. The believer is to seek to bring love where there is hate, peace where there is conflict, beauty where there is dreariness, truth where there is falsehood, good where there is evil. Christians are to stand, with God, against the ravages of natural evil, droughts, floods, earthquakes, famines, disease, and the human destruction of creation through waste, conspicuous consumption, and raping of the natural environment. As part of the sanctification process, we are to steward creation. As the apostle Paul reminds us, creation is waiting for the revealing of the sons of God.[11] It is waiting for those who have been declared children of God in their justification to begin to act like children of God in their sanctification.

Sanctification is broad and progressive. In all of this there is a "dance" between the believer and God. God leads in the dance, but the believer is responsible to willfully engage in response. In sanctification, the believer is active and intentional in this part of salvation.

We are not merely called out of darkness into light, we are also called to "walk in the light." As the catch phrase of my generation reminds us, "We are to walk our talk!"

God is love; we are to love our friends, neighbors, and even enemies. God is just; we are to pursue justice in a corrupt world. God is compassionate; we are to extend compassion to a broken world. God is true; we are to speak the truth in the face of lies and to live trustworthy lives in a world of betrayed promises. God is beautiful; we are to bring beauty into our communities in our buildings, landscape, art, and music.

Just as God's salvation is comprehensive, so is our service. Our service is to be expressed in worship of the King, love of our fellow man, and stewardship of creation.

FUTURE—I will be saved! (Glorification)

That which has begun in justification and has continued in the process of sanctification will be completed when Christ returns at the end of history. While we have the task of occupying until Christ returns, Christ has the task of returning with the kingdom.[12] At the end of history all of God's plans and purposes will be fulfilled. The return of Christ at the end of the age to complete the process that he has begun at the cross is known in theological terms as glorification. Therefore, in addition to saying, "I was saved!" and "I am being saved!" the believer can joyously say, "I will be saved!" Jesus will return in glory, and all the pain and suffering of the present life will be thrown off. The process, once begun, will be gloriously finished.

A word that captures the fullness of this in space and time and for the individual and the kingdom is *consummation.* The word speaks of coming to fullness, to completion, to fulfill an eternal purpose and glory. Paul speaks of this in 1 Corinthians 13:12: "For now we see through a glass, darkly; but then face to face: now I know in part; but then shall I know even as also I am known" (KJV). We see now in poor reflection a blurred image of that which will come. C. S. Lewis speaks of our existence now as the "Shadowlands." But when Christ returns, things will be as they were meant to be.

While in justification we are declared to be holy and just positionally, and in sanctification we are seeking to live just and holy lives in practice, in glorification we will be perfectly holy and just in reality. That which we have been declared to be will be finally and completely realized. We see examples of the promise of the completion of the process in Paul's writings:

> And you also were included in Christ when you heard the word of truth, the gospel of your salvation. Having believed, you were marked in him with a seal, the promised Holy Spirit, who is a deposit guaranteeing our inheritance until the redemption of those who are God's possession—to the praise of his glory. (Eph. 1:13–14)

Here Paul uses two images that speak of the completion of the process of salvation. First is that of being "marked with a seal." In ancient days if an important document or a treasured thing was to be transported to another destination, the king would put his own seal on the object. The seal would guarantee the safe arrival of the prized object. The second image is that of making a deposit. In many cultures, if you want an item held until you can complete the purchase, you may make a down payment or, in the case of property, pay earnest money. Again, the deposit is a show of commitment that the final transaction will be completed. Paul is saying in this passage that God the Father has sealed the final and perfect delivery of our salvation with the seal or deposit of the Holy Spirit.

We see a different image in Philippians 1:6: "being confident of this, that he who began a good work in you will carry it on to completion until the day of Christ Jesus." Paul is confident that the God who has begun the good work of our salvation has the ability and commitment to continue the process to its completion when Jesus Christ returns.

Our personal salvation is comprehensive. God will complete the good work he has begun in us personally, to making us holy, "mature and complete, not lacking anything" (James 1:4). But we must not forget God's big agenda: to restore all things, everything about each Christian, and all relationships. There will be the complete restoration of all things when Jesus returns with his kingdom. When the King returns, the kingdom is consummated. In the present time, we are to work in God's grace and power to see substantial healing in all of life. When Jesus returns, the climax of the process will be the consummation of the kingdom in all its glory.[13] The kingdom of God will exist in all its fullness and glory.

SALVATION'S RIPPLES

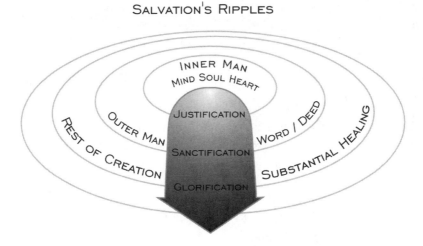

In short, salvation manifests ripples; it is part of the believer's past, present, and future.

The Nature of Salvation

Concept	Justification	Sanctification	Glorification
Time Frame	PAST I WAS saved	PRESENT I AM BEING saved	FUTURE I WILL BE saved
One's Position	DECLARED just AND Holy FREE FROM THE PENALTY OF SIN	BECOMING just AND Holy BECOMING FREE FROM THE POWER OF SIN	HOLY FREE
Example Texts	...IF ANYBODY DOES SIN, WE HAVE ONE WHO SPEAKS TO THE FATHER IN OUR DEFENSE—JESUS CHRIST, THE RIGHTEOUS ONE. I JOHN 2:1 GOD MADE HIM WHO HAD NO SIN TO BE SIN FOR US, SO THAT IN HIM WE MIGHT BECOME THE RIGHTEOUSNESS OF GOD. 2 CORINTHIANS 5:21	...FOR WE ARE GOD'S WORKMANSHIP, CREATED IN CHRIST JESUS TO DO GOOD WORKS, WHICH GOD PREPARED IN ADVANCE FOR US TO DO. EPHESIANS 2:10 THEREFORE, MY DEAR FRIENDS, AS YOU HAVE ALWAYS OBEYED...CONTINUE TO WORK OUT YOUR SALVATION WITH FEAR AND TREMBLING. PHILIPPIANS 2:12	...HAVING BELIEVED, YOU WERE MARKED IN HIM WITH A SEAL, THE PROMISED HOLY SPIRIT. EPHESIANS 1:13 ...BEING CONFIDENT OF THIS, THAT HE WHO BEGAN A GOOD WORK IN YOU WILL CARRY IT ON TO COMPLETION UNTIL THE DAY OF CHRIST JESUS. PHILIPPIANS 1:6

NOW AND NOT YET

Christ has come and Christ will come again. The King has come[14] and he will come again.[15] His kingdom is now and not yet. The kingdom is a present reality wherever Christ reigns[16] and yet it will be fully revealed in the future[17] when Christ returns. It is present now in its beginnings and will come in the future in all its glory. This is the dynamic of *HIS*-story, of redemption history.

Salvation encompasses all of each believer and all of his or her relationships, and it involves the past, present, and future of the believer's life. Not all Christians or church traditions have put an emphasis on the fullness of salvation. Some have stressed one or two elements at the expense of the others. Biblical theism, however, with its biblical worldview, stresses that salvation is our personal state before God as well as the process of bringing substantial healing in all of our relationships. This process will be completed when Christ returns.

The whole of our lives and work is intrinsically connected to God's work of reconciling all things to himself, advancing his kingdom of righteousness, peace, and joy, in time and in eternity.

The Scriptures reveal that we, having been called to life, have an assignment—our own unique calling in life and our specific place in the body of Christ. In the next chapter we will explore this second aspect of God's double call—our particular call to work.

CHAPTER 13

THE PARTICULAR CALL:

TO WORK

The Scriptures reveal that, having been called into the kingdom, we each have a unique role in manifesting and extending the kingdom. Whether God grants us many days or few, we are to use them to discover and live out our particular assignment. Whether he grants us "employment" or "unemployment," seasons of health or sickness, the assignment continues. Called by God, we must avoid the secular sense of "work" in which there is a time of work and a time for retirement. The concept of *retirement* is foreign to biblical culture. As citizens of the kingdom of God and members of the body of Christ, we are called to put feet, hands, and imaginations to the prayer "your kingdom come, your will be done on earth as it is in heaven." Ours is a life of passion and not apathy, of work and not of ease.

GOD'S WORKMANSHIP

If passivity or disengagement were God's norm, the inevitable would have happened: we would have been lost forever. Instead, as we have explored in Ephesians 2:1–9, at God's initiative, while we were dead, we were saved by grace, through faith. Not only have we been rescued from death, but also God has made us well and is making us whole. By his grace he is restoring us to the purpose and potential he instilled in us when he created us in his image. Paul writes in astounding contrast to the death that claims us outside of Christ: "For we are God's workmanship, created in Christ Jesus to do good works, which God prepared in advance for us to do" (Eph. 2:10). In keeping with the rest of Scripture, this verse testifies that work is central to our identity and purpose *in Christ*. We work in light of our creation and redemption *in Christ*.

Two terms in this powerful verse draw our attention, *workmanship* and *good works*. Found only here in Ephesians and in Romans 1:20, the word *workmanship* is the Greek word *poiema*, the root of the word *poem*.[1] In Romans 1:20, *poiema* is referring to all of creation—by "the things that are made" (KJV). God is the First Poet. His creation and my life are acts of his *poiema*. My good works are enabled by and in response to *him*. As always, God is the initiator, the starting point. My work is part of his workmanship.

The second word to explore is *ergon,* a Greek word used for a deed or action in contrast to inactivity or mere words. Found 169 times in the New Testament, it is used in a wide variety of ways, including the work of Christ, the work of the gospel, the good work of service to those in need, and the work of "employment" or "occupation."[2]

The Hebrew Old Testament equivalent is the word *abad,* to work or serve. It is used for the work of man as assigned by God and is part of the common work-rest cycles of the Decalogue.[3] This is the same word that we explored earlier that is part of the cultural mandate given to man to *abad* and *shamar* the garden.

We have been redeemed to work, and that work can be seen in a broad context from "spiritual work" to the works of service and compassion[4] and the common works given man in the cultural mandate. We must be careful not to read the word *works* in a narrow spiritual sense only. Every good work means every good work! It also means all our work is to be good work—done well; we are to do our work with excellence.

PART OF THE WHOLE

If we understand our work as something we were created and redeemed to do, then what we once saw as simply a job or a rung on the career ladder can become part of our vocation. While all of us share a common purpose, our own vocation, our *lifework,* is one of a kind. The nature of our unique "project of love and grace,"[5] as Pope John Paul II so aptly called our particular assignment, flows from the nature of our Creator and Caller. As Michael Novak writes,

> Each of us is as unique in our calling as we are in being made in the image of God. (It would take an infinite number of human beings, St. Thomas Aquinas once wrote, to mirror back the infinite facets of the Godhead. Each person reflects only a small—but beautiful—part of the whole.[6]

What an astounding picture to meditate on! Each of us is a unique reflection of his infinite image. Our own nature, and "the good works, which God prepared in advance for us to do" (Eph. 2:10), is rooted in the nature of God himself.

LISA ETTER'S AND HAYDEN SMITH'S STORIES

"You were created to be passionate and purposeful for God and others in this world!" These words, written by Lisa Etter's father to his daughter at age twelve, have shaped Lisa's life and impacted the lives of countless others along the way.

Years after her father's letter, Lisa met Hayden Smith at Calvin College in Grand Rapids, Michigan. The two quickly recognized their shared life vision and became best friends. After graduating from Calvin in 2002, they moved to a diverse Chicago neighborhood where Hayden taught first grade and Lisa worked as an intern at a homeless shelter for women. Living in the midst of this urban environment and interacting daily with individuals who looked different and who had life experiences very different from their own middle-class upbringing was eye-opening.

"As we built friendships with our neighbors and the people with whom we worked, we were saddened by the ways that these friends had been reduced to labels—'at risk,' 'low income,' 'homeless'—by the world around them. We realized that they were not really all that different from us. All of us, no matter our background or situation, have the same basic needs: to explore who we are, to be loved as we are, to use our gifts, to contribute. Our basic longings are the same, and ultimately they all point to God and how he made us. So many people are deprived of opportunities to explore these things and contribute their gifts to the world because they are looked upon or treated as if they have nothing of value to offer."

Faced with the reality of how so many people live, both women began asking questions: Who are we? How are we meant to live? What does this knowledge mean for our lives? Their desire to provide a place where *all* kinds of people would be welcomed and given space to explore their gifts began to grow.

In the midst of Lisa and Hayden's time in Chicago, Lisa's dad became terminally ill and she left the city to return home to care for him. One night, as her dad's health continued to deteriorate, Lisa was thinking about the questions she and Hayden had been wrestling with, the values that her parents had instilled in her, and her dreams and gifts. As she began putting these pieces together, she said, "Let's dream together, Lord." In time, she began envisioning a unique type of coffee shop that would allow many types of people in a community to come together and feel a part of a place where they were valued and loved for who they were. She wrote and sketched the details in her journal and later shared them with Hayden, who was equally excited about the idea as a way to be available to those around her while integrating many aspects of her life.

After the death of Lisa's dad, a series of improbable events and connections brought Lisa and Hayden to Seattle, where they were put in touch with a church searching for the right person to open a coffee shop to serve as a community outreach. In the spring of 2005, the Green Bean Coffee Shop opened its doors, with Hayden and Lisa as its managers. Now the Green Bean is established as a community gathering place, offering classes proposed and taught by customers, hosting neighborhood events, providing a place for local artists to display their work, and welcoming in and connecting a diverse group of customers with each other. Tips also are donated to local community organizations.

Hayden and Lisa overflow with stories of customers who have become part of the Green Bean community. "Chris," a well-to-do attorney, initially made his hostility toward Christianity well-known and left the shop a number of times saying that he would never come back. Over time, he has become part of their group of friends and, although he has not become a Christian, has begun to emulate the Christlike love he has witnessed from this group, recently asking his lawyer friends to get a laptop computer for another customer in need.

"Jay" became a regular customer soon after the Green Bean first opened but mostly kept to himself, sitting in the corner for hours and writing poetry. Over time, he began to open up and share his poetry with Lisa and Hayden, who promptly framed some of his compositions for the Green Bean's walls. When he received news that his cancer had returned, Lisa and Hayden offered him a place to stay while he went through treatment, recognizing that he had no other family to support him. The women and other customers drove him to his treatment appointments. When it became apparent that he wasn't going to recover, he asked the women to hold power of attorney for him, and they became a key part of making his medical decisions. In hospice, Lisa and Hayden shared the gospel with him, and Jay accepted the Lord.

The first time Hayden and Lisa met "Rex," he told them about the comic book heroes

The One and Many God

God is Trinity, the United-One God, not the Single-One (unitarian) God. Father, Son, and Holy Spirit are unique persons with unique roles and responsibilities, existing as three separate personalities. And yet, they are equally and indivisibly God: one God—three Persons. So, too, in the family and the larger society, there is diversity of gifts, talents, personalities, roles, and responsibilities; at the same time all members of the human family are equal in dignity and value because they equally are the image of God. And just as the members of the Trinity are defined both by their own uniqueness and by their relationship in community, so each person is equally defined both individually and corporately.

that he thought were real and mumbled nonsense much of the time. As the women have gotten to know him and continue to treat him as a valued human being, he has become a regular fixture at the shop, offering to wash windows, sweep the back porch, and help carry in groceries, also attending church with them on Sundays. When the two learned of his interest in music, they found a used keyboard, and now Rex can be found much of the time on the back porch of the Green Bean playing music.

These are just a few of the stories of lives transformed, and Lisa and Hayden recognize the importance of stepping back to recognize and celebrate these ways that God is at work in the Green Bean. "It's easy to get caught up in the day-to-day difficulties," Hayden explained. "But it's so much about my perspective. I make a major shopping trip to buy supplies for the Green Bean every week and can have an attitude of 'This is an annoying task,' or I can go realizing that I am serving God through it. It doesn't

matter what you're doing, you can glorify God through it. We need to get over this idea that some people are in ministry and others aren't. The glory of God is shared through our work."

Lisa agrees. "It always confuses me and makes me a little sad when people say things like, 'I'm an attorney but my ministry is working at the homeless shelter on the weekends.' We need to realize that every moment is significant and we have the power to impact the people around us in ways that we don't even realize, no matter what we do. Just today, I was chatting with the clerk at the grocery store, and something she said gave me the courage to face another hard visit to Jay in hospice.

"It's all about living in the joy of being redeemed. If you believe that you have been saved from something, you will live with that joy wherever you go, whether serving coffee or shopping or pastoring, and that joy will transform people."

The Church—the Body of Christ

It is no wonder that when God called forth the church, he called forth community. Paul uses the image of the body of Christ[7] to reflect the unity-diversity of community. And the church of Christ manifests its diverse parts and functions in the unity of one body. Paul describes the manifestation of the first principle of community in the body of Christ very fully in 1 Corinthians 12:12–27:

> The body is a unit, though it is made up of many parts; and though all its parts are many, they form one body. So it is with Christ. For we were all baptized by one Spirit into one body—whether Jews or Greeks, slave or free—and we were all given the one Spirit to drink.

Now the body is not made up of one part but of many. If the foot should say, "Because I am not a hand, I do not belong to the body," it would not for that reason cease to be part of the body. And if the ear should say, "Because I am not an eye, I do not belong to the body," it would not for that reason cease to be part of the body. If the whole body were an eye, where would the sense of hearing be? If the whole body were an ear, where would the sense of smell be? But in fact God has arranged the parts in the body, every one of them, just as he wanted them to be. If they were all one part, where would the body be? As it is, there are many parts, but one body.

The eye cannot say to the hand, "I don't need you!" And the head cannot say to the feet, "I don't need you!" On the contrary, those parts of the body that seem to be weaker are indispensable, and the parts that we think are less honorable we treat with special honor. And the parts that are unpresentable are treated with special modesty, while our presentable parts need no special treatment. But God has combined the members of the body and has given greater honor to the parts that lacked it, so that there should be no division in the body, but that its parts should have equal concern for each other. If one part suffers, every part suffers with it; if one part is honored, every part rejoices with it.

Now you are the body of Christ, and each one of you is a part of it.

As we reflect on this passage, we see that God has arranged the parts just as he wanted them to be for their own unique purpose (v. 18). Each part has a unique role to play in the body; each is indispensable (v. 22). While each has different roles and functions, each part has equal value and worth (vv. 24–25). Paul's description is similar in Romans 12:4–8 and Ephesians 4:11–13.

Unity and Diversity in the Giftings

Christ provides his body with a diversity of gifts. As 1 Corinthians 12:4–7, 11 reveals,

There are different kinds of gifts, but the same Spirit. There are different kinds of service, but the same Lord. There are different kinds of working, but the same God works all of them in all men.

Now to each one the manifestation of the Spirit is given for the common good....All these are the work of one and the same Spirit, and he gives them to each one, just as he determines.

In this passage we see the reference to the unity-diversity of God as foundational to the unity-diversity in the giving of the gifts to the body of Christ. We see one God and three Persons: the same Spirit (Holy Spirit), the same Lord (Jesus Christ), and the same God (the Father).

We also note that just as God created unity with diversity, he also established the principle of seed for multiplication. There is an organic quality about the gifts God has given. An African proverb reminds us of the natural miracle of the seed: "You can count the seeds in the mango, but you cannot count the mangoes in the seed." There is one seed in a mango. But that one seed would produce thousands of trees, millions of fruit, endlessly.

We see this multiplying effect of the dispensation of gifting: different kinds of gifts are multiplied by different kinds of service and different kinds of working. A particular gift given to one individual will have a different form of service than the same gift in another person. The outworking of ministry will have a different impact in different settings because of the uniqueness of each context.

While there is an infinite variety of effects from each gift, all the individual gifts are given for the common good (1 Cor. 12:7). The gifts are to be used not for a diversity of individual benefits but for the good of the whole body. This same emphasis is also found in Ephesians 4:11–13:

> It was he who gave some to be apostles, some to be prophets, some to be evangelists, and some to be pastors and teachers, to prepare God's people for works of service, so that the body of Christ may be built up until we all reach unity in the faith and in the knowledge of the Son of God and become mature, attaining to the whole measure of the fullness of Christ.

These unique vocations of leaders "in" the church were given so that the church will function in service, so that the unity, maturity, and the fullness of the body of Christ is established. As we have mentioned previously, these leadership gifts are unique functions but not higher functions than the other gifts given the body of Christ. In turn, a healthy church does not exist for itself. It exists to be God's instrument of healing in a broken world.

GOD INHABITS THE ORDINARY

It is as members of Christ's body that we can begin to understand ourselves and how we relate to others and the needs we meet in the world.

Pope John Paul II said that we each have our "own place in God's heart and in the history of humanity" and it is on this basis that we each are enabled to make a "personal and irreplaceable contribution to the progress of humanity on the path of justice and truth."[8] Do you believe that you have your own place in God's heart and in history?

Do you believe that God has enabled and called you to make a contribution that is irreplaceable? Can you truly hear what the apostle Paul says about your place in Christ's body? Listen again: "But in fact God has arranged the parts in the body, every one of them, just as he wanted them to be" (1 Cor. 12:18). Your part in the body is legitimate and necessary. God not only creates what we call the ordinary—the flowers of the field, the stars in the sky, the breath in our breast, and all those other things that are ordinary miracles—but he also inhabits the ordinary, working in and through every man and woman. We see throughout Scripture and through history how God uses shepherds and homemakers, shoemakers and farmers, to shape history. Dallas Willard captures this when he says, "The obviously well kept secret of the 'ordinary' is that it was made to be a receptacle of the divine, a place where the life of God flows."[9]

Two of my favorite examples of this come from the Old Testament. The prophet Jeremiah writes,

> "Go up and down the streets of Jerusalem,
>   look around and consider,
>   search through her squares.
> If you can find but one person
>   who deals honestly and seeks the truth,
>   I will forgive this city." (Jer. 5:1)

It is striking to think that God is looking for one person, not 10,000 or 1,000 or 100, or even 10. He can and will work with and through just one person. But note, this is not just a breathing body; it is a person who "deals honestly and seeks the truth." We see a similar picture in Ecclesiastes 9:13–18:

> I also saw under the sun this example of wisdom that greatly impressed me: There was once a small city with only a few people in it. And a powerful king came against it, surrounded it and built huge siegeworks against it. Now there lived in that city a man poor but wise, and he saved the city by his wisdom. But nobody remembered that poor man. So I said, "Wisdom is better than strength." But the poor man's wisdom is despised, and his words are no longer heeded.
>
> The quiet words of the wise are more to be heeded
>   than the shouts of a ruler of fools.
> Wisdom is better than weapons of war,
>   but one sinner destroys much good.

What a wonderful picture. God used one poor, unnamed man to save a small city against a powerful king and his siege. Wisdom and quiet words are more significant than weapons of war and the "shouts" of the powerful. God can even use the seemingly most insignificant people, whose names the world would not recognize, to reshape their community or even their world.

British theologian F. W. Farrar (1831–1903) captures the wonder of God's use of the ordinary when he writes,

> There is a greatness in unknown names, there is an immortality of quiet duties, attainable by the meanest of human kind; and when the Judge shall reverse the tables many of these last shall be first.... To fill a little space because God wills it; to go on cheerfully with a petty round of little duties, little avocations; to accept unmurmuring a low position; to be misunderstood, misrepresented, maligned, without complaint; to smile for the joys of others when the heart is aching;—to banish all ambition, all pride, and all restlessness, in a single regard to our Savior's work. To do this for a lifetime is a greater effort, and he who does this is a greater hero, than he who for one hour stems a breach, or for one day rushes onward undaunted in the flaming front of shot and shell. His works will follow him. He may not be a hero to the world, but he is one of God's heroes.[10]

The marks of greatness and success that the world recognizes are not what God seeks. We find in Paul, at one time a fiery enemy of the cross of Christ, the credentials of those called into kingdom service:

> Brothers, think of what you were when you were *called*. Not many of you were wise by human standards; not many were influential; not many were of noble birth. But God chose the foolish things of the world to shame the wise; God chose the weak things of the world to shame the strong. He chose the lowly things of this world and the despised things—and the things that are not—to nullify the things that are, so that no one may boast before him. It is because of him that you are in Christ Jesus, who has become for us wisdom from God—that is, our righteousness, holiness and redemption. Therefore, as it is written: "Let him who boasts boast in the Lord." (1 Cor. 1:26–31; italics added)

God's criteria are far different from the world's. He chooses the foolish, the weak, and the lowly people. He chooses people who have little significance in the world's eyes to do his work. Why? Because God's strength is best manifested through humble servants.

Imagine a candle placed in a clay jar. It is the cracks in the jar that let the light through. Similarly, the glory of God is best revealed through the foolish, weak, and lowly. Paul sees this in his own life. He writes in 2 Corinthians 12:9–10:

> But he said to me, "My grace is sufficient for you, for my power is made perfect in weakness." Therefore I will boast all the more gladly about my weaknesses, so that Christ's power may rest on me. That is why, for Christ's sake, I delight in weaknesses, in insults, in hardships, in persecutions, in difficulties. For when I am weak, then I am strong.

In his powerful sermon "I Qualify!" my friend and the pastor of Nairobi Lighthouse Church, Don Matheny, states,

> The Bible is an account of common, everyday individuals used of God to do the extraordinary—men and women who by natural standards and appearance seemed so unsuitable for the task to which they were called or chosen. God, however, considered them fit for the purpose or the position; therefore they became powerful tools in His hand. In the Scriptures we read of a shepherd boy who became Israel's greatest warrior and king. A simple cupbearer who rallied an entire city to rebuild its walls destroyed in war decades earlier. A man, who in his youth killed another man, yet would be raised up to deliver God's people from Egypt after 400 years of bitter bondage and hardship. Individuals qualified by God Himself.
>
> You must be reminded that the great men and women of God throughout the ages have all had imperfections, defects, faults and failures. Moses stammered. Sarah laughed. Gideon fleeced. Jonah sulked. Peter cursed. Thomas doubted. Yet each of these was chosen and called by God, thus qualified to do exploits in His name. What you must understand is that qualification is not based on performance or production. Qualification is based on position. God doesn't use a man based on the man's achievements. God always uses the man closest to Him![11]

Again, we catch the sense of the wonder of the ordinary, of how God uses ordinary people in extraordinary ways, from the apostle Paul when he writes to the church at Corinth:

> Our work as God's servants gets validated—or not—in the details. People are watching us as we stay at our post, alertly, unswervingly...in hard times, tough times, bad times; when we're beaten up, jailed, and mobbed; working

hard, working late, working without eating; with pure heart, clear head, steady hand; in gentleness, holiness, and honest love; when we're telling the truth, and when God's showing his power; when we're doing our best setting things right; when we're praised, and when we're blamed; slandered, and honored; true to our word, though distrusted; ignored by the world, but recognized by God; terrifically alive, though rumored to be dead; beaten within an inch of our lives, but refusing to die; immersed in tears, yet always filled with deep joy; living on handouts, yet enriching many; having nothing, having it all. (2 Cor. 6:4–10, The Message)

We have been made to make history. We have been made to fulfill a destiny in our time and our place that no one else has been made for. We are to live our ordinary lives in the midst of God's extraordinary call.

Commenting on Micah 6:8—"And what does the LORD require of you? To act justly and to love mercy and to walk humbly with your God"—my friend the educator and pastor Dr. George Grant describes God's use of ordinary people to shape the destiny of nations:

After all, the future of our culture does not depend upon political messiahs or institutional solutions. Neither does it depend on the emergence of some new brilliant spokesman or inspiring leader. Instead, the future of our culture depends upon ordinary men and women in the church who are willing to live lives of justice, mercy and humility before God.[12]

There is power not only in ordinary lives but also in ordinary days. The Battle of the Bulge, that battle that marked the extraordinary turning point of World War II in Europe, took place within the context of an ordinary day of war. Philip Yancey, writing in Christianity Today, reflects on a television special that interviewed survivors from the war in Europe:

The soldiers recall how they spent a particular day. One sat in a foxhole all day; once or twice, a German tank drove by, and he shot at it. Others played cards and frittered away the time. A few got involved in furious firefights. Mostly, the day passed like any other day for an infantryman on the front. Later, they learned they had just participated in one of the largest, most decisive engagements of the war, the Battle of the Bulge. It did not *feel* decisive to any of them at the time, because none had the big picture of what was happening elsewhere.

Great victories are won when ordinary people execute their assigned tasks, and a faithful person does not debate each day whether he or she is in the mood to follow the sergeant's orders or go to work at a boring job. We exercise faith by responding to the task that lies before us.[13]

Let's allow the extraordinary American heroine, the blind, deaf, and mute Helen Keller, to explain in her own words the power and significance of the ordinary life. Some people would have said Keller was "subordinary." In a culture like that of the Third Reich, she would have been branded a "life unworthy of life." Keller writes,

JEMIMAH WRIGHT'S STORY

Jemimah Wright wrote the story about infanticide in Brazil that is related at the beginning of chapter 8. Her article brought this atrocity to the attention of readers in Britain and beyond, and she has since written a book about Hakani and the Suzikis. Here she tells the story of how she found her calling as a freelance writer—eventually.

I did a BA degree in publishing and history at Oxford Brookes University, mainly because I wanted to be in Oxford. I didn't know much about publishing, but thought from what I knew that it sounded like a good career to have. After graduation I got temporary jobs in academic publishing, which I hated. I remember praying that I would prefer to go to heaven now than continue doing a job that didn't inspire me but seemed to suck the life out of me! To my relief, after a year, I found work at a local Christian newspaper. But after three years, I was made redundant, and once again I had no idea what to do with my life. Heaven seemed to be silent on the subject. In my own strength I tried to save

myself. I thought of every job under the sun, but I knew deep down I didn't want to do them, and they weren't me. Despair set in.

However, I did have a desire to work with AIDS orphans in South Africa. I e-mailed the pastor of a Vineyard church in Cape Town and asked if I could come out and help. But then I panicked, thinking I needed to get a "proper" job and start on a career ladder. In my confusion I asked God to make it clear if he wanted me to go to South Africa; he did by miraculously providing the money I needed.

I flew out to South Africa in 2003 and worked in a township called Imizamo Yethu helping the poorest of the poor. I was open to this being my calling, but I sensed it wasn't long term. I was still in the same place, asking God to show me what to do. I had been in Cape Town six months when I turned twenty-five. One day I was driving back home from the township when a thought popped into my head, *Be a freelance journalist.* It was quiet, not a resounding shout from heaven, but as I thought it, I knew it was from God.

I long to accomplish a great and noble task, but it is my chief duty to accomplish humble tasks as though they were great and noble. The world is moved along not by the mighty shoves of its heroes, but by the aggregate of the tiny pushes of each honest worker.[14]

What do all of these illustrate? Quite simply, God uses ordinary people in the ordinary part of the world that they inhabit to shape the destiny of nations. Your life counts for something in this broken world. God has made you to be a history maker. You are called to a unique role in the unfolding of God's kingdom.

So after a year in South Africa, I returned to London to be a freelance journalist. I had a deep conviction that God was in this, but had no idea how to go about it. I also had no money! I was told about a five-month journalism course. It usually cost £700, but since I was unemployed before I started the course, the government subsidized it and I only had to pay £10! After I finished the course, I applied for a job as a feature writer at a press agency. It seemed a perfect way to get more training and make contacts for the future.

I got the job but had a few months free before my work started. I had been in contact with Youth With A Mission (YWAM) in Haiti, and I e-mailed to ask if I could come out and help with the hurricane relief under way. When I got there, Terry Snow, the leader of the YWAM base, said, "Jemimah, you're a journalist. Do you want to write my book?" I laughed. I could hardly call myself a journalist. I had no experience, so I said *no way.* Terry tried to convince me, but I was adamant. Then, as the weeks went by, I started to have a desire to write the book. One morning I prayed and asked God that if he wanted me

to do this book, could he get Terry to ask me again that day. (I needed to know God was in it, because I knew I would need his help!) Terry was hardly ever at the YWAM base, and I had already said *no way,* so it wasn't looking likely. But then the first person I bumped into was Terry, and he said, "Jemimah, are you sure you don't want to write my book?" My mouth fell open. "Okay!" I replied.

After working on the book, I came home and started the job at the press agency in Bristol. I had the shock of my life. It was tabloid journalism and such a dirty world. The first day I went home thinking I had to leave. *Surely you can't want me here, Lord?* I prayed. But I felt God keep on confirming that I was where he wanted me by extraordinary blessing. I had to make a target each month of £3000 in stories sold. The first week I bicycled home worrying away about how I would ever make the target; it seemed impossible. Then suddenly I felt God say, "Who got you this job?" "Oh, yes. You, God," I replied. "Well, if I can get you this job, do you believe that I can provide the stories to meet your target?" A weight lifted off my shoulders as I realized it wasn't my problem. But God's blessing came with a price of obedience. I felt he was asking me to walk with such strong integrity—when it was so tempting not to.

Our salary was the minimum wage, but each month we got a bonus of £100 if we made our targets. However, to get the bonus, we had to lie and put it down as expenses to avoid tax. I knew God was saying I couldn't do this. I struggled, as I really needed the money, but at last I came to the realization that God was my provider and I needed to fear him. So I did, and in the first week I made £5000 for the company on one story. It was a miracle and unheard of—usually when people start they don't make anything for the first month as they learn the ropes. In the end my nickname was "Gold" because they said everything I touched turned to gold. I was able to tell them that it had nothing to do with me; it was simply the favor of God. I was the only Christian in the office, and I'm pretty sure they didn't know what to think!

After a year I felt God say it was time to go freelance. But everyone was saying it wouldn't work, that I had to go to London first to work for the nationals for a couple of years and then go freelance. I began to believe them, and thought they knew better than God! One evening I was home alone. I knew God was trying to speak to me, but I was ignoring him, tidying the house, distracting myself by doing anything but seeking him. Eventually I went to bed. Usually when I hit the pillow, I fall asleep straightaway. That night I couldn't sleep. I was tossing and turning, my head full of worried thoughts about freelancing. At 3:00 AM I finally gave in. I turned on my light and said, "Lord, please speak to me." I opened my Bible to Deuteronomy 11 and read: "Go into the land that God has given you, go and you will be blessed...." I knew God was saying he had gone ahead, I just had to follow and he would do the rest. After that, people still told me it wouldn't work, but I knew God had told me to do it, so I had to do it!

I went freelance on my birthday, March 20, 2006. It has been amazing. God has provided me stories, and my job is perfect for my character. I love the creativity of writing, and I love hearing people's stories. I also love the excitement of selling the stories, and the challenge of finding them. Being freelance also means I have time to leave the country to write more books like *Taking the High Places,* the story of Terry Snow's ministry in Haiti. I have just been in Brazil for a month writing the biography of two YWAM missionaries who are trying to stop infanticide in Brazil.

I feel as if God hid the calling and job he wanted me to do for a little while, to prepare me, to make me seek him, to teach me to trust. Then as I was seeking first his kingdom in South Africa—not my own career—he showed me what to do. He has provided amazingly at every turn, opening up doors I could never have imagined, and it is so exciting!

THE KING AND HIS WORK

We have surveyed the extraordinary significance of the ordinary human life. Now let us look for a moment at the ordinary significance of the most extraordinary human life, the God-Man, Jesus Christ.

When the God of the universe came to earth in human flesh, how did he come? He could have come as a political figure—a king, pharaoh, or emperor. He could have come as a priest, to affirm the superiority of spiritual work. He could have been born in a palace in a world-class city like Athens or Rome. How did he choose to come? He was born in what today would be called a third-world nation that was occupied by a conquering army. God came in human flesh; he was born into an ordinary family to a poor woman of the oppressed Jewish people. His first bed was a cattle-feeding trough; his first home was a stable. The God of the universe chose to be born into a common working-class family as a blue-collar worker—a carpenter.

We know that Jesus was and is a servant-king. He is King of kings and Lord of lords, yet as it says in Mark 10:45, "[He] did not come to be served, but to serve, and to give his life as a ransom for many." The full image of God was revealed in Christ through his service; while Christ's primary work was for our salvation, he carried out that work in the context of a common life two thousand years ago, through a number of vocational avenues. He was a carpenter who built furniture and framed doors and windows. He was a teacher who taught both children and adults. He was a "public health worker" who brought emotional, spiritual, and physical healing.

God is a working God. He works directly in history, and he worked distinctly in Christ during his thirty-three years on earth. He also is at work through the lives of believers in their work. The scope of his work is immense.

One of the heroes of our faith, the missionary stateswoman to India, Amy Carmichael, has captured the relationship between God's work and our work. In *Amma: The Life and Words of Amy Carmichael,* author Elizabeth R. Skoglund quotes from Carmichael. Here is an excerpt of Amy's words and the corresponding quote from Scripture:

> "What is your work? Whatever it be, the Lord, the King, has done that kind of work Himself, and you dwell with Him here for His work....
>
> "Is your work to 'mother,' comfort and strengthen? ('Gentle as a mother is when she tenderly nurses her own children.' I Thess. 2.7, Weymouth.)
> "As one whom his mother comforteth, so will I comfort you, saith the Lord....
>
> "Is your work in the sewing-room?
> "Unto Adam also and to his wife did the Lord God make coats of skin, and clothed them....

"Is your work cooking, lighting fires in the kitchen in the early morning, getting food ready for others?

"When the morning was now come, Jesus stood on the shore; but the disciples knew not that it was Jesus. As soon then as they were come to land, they saw a fire of coals there, and fish laid thereon, and bread. Jesus saith unto them, Come this way and have breakfast. (John 21.12, Weymouth.)...

"Is your work nursing, bandaging sores?
"He healeth the broken in heart, and bindeth up their wounds....

"Is your work account-keeping, teaching or learning arithmetic, or the names of things hard to remember?
"He telleth the number of the stars; He calleth them all by their names. Even the very hairs of your head are all numbered....

"Is your work in the farm with the animals?
"He shall feed His flock like a shepherd: He shall gather the lambs with His arm, and carry them in His bosom....

"He has done the work that you are doing. You dwell here with the King for His work."[15]

As Amy Carmichael recognized, God has done the work we are doing. God provides us with a principled archetype for all morally legitimate vocations. He was the First Farmer, the Divine Healer, the Water Engineer, the Accountant, the Investor/Entrepreneur.[16] God's nature is modeled and manifest in Christ through the Scriptures. Christ is the communicator, the agriculturalist, the construction worker, the healer, and the businessman. The most extraordinary human being of all time, Jesus of Nazareth infused dignity into what the world calls menial. He gloried in and glorified the ordinary.

New Testament scholar and author Paul S. Minear (1906–2007) writes of the impact of the God of the universe incarnating himself in the flesh of a humble carpenter:

One effect of this was to give workers in all trades a genuine equality before God and genuine importance in the life of the community.... No menial work was in itself beneath the dignity of prophet, priest, or king. In fact, God chose an obscure shepherd boy as king and an unheralded carpenter as Messiah.[17]

Dallas Willard also captures the essence of Christ and vocation:

If he were to come today as he did then, he could carry out his mission through most any decent and useful occupation. He could be a clerk or accountant in a hardware store, a computer repairman, a banker, an editor, doctor, waiter, teacher, farmhand, lab technician, or construction worker. He could run a housecleaning service or repair automobiles.

In other words, if he were to come today he could very well do what you do. He could very well live in your apartment or house, hold down your job.[18]

Christ wants to inhabit the world through his people in the place where they live and work. As a Christian, I am not discipled to do "spiritual things" either as a higher calling or to supplement my "secular work." No, I am to learn to live all of my life the way that Jesus would want it to be lived, in the house and in the vocation where he has deployed me. Again, Dallas Willard has captured this sense:

I am learning from Jesus to live my life as he would live my life if he were I. I am not necessarily learning to do everything he did, but I am learning how to do everything I do in the manner that he did all that he did.[19]

The God of the universe walked in the garden with our first parents, Adam and Eve. He commanded Moses to build a tabernacle because he wanted to "dwell among" his people.[20] In Christ, "the Word became flesh and made his dwelling among us."[21] Now he wants to dwell among the nations through his church.[22] I am to learn from Jesus how he would live my life, so that he would be substantially present in the place of my work and the place where I live. I am to occupy the territory and time of my life for Jesus Christ.

Brother Lawrence (c. 1614–1691), the author of the classic *The Practice of the Presence of God*, captures this sense of focus when he comments, "Our sanctification does not depend as much upon changing our activities as it does in doing them for God rather than ourselves."[23] It is no longer my work but God's work. It is not something I do merely to survive or to accumulate wealth or power. My work is the place through which his kingdom comes, his will is done. The ordinary is enlivened with the sacred.

As we have seen in this part of our journey, Christ has saved us for more than "going to heaven." While we have been saved for heaven, we have also been saved for earth; we have been saved to serve Christ and advance his kingdom on earth as it is in heaven. So far we have examined three fundamentals. First, we have been saved for a purpose and that purpose is our *life*work. Second, this call is a general call for all Christians to worship God, love their neighbors, and steward creation. Third, we each have a particular calling that we were made uniquely to discover and to live out.

Now we will explore more of the characteristics of our *life*work. As we continue to move forward, my hope is that you will see the potential of your life and work within the framework of the coming of the kingdom of God.

CHAPTER 14

CHARACTERISTICS
OF OUR *Life*WORK

God's story reveals that God is the King, the world is his kingdom, and we are his stewards. We are to have dominion over creation. We are to fulfill Christ's mandate to disciple the nations, so that the glory of the nations will be prepared for Christ's return. We are to do this as Christians not outside the context of our work, and not merely in our work. Our task is to manifest the kingdom of God *through* our work as a part of our calling.

As we seek to walk in our *life*work, we need to consider four important guideposts: the primacy of grace, the redemption of time and space, the manifestation of God's excellence, and the revelation of God's glory.

THE FRUITS OF OUR *Life*WORK
ARE THE RESULT OF GRACE

As we consider the fruits of our work, what constitutes "success"? Success, in simple terms, is realization of what one sets out to do. The goal may be good or bad, but it is achieved.

People often set wealth or power or both as the measure of success. In a biblical paradigm the goal is not wealth or poverty,[1] nor is it power; we are to be servants.[2] In a biblical paradigm the goal is an entrance into and advancement of the kingdom of God.[3] And the proper question for the Christian is, How can my life and work advance the kingdom of God?

As in so many things, there is a radical middle both in terms of goal—"give me nei-ther poverty nor riches" (Prov. 30:8)—and in terms of process, or the means. People in materialistic cultures assume that success is found in their efforts alone. The mantra is, "I did it myself!" or "I am a self-made man!" In fatalistic animistic cultures, people believe success is dependent on the whim of the gods or chance. In the biblical motif, God's grace and people's responsibility dance together. People have a responsibility to apply good effort and to discipline themselves in their lives and work. But it is by God's grace that success comes. This is articulated in Deuteronomy 8:18: "But remember the LORD your God, for it is he who gives you the ability to produce wealth, and so con-firms his covenant, which he swore to your forefathers, as it is today."

Reputedly, Charles Spurgeon, the great pastor and preacher of nineteenth-century England, told a story that articulates this balance. There were two girls, one of whom received very good grades in school and one who did not. The girl who was struggling asked the successful girl what the secret of her success was. The first girl answered that she worked very hard at her papers and in preparation for her tests. So the second girl applied more effort. After the next test, the second girl's scores had improved little. She asked the first girl why, after so much effort, she had not succeeded. The first girl asked, "Well, did you pray?" The second girl replied, "No!" The first girl answered that she both worked hard and sought God's favor. As the story goes, Spurgeon then says:

> We are to work as if it all depends on us,
> Pray as if it all depends on God, and
> Give God the glory for the results.

Throughout the Scriptures, we see that the relationship between God and human-kind is paramount. We see that God is sovereign and we are responsible. This is the biblical tension where life is lived out. The radical middle of the Scriptures reveals that human beings are *in*-dependent. This means they have personal freedom—indepen-dence—and responsibility to act, but they are also to be *in* relationship to both God and community and there find their true independence—in their *in*-dependence. And their success is all of grace.

While our salvation-justification is all of God,[4] our sanctification reflects the dance of responsibility and relationship. Paul reminds us in Philippians 2:12–13, "Work out your salvation with fear and trembling [personal discipline], for it is God who works in you to will and to act according to his good purpose [God's power]." Likewise we see this balance in James 1:5: "If any of you lacks wisdom, he should ask God, who gives generously to all without finding fault, and it will be given to him." As an "in-dependent" creature, a person has the responsibility to know his or her own limitations and to pray. God has the ability to provide wisdom, new insight, fortitude, and strength.

This radical middle was well articulated by the Reformers in Europe and later by the Puritans of North America. Martin Luther wrote,

> When riches come, the godless heart of man thinks: I have achieved this with my labors. It does not consider that these are purely blessings of God, blessings that at times come to us through our labors and at times without our labors, but never because of our labors; for God always gives them because of His undeserved mercy.[5]

Similarly, John Calvin wrote,

> Men in vain wear themselves out with toiling, and waste themselves by fasting to acquire riches, since these also are a benefit only by God.[6]

Cotton Mather (1663–1728) was an influential Puritan preacher and prolific writer, and sometimes even scientific pioneer and political leader, in early Massachusetts. He wrote, "In our occupation we spread our nets; but it is God who brings unto our nets all that comes into them."[7]

Professor of English Leland Ryken, writing in *Worldly Saints*, summarizes for us:

> The Puritan attitude was that wealth was a social good, not a personal possession—a gift from God, not the result of human effort alone or a sign of divine approval.[8]

As we walk in our *life*work, we are guided by these profound insights: our success is of divine grace, wealth is not a sign of divine approval but of grace, and our wealth is not for personal possession or consumption but for the good of the larger community. This is kingdom thinking.

OUR *Life*WORK REDEEMS TIME AND SPACE

Our very lives are God's first gift to us. In addition, he has given us both space and time with which to unfold our *life*work. He has given us the space of this planet, and the larger universe in which our small planet dwells, as a context for our lives. We have been given a soul and a body that allow us to engage the whole of creation, both the material and nonmaterial elements. Our bodies and their senses allow us the ability to enjoy, engage, and explore the universe. He has given us reasonable minds to explore and discover the secrets of the universe, and he has given us creativity with which to create whole new universes in the imagination.

As we have seen in the parable of the minas, Christ has capitalized his disciples to advance his kingdom.[9] One of the minas of his investment is the *time* of our lives. Jesus tells us that his *life*work—his life, death, and resurrection—was so that we "may have life, and have it to the full" (John 10:10b). He has given us time to explore, create, participate in his plan, and as significant agents, to write history. How we use our time, however, has been the critical question since the Fall. Will it be redeemed or squandered?

He has given us seven days a week and fifty-two weeks a year. This time is to be used to build lives that honor the Creator, enhance his creation, and create culture that reflects God and his created order. He has given us the sun, moon, and stars, to mark out the seasons to guide us in the process of having dominion over this world.[10]

The apostle Paul reminds us that we are to use the time and the opportunities wisely: "Be very careful, then, how you live—not as unwise but as wise, making the most of every opportunity, because the days are evil" (Eph. 5:15–16). Time cannot be brought back. Once it is gone, it is gone forever. Have we wasted it or have we redeemed it? Have we taken it as a precious gift or have we squandered it? Have we used it to build culture that reflects the Creator and the work he gave us in creation, or have we followed the lead of the liar—Satan—and built worlds that reflect counterfeit principles and that build on Satan's illusions?

John Wesley wrote,

> Lose no time. If you understand yourself and your relationship to God and man, you know that you have none to spare. If you understand your particular calling as you ought, you will have no time that hangs upon your hands.[11]

The span of our earthly lives is limited, as we are reminded in Isaiah 40: 6–7: "All men are like grass, and all their glory is like the flowers of the field. The grass withers and the flowers fall." Moreover, we can well say with Isaac, "I... don't know the day of my death" (Gen. 27:2). Will we live one day or a hundred days or a hundred years? Even more, we do not know when the Master, who has invested in us and charged us with the work of his kingdom, will return.[12] The Lord will not ask us the question, "How many years have you lived?" but "What did you do with the years I gave you?" How have we used our time?

As we seek to cultivate this kind of consciousness of the value of time, we may be pulled in a different direction by our culture. For the materialist, the chief value of time is economic: it is foremost a factor in productivity and in time-earnings ratios. What matters most is whom time belongs to. Because there is no God in a secular framework, there is only "clock time"; there is no transcendent time or fullness of time. The passage of time may have significance in developmental terms, but history has no eternal significance. Moreover, there is no lasting significance to time in an individual's life apart from accomplishing certain goals—economic, intellectual, or leisure. Ultimately, this lack of eternal value to time supports the hedonistic approach exemplified by the motto "Eat, drink and be merry, for tomorrow you die!" Time outside of work comes to be seen as meant for indulgence. You work all week so that you can live on the weekends in leisure. Life and work are often separated.

Interestingly, there is actually something that animism-informed cultures share in common with Scripture at this point, and that is the importance of relationships and the use of time for relationship. People in such cultures highly value relationships—often a very complex web of them—and will spend considerable time enjoying the companionship of people they know, even if there is no material gain in this use of time. Children, highly valued, are likely to be kept much more in the company of parents and other adults, in times both of leisure and of work. And often dependent members of society—small children, the sick, the elderly infirm—are cared for personally with little question rather than ignored or consigned only to the care of professionals. This all stands in stark contrast to materialistic societies whose production- and pleasure-oriented values often lead people to sacrifice relationships in order to seek success in the marketplace or unencumbered pursuit of pleasure.

Nevertheless, though people in animistic cultures may have time for relationship, time still lacks meaning in the larger context. Life is on the wheel. History is going nowhere. There is no sense of progress in the material world. Time is easily wasted. Time is largely seen in terms of the days we survive until we die and flee this passing world of space and time to be reunited with the spirit world, or the world of our ancestors.

In contrast, Scripture shows us that history has a beginning and an end. History is moving toward God's ordained purposes. We have already looked at the importance of salvation history as the metanarrative on which we should be basing our lives. A person's *life*work is to bring substantial healing into all of his life and to all of his relationships and to restore the created intent to his vocation. At the end of history, the healing, restoration, and rest that began with the first coming of Christ will be completed when he returns. History is going someplace! Between Christ's first and second coming, our *life*work is to redeem time and space.

OUR *Life*WORK MANIFESTS THE EXCELLENCE OF GOD

Os Guinness summarizes the nature of our call in his book *The Call*: "When Jesus calls, he calls us one by one.... We are each called individually, accountable to God alone, to please him alone, and eventually to be approved by him alone."[13]

Called by God, we have an employer worthy of our greatest efforts. Paul captures this in his first letter to the Thessalonians, where he writes that we are not to please man but God. "On the contrary, we speak as men approved by God to be entrusted with the gospel. We are not trying to please men but God, who tests our hearts" (1 Thess. 2:4). Likewise, he challenges the church in Colossae to work for the Lord, not for men: "Whatever you do, work at it with all your heart, as working for the Lord, not for men" (Col. 3:23).

Because redeemed man is working for God, to fulfill God's plans, the work is to be done with excellence. Our guidelines for excellence are found in God's own nature. God is true, just, and beautiful. Our work, in both its means and ends, is to manifest truth, justice, and beauty.

As we have observed earlier, Genesis 1 records that at each stage of creation God examines what he has made and declares it "good" or "just," "right" or "true." From the grandeur of the star-filled sky and the vast beauty of the Grand Canyon in Arizona to the exquisiteness of the tiniest flower, God's excellence is revealed. From the natural laws studied in astronomy, physics, geology, and biology to the capacity God created in man to express those laws variously in mathematics or poetry, God's exquisite skill is manifest. Psalm 104:1–5 reveals the wonder of God's artistry and skill:

Praise the LORD, O my soul.

O LORD my God, you are very great;
   you are clothed with splendor and majesty.
He wraps himself in light as with a garment;
   he stretches out the heavens like a tent
   and lays the beams of his upper chambers on their waters.
He makes the clouds his chariot
   and rides on the wings of the wind.
He makes winds his messengers,
   flames of fire his servants.

He set the earth on its foundations;
   it can never be moved.

As the poetry of this psalm conveys, God's excellence is reflected in creation and in the way he works to sustain the natural world. We also see God's excellence in redemption and the way he works to sustain his people, as expressed by the beautiful words of Psalm 111:

Praise the LORD.

I will extol the LORD with all my heart
   in the council of the upright and in the assembly.

Great are the works of the LORD;
   they are pondered by all who delight in them.
Glorious and majestic are his deeds,
   and his righteousness endures forever.
He has caused his wonders to be remembered;
   the LORD is gracious and compassionate.
He provides food for those who fear him;
   he remembers his covenant forever.
He has shown his people the power of his works,
   giving them the lands of other nations.
The works of his hands are faithful and just;
   all his precepts are trustworthy.
They are steadfast for ever and ever,
   done in faithfulness and uprightness.
He provided redemption for his people;
   he ordained his covenant forever—
holy and awesome is his name.

The fear of the LORD is the beginning of wisdom;
   all who follow his precepts have good understanding.
To him belongs eternal praise.

We read in this psalm a manifesto for excellence. As the psalmist says, when we ponder the works of the Lord, we see his delightfulness, glory, majesty, righteousness, grace, compassion, power, faithfulness, justice, trustworthiness, steadfastness, uprightness, holiness, and wisdom. As God enables us, and as we strive diligently to develop the capacity he has given us, our work should manifest this same excellent nature of God. Notice that this psalm of praise to God ends with a promise for us in our own labors: "The fear of the LORD is the beginning of wisdom; all who follow his precepts have good understanding" (Ps. 111:10).

In what kind of work does our excellent God call us to labor with him? Excellent work! Why? Because our work contributes, in some small way, to God's abode and to our future dwelling place—the kingdom of God. Let's explore this beautiful picture.

We have seen that there is a wonderful symmetry between the Old and the New Testament. In the Old Testament God reveals himself as the First Artist and First Craftsman; in the New Testament he *continues* his creative activity as the Architect and Builder of the eternal city.[14] In the Old Testament we see God and people colaboring to build first the tabernacle[15] and later the temple[16] for God's dwelling place.[17] In the New Testament we see God and people colaboring to build the present and future kingdom of God, where the redeemed will live with God forever.[18]

Building a dwelling place where God is manifest calls us to excellence. We see a picture of this excellence in the description of the building of the temple in 2 Chronicles 2:1–14:

> Solomon gave orders to build a temple for the Name of the LORD and a royal palace for himself. He conscripted seventy thousand men as carriers and eighty thousand as stonecutters in the hills and thirty-six hundred as foremen over them.
>
> Solomon sent this message to Hiram king of Tyre:
>
> "Send me cedar logs as you did for my father David when you sent him cedar to build a palace to live in. Now I am about to build a temple for the Name of the LORD my God and to dedicate it to him....
>
> "The temple I am going to build will be great, because our God is greater than all other gods. But who is able to build a temple for him, since the heavens, even the highest heavens, cannot contain him?...
>
> "Send me, therefore, a man skilled to work in gold and silver..., to work in Judah and Jerusalem with my skilled craftsmen, whom my father David provided.
>
> "Send me also cedar, pine and algum logs from Lebanon, for I know that your men are skilled in cutting timber there....
>
> Hiram king of Tyre replied by letter to Solomon:
>
> "Because the LORD loves his people, he has made you their king."
>
> And Hiram added:
>
> "Praise be to the LORD, the God of Israel, who made heaven and earth! He has given King David a wise son, endowed with intelligence and discernment, who will build a temple for the LORD....
>
> "I am sending you Huram-Abi, a man of great skill.... He is trained to work in gold and silver.... He is experienced in all kinds of engraving and can execute any design given to him. He will work with your craftsmen and with those of my lord, David your father.

Like Solomon, we have a great task in contributing to a dwelling place for God and his people and showing the excellence of his nature before a watching world. Our *lifework* is our contribution to the coming of the kingdom of God. With this king of Israel we can say, "The temple I am going to build will be great, because our God is greater than all" (v. 5). We might find ourselves wondering as he did, "Who is able to build a temple for him, since the heavens, even the highest heavens, cannot contain him? Who then am I to build a temple for him...?" (v. 6). Yet God has called us. We approach our work as Solomon did, with seriousness and creativity and resourcefulness, searching out what to us is the equivalent of the best designs, the materials of the greatest quality and beauty, and the most skilled craftsmen.

Previous generations of Christians have grasped the call to excellence better than we do today. The philosophy of the Shaker communities, who excelled in furniture making, reflects this kind of care:

> Make every product better than it's ever been done before. Make the parts you cannot see as well as the parts you can see. Use only the best of materials, even for the most everyday items. Give the same attention to the smallest detail as you do to the largest. Design every item you make to last forever.[19]

John Wesley, the reformer of England and founder of the Methodist movement, captured this same sense of excellence in his sermon on money:

> You should be continually learning, from the experience of others, or from your own experience, reading, and reflection, to do everything you have to do better to-day than you did yesterday. And see that you practice whatever you learn, that you may make the best of all that is in your hands.[20]

A story is told of a twelve-year-old Brazilian girl who also understood this need for excellence in all work because it is done for the Lord. Luiza's father volunteered to fix an old box used to collect offerings at the Capela da Videira. He did a great job, and the box was beautiful. Luiza added something extra, however. She made a little pillow to fit inside the box and adorned it with cross-stitch embroidery. Luiza's willingness to help and the care she took in making the pillow became an example and an inspiration that encouraged others in their service for the Lord.[21] As this Brazilian girl realized at a young age, the Bible calls us to faithfulness and excellence not only in the big things but also in those things we may think most inconsequential, superfluous, or common. Because there is dignity and wonder in the small things, we are called to sanctify the "menial," the small things. But because God is interested in the ordinary, the children of God are to appreciate the simple things and to bring dignity to them, working with excellence no matter how inconsequential the job may seem. When we understand the miracle of the ordinary, we acknowledge as one Puritan wrote, "that a Christian can regard 'his shop as well as his chapel as holy ground.'"[22]

Some thirty years ago, my wife Marilyn and I were driving from Phoenix, Arizona, to Denver, Colorado. In the high desert of southwestern Colorado, I pulled into the only gas station within miles to use the facilities. In the USA, at that time, gas station bathrooms were notorious for being filthy. As I opened the door to the men's room, I was expecting the worst. But what a surprise! The bathroom was spotless, and next to the sink was a vase of fresh-cut flowers. Whoever cared for this bathroom understood that we are to bring dignity and delight to the menial.

On another occasion, I was staying at a hotel. When I walked into the bathroom of my room, the tiny, packaged soaps were arranged artistically into a fan shape next to the sink. As I saw these, I thanked the Lord for the person who greeted me with this little bit of artistry in the midst of what is normally a utilitarian setting. This hotel maid had left her signature on the bathroom, choosing to bring dignity to the ordinary bathroom.

These little works of care and artistry are in keeping with a biblical worldview. A commitment to excellence and beauty stands in contrast to the pragmatic philosophy of the modern materialist, for whom efficiency, utility, and reproducibility are primary values. Nothing models this more than the fast-food industry. The McDonald's restaurant chain has built a whole business model on these values. Their stores look the same all over the world, the purchase and preparation of food is highly standardized, and workers are trained and judged accordingly to exact, standardized work methods, speed, and efficiency. While there are good things in these efficiencies, they do not tend to promote beauty or excellence.

There is also little in the animistic, fatalistic worldview, or in the corrupt systems so often associated with it, to foster excellence in work. If nothing in this life has any lasting meaning, or if workers or businesspeople have no sense that the quality of their work makes a difference either for themselves or for the individuals they serve, they have little reason to make that extra effort to have goods or service be regarded as excellent.

But if we know the kind of God for whom and with whom we are working, we have ample reason to pursue excellence. As John Politan of Scottsdale Bible Church has put it,

> The greatest single statement most people will ever make in their life for the cause of Christ—for good or bad—is how they do their work.[23]

And Chuck Colson writes,

> Excellence in our calling, which the Bible calls for, makes the most powerful witness for us in the workplace.... Those Christians already in the mission fields of accounting, sales, software, construction, and other honorable vocations, need to be equipped to work with integrity and thus share their faith in actions as well as words.[24]

As pictured in the parable of the minas, as Christ's followers we are workers on our master's estate, responsible for continuing to develop it, doing our day-to-day work according to his plans. We are called to do our work with the excellence fit for the One who has called us.

OUR *Life*WORK REVEALS GOD'S GLORY

The glory of God is revealed as his servants are obedient to his call upon their lives. As we seek, in some small way, to put our feet, hands, and imaginations into living the Lord's Prayer, the firstfruits of the kingdom are revealed and the King of the kingdom is glorified.

As Christ and his kingdom advance in this broken world, God has made each of us to fulfill a unique purpose. Out of a multitude of possibilities, we can illustrate this with two biblical figures, Moses and Jesus; with a godsend from recent history, William Wilberforce; and with one of today's heroes of the faith, Joni Eareckson Tada.

Let's look first at the prophet Moses, a Hebrew born of humble means, who through providential circumstances was raised to become a prince in Egypt. God used this man to lead the Hebrew people from slavery to the border of the Promised Land. As we have seen, during forty years of wilderness wandering, God instructed Moses to build a tabernacle. Exodus 25:8–9 reads, "Then have them [the people] make a sanctuary for me, and I will dwell among them. Make this tabernacle and all its furnishings exactly like the pattern I will show you." As the story unfolds, God reveals the plans, the provision of supplies and craftsmanship is accomplished, and the tabernacle is built. We pick up the narrative in Exodus 40:33: "Then Moses set up the courtyard around the tabernacle and altar and put up the curtain at the entrance to the courtyard. And so Moses finished the work." The tabernacle was completed just before he died.

Moses lived his life to the fullest, seeking to be obedient to the God of Abraham, Isaac, and Jacob. He had "finished well." He had completed his assignment. He had led the Hebrew people out of captivity in Egypt. He had completed the tabernacle. Now we find these remarkable words in Exodus 40:34–35: "Then the cloud covered the Tent of Meeting, and the glory of the LORD filled the tabernacle. Moses could not enter the Tent of Meeting because the cloud had settled upon it, and the glory of the LORD filled the tabernacle." We find that when Moses finished the assignment that God had for him, "the glory of the LORD" filled that space. When God's work is done in God's way, he is glorified and his glory animates—breathes life into—the work. Note two things here. First, God is glorified by our obedience, by our completing the task we have been given. Second, when the assignment is completed, God's glory transforms the work.

We see a similar pattern reflected in the life of Christ. Early in his life, Jesus recognized that he had an assignment from the Father. This is recorded in his public ministry:

> Meanwhile his disciples urged him, "Rabbi, eat something."
> But he said to them, "I have food to eat that you know nothing about."
> Then his disciples said to each other, "Could someone have brought him food?"
> "My food," said Jesus, "is to do the will of him who sent me and to finish *his work*." (John 4:31–34; italics added)

Jesus understood that he had work to do, work that his Father had delegated to him. We see this reflected in John 5:17: "Jesus said to them, 'My Father is always at his work to this very day, and I, too, am working.'" Jesus is an organic part of what God is doing. The call is similar in our lives. The call to Christ is a call to the Father's work. He is working now, and he wants to connect our lives to his work. Our *life*work is that connection.

Jesus reflects on his work. At the last supper he prays what we have come to know as his High Priestly Prayer. The first part of the prayer is instructive as we think about the need to connect our work to the kingdom of God. John 17:1, 4–5 says,

> After Jesus said this, he looked toward heaven and prayed:
> "Father, the time has come. Glorify your Son, that your Son may glorify you....I have brought you glory on earth by completing the work you gave me to do. And now, Father, glorify me in your presence with the glory I had with you before the world began."

We see that Jesus glorified the Father "by completing the work you gave *me* to do"! Jesus had a particular job. His completing that task brought glory to the Father. Do you want to bring glory to the Father? Then do the work that he has for you to do! We do not glorify God by doing someone else's work, but we glorify him when we do our own work that he gives us to do.

As a young Christian, studying at L'Abri Fellowship in Switzerland, I would become depressed when I woke up in the morning. I had three heroes at L'Abri— Francis Schaeffer, Udo Middelmann, and Os Guinness. I made a composite from each of their strengths and said, *This is the person I want to be.* I did not consider any of their faults in forming this caricature. As I compared myself with this "model man," I saw how lacking I was in meeting the standard. I became discouraged. One day I realized my sin in doing this and understood that God had made *me* for a purpose. We glorify

God as our life fulfills the purpose for which we have been made. We destroy ourselves when we compare ourselves with others. We do not glorify God by trying to do what he has made someone else to do.

We should also note that when Jesus completed the work the Father had for him, the Father glorified the Son. Each of us is absolutely unique. The wonder of our own special abilities is revealed as we are obedient to the call God has upon our own lives.

The life of one of my heroes, William Wilberforce, illustrates this. As we saw earlier, Wilberforce was an English Christian who was so concerned about the evils of slavery and the breakdown of civility in British society that he won a seat in Parliament in order to change both public policy and public demeanor. Wilberforce was challenged by a number of friends to seek "spiritual" work in the ministry. Fortunately for Britain and the world, he was not persuaded but followed God's call into political life.

For nearly a half century, Wilberforce campaigned for the emancipation of slaves. It was a daunting task, in that he had to stand, almost alone, against the political and economic powers in British society. Over the course of more than forty long years, a rising tide of public outcry finally developed. On July 26, 1833, three days before his death, the news reached Wilberforce that the House of Commons had passed the Slavery Abolition Act, freeing slaves throughout the empire.[25] In the end, it could be seen that throughout Wilberforce's life, God was glorified by his unrelenting courage and determination to do the particular work God had for him to do.

The life of our contemporary Joni Eareckson Tada also exemplifies how we glorify God as we do the unique work for which he has called us. As a teenager, Joni had her life before her. She was active and attractive, a young woman with dreams and aspirations. Then one day tragedy struck. Joni dove into shallow water in the Chesapeake Bay and broke her neck. In that brief moment her whole life was altered. Joni was left a quadriplegic, confined to a wheelchair for life.

In time, Joni emerged from despondency, and sought the Lord for what good he might wish to bring out of this tragedy. Joni began a worldwide ministry of encouragement and advocacy for handicapped people called Joni and Friends. She has become a writer and a gifted artist. She has also engaged in the public policy debate in the United States over embryonic stem cell research. As others advocate for the use and destruction of early human life, Joni has forcefully led the charge to protect the life of the unborn, even if it means that she herself will not walk again.

Charles Colson was at a meeting held at the White House where President George W. Bush laid out the rationale for the defense of human life and the case against destruction of embryonic stem cells even for the good end of helping heal spinal cord injuries. Joni Eareckson Tada was in the audience. Colson describes what he observed on the occasion:

Several times during his talk, I saw President Bush look directly at Joni. At the end of his speech, the president surprised everyone. Stepping from the podium, he put his arms around Joni and embraced her and kissed her. It was a moving moment. Surely, I thought, this was the moment and issue for which Joni had been born. There was a purpose for all of her suffering.[26]

Joni could have turned inward after the accident. Her life could have been marked by self-pity, bitterness, and despair. And yet it was not. What could have made the difference? Instead of endlessly asking the question, "Why, Lord?" Joni began to ask the questions, "Lord, what do you want me to do? How can I respond to this tragedy in a way that will honor you?" By seeking to hear the call of God in her *life*work, Joni's life has been transformed and has been used of God to advance his kingdom. As Joni was sitting in her wheelchair in the White House, the voice of Mordecai could be heard through history: "for such a time as this!" (Esther 4:14).

God is glorified through our work—when we walk in the particular call he has placed on our lives. He is glorified when we finish the task that he has made us for, when we fulfill our destiny. He is glorified when we are godly carpenters, politicians, and artists; when we are godly sons and daughters, mothers and fathers, sisters and brothers, husbands and wives. He is glorified when we manifest truth, beauty, and justice in our communities, workplaces, and nations. He is glorified when we walk confidently in our *life*work.

PART 5 : THE ECONOMICS OF OUR *Life*WORK

CHAPTER 15

STEWARDSHIP:

THE PROTESTANT ETHIC

A hallmark of our *lifework* clearly must be a biblical understanding of economics. If you were to read the Bible from Genesis to Revelation and record in a journal every passage you found on the salvation of the soul or on business and economics, which list would be longer at the end of the survey? The passages on business and economics would be far more numerous than those on spiritual salvation. Is this a sign that spiritual salvation is secondary? No! Quite the contrary; a person's salvation is fundamental to everything else. But it does point out that God is interested in economics and has given us first principles to help us steward creation and promote healthy economic activity.

"ECONOMIC MAN"

Economic activity under God is about the value found in producing, saving, and giving. In Genesis God mandates the stewardship of creation.[1] Stewardship implies both progressing (producing bounty) and conserving (being careful with creation). We see this sense of good stewarding in the Greek root for the word *economy*, which is *oikonomia* and means "to manage a house" or "to steward an estate." (*Oikos* can mean "house" or "temple," and *nomia* comes from *nemein*, which means "to allot" or "to manage.") If we think of the world that God created as his "house," then we can think of ourselves as the stewards he has placed in it to manage it. This is why I often say that man is *homo oikonomia*—"economic man." Economics, therefore, could be said to be the wise management of God's household (the world) with moral imagination, or to put it another way, the stewardship of resources within the boundaries of God's laws.

AVOIDING TWO ERRORS

God has entrusted us with his household, and as we see with the parable of the shrewd manager[2] and the parable of the ten minas,[3] he expects us to be responsible managers. In the parable of the shrewd manager, the master commended the dishonest manager because of his "prudent" management.[4] This is not a call to be dishonest but a call to be wise in the economic arena. In the parable of the ten minas, the master commends the godly stewards who returned tenfold[5] and fivefold[6] on their investments. He condemns the one who hid the capital and did not turn a profit.[7] What was the focus of the master's interest? He was looking for wise and intelligent use of his capital investment. Such prudent investment will produce a "profit" for the master and the kingdom of God.

As we discussed earlier in the book, parables like that of the ten minas are not solely about economics but serve as metaphors for spiritual realities. Yet part of how God created us, and how God has called and equipped us to manifest and extend the kingdom, is in our literal work in the economic arena, through how we manage what he has entrusted to us, including time, space, and resources, both those of the earth and those of our own individual households.

It might be easy for us to overlook Scripture's very practical teachings about God's intentions for our economic life. On one hand, if we are steeped in the mindset of evangelical dualism, we will see the material world as irrelevant to, or only a shadow of, the spiritual, "real" world. There would be no sense in discussing something as "worldly" as economics in a book about theology; we would not see a connection between our faith and our economic lives. On the other hand, in recognizing that there is no such dichotomy—that the physical is infused with the sacred—we may be tempted to fall into another error and subsume the material into the spiritual. We may end up overspiritualizing the issue so that it no longer has its own physical nature as God created it. In this scenario also there would be no sense in discussing economics. Instead of falling into either error, we want our thinking to be shaped by a biblical understanding of the relationship between the material and spiritual worlds, in which both are inextricably connected parts of the one reality God has made. Only then can we be the kind of stewards God intends us to be, excluding nothing and no one from the reach of his care and redemption.

THE PROTESTANT ETHIC AND JOHN WESLEY'S THREE PLAIN RULES

The Reformers of the Protestant movement recognized the importance of our economic lives as citizens of God's kingdom. Their teaching on this vital topic changed the world. In fact, as we'll discuss in chapter 19, The Domains, it was the biblical worldview taught by the Reformers that economic historians have recognized as a major factor in lifting whole nations out of poverty through the development of middle-class society. Through the new economies of Europe, multitudes were freed to live a life very different from that of the old indentured servants and serfs, to enjoy broader opportunities in their lives, and to have a significant effect on the life of the nation.

The Reformers' teachings on work have had such a major and lasting influence that they have come to be known as the Protestant ethic. Just as our Savior inculcates the virtues of humility and forgiveness in his followers, so the Reformers impressed by frequent admonition a series of economic principles. These were imprinted on the mind, breaking down the strongholds of counterfeit worldviews and the vices that stem from them. As minds and hearts were inculcated with the biblical virtues, cultures were transformed.[8]

What did the Reformers teach in the realm of the marketplace that transformed economies and social structures over most of Northern Europe? We have already seen that they abolished the Gnostic paradigm of the perfect life and the permitted life; they abolished the distinction between *vita contemplativa* (the contemplative life) and *vita activa* (the active life). With the understanding that all of life is sacred and that we are to live *coram Deo* (before God), what did the Reformers teach about work?

John Wesley's motto concerning work and the use of money can offer a simple framework for analyzing the economic teachings of the Reformers in Europe. God used John Wesley to start a revival in England in the mid-1700s, one that transformed the nation in a little more than one generation, similar to the transformations initiated by Luther and Calvin in their regions two hundred years before. Wesley preached the cross of Christ for personal salvation and then drew the social implications of the gospel for national transformation. Wesley's three plain rules concerning the use of money are

> Gain all you can!
> Save all you can!
> Give all you can!

These admonitions need to be infused again into Western nations, which are rapidly losing their soul, and into the developing world, which is longing for the fulfillment and elusive material health granted by these principles. Let's examine each of these in turn.

GAIN ALL YOU CAN: THREE REASONS TO WORK

The first part of Wesley's call is to work: "Gain all you can, without hurting either your-self or your neighbor, in soul or body, by applying hereto with unintermitted diligence, and with all the understanding which God has given you."[9] Wesley's call is to work that is healthy and moral, to work that edifies self and neighbor in a wholistic fashion. It should be performed with diligence; people are to work hard and employ all the gifts and skills given them by God. We are called to cultivate the virtues of industry and diligence and to root out the vices of idleness, sloth, and laziness.

Martin Luther captured the essence of this in his exposition of Exodus 13:18: "God does not want to have success come without work.... He does not want me to sit at home, to loaf, to commit matters to God, and to wait till a fried chicken flies into my mouth. That would be tempting God."[10] We are to work hard, with industry and diligence.

Puritan preacher Robert Bolton (1572–1631) wrote, "Be diligent with conscience and faithfulness in some lawful, honest particular calling...not so much to gather gold and engross wealth, as for necessary and moderate provision for family and posterity: and in conscience and obedience to that common charge laid upon all the sons and daughters of Adam to the world's end."[11]

At the heart of the Protestant ethic we find that work has intrinsic value. Our work, along with our citizenship, is the place where we contribute to the building of culture. Our work is not just what we do to survive (animism), to consume (materialism), or to have a platform for witness (evangelical Gnosticism). Instead, Scripture reveals three reasons to work.

God Works

God is a working God. As we have established, work is not a part of the curse, as many assume. When we think that work is a curse, the words of Genesis 2:2–3 are startling:

> By the seventh day God had finished the work he had been doing; so on the seventh day he rested from all his work. And God blessed the seventh day and made it holy, because on it he rested from all the work of creating that he had done.

The creation of the universe was work. And it was God who did that work. God worked for six days in creation and then rested the seventh day. It is in God's nature to work. Note that the word for *work* here is the Hebrew *melakah*. It is used 167 times in the Old Testament and is translated "occupation," "work," or "business."[12] This is the same Hebrew word[13] used in the Ten Commandments when speaking of the work and rest cycle we should maintain.[14]

We find that God not only worked at the time of creation but continues to work in the sustaining of creation. Psalm 104:10–16 is a testimony to his ongoing work:

> He makes springs pour water into the ravines;
>   it flows between the mountains.
> They give water to all the beasts of the field;
>   the wild donkeys quench their thirst.
> The birds of the air nest by the waters;
>   they sing among the branches.
> He waters the mountains from his upper chambers;
>   the earth is satisfied by the fruit of his work.
> He makes grass grow for the cattle,
>   and plants for man to cultivate—
> bringing forth food from the earth:
> wine that gladdens the heart of man,
>   oil to make his face shine,
>   and bread that sustains his heart.
> The trees of the LORD are well watered,
>   the cedars of Lebanon that he planted.

We also see in the words of our Lord and Savior, Jesus Christ, that his Father is continually at work. "Jesus said to them, 'My Father is always at his work to this very day, and I, too, am working'" (John 5:17), and in John 4:34, "My food . . . is to do the will of him who sent me and to finish his work." The work that Jesus came to do is the Father's work. Our salvation and the advancement of the kingdom is God's ongoing work. Note that God continues to work today. His work of common grace sustains the universe. His work of special grace is his work for our salvation. God is a working God. It is part of his nature.

Man Was Made to Work

The second reason we work is that man was made to work. Scripture makes it clear that work is not part of the curse but part of the blessing; it is part of the dignity of man. We saw this in the discussion on the cultural mandate. Because God is a working God, when he makes man in his image, part of what that means is that man is to work as well. We find in Genesis the first job description. The nature of man's work is to have dominion (stewardship) over creation.[15] This is not only the first job description but also the job description out of which all other legitimate job descriptions come.

This first job description was given before the Fall, and the Lord confirms his command to work after the Fall. Exodus 20:9–10 says, "Six days *you shall labor* and *do all your work,* but the seventh day is a Sabbath to the LORD your God. On it you shall not do any work, neither you, nor your son or daughter, nor your manservant or maidservant, nor your animals, nor the alien within your gates [italics added]." We normally think of the fourth commandment as the commandment to keep the Sabbath. And so it is. However, it is larger than the Sabbath issue alone; it commands both work and rest. Just as God labored for six days and rested on the seventh, so shall you. Work is commanded. Man is to have the same work-rest pattern as his Creator.

The Psalms testify to the fact that work is part of man's dignity, part of what it means to be human. Psalm 104:19–24 says,

> The moon marks off the seasons,
>   and the sun knows when to go down.
> You bring darkness, it becomes night,
>   and all the beasts of the forest prowl.
> The lions roar for their prey
>   and seek their food from God.
> The sun rises, and they steal away;
>   they return and lie down in their dens.
> Then man goes out to his work,
>   to his labor until evening.
>
> How many are your works, O LORD!
>   In wisdom you made them all;
>   the earth is full of your creatures.

John Milton captured the sense of the dignity of work when he wrote in *Paradise Lost,*

> Man hath his daily work of body or mind
> Appointed, which declares his dignity
> And the regard of Heaven on all his ways.[16]

Work is a normal activity. As the moon marks the seasons, as the lion hunts for its prey, so man goes out to work. God works and man works. Similarly Psalm 128:1–2 states,

> Blessed are all who fear the LORD,
>   who walk in his ways.
> You will eat the fruit of your labor;
>   blessings and prosperity will be yours.

We find here the sense of contentment, satisfaction, and fulfillment of work. There is a blessing in the contentment of the soul and the satisfaction of work well done.

We Are Coworkers with God

There is a third reason to work: we are coworkers with God. God is a working God, and he has a plan for creation that he is bringing about. He has made man to work, but not just to work on his own for his own purposes; he has made humankind to labor with him in his grand scheme for the universe. As we learned in the discussion of the cultural mandate, being made in the image of the Creator God, people are to use their creativity and enterprise to cultivate the world, to shape it, to draw out its potential. Genesis 1:26–28, along with Genesis 2:15 and 2:19, reflects that we are to create culture. God was not finished with creation when he rested. Now it is our turn to work alongside God. We are to use our hands, hearts, and minds to expand the garden and to bring forth all the potential latent in creation, to the glory of God.

We've also studied Ephesians 2:10: "For we are God's workmanship, created in Christ Jesus to do good works, which God prepared in advance for us to do." Why were we saved? We were saved from our sins in order to rejoin God in his work. God is at work today. Our work is to be a vehicle for God's work. It is a communal and relational activity. Our life and work are to be connected to the coming of the kingdom. As we saw in Colossians 3:23, we are to do all that we do "as working for the Lord"! Why? Because God is at work and he has called us to be part of his work.

Why, then, are we to work? First, we work because God works. Second, we work because man was made to work. Third, we work because man was made to be a coworker with God in his enterprise.

SAVE ALL YOU CAN: SIX REASONS TO SAVE

The second part of John Wesley's call was to savings: "Save all you can, by cutting off every expense which serves only to indulge foolish desires; to gratify either the desire of the flesh, the desire of the eye, or the pride of life; waste nothing, living or dying, on sin or folly, whether for yourself or your children."[17]

For a Westerner who has been smitten by the "spirit of the age" of consumption culture, this is language from another era. Do not feed base passions; waste nothing in living or dying. Here we find a call to frugality, a simple lifestyle, and the practice of an external asceticism. We are called to cultivate the virtues of thrift, frugality, contentment, and moderation and root out the vices of envy and waste.

Some Christians are, at the core, materialists; they idolize wealth. The prosperity gospel teaches that we are children of the King, and the King wants his children to be wealthy, healthy, and happy—so indulge! Other Christians idolize poverty. Matthew 19:24 tells how hard it is for the rich to get into the kingdom of heaven. Luke 6:20 says, "Blessed are you who are poor, for yours is the kingdom of God." These Christians see wealth as a sign of ungodliness, and poverty as a virtue, a sign of godliness. Some so identify with the poor that they become impoverished themselves. There is no reason to save but every reason to give.

In contrast to these faulty understandings held by many Christians, the Bible reveals six reasons to save. The principles that lead to savings demand a community of people who are progressive enough to generate wealth and conservative enough to care for creation and the needs of the larger community.

God Cares for Creation

First, as God manages his creation with care, we too are to manage with care what God has given into our stewardship. We know that through his common grace, God sustains all things, today.[18] We can picture God as the First Husbandman. The meanings of the old word *husbandry* include "the care of a household," "control or judicious use of resources," and "the cultivation or production of plants or animals."[19] As the First Husbandman, God tends and cares for his creation judiciously, or with sound judgment.

The words of Walter Chalmers Smith's great hymn "Immortal, Invisible, God Only Wise" capture the sense of God as Husbandman: "Unresting, unhasting, and silent as light, Nor wanting, nor wasting, Thou rulest in might." God cares for his creation. He rules in might, not wanting or wasting. He wants his children to do the same.[20] The judgment comes upon those who bring want and waste to the earth.[21]

So the first reason for saving is that it is a reflection of God's husbandry of creation, manifested in the virtue of thrift. We see the instruction given to humankind in Genesis 2:15 when Adam and Eve were put in the garden to "work it" (progressing) and to "take care of it" (conserving). As good "husbandmen" we are to exhibit thrift.

Work Six Days—Live Seven

The second reason to save is that we work six days and live seven. Genesis 2:2 establishes that God modeled the work-rest pattern. He worked for six days at creation and then rested on the seventh day. This same pattern is commanded of man. We see this in Exodus 20:8–11, where the fourth commandment mandates both holy work and holy rest. We are to work six days and rest on the seventh. The reason to save is that if we are going to live seven days but only work six, then we need to save during the working days for the day of Sabbath rest. While this reason to save may have little application in the world of the middle class, it has significant force for people still living in poverty.

We Live in a Fallen World

The third reason to save is that we live in a fallen world. Genesis 3 reveals that there were consequences to man's rebellion. The ground is now cursed, and there will be weeds in the garden. What theologians call "natural evil" is now part of the landscape. There will be droughts and floods, earthquakes and famines. In order to prepare for the bad years (and there will be bad years) we need to save in the good years. If we do not save in the good years, we will starve in the bad years.

The classic illustration of this is found in Genesis 41 and the story of Joseph. The Pharaoh in Egypt had a dream in which he saw seven fat cows and seven skinny cows. These represented seven bountiful years and seven lean years. Joseph developed what was probably the first disaster preparedness plan in history. The plan called for saving in the good years and distributing food in the bad years. Prudent people will save in the good years, because they know that the bad years will come. This has real application in both economically developed and developing nations, as we face natural disasters, recession, and personal crises.

Provision for the Future

The fourth reason is similar to the third, to make provision for the future. In contrast to materialistic and animistic societies in which there is no belief in the future, in the biblical economy—in reality—there is a future. In fact, one of the facets of the biblical worldview is that history is going somewhere. There was a past, there is a present, and there is a future in which Christ is coming back with his kingdom. In the meantime, we live on the kingdom continuum. We are to appreciate the past, enjoy the present, and build for and contribute to the coming of the kingdom. There is a future in my life. There is a future for my children and for their children. There is a future for society. We need to *delay* gratification for the good of others. We need to save now for our children's education or to capitalize a business, purchase a home, or endow the arts or to build libraries, universities, clinics, and hospitals.

We see this principle illustrated in the example of the ant in Proverbs 6:6–8:

Go to the ant, you sluggard;
consider its ways and be wise!
It has no commander,
no overseer or ruler,
yet it stores its provisions in summer
and gathers its food at harvest.

Even the ant is wise (read shrewd) in this regard. It stores provisions in the summer for the winter. If the ant is prudent, surely people ought to be more so.

Virtue in a Simple Life

The fifth reason to save is that there is virtue in moderation and simplicity. We will take an extended time to review this point because it is necessary to establish two truths held in tension in the biblical worldview: Scripture affirms both that people have a right to the fruit of their labors *and* that as Christians we are called to choose a moderate lifestyle, seeking to be creators, savers, and givers of wealth, not simply consumers of wealth.

To understand our call to a simple life, it is important first to recognize that God intends for humankind to receive the fruit of our labors. The principle that "the worker deserves his wages" (Luke 10:7) or, as the King James Version translates it, "the labourer is worthy of his hire," was established by God in the very beginning:

> The LORD God took the man and put him in the Garden of Eden to work it and take care of it. And the LORD God commanded the man, "You are free to eat from any tree in the garden; but you must not eat from the tree of the knowledge of good and evil, for when you eat of it you will surely die." (Gen. 2:15–17)

In these verses we naturally hear God's commandment of what the man is *not* to eat. But these verses also show that with the exception of the one tree, the fruit of all the other trees *is* for the man to eat. The man is cultivating and caring for the garden, and the fruit of his labor is his provision. Similarly, Genesis 1:29–30 records,

> Then God said, "I give you every seed-bearing plant on the face of the whole earth and every tree that has fruit with seed in it. They will be yours for food. And to all the beasts of the earth and all the birds of the air and all the creatures that move on the ground—everything that has the breath of life in it—I give every green plant for food." And it was so.

Here, too, we see that God ordained that humankind's work in the garden would sustain them. He made seed-bearing plants. If you plant one seed, you get back a hundredfold or a thousandfold. God made the world to produce bountifully, providing for the expanding human community.

God confirmed the truth that the worker deserves his wages in the commandments he gave his people through Moses after bringing them out of slavery in Egypt.

The eighth and the tenth commandments are founded on the principle that a person has a right to the fruit of his or her labors:

> You shall not steal.... You shall not covet your neighbor's house. You shall not covet your neighbor's wife, or his manservant or maidservant, his ox or donkey, or anything that belongs to your neighbor. (Exod. 20:15, 17)

These commandments establish the right to "private property." While in an absolute sense, everything belongs to God, people have the right to the fruit of their labors. Private property is to hold in trust that which ultimately belongs to God.

Similarly, the New Testament also teaches that a worker is worthy of his hire. James 5:4 states, "Look! The wages you failed to pay the workmen who mowed your fields are crying out against you. The cries of the harvesters have reached the ears of the Lord Almighty." A person has a right to his or her wages. To withhold someone's wages is fraud and theft.

While the Bible affirms that we have a right to the fruit of our labor and that we are to appreciate the goodness of the physical things of God's creation, it also calls us to moderation. Moderation establishes a balance between idolizing wealth (materialism) and being condemned to poverty (animism). We see this articulated in Proverbs 30:7–9:

> Two things I ask of you, O LORD;
>   do not refuse me before I die:
> Keep falsehood and lies far from me;
>   give me neither poverty nor riches,
>   but give me only my daily bread.
> Otherwise, I may have too much and disown you
>   and say, 'Who is the LORD?'
> Or I may become poor and steal,
>   and so dishonor the name of my God.

Give me neither poverty nor riches. There is a balance here. Neither riches so I no longer perceive a need for God, nor poverty so that I dishonor the name of the Lord by stealing. The scripture establishes the goal of "adequacy"—sufficiency in all realms of life. It calls for a simple lifestyle based on an external asceticism. Some have called this a "theology of enough."

Some see wealth as a sign of favor with God. But the Reformers and Puritans did not. Ryken writes,

It will come as a shock to the debunkers of the Protestant ethic to learn that the original Protestants saw an inverse relationship between wealth and godliness. Given their position as an often persecuted minority, the early Protestants regarded persecution and suffering, not earthly success, as the most likely result of godly living.[22]

This echoes colonial pastor Samuel Willard, who wrote in *A Complete Body of Divinity*, "As riches are not evidences of God's love, so neither is poverty of his anger or hatred."[23] Poverty does not indicate God's disapproval or a lack of faith; neither is poverty a sign of godliness, as the ascetic would say. Nor is wealth a sign of God's favor. Christians impacted by a materialistic value system have idolized wealth (served mammon), while those who have identified with the poor have romanticized poverty.

The balance is to appreciate the material world without having an idolatrous or covetous relationship with it. We are to pursue a simple lifestyle. Jesus gives a warning in Luke 12:15: "Then he said to them, 'Watch out! Be on your guard against all kinds of greed; a man's life does not consist in the abundance of his possessions.'" Jesus' warning is that life is not determined by how many things a person owns. We are not to seek to be rich. Rather we are to seek first his kingdom and his righteousness.[24]

Contentment

The sixth principle that drives savings is to learn contentment in every situation. The apostle Paul describes the principle in Philippians 4:10–13:

> I rejoice greatly in the Lord that at last you have renewed your concern for me. Indeed, you have been concerned, but you had no opportunity to show it. I am not saying this because I am in need, for I have learned to be content whatever the circumstances. I know what it is to be in need, and I know what it is to have plenty. I have learned the secret of being content in any and every situation, whether well fed or hungry, whether living in plenty or in want. I can do everything through him who gives me strength.

Paul had a secret. He could be content in any and every situation. He had the ability to be "comfortable" in the emperor's palace and in the home of a hungry person. He could be content in wealth or poverty. It is easy to be content in wealth or to be resigned in poverty. It is difficult to be content in any and every situation.

Again Paul writes, this time to his young disciple Timothy,

> But godliness with contentment is great gain. For we brought nothing into the world, and we can take nothing out of it. But if we have food and clothing,

we will be content with that. People who want to get rich fall into temptation and a trap and into many foolish and harmful desires that plunge men into ruin and destruction. For the love of money is a root of all kinds of evil. Some people, eager for money, have wandered from the faith and pierced themselves with many griefs. (1 Tim. 6:6–10)

Note it is not money that is evil. It is the love of money that is evil. Do we hold our money in trust to God? Or does our money hold us hostage? Do we possess our money or does our money own us? As Jesus has reminded us, we cannot serve two masters. We cannot love God and money at the same time. Godliness with contentment, and not wealth, is the virtue.

Hebrews 13:5 says to "keep [our] lives free from the love of money and be content with what [we] have, because God has said, 'Never will I leave you; never will I forsake you.'" Dr. Howard Hendricks, Chair of the Center of Christian Leadership at Dallas Theological Seminary, comments on the human error of "longing for money as the way to get 'enough,' instead of longing for God as the Provider of 'enough.'"[25] The issue here is not one of income but one of consumption. It is an issue of an attitude and lifestyle of contentment.

What happens when the virtues of hard work and thrift are practiced? Wealth or "capital" is created! But the wealth is not for consumption. The principles of moderation—simple living and contentment—define the use of the wealth. What is to be done with all this wealth? It is to be given away to advance the kingdom.

GIVE ALL YOU CAN: THREE REASONS TO GIVE

The third part of John Wesley's call is to giving: "Give all you can, or, in other words, give all you have to God. Do not stint yourself...to this or that proportion. 'Render unto God,' not a tenth, not a third, not a half, but all that is God's, be it more or less; by employing all on yourself, your household, the household of faith, and all mankind, in such a manner, that you may give a good account of your stewardship when you can no longer steward."[26]

All that we have, not just the capital that has been created through hard work and savings, belongs to God and is to be employed in the service of Christ and his kingdom. Wesley writes,

> "When the Possessor of heaven and earth brought you into being, and placed you in this world, he placed you here not as a proprietor, but a steward: As such he entrusted you, for a season, with goods of various kinds; but the sole

property of these rests in him, nor can be alienated from him. As you yourself are not your own, but his, such is, likewise, all that you enjoy. Such is your soul and your body, not your own, but God's.... And he has told you, in the most clear and express terms, how you are to employ it for him, in such a manner that it may be all an holy sacrifice, acceptable through Christ Jesus."[27]

As Wesley recognized, God is the owner of *all* things. We are to cultivate the virtues of community, benevolence, charity, generosity, and compassion and to root out the vices of stinginess, covetousness, greed, and selfishness. At the heart of the matter, selfishness gets in the way of giving. "Selfishness, in its worst or unqualified sense, is the very essence of human depravity, and it stands in direct opposition to benevolence, which is the essence of the divine character. As God is love, so man, in his natural state, is selfishness."[28] As believers we want an attitude of self-sacrifice for others, not of sacrificing others for the self. The biblical focus throughout the Old and New Testaments is always outward to the larger community. Scripture reveals three reasons to give: thankfulness, pragmatism, and obedience.

Thankfulness

The first reason to give is in thankfulness to God for his love and grace.[29] He has given us what we do not deserve: eternal and abundant life. And he is merciful, not giving us what we do deserve: death.

How are we to respond to such mercy and grace? With thankfulness! The apostle Paul reminds us of the logical response to the mercy of God in Romans 12:1 (KJV): "I beseech you therefore, brethren, by the mercies of God, that ye present your bodies a living sacrifice, holy, acceptable unto God, which is your reasonable service." It is reasonable. Paul commended the Macedonian church when writing to the Corinthians:

And now, brothers, we want you to know about the grace that God has given the Macedonian churches. Out of the most severe trial, their overflowing joy and their extreme poverty welled up in rich generosity. (2 Cor. 8:1–2)

Paul continues in 2 Corinthians 9:6–7:

Remember this: Whoever sows sparingly will also reap sparingly, and whoever sows generously will also reap generously. Each man should give what he has decided in his heart to give, not reluctantly or under compulsion, for God loves a cheerful giver.

Giving is to be done freely and cheerfully out of a thankful heart.

Pragmatism

The second reason to give is pragmatic; we were designed to give. God is a serving God.[30] The very nature of his love is that it is self-sacrificing.[31] And again, we are made in his image. We have been designed to serve. We are most fully ourselves and most fully human when we are sharing with others.

Because God is community, we were made for community. We have been made to connect with other people. As such we are to look out not only for our own interests but also for the interests of others.[32]

In Isaiah 58 we read that the nation of Israel is "depressed." She is out of favor with God. In verses 6–10, God gives his prescription for lifting the "darkness":

> "Is not this the kind of fasting I have chosen:
>   to loose the chains of injustice
>   and untie the cords of the yoke,
>   to set the oppressed free
>   and break every yoke?
> Is it not to share your food with the hungry
>   and to provide the poor wanderer with shelter—
> when you see the naked, to clothe him,
>   and not to turn away from your own flesh and blood?
> Then your light will break forth like the dawn,
>   and your healing will quickly appear;
> then your righteousness will go before you,
>   and the glory of the LORD will be your rear guard.
> Then you will call, and the LORD will answer;
>   you will cry for help, and he will say: Here am I.
>
> "If you do away with the yoke of oppression,
>   with the pointing finger and malicious talk,
>   and if you spend yourselves in behalf of the hungry
>   and satisfy the needs of the oppressed,
> then your light will rise in the darkness,
>   and your night will become like the noonday."

Why did God say that when the people of Israel fed the hungry and clothed the naked, their light would rise in darkness? Because they were designed to give. If they gave to others, they would fulfill one of the central purposes of their lives, affirming the image of God within them and within others.

When we function on the basis of our design, life works better than when we try to deny our design. When we give, we are blessed and the community is blessed. Paul reminds us of this in his farewell address to his Ephesian friends, "In everything I did, I showed you that by this kind of hard work we must help the weak, remembering the words the Lord Jesus himself said: 'It is more blessed to give than to receive'" (Acts 20:35).

Obedience to God's Command

The third reason to give is out of obedience to God's command. Sometimes, most of the time, we do not function out of thankfulness. Sometimes we do not function because it is best for us. Well, God has provided a safety net to catch us when we fall. He says we are to give "because I command it!"

Christians often quote Jesus' words to his disciples in Matthew 26:11: "The poor you will always have with you." Too many Christians take this as an excuse not to care for the poor and needy, and few take the time to study the passage that Jesus was referring to in his statement. It comes from Deuteronomy 15:7–11, where God is calling his people to give generously to the poor people in their midst. The passage ends with these words: "There will always be poor people in the land. Therefore I command you to be openhanded toward your brothers and toward the poor and needy in your land." God's people are commanded to care for the poor and needy. It is not an option. Those Christians who misconstrue Jesus' words in order to serve their own selfishness fail to hear the heart and command of God.

It was said of Dr. Larry Ward, the founder of the Christian relief and development organization Food for the Hungry, that no one in the world had looked into more hungry faces than he had. Once during an interview, a reporter asked why Dr. Ward was so passionate about helping the poor and hungry. Was it because he had seen so many hungry people, the reporter asked? Larry Ward responded by holding up his Bible. He said it was because of this book. From beginning to end, the Bible tells of a compassionate God who loves the poor and who commands his people to care for the destitute and hungry.

So, we may give in thankfulness for God's grace in our lives, for the pragmatic reason that we were designed to do so, or out of obedience.

Let Wesley summarize:

I entreat you, in the name of the Lord Jesus, act up to the dignity of your calling! No more sloth! Whatsoever your hand findeth to do, do it with all your might! No more waste! Cut off every expense which fashion, caprice, or flesh and blood demand! No more covetousness! But employ whatever God has entrusted you with, in doing good, all possible good, in every possible kind and degree to the household of faith, to all men! This is no small part of "the wisdom of the just." Give all ye have, as well as all ye are, a spiritual sacrifice to Him who withheld not from you his Son, his only Son.[33]

As Wesley and other Protestant Reformers recognized, we are called to live as economic citizens of God's kingdom. We have been made not simply to be spiritual beings but also to be economic beings. As Christians before us have, let's embrace the biblical work ethic. Let's pursue a lifestyle of generous compassion.

CHAPTER 16

THE ECONOMICS OF GIVING:

GENEROUS COMPASSION

Grasping the economics of giving—so often misunderstood—is vital to walking in our *life*work. So before we move on from the biblical concept of stewardship found in John Wesley's three plain rules, I want to expand on the theme of generous giving.

GIVING: A REFLECTION OF GOD'S BIG AGENDA

Remembering that God has a big agenda—nothing less than reconciling all things to himself[1] and seeing all nations transformed through discipleship[2]—we are called to be nothing less than the ambassadors of his kingdom. It is our privilege and responsibility to give in a way that reflects God's big agenda.

THE KINSHIP TRIANGLE

There are three relationships that are at the heart of our giving. We are to give to God in worship, to creation in stewardship, and to our fellow human beings in charity.

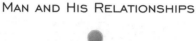

MAN AND HIS RELATIONSHIPS

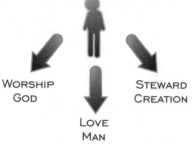

WORSHIP
GOD

STEWARD
CREATION

LOVE
MAN

To God in Worship

Paul writes of the generous giving of the Macedonians to the church in Jerusalem despite their own poverty: "They did not do as we expected, but they gave themselves first to the Lord and then to us in keeping with God's will" (2 Cor. 8:5).

The Puritan Richard Baxter wrote,

> Choose that employment or calling…in which you may be most serviceable to God. Choose not that in which you may be most rich or honorable in the world; but that in which you may do most good, and best escape sinning.[3]

What a wonderful picture! We are to choose work that allows us to maximize our use to God, and allows us the greatest opportunity for doing good in the larger community. Our work is to be such that it does not tempt us into overconsumption but facilitates our giving to the kingdom of God. Do we work for money? Or do we work for the kingdom? Are we kingdomizing our work to make the most good for the kingdom?

To Creation in Stewardship

We have seen that the cross of Christ restored the creation mandate. Our work and giving is meant to steward creation, first in doing no harm and second in pushing back natural evil. The creation is waiting "for the sons of God to be revealed," to be "brought into the glorious freedom of the children of God" (Rom. 8:19, 21). Our time, talents, resources, and lifestyle are to reflect our stewardship of creation.

To the Community in Charity

Because, through creation, we are related to the larger community, we have a responsibility for bringing kingdom culture—truth, justice, and beauty—into that community. Christ put the interests of others before his own, and we are called to follow his example.[4] When Jesus returns, he will judge how well we cared for the larger society through our labors as well as the fruit of our labors.[5]

Puritan William Perkins wrote,

> The main end of our lives ... is to serve God in the serving of men in the works of our callings.... Some man will say perchance: What, must we not labor in our callings to maintain our families? I answer: this must be done: but this is not the scope and end of our lives. The main end of our lives is to do service to God in serving of man.[6]

This is what Dr. Bob Moffitt of the Harvest Foundation has called the "Irreducible Minimum." If we boil down God's commandments to us to their very essence, the irreducible minimum is that we demonstrate our love and service to God by loving and serving man. The apostle John captures a portion of this in 1 John 3:17–18: "If anyone has material possessions and sees his brother in need but has no pity on him, how can the love of God be in him? Dear children, let us not love with words or tongue but with actions and in truth."

The prince of preachers, Charles Haddon Spurgeon, said,

> God's intent in endowing any person with more substance than he needs is that the man have the pleasurable office, or rather the delightful privilege, of relieving want and woe.[7]

When we give to God in worship, to creation in stewardship, and to our community in charity, we participate in the breadth of God's big agenda. Throughout this book we've explored our *life*work as both worship and stewardship. Here we'll focus on charity—generous giving to the community.

GIVING IS TO BE BASED ON REALITY

We live in a universe with fixed moral and metaphysical boundaries. The universe is *moral,* and thus we have a responsibility to be both "our brother's keeper" and stewards of creation. This stands in stark contrast to the amoral view of both secularism and animism.[8]

The universe is also an *open system*. It is open to the intervention of God, its Creator, as well as the intervention of angels, the demonic, and man. Because human beings have minds for problem solving and discovery, and hearts for imagination and invention, and because they are free moral agents,[9] resources are first and foremost a factor of human abilities, the product of human imagination and moral stewardship.[10]

The biblical concept that resources are first and foremost a factor of human abilities stands in contrast to secularism, or naturalism, in which there is no God, nor angels nor demons. In secularism, man is only a biological being, an animal—part of the great "cosmic machine." He is a consumer of resources. There is no transcendent reality. Nature is all there is. So the universe is a "closed system." In this paradigm, resources are limited. They are finite, only "in the ground." The economic "pie" is fixed—*zero-sum*.[11] As there are more and more people on the earth to share the pie, the pieces of the pie get smaller and smaller.

Most modern schemes of giving are based on this materialistic assumption. In this paradigm, how do you help the poor? What's left for us to do is simply to divvy up the slices of the pie. If one person's or one nation's slice of the pie is large, then another's is necessarily smaller. According to this thinking, the reason that the poor are poor is that the rich have too much of the pie. The way to help the poor is to redistribute the pie from the rich and give it to the poor. When I started my work for Food for the Hungry in 1981, this was the model I held for solving the problems of hunger and poverty.

But the biblical view of economics—born out of both biblical study and what I've experienced in nation after nation in the field—shows a universe that is *open*. Because God created the universe, it is "open" to his intervention. It is also open to the intrusion of angels, demons, and human beings. The physical creation is governed by physical laws, but God, angels and demons, and humankind can all impact this world by their decisions and actions. Because of this, economics is a *positive-sum* system (think of the principle of the seed in which a vast, unending harvest is delivered from a single seed). Wealth is not fixed; wealth is created. In this open system, resources are created and discovered and thus wealth can grow exponentially.

To be effective in our stewardship, we as Christians need to reject the naturalistic view of the universe in favor of our call in the cultural mandate to be subcreators, drawing out the potential that is latent in God's primary creation. We need to accept the biblical and practical evidence that managing God's household is not analogous to dividing up pieces of a finite pie.

Equally, in our consumer age we need to hear that the open nature of the universe does not mean that we can afford to be reckless or selfish with the resources that God has entrusted to our stewardship. There is a reason so many people are concerned about divvying up the pie: we are right to care about others; we are right to want all people to share the bounty of God's creation. This concern for justice and the well-being of others is the kernel of truth in the faulty "pie" paradigm.

Perhaps a graphic will help to explain what I am saying.

ECONOMIC PHILOSOPHY

	OPEN SYSTEM	CLOSED SYSTEM
MORAL UNIVERSE	OIKONOMIA (STEWARDSHIP OF CREATION)	IDEALISTIC SOCIALISM (MATERIAL MECHANICAL UNIVERSE)
AMORAL UNIVERSE	PREDATORY CAPITALISM (HEDONISTIC CONSUMERISM)	CLASSIC COMMUNISM (INSTITUTIONALIZED CONTROL)

Along the top of the graphic we have the open system of biblical theism and the closed system of atheistic materialism. Down the side we have the moral universe of biblical theism and the amoral universe of atheistic materialism.

Of the four quadrants of this graphic, which two are inconsistent with their assumptions? The upper right, which might be called idealistic socialism, and the lower left, which might be called predatory capitalism.

Idealistic socialism inconsistently marries a closed naturalistic system with a morality that can exist only if there is a transcendent, moral God. This morality brings a correct sense of responsibility to care for creation and our fellow man. But inconsistently it makes the materialist assumption that the universe is a closed system and thus resources are finite and human beings are seen as mouths to be fed. The solution to the problem of poverty, viewed from this paradigm, has to be the redistribution of resources. This socialistic solution is too often the solution of Christians working from a liberation theology or social gospel mindset. If we want to be economic citizens of

God's kingdom, we must ask if we are treating people who are poor as people, image bearers of God, with imagination for discovering and creating resources, or as a class of people who are simply "mouths to be fed."

The second inconsistent position is the view of many modern Westerners. It marries an atheistic, amoral universe with an open, transcendent system. Because the primary assumption is amoral, there is no responsibility to care for our neighbors and we are free to rape nature for our own conspicuous consumption. Incompatibly this position borrows from a memory of a biblical paradigm where wealth can be created. In the end, those who hold this view subscribe to the hedonistic mantra of "Eat, drink, and be merry, for tomorrow we die!" This is the focus of modern consumer-oriented economic systems. It is what the ancients called *chrematistics* and I call predatory capitalism.

When materialism recognizes no absolute moral code, it observes no restraints on how a person gains or uses wealth. Greed and corruption flourish in the gaining of wealth, and hedonism governs the use of the wealth. If we want to be economic citizens of God's kingdom, we will put ourselves honestly before two serious questions: How do we gain wealth? How do we use our wealth?

Going back to the graphic on page 193, the two quadrants that are consistent with their assumptions may be called classic communism or fascism, in the lower right quadrant, and stewardship economy, in the upper left quadrant. Classical communism or fascism is a social-economic system based on a consistent atheistic-materialistic paradigm. The universe is closed and there are no moral constraints. This scheme is closely aligned with social Darwinism—survival of the fittest—at its best (or worst). This system is all about power. We see failed models of this in the Third Reich in Germany and the Marxism of the Soviet Union.

The second consistent position is what the Bible and the ancients knew as the *oikonomia*. This can be called the stewardship economy of biblical theism. The system is open and the universe is moral. Therefore we are truly our brother's keeper and we are mandated to be moral stewards of God creation.

We said earlier that economics is the wise management of God's household with imagination and the stewardship of resources within the boundaries of God's laws. This means that there are moral constraints on how we gain and use wealth. In God's economy, gaining of wealth needs to take place within the framework of caring for creation, and the use of wealth must take place within the framework of caring for the larger community. This is important for us to hear in the midst of our materialistic culture.

Do we gain money and other resources honestly and without harm to self, family, neighbors, and the environment? And do we spend what we've gained on ourselves or include others in our bounty, and for the sake of Christ and his kingdom?

How do we take into account the humanity of people who are poor when we engage in sharing our gains? Because all human beings are made in the image of God, they are not just mouths to feed; they are people with minds and hearts to be given opportunity to reach their God-given potential as developers of their communities, creators of godly culture. They may use their minds and hearts to create their own bounty and exercise moral stewardship to share that bounty with their neighbors and to care for creation.

When we develop our ministries or create charities or practice personal charity in caring for our neighbor, are we consciously seeking to function from the reality of an open system and a moral universe?

PRINCIPLES OF COMPASSION

It is a truism that God's character informs all the good things of life. When we think of articulating principles of generous giving, we need look no further than to that character. God's nature should always inform principles of ministry.

One of the books that proved instrumental in my own journey of understanding was Dr. Marvin Olasky's *The Tragedy of American Compassion*.[12] Olasky traces how the American concept of compassion changed as we moved from a biblical worldview to an atheistic-materialistic worldview. Olasky's book has been one of the profound shapers of my own thinking. One of the chapters in the book is titled "Seven Marks of Compassion," and it shows principles of an older generation of compassion workers who functioned from a biblical paradigm.

Daniel A. Bazikian has written a review of Dr. Olasky's book for the Foundation for Economic Education. His review summarizes the seven marks derived from biblical principles:

> "The Seven Marks of Compassion" constitutes the heart of [Olasky's] study and of his critique. Seven basic ideas motivated the charity workers of a century ago: *affiliation,* that is keeping the individual's family, religious, or community ties strong so as to strengthen his sense of belonging; *bonding,* or developing a close personal relationship between the charity volunteer and the recipient, in order to coax and encourage the latter to self-sufficient status; *categorization,* or assigning individuals to different categories of need (e.g., the need for continuous relief, relief on a temporary basis, aid in a job search, or just designating someone as unfit for relief due to unwillingness to work); along with this went *discernment,* the willingness to separate worthy objects of charity from fraudulent ones; seeking the goal of long-term *employment* of all able-bodied heads of household so as to instill self-sufficiency and responsibility

in the individual; placing emphasis on *freedom,* or the ability to work without governmental restrictions so as to improve one's lot in life over a period of time; finally, recognizing the relationship of the person to *God,* since men and women had spiritual as well as physical needs.

The presence of these principles gave traditional charities their great strength. Conversely, their absence in contemporary charity does so much to explain the spiritual and moral poverty of American compassion and its tragic social consequences: the decline in upward mobility of the poor; the weakened state of private charity; and the disintegrating state of marriage. These principles, Olasky contends, need to be re-inserted and reintegrated into programs to aid the poor.[13]

As God's people, let's not participate in the tragedy Olasky describes. We are to be a people of compassion, and it matters that we articulate and apply *biblical* principles of compassion, because people, cultures, and charities become like the God or god(s) they worship.

The wellspring of compassion is the heart of God. In fact, it can be said that a world without Christ is a world with limited compassion. God manifested his compassion in the incarnation, when Christ, the suffering servant, "came alongside" the people in their need.

Count Zinzendorf, who led the influential Moravian renewal in Germany in the eighteenth century, was stirred by the Domenico Feti masterpiece *Ecce Homo,* "Behold the Man." The painting depicts Christ before Pilate and the Jewish mob, wearing his crown of thorns. Beneath the famous picture were inscribed the words "This have I done for thee; What hast thou done for me?" From the moment he read these words, Zinzendorf took as his life motto "I have but one passion, and that is He and only He."[14]

When I first read this, it struck me to the core of my being. How do I answer the question, "This have I done for thee; What hast thou done for me?"

Christians, recognizing they are made in the image of God, and in gratitude for God's compassion, are called to "suffer with" those in need. God chooses to manifest his compassion through his people. Scripture is replete with admonitions to represent the extravagant compassion of God, not simply by giving money but by identifying with and serving the poor. Examples abound.

We read in Isaiah 58:6–7,

Is not this the kind of fasting I have chosen:
to loose the chains of injustice
    and untie the cords of the yoke ...?

Is it not to share your food with the hungry
  and to provide the poor wanderer with shelter—
when you see the naked, to clothe him,
  and not to turn away from your own flesh and blood?

The well-known story of the Good Samaritan in Luke 10 is also a perfect word picture of the compassion that God longs to see in his people. This passage changes the word *neighbor* from a noun to a verb.[15]

In Matthew 25:34–36, Jesus reinforces the need for Christians to act neighborly when he describes what he will be looking for when he returns:

> Then the King will say to those on his right, "Come, you who are blessed by my Father; take your inheritance, the kingdom prepared for you since the creation of the world. For I was hungry and you gave me something to eat, I was thirsty and you gave me something to drink, I was a stranger and you invited me in, I needed clothes and you clothed me, I was sick and you looked after me, I was in prison and you came to visit me."

When we live out Christ's compassion, the result is striking. During the third century, Emperor Julian recognized that the early Christians were a whole new breed of people. Compassion did not exist as a concept in the Greco-Roman world until Christians came along. Julian wrote,

> [Christian faith] has been specially advanced through the loving service rendered to strangers, and through their care for the burial of the dead. It is a scandal that there is not a single Jew who is a beggar, and that the godless Galileans care not only for their own poor but for ours as well; while those who belong to us look in vain for the help that we should render them.[16]

We can be inspired by the story of the generous giving of merchant Stephen Girard of Philadelphia in the 1790s, as related by Marvin Olasky:

> Born in France in 1750, Girard left home as a boy, sailed for a dozen years, settled in Philadelphia at the start of the Revolution, and accumulated a fortune in the shipping business over the next two decades. But it was his work during the yellow fever epidemic of 1793, rather than his business acumen, that won him wide renown. Girard, who had received previous exposure to the disease, took charge of and paid bills for a hospital during that and subsequent epidemics. But he also spent months nursing the inmates himself, and supplied

food and fuel to sufferers and their families. Later, he took many orphans into his own home, and upon his death made a bequest that established a school for poor orphan boys.[17]

Each of these scriptures and examples reflects that we are to give ourselves—our time and talent—as well as our treasure. God's compassion made great demands on him; he sacrificed his son. Generosity of compassion is measured not by the amount of dollars given but by Scripture's admonitions to represent the extravagant compassion of God by identifying with and serving the poor. As Professor Robert Thompson of the University of Pennsylvania wrote in the late nineteenth century,

> You can judge the scale on which any scheme of help for the needy stands by this single quality, Does it make great demands on men to give themselves to their brethren?[18]

LESSONS FROM THE BOOK OF RUTH

Finally let's take a lesson from Scripture on how we can best give help to those in need. The story of Ruth and Boaz beautifully demonstrates biblical giving:

> At mealtime Boaz said to her, "Come over here. Have some bread and dip it in the wine vinegar." When she sat down with the harvesters, he offered her some roasted grain. She ate all she wanted and had some left over. As she got up to glean, Boaz gave orders to his men, "Even if she gathers among the sheaves, don't embarrass her. Rather, pull out some stalks for her from the bundles and leave them for her to pick up, and don't rebuke her." (Ruth 2:14–16)

The Moabite Ruth was among the poorest of the poor in her day. During a major famine in Israel, her husband's family had fled as refugees to Moab, where she joined the family. After about ten years Ruth's husband, father-in-law, and brother-in-law all died, so Ruth accompanied her mother-in-law, Naomi, when she returned to Israel.

In this foreign land, Ruth came destitute to the house of Boaz. It is to be noted that Boaz treated her personally, as a human being. He invited her to eat in his home. After the meal he devised provision for Ruth and Naomi. The way he does this is very instructive. Our dignity is tied up with our work. If you strip a person of his or her work, you strip the person of his or her dignity. So Boaz followed God's injunction[19] for landowners to leave unharvested margins—gleanings for the poor to harvest. Rather than do the easy thing for himself and Ruth (have his laborers bring bundles of harvested grain to give to her), Boaz chose to allow Ruth to labor for her sustenance. He instructed his laborers to return to the field and "pull out some stalks for her from the bundles and leave them for her to pick up." Boaz was concerned for Ruth's physical health but also for her dignity. If he stripped her of that, he would actually leave her in greater poverty.

This portion of the wonderful and tender story of Ruth illustrates one of God's principles of compassion: that the poor are to be cared for, but also that their dignity is to be preserved in the provision.

Let us put these biblical principles firmly in our minds as we consider our role as compassionate givers, a mark of the *life*work of a Christian.

We will now turn our attention to the potential of our *life*work for advancing the kingdom of God in our communities and nations through our participation in the domains of society: the exciting arenas to which we may be called, such as business, the arts, education, and science.

PART 6 : INTO THE WORLD

CHAPTER 17

THE KINGDOM ADVANCES FROM THE INSIDE OUT

The kingdoms of this world expand their territories through warfare, bloodshed, and colonialism. Unlike the kingdoms of this world, the kingdom of God does not invade a country militarily in order to impose a godly culture—that is, a culture that reflects the true nature of God and his creation.

A quotation attributed to the Russian novelist Alexander Solzhenitsyn reminds us what the Bible makes clear:[1] "The line between good and evil is drawn not between nations or parties, but through every human heart." We will not see societies transformed until we see the human heart transformed. Jesus illustrated this in his discussion with the inquiring Nicodemus: "I tell you the truth, no one can see the kingdom of God unless he is born again" (John 3:3).

The transformation of nations takes place as Christians of all stripes are obedient to God's ordinances, love their neighbors, serve their communities, engage in the marketplace of ideas, and share in word and deed the good news of Jesus Christ. These words and deeds create an opportunity for individuals and ultimately communities and nations to become forces for the kingdom of God.

The transformation of one human being works its way outward, through the institutions of the family and the church, into the structures and institutions of communities, nations, and, eventually, the world. Jesus painted a picture of the spreading, infusing, transforming extension of the kingdom as he compared it to yeast: "The kingdom of heaven is like yeast that a woman took and mixed into a large amount of flour until it worked all through the dough" (Matt. 13:33). Each of us is tied to this mysterious transformation.

As we consider both the setting and the substance of our *life*work, we can imagine any culture as a series of concentric circles. The innermost circle is the individual human heart and mind. The surrounding circles represent, in order, the family, the church, the nation, and the world.

THE PROCESS OF KINGDOM ADVANCEMENT

INDIVIDUAL
FAMILY
CHURCH COMMUNITY
THE NATION
THE WORLD

THE HUMAN HEART

The first and fundamental battle for the advancement of the kingdom of God is within the human heart. One observer has noted, "God's law must be written on the individual's heart, then later on the stone tablets of the institutions of society."[2] When a war is waged, the attacking army needs to determine the first point of engagement. In the Old Testament account of the conquest of Canaan, the initial point of invasion was at the battle of Jericho. The offensive for the heart of a nation begins with the battle for the heart of the individual citizens. We see this in that Jesus Christ himself invades the heart and calls us to a new nature[3] and a new order—the kingdom of God. It is the work of the Holy Spirit and the winsomeness of the deeds and words of Christians that are the key to the opening of other human hearts.

God uses many ways to reach the human heart, but it is important to remember that in most contexts the entrance to human hearts is through the demonstration of God's love, which represents nothing less than our service to Christ himself.[4] Do we seek to advance God's kingdom? Then we must go to the place where people are wounded. God is a God of compassion. He wants to meet people at the place where they are bleeding. This is the meaning of the Samaritan Strategy—God's plan for his people to show compassion to people at their point of need.[5]

Another critical piece of the believer's winsomeness is to manifest kingdom culture—truth, beauty, and justice. People who are enslaved by ignorance and lies are longing for someone to bring knowledge and truth to them. People who are surrounded by darkness and drabness long to see beauty. People who are crushed by corruption long for justice. The key to the human heart is to demonstrate God's love and to manifest his truth, beauty, and justice.

Once our hearts have been regenerated through the power of the Holy Spirit—once we have been "born again"—we are to be given opportunity to enroll in God's "Bible school." The call to repentance is the call to be (literally) "re-minded" from "hollow and deceptive philosophy, which depends on human tradition and the basic principles of this world rather than on Christ" (Col. 2:8). We are called to love God not only with our whole heart (emotions) but also with our entire mind. The apostle Paul reminds us to "not conform any longer to the pattern of this world, but be transformed by the renewing of [the] mind" (Rom. 12:2). We are to begin a lifelong journey to consciously uncover assumptions that do not align with God's Word and replace them with biblical truth. Human behavior will change only as our minds are transformed by the biblical worldview. There will be transformation in families and societies when human minds and behaviors are turned toward God.

People all over the world long for communities and nations that reflect justice, beauty, and truth. But you cannot have justice in the community until there is the concept of justice in the mind. You cannot have beauty in the community until there is beauty in the heart. You cannot have truth in the community until there is truth in the mind. People long to see their communities and nations develop. But this development occurs when there is renewal in the hearts and minds of a critical mass of people—renewal that will work its way outward into society.

There are three fundamental institutions in any society: the family, the church, and the civil government. We will look at the family and the church in this chapter and examine government in chapter 19.

THE FAMILY

The family is God's first fundamental institution. It exists to fulfill in two ways the creation mandate given in Genesis. The first is the *social function* of the mandate—fill the earth with image bearers of God, to create extended families, communities, and ultimately nations of people. The second is the *developmental function* of the mandate—to be stewards of creation.

It is the parents' responsibility, not the state's, to nurture and educate children, to prepare them to live as free and productive citizens in society. This education is to feed the soul through developing the intellect to be inquisitive and innovative. Parents prepare their children's hearts for creativity and their wills for virtue. Parents have the wonderful opportunity to shape the next generation of a nation's citizens and leaders. If parents do this well, the family will be healthy and the nations will prosper morally and materially. There will be social peace, economic sufficiency, and civic justice. If the family is not healthy, the society will become increasingly dysfunctional, corrupt, and impoverished.

The modern Western world is dominated by both individualism and self-absorption. Because of this, we find on the micro level a disintegration of the family and on the national level the growth of an antimaternal movement that is resulting in cultural suicide through many of the nations of Europe.[6]

So if we want to see a nation transformed, it must first begin with the internal transformation of individuals and then move outward to the immediate and extended families. From there it moves to the next fundamental institution, the community of believers, the church.

THE CHURCH

The church is God's chosen community, selected to advance his kingdom on earth. Unlike the government, which is to "wield the sword"—protect the nation and provide for social peace and justice—the church is to use the "sword of the Spirit, which is the word of God" (Eph. 6:17). It is God's essential agent for the development of communities and the building of nations.

The mission of the church is to lead humankind to its final destiny, revealing the hidden plan of God through the ages. The apostle Paul speaks of the mystery of the ages, the divine purpose of the church:

> The mystery of Christ, which was not made known to men in other generations …is that through the gospel the Gentiles are heirs together with Israel, members together of one body, and sharers together in the promise in Christ Jesus.
>
> I became a servant of this gospel…to make plain to everyone the administration of this mystery, which for ages past was kept hidden in God, who created all things. His intent was that now, *through the church,* the manifold wisdom of God should be made known to the rulers and authorities in the heavenly realms, according to his eternal purpose which he accomplished in Christ Jesus our Lord. (Eph. 3:4–11; italics added)

God has a goal for people and nations. The church, in all her finiteness and weakness, is the bride of Christ and the ordained steward of that purpose. She is called to incarnate—"put flesh on"—the Word of God before a watching world. As the church manifests the right-side-up values of the kingdom of God through acts of obedience and service in society, the society will be impacted and significantly healed.

We will explore further the role of the church in societal transformation in chapter 22.

THE WORLD

Leaving the discussion of civil government and the nation to a later chapter, we now come to the outer circle of the kingdom advancement, the "world." How are we to think of this outermost circle? Too often we simply picture a globe in our mind's eye. But let's be more specific. First we will look at the extent of the Great Commission, and second we will look at the extent of the task in our societies.

The Great Commission

When I was a young Christian, I had the impression that the Great Commission was one thing: go into all the world, preach the gospel, and save souls for heaven. You can see, by the nature of this book, that my mind has been expanded on this issue in a very dramatic way.

First, as we have seen previously, God has a big agenda. Paul states that Christ died on the cross to reconcile *all things,* in heaven and earth, to himself.[7] This includes my soul and your soul, but Christ's death was for reconciling all things.

Second, the Great Commission is comprehensive. There are three passages in the Bible where Christ gives the commission; they are Acts 1:8, Matthew 28:18–20, and Mark 16:15. Each provides us with a different facet of the Lord's commission. These may be called the three dimensions of the Great Commission.

THREE DIMENSIONS OF THE GREAT COMMISSION

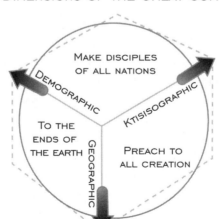

Acts 1:8 reveals that we are to take the gospel to Jerusalem, to Judea, to Samaria, and to the "ends of the earth." This is a *geographic* commission calling for the gospel to travel around the world. It is a horizontal perspective of the Great Commission.

In Matthew 28:18–20, there is a different focus: "make disciples of all nations." Note that the focus here is not individual souls. The Greek word for *nations* is *ethne;* it means people group or ethnic group. Note as well that it does not say "evangelize"; it says "disciple." Of course evangelism often precedes discipleship. But you can evangelize people and never disciple them. Here Christ is telling us to disciple nations. The gospel is not only to go around the world but also to penetrate culture. This is the vertical aspect of the Great Commission; it is the *demographic* component of the mandate. We will discuss this more below.

The Gospel of Mark has a very different perspective. Here Christ tells us to "preach the good news to all *creation!*"[8] Again, it does not say souls. And in this text it does not say nations. This is the Greek word *ktisis*—creature or creation. We might coin the term *ktisisographic* to describe this perspective of the Great Commission. God is interested in all of his creation. Remember, Christ died to reconcile all things to himself.[9] Paul reminds us of this when he says that all creation is waiting redemption.[10] The apostle John says it this way: "For God so loved the world [*kosmos*—universe] that he gave his one and only Son" (John 3:16).

So as we think of the Great Commission, we must understand that it is a comprehensive mandate that goes to the ends of the earth, penetrates culture, and brings good news for all creation.

All the Domains of Society

In the final step of unfolding God's kingdom, we want to go back and focus on the vertical component of the Great Commission. How does the church disciple a nation? She penetrates the nation's culture with kingdom culture—truth, beauty, and goodness. She brings biblical order and principles into all spheres of society. This is done as the people of God live *coram Deo*—before the face of God—in all areas of their lives. As this happens, the biblical worldview will flow through the church, outward to the world. As believers, our engagement with the world is determined to a large extent by our specific callings in life—our vocations. We have the opportunity to examine our lives, understand our gifts, and recognize God-given opportunities to exercise them for the advancement of his kingdom. Most Christians will be called into small arenas, where we exercise some degree of influence. By God's grace we have the ability to mature in our abilities for the glory of Christ and his kingdom.

Every valid vocational area offers unique opportunities to advance God's kingdom. Christians engaged in politics and legislation can acknowledge God as the supreme authority and his laws as the highest laws. Christian businesspeople can work with honesty and integrity. Christian doctors can defend the sanctity of human life and bring healing to their patients. Christian artists can reflect God's nature and the glory of his creation through their art. Christians engaged in science can seek to understand the intricacies of God's created order and develop innovations to help fight hunger and disease. In all cases, Christians are to be citizens looking for opportunities to provide leadership and service in the neighborhood and community and, in doing so, represent the "right-side-up" culture of God's kingdom. Some Christians will bring about institutional reform within their vocations—reform that is consistent with the kingdom of God. Others will respond to God's calling to confront institutionalized evil within their cultures. In all cases, Christians' activities must be linked to the message and power of the gospel and to the understanding that the kingdom advances from the "inside out."[11]

Where can we be agents of cultural change? The possibilities are nearly endless. Remember what we read earlier from Dallas Willard:

> If he [Jesus] were to come today as he did then, he could carry out his mission through most any decent and useful occupation. He could be a clerk or accountant in a hardware store, a computer repairman, a banker, an editor, doctor, waiter, teacher, farmhand, lab technician, or construction worker. He could run a housecleaning service or repair automobiles.
>
> In other words, if he were to come today he could very well do what you do. He could very well live in your apartment or house, hold down your job.[12]

In the next chapter we'll draw wisdom from Scripture for living out our callings in the "gates of the city," and in chapters 19 and 20 we'll explore the vast potential for meaningful, life-giving, and transforming work in the modern domains.

CHAPTER 18

THE GATES
OF THE CITY

As we have seen, God's work of redemption—his advancement of his kingdom—works from the inside out. Like yeast working its transforming way all the way through dough, the transformation of an individual's heart and mind by God works its way outward into the family, into Christ's church, and through the church into the world at large.

TAKING RESPONSIBILITY FOR THE GATES

Borrowing a metaphor (and a reality) from biblical times, the concept of "the gates of the city" expresses the setting of our *life*work. As citizens of God's kingdom, we are to occupy the gates of our cities as his stewards through our *life*work. For us, the purpose of gatekeeping is not to command and control society. Rather, it is to send servant leaders into the marketplace and public square to bring truth, beauty, and justice into our societies. In occupying its gates, the kingdom of God can be made manifest in the city.

This metaphorical application of the concept of city gates comes from the very real-world importance of these structures in Bible times. The gates of the city played a critical social and civic function in the ancient world. Throughout history, when the Jews erected fences and walls to delineate the boundaries of their property, gates were built at strategic places along the walls to provide access. When the Jews were nomadic, they had gates at the entrances of their camps.[1] And when they were living in the Promised Land, they had gates to the royal palace,[2] to the temple,[3] and especially into the cities.[4] All kinds of public life and discourse took place at these gates, in addition to providing for the defense of a city. Reference to "the gates" might also refer to the area around the gates, to the land just inside and outside the gates. In fact, people often used the term *the gates* for the city as a whole.

Today, our societies are languishing because the metaphorical gates of our cities have largely been abandoned by the very people who can bring the person of Christ and the transforming power of the gospel into the lifeblood of society. God wants the descendants of Abraham to occupy the gates of the cities for the purpose of blessing the nations.[5] When we combine this calling with being Christians who have a gospel that saves, redeems, renews, and restores, and with the worldview of Scripture, which instructs us about working out its transforming vision for the world through our callings in every area of life, then we get a glimpse of the potential. Vision like this has brought unprecedented economic development, political freedom, the rule of law, and the concept of universal education into much of the world. It has brought the emancipation of slaves and dignity to women. In other words, it has given humankind its humanity.

Christian stewardship of "the gates," therefore, is vital for the life of our societies. Whoever takes responsibility for the gates will set the agenda for the health or destruction of society.

THE GATES AS THE PLACE OF PUBLIC LIFE

The setting for much of our *life*work can be pictured as the gates of the city—the place of public life in Bible times. In many European and Latin American cities, the city square has been the place of public life. The town's church or cathedral could be found on one side of the square and local government buildings on another, with stalls for markets and commerce located elsewhere around the square. This is where the public life of the city took place. In the Western world today, the "high streets" of towns in Britain and Europe and the downtown areas of American cities perform a similar function, as do large suburban sports arenas, which are often hired for public events such as political conventions, trade shows, religious gatherings, and music concerts and other forms of entertainment.

The vital aspects of public life that occurred at the gates of a city in biblical times include the following:

- transacting business and commerce[6]
- listening to the reading of the Law[7]
- hearing and settling legal disputes[8]
- maintaining governance and civic administration[9]
- hearing news and public announcements[10]
- attending public meetings and having public discourse[11]

In each of these areas of public life, Scripture gives us insights into ways Christians can be faithful with their work in "the gates of the city." Let's explore life in the ancient city gates with an eye out for fresh and creative ideas for thinking about our own callings today.

Business and Commerce

The gates of the city were places of business and commerce. Some gates were named for the major markets that took place at them, such as the Sheep Gate (Neh. 3:1), the Fish Gate (Neh. 3:3), and the Horse Gate (Neh. 3:28). Second Kings 7:1 describes the marketing of flour and barley. We can imagine vendors, with their stalls of goods and their kiosks of food, spices, and household implements, bartering and selling their products around the city gates. To this day, the old city of Jerusalem (the area of Jerusalem contained in the ancient walls) retains some of the names of the gates. One is the Dung Gate,[12] where refuse from the ancient city passed on its way to be burned outside the walls. The Sheep Gate is now also known as the Lion's Gate and St. Stephen's Gate.

Much larger business transactions, such as the buying and selling of property, also occurred at the gates. In Genesis, it was at "the gate of his city" where Abraham struck a deal with a man named Ephron and for "four hundred shekels of silver" purchased some real estate where he would bury his beloved wife Sarah (Gen. 23:1–20). Characteristics of a modern business transaction can be found in this story: it was private property, a "survey" of the property was given, there was public discussion and open negotiations to establish a fair market price, money changed hands, and there were witnesses to the transaction. Public transactions like this made it difficult for fraud, corruption, or false scales, a reminder that business transactions are to be just, clean, and fair. Business was a godly activity. Enterprise was encouraged and wealth generated.

Today as well, some are called to the gates of the city as marketplace Christians to ensure that the markets are free and just. Marketplace Christians can do business with integrity. They can occupy the gates of the city with truth and justice, service and provision, creativity and innovation.

SHERRON WATKINS'S STORY

Raised in the obscure town of Tomball, Texas, by parents who were secondary-school teachers, Sherron Watkins was an accountant (what some people lightly refer to as a "bean-counter") whose gifts and skills led her to become the vice president of corporate development for the now-infamous Enron Corporation. At the time, Enron was the seventh largest company in the United States. A member of the First Presbyterian Church of Houston, Texas, Sherron had a heart to live out her faith at work but had no idea what this would mean.

In 2001, after working at Enron for eight years, Watkins became concerned with the financial health of the company. She came to realize that much of the company's wealth was built through fraud. When the hoax was exposed, the company would likely collapse. Sherron watched as a good friend and coworker, the company treasurer Jeff McMahon, was punished by his boss, CEO Jeffrey Skilling, when he tried to expose the accounting problems in Enron. Sherron did not want to be punished if she were to speak up. But what should she do? She wanted to do what was right. She wanted to be a person of integrity.

Watkins was afraid to speak publicly. So she wrote an anonymous letter detailing her concerns and dropped it in a company suggestion box. Noting happened. So in August of 2001, in order to "do the right thing," she wrote a seven-page letter to Ken Lay, the Chairman of the Board of Enron. The letter detailed her charges concerning the financial hoax perpetuated on the public, employees, and shareholders. Watkins then hand carried the letter to Ken Lay. At the time, Sherron did not know that two days before, Lay had sold his stock in the company for a cool $1.5 million profit. As it turned out, Skilling and Lay were at the heart of the fraud. Enron soon collapsed, bringing down the once-reputable accounting firm Arthur Andersen with it.

Five months later, after Enron collapsed, Watkins's letter became part of the public record, and Sherron became a hero to millions of people around the world for standing and confronting Lay with the truth of what was happening at Enron. There had been a profound moral failure in the leadership and culture of Enron. People were more interested in short-term economic gain than in truth, accountability, and the long-term health of the company.

This moral failure, if endemic in American citizens, will end up bringing down the country. (Great civilizations are not often conquered from without but die from within from moral and spiritual bankruptcy.) One woman had the moral character and courage to confront the problem. For this, she was recognized as one of *Time* magazine's three Persons of the Year for 2002. Her picture made the cover of *Time* twice that year. Watkins had no desire for notoriety; as a Christian, she simply wanted to do the right thing, even if it meant losing her job.

The Reading of the Law

The city gates were also places where the Law was read, such as in Nehemiah 8:

> All the people assembled as one man in the square before the Water Gate. They told Ezra the scribe to bring out the Book of the Law of Moses, which the Lord had commanded for Israel. So on the first day of the seventh month Ezra the priest brought the Law before the assembly, which was made up of men and women and all who were able to understand. He read it aloud from daybreak till noon as he faced the square before the Water Gate in the presence of the men, women and others who could understand. And all the people listened attentively to the Book of the Law.... On the second day of the month, the heads of all the families, along with the priests and the Levites, gathered around Ezra the scribe to give attention to the words of the Law. (Neh. 8:1–3, 13)

The square before the Water Gate was large enough for all the people of the city to gather in one place. Note that they gathered "as one man," both "men and women." There was unity among them. And there was to be no distinction before the Law; both men and women were to listen to its reading. Both men and women were to be responsible citizens.

Notice also that the Law was read in a public place. Why? The reason is that the reading of God's Law, for them, was not merely a private, religious event. The Book of the Law was given to the Hebrews to help them to be good stewards of their nation. That is, the Law of the Lord laid a foundation for a just society, providing the foundation for individual character development and for civil law, both of which are vital for building a just society.

Modern democratic societies are based on the rule of law, but instead of being based on God's Law, they have often instituted laws of their own making because of selfish or pragmatic considerations or because of the strong pressures of secularism and shifting perceptions of "the public good." In reality, God's laws are always for the true public good. They lead without fail to justice and life.

In the United States, because many people have forgotten or not been taught that biblical laws helped to formulate a large and vital part of our judicial system, controversy easily arises. For instance, in 2001, Alabama Supreme Court Justice Roy Moore had a large granite monument of the Ten Commandments installed and displayed overnight in the rotunda of the Alabama State Judicial Building, where a number of courts and the state's law library reside and where Judge Moore presided. He believed that it was of paramount importance to acknowledge and pay tribute to the Ten

Commandments as a historical reality and the moral foundations for the system of laws that has made America one of the most just nations in the world. Legal, political, and religious battles ensued on both sides of this issue to determine whether the monument could stay or must be removed. In November 2002 a U.S. District Court ruled against the monument, claiming that it violated the Establishment Clause of the First Amendment to the U.S. Constitution. When Chief Justice Moore refused to obey a federal court order to remove the monument, a legal ethics panel voted to remove him from the bench. Moore's subsequent appeals failed, with the U.S. Supreme Court deciding not to consider the case.

Yet Moore's stance has prompted debate all across the nation, among Christians and non-Christians alike. Despite the personal and professional cost, as noted in his book *So Help Me God,* former Chief Justice Moore stands firm in his conviction that "by refusing to follow the unlawful demands of a federal judge, he denied the rule of man and upheld the Constitution of the United States, the true rule of law, as his oath required."[13] Like Martin Luther King Jr., who was jailed for civil disobedience, Moore made a knowing choice many reformers have made, positively accepting the legal consequences of his actions. As the issues brought into the public eye by Moore continue to be debated by the people and courts of the United States, Judge Moore could be considered a twenty-first century gatekeeper for law and justice in America. Whether we work within the judicial system as Moore did or in another domain altogether, God calls all of us to be responsible citizens and good stewards of our nations in light of the law of the Lord.

Legal Disputes

In addition to being the place for the public reading of the law, the city gates were places for settling legal disputes. When God led the people out of Egypt into the wilderness, he instituted a system of governance and justice that functioned through a delegation of authority, with leaders and officials being appointed by Moses "over thousands, hundreds, fifties and tens" (Exod. 18:25). This delegation of authority arose as a result of Moses being burnt out from trying (foolishly) to resolve everyone's disputes himself (as we read earlier in Exodus 18). This is how an effective system of justice was begun for ancient Israel. Not long afterward, "judges and officers" were assigned to settle disputes at the gates. In Deuteronomy 16:18–20 we read,

> Appoint judges and officials for each of your tribes in every town [sha'ar: gate] the LORD your God is giving you, and they shall judge the people fairly. Do not pervert justice or show partiality. Do not accept a bribe, for a bribe blinds the eyes of the wise and twists the words of the righteous. Follow justice and

justice alone, so that you may live and possess the land the LORD your God
is giving you.

A number of principles are established in this passage. Each city is to have its own judge,
and everyone should have access to a fair trial. Gifts and bribes are taboo, because this
perverts justice. And because God "shows no partiality" (Deut. 10:17), judges should be
impartial. Such principles are particularly vital for the poor, who, simply because they
are poor, may have no access to justice. For instance, because they lack money, they may
lack legal power to redress injustices committed against them. In our day, we would say
that "they cannot afford an attorney." The prophet Amos warns against leaving the poor
to face injustice (note, too, that the poor have come to the gate to seek justice):

> You hate the one who reproves in court [sha'ar: gate]
>   and despise him who tells the truth.
> You trample on the poor
>   and force him to give you grain.
> Therefore, though you have built stone mansions,
>   you will not live in them;
> though you have planted lush vineyards,
>   you will not drink their wine.
> For I know how many are your offenses
>   and how great your sins.
>
> You oppress the righteous and take bribes
>   and you deprive the poor of justice in the courts [sha'ar: gate].
> Therefore the prudent man keeps quiet in such times,
>   for the times are evil.
>
> Seek good, not evil,
>   that you may live.
> Then the LORD God Almighty will be with you,
>   just as you say he is.
> Hate evil, love good;
>   maintain justice in the courts.
> Perhaps the LORD God Almighty will have mercy
>   on the remnant of Joseph. (Amos 5:10–15)

In this setting, the nation has exchanged the truth of God for a lie and the worship
of the living God for the worship of idols. This false worship is not without consequences

in the courts. From the worship of pagan gods, justice gets perverted through bribery and other means. Thus the poor are made poorer and are further oppressed, because the judge takes bribes. Note, too, that in Amos 5:15 the righteous are not to stay away from the gates because of the corruption there. In fact, it is precisely because of the corruption that they are to get righteously involved. They are to go into the courts fighting evil, loving good, and establishing justice.

Unfortunately, in many materialistic societies, the legal profession becomes a means to stir up inordinate amounts of litigation to secure large incomes for the lawyers. Too often in today's world Christians join others in society in entering law only because it is financially lucrative. These Christians live a divided life, separating their faith from their work.

Christians can be called by God to work in the court systems. Judges, lawyers, legal aids, and other legal experts can work to bring justice and to serve as advocates for the poor and the oppressed. Some lawyers are court-appointed to defend people who don't have the money to hire their own lawyers; these legal representatives don't get rich, but they work for justice. Other lawyers work some of their cases pro bono, without charge, dedicated to seeing that justice is served for the poor. Even ordinary citizens can work or volunteer as court companions for children in the court system, becoming their advocate and a constant familiar face in the intimidating legal system. Clearly, working in the legal system can be a sacred calling.

Governing and Administration

Today in animistic cultures, the chief's palace is the place where all major decisions are made for the good of the community. The equivalent in Bible times was the city gate, which functioned as a seat of government. Scripture therefore speaks of the "elders at the gate" (Deut. 21:19; 25:7) whose function was to influence and provide civil oversight of the city. A simple biblical example is found in Proverbs 31:23: "Her husband is respected at the city gate, where he takes his seat among the elders of the land." Here the elders gather at the gate to oversee the affairs of the city, and this man is respected for his abilities. Daniel 2:47–49 is a striking illustration of governance at the gates:

> The king said to Daniel, "Surely your God is the God of gods and the Lord of kings and a revealer of mysteries, for you were able to reveal this mystery."
>
> Then the king placed Daniel in a high position and lavished many gifts on him. He made him ruler over the entire province of Babylon and placed him in charge of all its wise men. Moreover, at Daniel's request the king appointed Shadrach, Meshach and Abednego administrators over the province of Babylon, while Daniel himself remained at the royal court [tera': Chaldean for "gate"].

The king of Babylon acknowledged the God of the universe and recognized that Daniel served this God. Nebuchadnezzar then appointed Daniel to rule over the entire province of Babylon, making him the head over all the other governors, what today we might call a prime minister. Daniel took his appointed place in the gate of the city, from which the king governed the people through Daniel. Note also that Daniel secured positions in the government for three other qualified and godly men: Shadrach, Meshach, and Abednego (see also Dan. 1:17).

In modern life, godly men and women need to stand ready to serve in government, either at a local level, such as on the school board or the city council, at the state or provincial level, or even at the national level. By this I don't mean that Christians need only to become politicians or elected officials. Elected officials need many kinds of assistants and associates working with them, and Christians can occupy for the kingdom in such positions.

In much of the world today where the gospel of salvation has gone forth, some Christians, unfortunately, seek positions in government merely for the sake of gaining political power. There may also be a sense of triumphalism in Christian views of governance. For instance, people may think, "If only we can get a Christian into the presidency, then all the nation's problems would be solved." It is enough to look at Kenya, Guatemala, and South Korea, where evangelical Christians have gotten into positions of political power and have been corrupted by that power, to see that simply having Christian leaders does not guarantee transformation in a nation.

Political power may also corrupt in other ways. My Ghanaian friend Chris Ampadu has said that in some societies in Africa, after one is made a traditional chief, he becomes adored, and his views are suddenly considered to be always right. The chief must be respected by all, and there is to be no internal dissent or forums even for appropriate criticism of policies. Chiefs, then, can easily dominate rather than serve their people. Also, many highly educated people get involved in politics simply for the respect that it brings and because it will give them access to tribal properties rich in mineral deposits or forest timber, which they seek to exploit for selfish ambition.

Corruption like this has been known to keep Christians from entering politics in such societies, because they ask, "If the political system is corrupt, what will prevent me from being corrupted?" Many of us are familiar with Lord Acton's truism, "Power tends to corrupt; absolute power corrupts absolutely." The key is that we should not seek political "power," but that Christians who are called into politics should come in order to serve others. They are to seek God, as Daniel did in Babylon and as Joseph did in Egypt. As these men sought God, he placed them in their national "political" callings, through which they served the people.

On the other hand, many Christians see politics as worldly, and they argue that "good" Christians should not get into government, because they will be tarnished by the world. This is not a biblical attitude. God established government[14] as one of the most basic institutions of society. For far too long, because of their pietistic attitudes, Christians evacuated the realm of politics, which has left a great moral vacuum in our societies and contributed to their decay. Christians answering the call to government and civil administration can help to change that.

News and Public Announcements

In ancient times the gates were also hubs of communication for a constant flow of news and important public information. We see an example of a major announcement made when Sennacherib, the king of Assyria, invades Judah. King Hezekiah organizes the defense of the city and then calls the people to assemble in the square at the gate of the city of Jerusalem to hear his message of encouragement concerning the defense of the city. Second Chronicles 32:6–8 records this event:

> He appointed military officers over the people and assembled them before him in the square at the city gate and encouraged them with these words: "Be strong and courageous. Do not be afraid or discouraged because of the king of Assyria and the vast army with him, for there is a greater power with us than with him. With him is only the arm of flesh, but with us is the LORD our God to help us and to fight our battles." And the people gained confidence from what Hezekiah the king of Judah said.

More than just regular news was proclaimed at the gates. Prophets proclaimed messages there as well.[15] And in Proverbs 1:20–21 we see a personification of wisdom at the gates: "Wisdom calls aloud in the street, she raises her voice in the public squares; at the head of the noisy streets she cries out, in the gateways of the city she makes her speech,"[16] while in Proverbs 31:28–31, news honoring the virtuous woman is made public at the gates of the city.

In today's world, we have newspapers, magazines, mail service, telephone, television, fax, radio, the Internet, e-mail, YouTube, and blogs to spread news and make public announcements. Who controls these "gates" (the media) in your country? Who controls the mechanisms of public information? People are sitting in the gates of these industries, but who do they represent and what ideas are they peddling? It is not stretching the point to say that Christians are called first and foremost to be communicators. This means that many of us should be involved in communications industries, helping to redeem our societies by working under God to communicate the truth through all forms of the media and the press.

MARVIN OLASKY'S STORY

Born into a Russian Jewish family, Marvin Olasky became an atheist at age fourteen and then a communist in the early 1970s. In 1976, while reading both Lenin and the New Testament, Olasky became a believer in Jesus Christ. He received his Ph.D. in 1976 and began to teach journalism at the University of Texas in 1983. Because of his newfound faith in Christ and his profound understanding of the Bible, Olasky sought to live *coram Deo*, "before the face of God."

Olasky had a heart for the poor and understood the power of a biblical worldview. In 1992 his laser-like mind focused on the issue of poverty in the USA. In his book *The Tragedy of American Compassion*,[1] he showed how as our nation moved from a biblical worldview at its founding to a secular worldview today, the concept of compassion changed as well. At the founding of the United States, caring for the poor was the responsibility of individuals, the church, and private social organizations. As the worldview of the nation shifted, so did its understanding of the causes and solutions of poverty; under the secular paradigm it became the role of the state to solve the problems of poverty. Olasky's book was, above all, a call to return to biblical foundations and thus to a revival of private personal and corporate charitable engagement. It was Olasky who began to call forth a need for "compassionate conservativism" that so influenced national leaders such as William Bennett, Newt Gingrich, and President George W. Bush.

Because Olasky understands that Christians need to speak into the marketplace of ideas and seek to engage the social, political, and economic debate in this country, in 1992 he became the editor-in-chief of *World* magazine, the fifth most-read U.S. newsweekly. He continues in this work and has been a catalyst in creating the World Journalism Institute to train Christian journalists to approach their craft from a distinctly biblical (rather than a secular) point of view.

Not content to abandon the gates of the city, Marvin Olasky is a model of the influence we can have in society if we reject a divided mind and a divided life and live all of life *coram Deo*, working faithfully in the sphere to which God has called us.

Public Meetings and Discourse

The biblical gates of the city, as we noted, were places where people were active in commerce, law, government, civil affairs, and legal matters. They were also places where friends and neighbors came from their homes to gather and to talk, or where travelers met friends and secured information on lodging and learned about the city. We find an example in Genesis 19:1–2:

> The two angels arrived at Sodom in the evening, and Lot was sitting in the gateway of the city. When he saw them, he got up to meet them and bowed down with his face to the ground. "My lords," he said, "please turn aside to your servant's house. You can wash your feet and spend the night and then go on your way early in the morning."
>
> "No," they answered, "we will spend the night in the square."

Lot, as he may often have done, was sitting at the gate of Sodom, perhaps enjoying the cool evening and the coming of a beautiful and clear desert night sky. He may even have been enjoying social intercourse with friends and neighbors when two strangers arrived. Lot graciously greeted them and offered them lodging for the night. Hosting strangers like this was a normal practice in Middle Eastern culture.

We Western Christians often meet coworkers, friends, and neighbors in public places, perhaps in coffee shops, restaurants, shopping malls, libraries, grocery stores, or on the Internet in chat rooms and electronic communities. There our lives mingle and words are spoken. Are we occupying those "gates" by honoring in word and deed those who are not there with us? Do we speak of our leaders with dignity and honor, even if we don't agree with some of their policies? How do we speak to others about our friends and neighbors? Do we build them up or strip them of their humanity? As we meet in the public places of our cities, whether in our occupations, as citizens, or in our private lives, we can manifest the character of God and attest to the value of each human being by the way we treat each other.

THE GATES AS A METAPHOR FOR THE CITY

Until Jesus comes again, the gates will remain a strategic place of occupation. In keeping with the way the gates represent the public life, the term *the gates* in the Old Testament is occasionally used to refer to the whole city—for what was good and bad, or glorious and weak about it. What was said about the gates was a reflection on the power and glory of the city, or its lack thereof.

Sometimes *sha'ar* is even translated "city," such as the New International Version does in Genesis 22:17–18: "I will surely bless you and make your descendants as numerous as the stars in the sky and as the sand on the seashore. Your descendants will take possession of the cities [sha'ar] of their enemies, and through your offspring all nations on earth will be blessed, because you have obeyed me." Here we find the restatement of the Abrahamic Covenant that God would bless Abraham as a vehicle for the blessing of the nations. In this restatement of that promise, we see that God's blessing through Abraham extends into cities themselves.

But many times even when *sha'ar* is translated "the gates," it is an obvious metaphorical reference to the city (or cities) in question. Take, for instance, Genesis 24:60, when Rebekah's family blesses her as she is betrothed to Abraham's son Isaac: "And they blessed Rebekah and said to her, 'Our sister, may you increase to thousands upon thousands; may your offspring possess the gates [sha'ar] of their enemies.'" Since to possess the gates meant having control of the city itself, we can see the metaphorical meaning of the verse.

Further, when a city is flourishing, its gates are said to be flourishing. When the city is languishing, its gates languish. When a city is in its glory and power, its gates are physically maintained in a way that befits the city's glory. In contrast, when a city is filled with lamentation, its gates betray that. The entrances to the city reveal its run-down condition, its loss of glory and power. For instance, in the book of Jeremiah, we find the nation Judah under divine judgment after the reign of the evil King Manasseh. Judgment will come through drought, famine, and invading armies. In Jeremiah 14:2–7 we can see the metaphorical understanding of "the gates" in the record of the word of the Lord concerning the impact of the drought:

"Judah mourns,
  her cities [sha'ar] languish;
they wail for the land,
  and a cry goes up from Jerusalem.
The nobles send their servants for water;
  they go to the cisterns
  but find no water.
They return with their jars unfilled;
  dismayed and despairing,
  they cover their heads.
The ground is cracked
  because there is no rain in the land;
the farmers are dismayed
  and cover their heads.
Even the doe in the field
  deserts her newborn fawn
  because there is no grass.
Wild donkeys stand on the barren heights
  and pant like jackals;
their eyesight fails
  for lack of pasture."

Although our sins testify against us,
    O LORD, do something for the sake of your name.
For our backsliding is great;
    we have sinned against you.

Prosperous cities once filled with vendors selling grain and engaging in much commerce now "languish," as Jeremiah records using the term for the city's gates.

THAT THE KING OF GLORY MAY COME IN

Not only do examples like that in Jeremiah show how the gates represent the city metaphorically; they also underscore the depth of a people's mourning for the loss of the glory of God within their cities. A bitter description of such mourning is found in Lamentations 4:6–9:

The punishment of my people
    is greater than that of Sodom,
which was overthrown in a moment
    without a hand turned to help her.

Their princes were brighter than snow
    and whiter than milk,
their bodies more ruddy than rubies,
    their appearance like sapphires.

But now they are blacker than soot;
    they are not recognized in the streets.
Their skin has shriveled on their bones;
    it has become as dry as a stick.

Those killed by the sword are better off
    than those who die of famine;
racked with hunger, they waste away
    for lack of food from the field.

Note the dramatic contrast drawn by describing princes who were once "brighter than snow and whiter than milk" but are now "blacker than soot," and the bitter observation that it's better to die by the sword than by famine.

It can get very dark and degenerate in cities, societies, and nations when "the lights" dim or go out. Many kings and others in authority during Old Testament times brought great darkness upon their cities and lands when they wandered far from God to worship "other gods." In the language of the New Testament, these kings "exchanged the truth of God for a lie, and worshiped and served created things rather than the Creator" (Rom. 1:25). Instead of looking to the living God for the strength, prosperity, and protection of their societies, they worshiped and followed the dictates of idols for religious, economic, and political life. In the song of Deborah, during the time of the Judges, we find these tragic words:

> "In the days of Shamgar son of Anath,
>   in the days of Jael, the roads were abandoned;
>   travelers took to winding paths.
> Village life in Israel ceased,
>   ceased until I, Deborah, arose,
>   arose a mother in Israel.
> When they chose new gods,
>   war came to the city gates,
> and not a shield or spear was seen
>   among forty thousand in Israel." (Judg. 5:6–8)

God brought judgment upon his people when they worshiped the animistic deities Baal and his consort Ashtoreth. When war came, defenses were overcome, the roads were abandoned, people stopped traveling, commerce dried up, and village life ceased. Farmers abandoned their fields for the relative protection within the walls of the city. They became a defeated and depressed people. Normal life had ground to a halt. Even today, when God is refused and denied, societies break down. They become organized around the cultic worship, whether of the pagan animism or the pagan humanism variety,[17] that dictates to the people how their social, economic, and political lives must be lived. This greatly harms a society because the life of its people is not "ordered" by the wisdom of Scripture.

Striking present-day illustrations of this can be found in animistic Africa, where patterns of work are based on belief systems derived from the spirits. So there are days in which farming and fishing are prohibited because on those days the gods need peace and rest and no one is to disturb them. This, of course, greatly disrupts economic activity. Further, there are rivers and streams in which people are always prohibited from fishing because the waterways are believed to be permanently inhabited by the spirits. Even though the health of the families who live near these rivers and streams would benefit greatly from the fish, the dictates of the spirits (gods) prevent this, even during times of famine.

In the pagan secular West, we are witnessing the slow death of our nations. There is no transcendent standard for truth and morality, so each person does what is right in his or her own eyes. Addiction to drugs, alcohol, gambling, and pornography are rampant. Abortion and homosexuality, which in the mid-twentieth century were shunned, are promoted and practiced as normal. As Europeans and North Americans abandon their roots in the Judeo-Christian faith, they no longer know their identity. This leads to an antinatal practice; most countries in Europe and some states in the USA have birthrates (1.2–1.5 children per mother) that will not sustain their societies. As a result, there will be cultural suicide in a little more than one generation.

Like Deborah, Nehemiah, and many other biblical reformers, Christians are called to change such cultural patterns. We are to rise and discover our callings and live them out, for the good of our societies, for the advancing of God's kingdom. We are to do this whether we live in the West or in the developing countries. The cry of Psalm 24:7–10 can be our cry:

> Lift up your heads, O you gates;
> be lifted up, you ancient doors,
> that the King of glory may come in.
> Who is this King of glory?
> The LORD strong and mighty,
> the LORD mighty in battle.
> Lift up your heads, O you gates;
> lift them up, you ancient doors,
> that the King of glory may come in.
> Who is he, this King of glory?
> The LORD Almighty—
> he is the King of glory.

As this psalm declares in its opening verses, the Lord is the Creator and the Owner of the earth and everything in it. Here, the gates refer to the glorious City of Zion, whose glorious King is entering them. He is taking possession to rule and reign.

When we work in the gates of the city, we work for and with the King. We work to see his redemption come, to see his kingdom come, and with it to see the fulfillment of his original intentions for his creation and all who live in it.

To explore the vast potential for transforming work in the gates of the city today, we will see in the following chapters how Christians throughout history have occupied the gates and helped to transform their societies.

CHAPTER 19

THE DOMAINS

Let's explore the vast potential for transforming work in the "gates of the city" today by learning how Christians through history have occupied the gates, helping to transform their societies.

What was represented by the gates of the city in biblical times has come to be conceptualized in today's world as the domains, or spheres, of society. Jesus Christ and the Christians that have followed him have done more to transform the domains of society for the good than any other kind of religious and social movement in the world. I don't mean that Christianity has made life in the world perfect or that there have not been many terrible injustices and atrocities committed in the name of Christianity. Nevertheless, I think the historical record shows that Christianity has shaped societies for the good like nothing else has. In his book *The Rise of Christianity: A Sociologist Reconsiders History*, evangelical sociologist Rodney Stark writes,

> I believe that it was the religion's particular doctrines that permitted Christianity to be among the most sweeping and successful revitalization movements in history. And it was the way these doctrines took on *actual flesh*, the way they directed organizational actions and individual behavior, that led to the rise of Christianity [italics added].[1]

As Christians put flesh on the gospel, society changed. Historian Thomas Cahill points out that "Christianity's 'initial thrust' has hurled 'acts and ideas' not only 'across the centuries' but also around the world."[2] Such Christian "ideas and acts" have transformed many areas within life's domains as disciples of Christ have occupied for the kingdom and lived out their callings down through history. In his foreword to Alvin Schmidt's book *Under the Influence: How Christianity Transformed Civilization*, Paul L. Maier, professor of ancient history at Western Michigan University, describes how Christ and his followers shaped history:

> Not only countless individual lives but civilization itself was transformed by Jesus Christ. In the ancient world, his teachings elevated brutish standards of morality, halted infanticide, enhanced human life, emancipated women, abolished slavery, inspired charities and relief organizations, created hospitals, established orphanages, and founded schools.
>
> In medieval times, Christianity almost single-handedly kept classical culture alive through recopying manuscripts, building libraries, moderating warfare through truce days, and providing dispute arbitration. It was Christians who invented colleges and universities, dignified labor as a divine vocation, and extended the light of civilization to barbarians on the frontiers.
>
> In the modern era, Christian teaching, properly expressed, advanced science, instilled concepts of political and social and economic freedom, fostered justice, and provided the greatest single source of inspiration for the magnificent achievements in art, architecture, music, and literature that we treasure to the present day.[3]

We too can find our callings in any of these areas. As the people of Israel participated in the dynamic life of their community at the gates, and as followers of Christ have walked in his footsteps in every kind of human endeavor, we too have an unbounded scope to live out our callings. We too can be part of transforming communities and whole societies. The possibilities stretch the imagination; the potential is inexhaustible.

In discussing the domains, I will be relying heavily on Alvin Schmidt's book *Under the Influence*, Stark's book *The Rise of Christianity*, and the book by D. James Kennedy and Jerry Newcombe, *What If Jesus Had Never Been Born?* These books draw from several eras of history to show many and varied domains transformed by the *life*work of Christians. My goal is that we would learn from the past in a way that will inspire us for our callings today. In this chapter we'll explore six of the modern domains: government, education, health, art, economic activity, and science.

GOVERNMENT

We have seen that kingdom transformation works its way from individual hearts and minds, through the family, into the church, and through the church into the other domains of society. In considering society at large, we'll begin with the domain of government because God has ordained three primary institutions in society: families,[4] churches,[5] and civil government—the state.[6] These are the foundational institutions of any society. For a society to be healthy, each of these institutions must be healthy. To be healthy, these institutions must be in right relationship with each other.

Recognizing these right relationships begins with understanding that God is sovereign over his entire creation. Therefore, God and his laws and ordinances are sovereign over each of these institutions. Each institution derives its life, boundaries, and authority from God alone. The health of each institution is determined by its free obedience to God's laws and ordinances. We say free, because obedience is not coerced by external tyranny. Human beings are born free; thus the obedience is born from internal motivation and self-governance. Each of these fundamental institutions is responsible to God alone. While these realms relate to one another and while individual members of society may be engaged in all three institutions, the integrity of each is protected from the abuses of the others by being responsible to God alone. Theologian J. I. Packer captures this when he writes:

> Each such means [the family, the church, and the state] has its own sphere of authority under Christ, who now rules the universe on his Father's behalf, and each sphere has to be delimited by reference to the others. In our fallen world these bulwark against anarchy, the law of the jungle, and the dissolution of ordered society.[7]

The state has the power of the sword, and the church has the power of the Word of God. The church is not to wield the sword, and the state is not to usurp the Word of God. The family has the responsibility for nurturing and educating the next generation of citizens. This is not the job of the state, as has been assumed in too many societies today.

The biblical pattern of relating the three fundamental institutions recognizes that God is sovereign over the universe and the affairs of man. Here liberty and self-government reign. God is sovereign over free, self-governing individuals. These individuals are members of families, churches, and civil government. Law, rather than men, governs the state.

Each of the three institutions functions in its own sphere under God's laws, to the glory of God. Each has its own area of authority under God but has no ultimate authority over the other spheres. The family has the delegated responsibility for nurturing children physically, emotionally, and socially and for educating children in the development of knowledge, wisdom, and virtue—all this so that children might become free, self-governing citizens of their nations.

The church has the delegated responsibility for proclaiming in word and deed the Word of God. She is responsible for corporate worship and for equipping the saints to be free citizens in the marketplace and in the public square and to serve the welfare of the larger community.

The state has the primary responsibility for wielding the sword. Because we live in a fallen world and we are sinful men and women, the state has the responsibility to defend her citizens against foreign threats and to provide for the peace and tranquility of society. She is to uphold the rule of law and establish a framework of free commerce and civil liberties.

As free men and women take up their roles as parents of families, members of churches, and citizens of communities, they influence the gates of the city—the various sectors of societies—with the kingdom culture of truth, beauty, and goodness. The result is the most free, just, and wholesome society imaginable. This kind of society might be identified as a "constitutional republic." Here, free, self-governing citizens sit at the gates of the city.

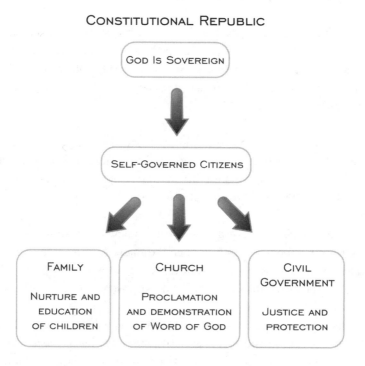

CONSTITUTIONAL REPUBLIC

GOD IS SOVEREIGN

SELF-GOVERNED CITIZENS

FAMILY	CHURCH	CIVIL GOVERNMENT
NURTURE AND EDUCATION OF CHILDREN	PROCLAMATION AND DEMONSTRATION OF WORD OF GOD	JUSTICE AND PROTECTION

This pattern of social order acknowledges that freedom is born within men; it is granted by God and not the state. It recognizes that the highest form of governance is internal self-governance. The Dutch lawyer and theologian Hugo Grotius summarized the principle of self-government:

> He knows not how to rule a kingdom, that cannot manage a Province; nor can he wield a Province, that cannot order a City; nor he order a City, that knows not how to regulate a Village; nor he a Village, that cannot guide a Family; nor can that man Govern well a Family that knows not how to Govern himself; neither can any Govern himself unless his Reason be Lord, Will and Appetite her Vassals; nor can Reason rule unless herself be ruled by God and (wholly) be obedient to Him.[8]

My good friend and the founder of Chrysalis International, Dr. Elizabeth Youmans, helps to clarify this principle:

> The Christian principle of self-government is God ruling internally from the heart of the believer. In order to have true liberty, man must *WILLINGLY* (voluntarily) be governed *INTERNALLY* by the Spirit and Word of God rather than by external forces. Government is first internal (causative), then extends outwardly (effect).[9]

The more self-governed a people, the freer the state. The less people govern themselves, the greater is the need for the power of the state. The founder of Pennsylvania, William Penn, wrote, "Those people who are not governed by God will be ruled by tyrants."[10] Those who allow themselves to be governed internally by God can be participants in a civil government that fosters liberty and justice and respects the integrity of the family, the church, and all the other domains of society.

The principles that lead to this kind of government are found in the biblical worldview. Like individuals, families, and churches, governments reach their greatest potential when they serve the living God. The health of any government is determined by its obedience to God's laws and ordinances. If civil laws are based on God's moral law—the Ten Commandments—and if they are obeyed by free, self-governing citizens, the result is truth, justice, and liberty.

God has made patterning human government on truth, justice, and liberty attainable by revealing himself and his ways to us. As we have discussed earlier, God has revealed himself through both creation and revelation. His ordinances are built into reality and establish the natural, metaphysical, and moral order. God speaks clearly through his creation so that all people can know that God exists and can know something of his nature through the things that he has made.[11] In theological terms this is known as general revelation.

Likewise, God's moral law is revealed in creation and in his Word. Paul speaks of the "law...written on their hearts, their consciences also bearing witness" (Rom. 2:15). This revelation is built into creation. The ancients called this form of revelation of right and wrong "natural law." The Bible also reveals God's moral nature through the Ten Commandments and the life of Christ.

As Paul testifies in Romans, the ancient Greco-Roman world could "read" the law revealed in creation and in the human conscience—natural law. Schmidt writes,

> Natural law was understood as that process in nature by which human beings, through the use of sound reason, were able to perceive what was morally right and wrong. This natural law was seen as the eternal, unchangeable foundation of all human laws.[12]

But even natural law had to be "interpreted" and applied, and it was done so by fallen people often seeking their own self-interests and working without the revelation and guidelines of Scripture. So lawmaking was often unjust and cruel and done according to the wishes, dictates, or whims of rulers and kings.

The Law of Moses, however, was quite different from Greco-Roman law. In it, the divine origin of law was stressed. This led to significant differences in the understanding of law held by Israel and by the other nations. It meant that for the nation of Israel, ultimate authority for law resided in God, unlike other nations, whose ultimate authority for law resided in the king, the dictator, or the state (in today's Western democracies, it resides in "the people").

Perhaps the most fundamental difference appeared when the Ten Commandments were announced, beginning with the preface "I am the LORD your God, who brought you out of Egypt, out of the land of slavery" (Exod. 20:2). This often overlooked statement is actually indispensable to what follows, for it means that God's Law began with the great truth of deliverance (from slavery in Egypt) and that the commandments and laws that follow therefore had a redemptive character to them. In other words, the Law was founded on the people's salvation experience, on the divine favor that ancient Israel had received from Yahweh, which no other nation had.[13]

Further, the Ten Commandments were not just about personal piety. They were also about the development of a social order for the people, who up to that point had no laws to govern them as a people and, later, as a nation. Previously they had been dependent on the laws of Egypt for their social and political life.

Israel's understanding of law also differed in scope from that of other nations. Many ancient law codes dealt only with legal matters, leaving moral and religious matters for other branches of literature. But in the Law of Moses, also called the Torah, legal, moral, and religious commands form an inseparable unit.

Since the time of Christ, Christians have sought to interpret biblical law and institute it to change unjust and oppressive policies and laws in their own cities and nations. For instance, typically throughout history, the chief, king, emperor, or czar was a law unto himself, what we today would call a dictator. He would make the laws and everyone would be bound to them except him. The first known incident of someone holding the emperor accountable to the law is recorded in Ambrose (c. 340–397), the bishop of Milan, who challenged the unjust slaughter of the innocent by Emperor Theodosius the Great (r. 379–395).[14]

In the early thirteenth century, Stephen Langton, the archbishop of Canterbury, led the effort which eventually forced King John to agree to the Magna Carta, which is one of the most pivotal documents of freedom ever written.[15] This charter, building on earlier efforts, made even a king subject to the rule of law and granted a few basic rights to citizens. Among other principles, it established that justice could no longer be bought or sold, that there could be no taxation without representation and no imprisonment without a trial, and that property could not be confiscated without just compensation.[16]

In 1520 Martin Luther called for the policy of the separation of church and state. Christ distinguished between two kingdoms—God and Caesar[17]—and Luther argued from this biblical point of view. A Christian, he said, is a member of both kingdoms, having obligations of obedience to fulfill both as a good citizen of his country and as a citizen of heaven. Another Reformer, John Calvin, did massive studies on how biblical law and covenant could be interpreted and applied in Europe.

The ideas of the Reformers spread across the Atlantic and were crucial in the formation of governance in the colonies and ultimately in the formation of the United States of America. For instance, the renowned English legal scholar Sir William Blackstone (1723–1780) drew heavily from natural law concepts passed down from Paul[18] and the Greeks through the church fathers. His *Commentaries on the Laws of England* (1765) was common reading for founding fathers of the United States. The Constitution of the United States—called by many "the world's greatest charter of liberty and justice"—was signed by thirty-nine of the nation's founders, the majority of whom were Christian.[19]

Many characteristics that we take for granted today in Western society can be traced to a biblical worldview. We have already discussed the separation of church and state, in which both spheres are responsible to God without power over the other, and the principle of self-government. In addition, the rule of law and the checks and balances in governance (the separation of powers) are tied to the biblical understanding of the depravity of man. Also the equality of the individual before the law is linked to the fact that all men and women are made in the image of God and are thus equal in dignity and worth.

God has ordained government—his government, self-government, and civil government. He has shown us how to govern and be governed in liberty and justice. And he calls Christians into this influential domain to manifest his redeeming reign, the kingdom of God.

Our Callings Today

- Promote freedom, justice, and the concept of self-government. This is a calling we can respond to whether we are working in one of the branches of government or in our families, schools, media, businesses, or church or community outreach programs.
- Be law-abiding citizens.
- Become educated voters, knowing the issues and the candidates.
- Engage in the political process in other ways on either a local, regional, or national level; for example, participate in town hall or school-board meetings,

JOHN W. WHITEHEAD'S STORY

A number of years ago I heard a story about my mentor Francis Schaeffer speaking to a group of Christian lawyers. He asked them what makes a lawyer a Christian in his or her law practice. Was it enough to have Christian magazines on the coffee table in the waiting room? Schaeffer then asked these young lawyers the provocative question, "What have you done before the Supreme Court lately?"

As I heard the story, a young lawyer named John Whitehead was in the audience. Schaeffer's question prompted Whitehead to examine his own life and work. In response to Schaeffer's challenge, in 1982 Whitehead founded the Rutherford Institute, a public interest law firm that specializes in civil and human rights issues. For more than twenty-five years, the Rutherford Institute

has provided free legal services for people seeking the protection of their rights. The Rutherford Institute has been a counterweight in American society to the American Civil Liberties Union (ACLU).

John Whitehead himself would be the first to admit that his actions went against the current thinking about being both a Christian and a lawyer. "Religious people had mostly withdrawn and were not participating in their culture," says Whitehead. Indeed, Whitehead was even told by some believers that "Christian involvement in the courts was unbiblical."[1]

Today, following many years of perseverance, faith, and action, John Whitehead's Rutherford Institute can answer Schaeffer's challenge in the affirmative. In 2007, the Rutherford Institute received 1,594 requests communicate with your elected representatives, volunteer as a poll worker, or work for a campaign.

- Protest to the authorities where government actions or local, regional, national, or international law opposes God's laws. Voice support for actions and proposed legislation that manifest truth and justice.
- Work with skill and integrity in civil service in city, regional, or national government.
- Serve in public office, from the city council and local water boards to state and national office.
- Fight against corruption in government and its institutions, whether from the inside or outside.
- Participate in civil disobedience, should the responsibility arise.

for legal assistance, and 66 cases dealing with various violations of civil and human rights made their way through the pre-litigation and litigation stages, including a number that were appealed directly to the United States Supreme Court.[2]

In twenty-five years, the Rutherford Institute has secured for America a huge number of successes in areas such as free speech, religious freedom, church rights, parental rights, and sexual harassment. Recently, in a move to protect the right of nonviolent, pro-life activists to free speech, the members of the Rutherford Institute stated their belief that "[s]peech in our republic must remain free not only for popular speakers, but also for the unpopular and the dissidents."[3]

In a different case, the Rutherford Institute filed a friend of the court brief urging the Supreme Court to invalidate a lower court's ruling that parental permission is not needed for a minor to have an abortion. Responding to the Supreme Court's positive decision, Rutherford stated, "We are pleased that the Supreme Court affirmed the rights reserved to states and the people to protect minors who confront serious life-changing decisions such as abortion. ... After all, if minors require parental consent in order to have their bodies pierced, tattooed, or tanned, why shouldn't their parents be notified about something as life-changing as abortion?"[4]

It is important to note that the Rutherford Institute is committed to protecting the individual rights of every person in the United States, not just those whose views and actions they agree with. This is bound to make everyone uncomfortable at one time or another. In the words of Whitehead: "It is our hope that all Americans would remember that our constitutional rights and freedoms must apply to all citizens, not just to those to whom our government decides to grant them."[5]

In September 2008, as part of his continued "sitting in the gate of law," Whitehead responded to a call to provide testimony to the Constitution Subcommittee of the Senate Judiciary Committee of the United States. The issue that Whitehead was asked to address was the weakening of the rule of law in the United States. In his written testimony, he stated: "Never before in American history has there been a more pressing need to abide by the rule of law, respect the sepa-ration of powers, and check governmental power and abuse....This is especially critical now, as the effects of the U.S. government's ongoing war on terror continue to be felt at home and abroad."[6]

The Rutherford Institute has been a strong voice for liberty, holding the nation accountable to its Constitution and particularly the Bill of Rights. As John Whitehead's *life*work has shown, it is possible—and vital—for Christians to engage the culture at all levels, in his case in the complexities of law and governance that affect us all.

EDUCATION

Broadly speaking, the domain of education seeks to develop people's innate capacities through various forms of schooling or other instruction, in moral and religious matters as well as so-called secular ones. The Latin for *educate* is *educare*: "to draw, or lead, out." This reminds us that education is primarily about drawing out the God-given potential found in each human being. As they would with all the others, Christians would want to enter this domain with the Bible in one hand and their books in the other. The Bible and education go back a long way. Scripture establishes fundamental principles for life, work, and worldview, providing the framework in which a good education can be unfolded. Even before the Christian era, the Old Testament itself was formed through an educational process that included handing down from generation to generation God's revelation in all matters of life and thought.

Unfortunately, many societies throughout history have not been instructed from and informed by Scripture's worldview. This means, to come straight to the point, and to use the apostle Paul's language, they worship and serve created idols rather than God.[20] As a result, they have little understanding of the revelation of God as Creator, or of sin and redemption, or of the relation of these facts of life to their educational paradigms. Such societies, therefore, have an exalted view of themselves (over that of the Creator), and education becomes yet another domain that develops in an idolatrous manner.

A biblical Christian view of education seeks to train children, young people, and adults to bring good potential and resources out of the creation that God has commanded us to steward. As we seek to "draw out" children and students into obedience to God's laws and truth, then we will be raising people who will, in their adult years, be helping to redeem, renew, and transform aspects of their societies. This is the great contribution that Christian educators can make to their schools and societies. Occupying for the kingdom, educationally, has always been a chief aim of Christianity throughout history.

At the start of the Christian era, Christian education focused on religious and moral instruction and its application in daily life. We see this in many of the Epistles that combine theology with exhortations to practical obedience to the theological truths. More sophisticated and structured forms of this kind of education appeared soon afterward in educational booklets such as the Didache, which instructed new converts,[21] and in Justin Martyr's "catechetical" schools of the second century, which provided instruction in faith and practice.[22]

Following the pattern of catechetical schools founded by the church fathers, "cathedral" and "episcopal" schools administered by the bishops were built alongside church buildings and cathedrals. These schools taught both doctrine and what has been called the seven liberal arts. The curriculum had two parts: the trivium (grammar, rhetoric, and logic) and the quadrivium (arithmetic, music, geometry, and astronomy).[23] Note that in this, Christian education is moving beyond religious and moral instruction and is beginning to reach into all areas of life. This has become known as classical Christian education, but to societies that have abandoned the foundations of the Scripture, it is known as the liberal arts.

Expanding beyond classical Christian education, followers of Christ founded the first universities during the Middle Ages. Although the Greeks and Romans have produced some of the world's great philosophers, poets, and scholars, they created no lasting institutions of higher education.[24] It was the followers of Christ who, with their passion for pursuing biblical knowledge in all domains, formed the taproot for higher education. During the early Middle Ages in Europe, a number of Christian monastic orders developed libraries, which drew scholars to them and laid the foundations for the first universities. The first was the University of Bologna, Italy, started in 1158. Not long afterward universities arose in Spain, Scotland, Sweden, Poland, and more in Italy. The University of Paris in France followed in 1200, and then came Oxford in England and universities in Portugal, Germany, and Austria.[25]

On the other side of the Atlantic, the first American universities prior to the Revolutionary War, with the exception of the University of Pennsylvania, were also founded by Christians and based on biblical principles for kingdom purposes.[26] Harvard, Yale, and Princeton were among those. In fact, well over one hundred of the first colleges and universities founded in the United States had Christian roots.[27]

Clearly, Christians through the centuries have had a great passion for learning and for the intergenerational responsibility they have to pass on that learning.

Another aspect of education that we take for granted today is "universal education," in which everyone should have access to basic learning, regardless of their gender, race, or social station. This unrestricted access to education is another legacy of the sixteenth-century Reformers. They believed that everyone, including peasants and shopkeepers, should be able to receive elementary education in subjects like grammar, reading, arithmetic, and religion, as well as a secondary education for the purpose of training citizens for civil and ecclesiastical leadership. This began with the Reformers' deep belief that the Bible should be translated into many languages and therefore made available to everyone, not just to church officials, to read. Kennedy and Newcombe write, "It wasn't until the Bible became the focal point of Christianity again that education for the masses was born."[28] Historian of education William Boyd notes, "Luther, in fact, wanted a system of education as free and unrestricted as the Gospel he preached [and] indifferent, like the Gospel, to distinctions of sex or of social class."[29]

Today in the educational domain, both the problems and opportunities are vast. Across many nations in Africa, the HIV/AIDS epidemic is halting or reversing progress in education. Teachers are in short supply, and children and their families are forced to choose daily survival over preparing for the future. Even where tuition is free, the cost of uniforms, books, supplies, and transportation makes education unobtainable. Far from being able to afford these things, many children—both orphans and those fortunate to still have their parents—must enter the workforce to acquire basic necessities. Even in the absence of the specter of HIV/AIDS, lack of access, unequal opportunities for girls, and a need to work keep millions of children all over the world from obtaining an education. While I was visiting one of the poorest regions in Guatemala, a friend told me about one of the local schools. This school had existed for thirty years and could handle four hundred elementary students. But in those thirty years, only a dozen boys had graduated from sixth grade and only one girl had attended the school. This is a typical picture of schooling today throughout much of the developing world, where more Christian influence and many more Christian workers in education are needed.

Wealthier countries have their own educational dilemmas. They long ago abandoned training in virtue and character development, becoming militant promoters of the atheistic-materialistic worldview, Darwinian "science," and moral and cultural relativism.

When you consider the needs at home and across the world and the many kinds of educational methods, such as homeschooling, state schools, and private education, Christians have countless opportunities to discover their *life*work in the domain of education.

ELIZABETH YOUMANS'S STORY

Dr. Elizabeth Youmans is an educator who has come to see that the Bible is not only a "spiritual" book but also the "owner's manual" for all of life. She understands that the Word of God establishes the true nature of what it means to be a human being and a child and thus has something to say about education.

Too often Christian educators, having been raised in a secular environment, begin with an atheistic understanding of a child and human nature and thus consciously or unconsciously subscribe to a secular philosophy and pedagogy of education. On this foundation they hire Christians to teach in their schools, add chapel and a class in the Bible, and conclude that this is Christian education.

Elizabeth Youmans understands that we need to go to the Book as a foundation for developing a theology of the child and then develop an educational philosophy and pedagogy that is grounded in a biblical, Christian worldview. She writes,

> The first question is whether God created children empty or full. If the answer is empty, then the philosophy of education is to pour information into the child's head for him to memorize and parrot back the "right" answer. If the answer is full, then the philosophy of education is to lead the potential of Christ out of the child, so he can develop his ability to think

and reason from a Biblical perspective or basis of truth. The role of education is to lead out the full potential of every child so he can attain God's destiny for his life.

> All thinking and reasoning begins with some basis, some assumption, some philosophy. The basis for thinking and reasoning from God's perspective is God's revealed truth and word. The word of God is central to Christian education.[1]

Accordingly, Dr. Youmans has pioneered in Word-centered education. She is a leader in the Principle Approach, which uses America's historical method of biblical reasoning and places the truth of God's Word at the center of education. She has served as a classroom teacher, school administrator, teacher trainer, graduate school professor, curriculum writer, and editor of The Noah Plan, a K–12 Principle Approach curriculum for Christian schools and homeschools.

This passionate educator has embraced God's call upon her life to bring the Principle Approach to education to the developing world. A visiting professor at Regent University in Virginia, Youmans has trained international students who return to their home countries to be leaders in education. She has also founded and leads Chrysalis International, a nonprofit educational institute that seeks to teach Christian global leaders to apply biblical principles to education. She travels globally, imparting vision for education that is based on a biblical worldview, training Christian teachers, and helping to start schools and Christian educator associations in some of the poorest countries in the world. She has also developed a principle-based curriculum for children called AMO.

Elizabeth Youmans, herself the mother of four and grandmother of seven, has a *lifework* that embraces the world's children. Her work recognizes that "each child is made in God's image and is destined for immortality" and that "every child is a promise with a name, a passion, a story, and a place in His Story!"[2]

Our Callings Today

- Codify languages so that all peoples can have access to Scripture. This has been the calling of men and women in Christian organizations such as Wycliffe Bible Translators.
- Start libraries in poor communities and neighborhoods to encourage literacy and learning.
- Establish literacy programs for both children and adults in nonliterate societies as well as among nonliterates in literate societies.
- Establish skills programs for the undertrained.
- Tutor children or adult learners who need extra encouragement and training to reach their potential.
- Show parents how to take responsibility for their children's education.
- Establish schools that are consciously founded on a biblical worldview, and use a biblically based curriculum for the whole of life, not just for religious instruction.
- Support your children's or community schools by donating time, money, or other resources.
- Provide internships and mentoring for students in your field of work.
- Work as Christian scholars, being the best professors and researchers possible.
- Work as teachers and administrators, whether in state schools, private schools, or homeschools, educating the next generation for their roles as servant-leaders in their places of deployment.
- Work as support staff in schools and universities, helping to facilitate the best possible education for the students served.

HEALTH

Matters of health and illness are viewed quite differently today than in Jesus' time. You can imagine what it must have been like if you consider that in the Greco-Roman world, cruelty and violence were like virtues and compassion was a sign of weakness (we'll discuss this more in the next chapter). "Health care" was certainly not a priority as it is in the modern world. There were few Greek and Roman institutions of healing. Author John Jefferson Davis writes,

> In the pre-Christian Roman Empire, hospitals existed only for soldiers, gladiators, and slaves. Manual laborers and other poor individuals had no place of refuge. Men...took little interest in the sick, but often drove them out of the house, and left them to their fate.[30]

The Hebrew, or Jewish, world at the time of Christ (and before) was called by God to abandon pagan thinking about health and to follow his laws. Obedience was the key to a healthy life (see, for example, Deut. 7:11–15). The book of Leviticus is filled with practical wisdom for sustaining the health of people and their communities. Chapters 11 to 15, for instance, instruct in principles of nutrition, diet, sanitation, hygiene, infectious disease, childbearing, and childcare.

By the time Jesus came, we can see just how great a clash there was between the Hebrew and Greco-Roman worldviews when we look at their different attitudes toward caring for the sick. Although the famous Greek physician Hippocrates (460?–377? BC), "The Father of Medicine," brought ethics to health-care professionals through the Hippocratic Oath, and although he did much to place medicine on an early scientific basis by separating it from superstition, these benefits mainly affected the rich and the free.

In contrast, Jesus and his followers made universal mercy and compassion for the sick into one of the highest values of Christian obedience and discipleship. Jesus is often called the Great Physician because of his determined emphasis on healing people of any race or social station. Early Christian mercy, compassion, and care for the sick were nothing short of revolutionary in the Greco-Roman world, and they have been redemptively countering cruel and uncompassionate attitudes toward the sick ever since. Jesus even went so far as to teach that when we care for the sick, we are caring for him.[31]

During the early Christian era, Christians stood out from the pagan culture by taking the sick and the dying into their homes to care for them. Many pagans fled the plagues that swept through the Empire in the second and third centuries, while Christians stayed to care for the suffering and dying. They knew that God's kingdom advances even in the midst of suffering. Cyprian, the bishop of Carthage, wrote in 251,

> How suitable, how necessary it is that this plague and pestilence, which seems horrible and deadly, searches out the justice of each and every one and *examines the minds of the human race; whether the well care for the sick,* whether relatives dutifully love their kinsmen as they should, whether masters show compassion for their ailing slaves, whether physicians do not desert the afflicted [italics added].[32]

Keep in mind that most of these Christians were not trained medical personnel. They were common people who simply provided what they could. By offering simple comforts like water, blankets, a human touch, as well as their time, care, compassion, and, yes, sometimes even their lives, these Christians carried thousands who had been abandoned by pagan society through the difficult stages of the plague. The gospel, you see, is a rescue operation, and these Christians knew what that meant.

In 325 the Council of Nicaea, in addition to dealing with issues of theology, mandated that a hospital should be established in every city where a cathedral was built.[33] By the sixth century, hospitals had become as common as monasteries.[34] And by the time of the early Middle Ages, there were so many hospitals run by Christians that the Arab world—so impressed with the care of the sick provided by Christians—began in the eighth century to build hospitals in their own lands. The term often used to refer to these hospitals was *God's house.*

Henry Dunant (1828–1910), a follower of Christ from Switzerland and one of the founders of the YMCA, witnessed a battle in Solferino, Italy, that proved to be a milestone in his life. From this experience he saw the need for a neutral, international volunteer organization that would care for the wounded in time of war.[35] In 1864, the International Red Cross was formed as a result. It was Dunant's Christian faith that led him to use the cross as a symbol for the new organization. In 1876, the Muslim Red Crescent Society was founded in the Ottoman Empire, in present-day Turkey. This humanitarian initiative established by non-Christians was an outgrowth of Christian obedience to Jesus.[36]

In France, Dr. Louis Pasteur (1822–1895), another follower of Christ, was one of the greatest biologists of all time. Kennedy writes that Pasteur's "research into bacteriology gave rise to pasteurization, sterilization, and the development of vaccines against many deadly diseases—including rabies, diphtheria, and anthrax."[37] Millions around the world today enjoy good health because Pasteur heeded the words of Christ to help the infirm.

After the U.S. Civil War, hospitals began to flourish in America, usually founded by denominations or by individual churches. Their Protestant and Catholic roots are often seen in their names even today: Baptist Hospital, Lutheran Hospital, Methodist Hospital, Presbyterian Hospital, St. John's, St. Luke's, St. Mary's, and St. Joseph's.[38]

Medical nursing is also a legacy of Jesus' followers. While there were no "professional" nurses during the early years of the Christian era, evidence "indicates that widows, deaconesses, and virgins commonly served as nurses in the early Christian hospitals."[39] For centuries thereafter, religious communities were caregivers to the sick, and even today, many of the hospitals around us were founded by nursing sisters. Florence Nightingale (1820–1910) is known as the founder of modern nursing. A devout Christian, she started leading teams of women to care for the dying and to tend the wounded during the Crimean War. Schmidt writes,

> This humble, compassionate woman, who was propelled by her love for Christ to help the sick and dying, lifted the art of nursing to a level of dignity, honor, and medical expertise not previously known. Today there are thousands of nursing schools indebted to her principles. She accomplished what she did because she never doubted her own words: "The kingdom of heaven is within, but we must also make it so without."[40]

Much of the reason for increased life spans for human beings around the world is Christian medical missionaries and Christian relief and development agencies, which bring quality health care and education to millions around the world. They establish clinics and hospitals that seek to restore to health those who suffer from deprivation caused by war and poverty. They care for the blind, the crippled, the deaf, the deformed, the leprous, and the malnourished in thousands of facilities, from major cities to the remotest jungles. I think of Mercy Ships, whose vessels and staff travel the world, staying for months in one port offering quality free health care and other services to poor communities. The list goes on and on, as do the potential parts Christians can play when they are called to the medical and health professions. Millions of people are alive today and have better lives because of compassionate Christian health care.

Our Callings Today

- Work for caring as well as for curing.
- Work as medical and health professionals in hospitals, clinics, and home health services, providing the highest quality care possible for the whole person.
- Educate people in the public health arena about basic health-care issues and healthy lifestyle choices in order to prevent sickness.
- Work as administrators and support staff in the medical field, helping facilitate the best care possible and assisting people in navigating the system and obtaining the care and support they need.
- Serve as hospital chaplains.
- Facilitate support groups for people facing a particular disease or health issue.

MARY HOLMGREN'S STORY

In a *life*work that has encompassed being a pastor's wife, mother of six, and grandmother of more than a dozen, God has weaved throughout it all a special calling of caring for the sick and aging. Through one woman's lifetime vocation to serve the elderly, God has made himself known in the ordinary.

Looking back over the life of Mary Holmgren, a pattern emerges. She was at home with the elderly already as a teenager. Her mother ran a nursing home in the family home in the 1950s, a business that today would be called an adult family home. This was one of the many ways Mary's mother supported the family after being widowed, and Mary was counted on to help out. She recalls that many of the residents were like grandparents. This pattern of calling in Mary's life continued when she left home. After high school, while earning a degree in social work, Mary boarded with elderly women who welcomed a companion. A few years later, Mary married Alvin Holmgren, and as a pastor's wife, both as a young woman and as she herself matured, she found that her work often centered on the many elderly people in the congregation. While she and Alvin raised a young family and cared for their own parents, their home was often filled with elderly visitors, and their children can attest to hours spent at nursing homes, hospitals, and funerals.

Later, when most of their children were grown, the Holmgrens housed and cared for a family friend with advanced bone cancer.

Following this experience, while still pastoring, they decided to open an adult family home, a model of care that was making a comeback from the old days. They remodeled a portion of the first level of their house and did all that was necessary to gain licensing from the state.

As many as five elderly residents lived with the Holmgrens at any one time. Some residents stayed a few months; others were part of the family for years. During her ten years of operating the business, Mary performed many routine tasks. She visited with residents, made three meals a day on schedule without fail, helped people walk to the bathroom, emptied commode buckets, gave baths, dispensed medications, answered call bells in the middle of the night, and attended association meetings to keep up on state regulations and to network for new clients. Above all, Mary was home and available twenty-four hours a day, needing to arrange and pay for qualified replacement help if she wanted to go out for any reason. The routine was relentless, 24/7, and it affected the family in challenging ways. It was definitely *work*. But it was work with a purpose. The business both helped support her family and provided a homelike alternative to institutional care for twenty-nine people.

Mary knew the residents' stories, where they came from and how they had spent their lives. She knew what they liked to eat and what made them nervous. At ease with the elderly in a way many people aren't, she treated those in her care with love and respect, as individuals, not as generic "nice old people." When family and friends were around or when church members gathered in the Holmgren home for fellowship or a celebration, she often invited residents to join in, helping them maneuver their walkers into the family living room.

Mary knew that caring for residents involved caring for their families even if she was busy or worn out. She listened to family members' memories and concerns, helping them navigate the aging of their loved ones. She heard the ins and outs of family relations, first one side and then the other, depending on who was visiting. For those residents blessed with attentive families—whether sons and daughters, grandchildren, siblings, or nieces and nephews—all became familiar. One elderly wife spent hours talking with Mary each week. When she could no longer live independently, she moved in, already at home.

Perhaps the most unique part of Mary's work came as residents grew weak or sick. If hospitalization wouldn't help and it was possible for her to continue care, Mary allowed people to stay on, even as the workload increased. Rather than send people away as death approached, she was able to provide a familiar environment for residents and their families. Beginning with their friend with cancer, several people passed away in the Holmgren home. For Mary as a caregiver and Alvin as a pastor, helping people at the end of life was integral to their calling. What was bewildering and frightening to others had become familiar to them, though never mundane. Confident of the sacredness of life and our passage into the next life, they were able to help families negotiate both the practicalities and the emotions of a loved one's death.

In order to both be financially viable and provide quality care, this work was extremely confining, requiring Mary herself to be on duty most of the time. But she was able to dedicate herself to caregiving for this season of her life while, for a variety of reasons, family members were unable to provide twenty-four-hour care for their loved ones.

In the years after Mary retired from adult family home work, she and Alvin provided care in their home for a family member whose multiple sclerosis and aging made it impossible for her to live alone. Now in their seventies, the Holmgrens are facing—earlier than they had imagined—the things they have helped other individuals and families find their way through with grace and hope. As they experience the progressive changes brought by Alvin's Alzheimer's disease, they rely on the same God who called them to salvation in Christ and sustains them in faith, the God who also prepared them for and sustains them in their *life*works.

Looking over these two ordinary lives that God brought together, it's clear to see that just as God prepared and called Alvin for his *life*work of pastoring, God prepared and called Mary for a *life*work in which he continues to make himself known in ordinary days, in ordinary ways.

- Care for those with AIDS.
- Care for elderly relatives. Work against institutionalizing them unless it is absolutely necessary.
- Establish or work in a business providing short-term "day care" services to relieve those caring for elderly, sick, or disabled family members, or volunteer time to relieve family caregivers that you know.
- Volunteer time to go on short-term medical missions trips. Doctors, nurses, dentists, and support staff are needed.
- Provide training to medical personnel in developing countries to increase their skills.
- Tithe your time to care for the impoverished sick in your own community.
- Continue research to fight diseases, which helps push back more of the results of the Fall.
- Work to change unjust health-care laws, whether as a lawyer, a politician, or a concerned citizen.

ART

With the exception of Islam, Judaism, and Christianity, the major world religions and religious philosophies posit a world without beginnings, a world without a Creator. But if the act of creation does not exist, where does the creative impulse that we see in people all around the world come from? Why do dance, music, sculpture, drama, poetry, and painting exist? What framework acknowledges and makes sense of humanity's creativity? In contrast to a world without beginnings, the opening line of the biblical narrative explodes into the longings of artists around the world: "In the beginning God created the heavens and the earth" (Gen. 1:1). These revolutionary words establish the "storyline" for The Story. A metanarrative that begins with these words creates a very different world and a very different context for our lives than do the stories of other worldviews. Among other things, it answers the questions of our longings to draw, write, paint, sculpt, make music, act, and dance.

God has made man in his image; as such, man is both a word maker[41] and an art maker.[42] The English author J. R. R. Tolkien writes that art is the "operative link between Imagination and the final result, Sub-creation."[43]

The wonder of man, the *imago Dei*, is that beginning with what God has provided, man is able to make *new* things. A composer can create a symphony that no one has ever heard before. A painter can create a painting that no eye has ever seen before. A poet can write a poem that no one has ever read before. While all of this is original, none of it surprises God.

We are destined to be creators. As Edith Schaeffer writes,

We are created in the likeness of *the Creator*. We are created in the image of a *Creator*.

So we are, on a finite level, people who can create. Why does man have creativity? Why can man think of many things in his mind [imagination], and choose, and then bring forth something that other people can taste, smell, feel, hear, and see? Because man was created in the image of a Creator. Man was created that he might create. It is not a waste of man's time to be creative. It is not a waste to pursue artistic or scientific pursuits in creativity, because that is what man was *made* to be able to do.[44]

A call to the arts goes back, as Schaeffer recognizes, to the very beginning, to creation. As with all vocations, the artist's vocation is tied to our corporate calling to create culture. Just as culture is a manifestation of worship, all art could be said to be religious, rather than only art explicitly treating a religious theme. And just as an individual society has varying degrees of kingdom culture, counterfeit culture, and natural culture, the same can be said of its art.[45]

As with the art of every culture, the creative expression of God's people, Israel, reflected their worship. In the Hebrew world, clear restrictions by Jewish law determined how God could or could not be depicted in their art. For instance, ancient Israel was commanded not to make religious images that could usurp their worship of God.[46] However, the people *were* permitted to be artistic in other ways. They could draw from the resources of creation and the laws of aesthetics that God has given all of us. One writer points out that while God did not forbid all representational art,[47] "the ancient Hebrews were still leery about making 'likenesses' of the sort that their nature-worshipping neighbors venerated as manifestations of their gods. This did not mean, as is often charged, that they made no art. Whereas the pagans adorned their pottery and other artifacts with pictures of animals, human beings, and deities, the Hebrews favored nonrepresentational designs: intricate patterns, interlocking shapes, and pleasing colors."[48] Further, we know from the Old Testament that the Jews filled their culture with dance, music, poetry, and song in their worship of the living God. The poetic sections of Scripture such as the Psalms and Song of Solomon are a testimony of this. We also see a striking example of artistic creativity in the book of Exodus, where God calls and equips many diverse kinds of artisans to build his tabernacle (a dwelling for God) in the wilderness.[49] When this great artistic endeavor was finished, God richly blessed it with his presence.[50]

With the exception of the Hebrew culture, the art of the Greco-Roman world that Christ entered revealed the people's worship of the things of creation, depicting their gods and goddesses and the forces of nature. The Infinite or the Divine, in the sense of what Jews and Christians mean by "God," was not depicted, because the transcendent God was not a part of their worldview.

Since God's revelation of himself in Christ, Christians faithfully living out their vocations in the arts have been exhibiting the nature of God, the nature of his creation, and the nature of his people. They have been telling the true Story, *HIS*-story. Cynthia Pearl Maus, in her book *Christ and the Fine Arts,* writes, "More poems have been written, more stories told, more pictures painted, and more songs sung about Christ than any other person in human history, because through such avenues as these the deepest appreciation of the human heart can be more adequately expressed."[51] This has been done throughout church history in many ways and shapes, from the simple "hymns and spiritual songs" recorded in Ephesians 5:19, to the basilicas and cathedrals of Europe, to the work of Michelangelo.

One artistic discipline in which Christians throughout history have made significant contributions is music. Music that serves the Word of God has been created to lift the soul toward God.[52] Pope Gregory the Great (c. 540–604) restructured the liturgy and music of the church, creating the Gregorian chant. In the early ninth century, "church operas" (biblical stories turned into drama) were written and sung near the altars of French churches. These were precursors of the operas that developed five hundred years later during the Renaissance.[53] And in the eleventh century, a monk named Guido of Arezzo (c. 990–1050) became "the father of the modern musical notation." From this time forward, Western music was freed from dependency on oral tradition alone, which was a crucial step in turning music into a "written language."[54]

Many great hymns, such as Luther's "A Mighty Fortress Is Our God," came out of the Reformation period. George Frideric Handel (1685–1759), a follower of Christ, gave the world *Messiah,* which he wrote in less than a month, saying he was under the inspiration of God.[55] And the renowned Johann Sebastian Bach (1685–1750), considered "the father of modern music," was also a Christian. For Bach, music was an act of worship. Throughout his manuscripts and musical scores, one finds the following notations many times: "S.D.G." for *soli Deo gloria,* meaning "solely to the glory of God"; "J.J." for *Jesu Juban,* meaning "help me, Jesus"; and "I.N.J." for *In Nomine Jesu,* meaning "in the name of Jesus."[56]

Music is just one facet of the creative work of Christians in the arts. Christians have led in the arts in the past, and they can lead again. For this to occur, the body of Christ must recognize that art is a God-given gift. Artists need no other justification than that they are called to the arts. There are, of course, many valid justifications; the Greek philosopher Plato summarized the importance of the arts in shaping the future of the nation: "Give me the songs of a nation and it matters not who writes its laws."[57] However, at root, no other validation than God's call is needed.

STEFAN EICHER'S STORY

Stefan Eicher is an artist from India. He is very aware of the injustices perpetuated on the poor because of the Hindu caste system and on women simply because they are female and are considered far inferior to men. For him, loving God and loving his neighbor through his work has taken different forms along his journey, ultimately leading to a vocation he didn't foresee. Here he tells the story of how he found his calling and a connection between art, faith, and justice.

I studied physics in college because physics, of all the different sciences, came easiest to me. The fact that I felt I had only the sciences to choose from had much to do with my family's history of three generations of missions work in India. The sciences felt legitimate because the only precedent was my older brother's choice to study biology in college. I was grateful for the history that rooted my family in this nation, as well as my parents' teaching me to believe in God and modeling a love for people, but as I entered college I did so with the decision that I would disassociate myself from what was, and still is, widely called "full-time ministry," in other words, being an evangelist or pastor.

In my last year of college I came across the concept of Christian development work and was thrilled with the idea that God calls us to serve the poor, as I had seen much poverty growing up. I was thrilled, in fact, that there were opportunities to do so professionally in a "real job," without having to "raise support" as I had seen my parents do.

After seven years of work with a Christian relief and development agency, I experienced burnout and took a sabbatical. One of my prayers for my recovery was that God would give me opportunities to be creative because from early childhood I have loved art. I had finally had a chance to study art at college, along with my physics major, and the art studio had provided me great relief from the physics lab. During my sabbatical, a group of four of my former art classmates decided to reunite for a week of community in which we picked a theme and painted from the perspective of our faith, the week ending with an exhibition in which we sold our paintings. The week was such a deeply satisfying experience it became an annual event for us and we gave our group a name: the Limner Society.

In my work I had shifted from community health to directly trying to get churches to respond to the poor, and yet I was increasingly excited about the idea of artists being disciplers of nations. One day I faced a dilemma on discovering that the annual Limner workshop was scheduled on the very same week as a critical ten-year planning retreat for our church-training team. I was in mental gridlock as to what I should do. My team leader pointed out that if I was clearer on what my overall calling was, making these smaller decisions would flow naturally. He advised me to take the day off and ask God. Sitting on my rocking chair I had a sense, for the first time in my life, that when God looked at me he saw an artist. I had never before considered this, as it went against what people all my life had deemed "important," "urgent," or "spiritual." I also had a vision that if I locked myself up in that room and spent the next thirty years painting pictures of Jesus in the here-and-now of India, simply to help me know him better, and nobody ever saw those paintings, my life would be a complete success. Needless to say I went to the art gathering instead of the planning retreat. Since then I have started organizing an annual workshop in India called "Creative Conscience,"

modeled on the Limner Society, in which Christ-following artists paint about social issues with a biblical worldview and then share their work with the public.

My desire to paint only increases, as does my conviction that just as the church pursues evangelism because of God's heart for the lost, or social ministry because of God's concern for the poor, the church should also set aside resources and people for creating art, because God is Creator. I have a vision to start an art foundation that would create spaces for Christ-following artists in India to pursue art, discover their calling, and connect their art, their faith, and the realities of a broken world around them. And it would allow me to paint!

Unfortunately, contrary to a biblical worldview, many artists receive little support for their calling, and often discouragement instead, from their churches, pastors, and Christian peers. Too often the church has abandoned her rich calling to the arts in favor of a sort of superspirituality. For art to have any value in many evangelical circles, it must deal overtly and unambiguously with spiritual or religious themes. It may also be justified if it is employed in worship or evangelism. Apart from this, there is little space for the Christian artist to be an artist. There is also little concept of, and virtually no place for the *balladeer*[58]—the prophetic artist—to speak into the world.

It is yet another consequence of the sacred-secular mindset that the church itself perpetuates narrowly defined categories of "religious art" and "Christian art," truncating the calling God has given his people. Novelist and short story writer Flannery O'Connor, a devout Catholic, comes at the problem from both a biblical and an artistic point of view:

The very term "Catholic novel" is, of course, suspect, and people who are conscious of its complications don't use it except in quotation marks. If I had to say what a "Catholic novel" is, I could only say that it is one that represents reality adequately as we see it manifested in this world of things and human relationships....The Church we see, even the universal Church, is a small segment of the whole of creation....All of reality is the potential kingdom of Christ, and the face of the earth is waiting to be recreated by his spirit. This all means that what we roughly call the Catholic novel is not necessarily about a Christianized or Catholicized world, but simply that it is one in which the truth as Christians know it has been used as a light to see the world by. This may or may not be a Catholic world, and it may or may not have been seen by a Catholic."[59]

The scope of the artist's work is all of reality. It is the potential kingdom of Christ; it is "the face of the earth." What distinguishes it is *worldview.*

Instead, the term *Christian art* often brings to mind a subculture of subpar work, whether fiction or painting or music. In her essay "Why Work?" the English writer Dorothy Sayers says,

> In her own buildings, in her own ecclesiastical art and music, in her hymns and prayers, in her sermons and in her little books of devotion, the Church will tolerate, or permit a pious intention to excuse, work so ugly, so pretentious, so tawdry and twaddling, so insincere and insipid, so *bad* as to shock and horrify any decent draftsman. And why? Simply because she has lost all sense of the fact that the living and eternal truth is expressed in work only so far as that work is true in itself, to itself, to the standards of its own technique. She has forgotten that the secular vocation is sacred. Forgotten that a building must be good architecture before it can be a good church; that a painting must be well painted before it can be a good sacred picture; that work must be good work before it can call itself God's work.
>
> Let the Church remember this: that every maker and worker is called to serve God *in* his profession or trade—not outside it.[60]

O'Connor sheds light on this same point. After talking about those who consciously distort their talents for popularity or money, O'Connor says,

> Even oftener, I think, we see people distorting their talents in the name of God for reasons they think are good—to reform or to teach or to lead people to the Church. And it is much less easy to say that this is reprehensible. None of us is able to judge such people themselves, but we must, for the sake of truth, judge the products they make. We must say whether this or that novel truthfully portrays the aspect of reality that it sets out to portray. The novelist who deliberately misuses his talent for some good purpose may be committing no

sin, but he is certainly committing a grave inconsistency, for he is trying to reflect God with what amounts to practical untruth. Poorly written novels— no matter how pious and edifying the behavior of the characters—are not good in themselves and therefore are not really edifying.[61]

O'Connor goes on to acknowledge that God can use poor work, but she points out that that is God's business, not that of any human being.

Sadly, there is an aesthetic poverty in the church that is also found in the larger culture. "Christian art" often falls far short of the incarnational or sacramental nature that can hold truth and beauty and mystery. As Western culture turns its back on the Living God, it becomes utilitarian in imagination and taste. The modern world asks the pragmatic questions, "Will it work?" instead of "Is it true?" "Is it valuable?" instead of "Is it good?" and "Is it functional?" instead of "Is it beautiful?"

In the midst of material wealth, the West today is in many cases morally, spiritually, and aesthetically bankrupt because we have abandoned the Living God and the beauty of his holiness. As we have moved from an objective standard for beauty found in the beauty and holiness of God to a standard steeped in relativism, beauty is truly "in the eye of the beholder."

This bankruptcy in the general culture has spread into the church. While there is still a form of spirituality (or in some cases religiosity), the church today is plagued by Greek Gnosticism, which leads to anti-intellectualism, rising immorality, and an anti-aestheticism. As the church in the West lives in a post-Christian culture that denies the God who is Truth, Goodness, and Beauty, she takes on the values of the general culture. Both the church and the world need the vision and leadership of Christians in the arts who understand the nature of God and his creation.

Our Callings Today

- Buy original art to encourage and support Christian artists.
- Create art of all forms that reflects the nature of God and his creation.
- Bring beauty into the mundane, the simple, and the ordinary, including homes and offices.
- Establish schools where all forms of art and biblical theology are fused, so that art can be both for the glory of God and for the advancement of his kingdom.
- Make our places of worship more beautiful and thought-provoking and less utilitarian.
- Promote art and art history classes in schools.
- Write and produce good drama of great biblical themes.
- Plant beautiful flower gardens.

- Promote the use of art in public spaces like parks, convention centers, and concert halls.
- Personally engage in some form of the arts: write poetry or prose; compose, play, or sing music; paint; sculpt; or dance.
- Encourage your children to develop their creative abilities.

MAKOTO FUJIMURA'S STORY

Makoto Fujimura is an American painter whose works are exhibited all over the world. He lives in what was the shadow of the World Trade Center. On 9/11 he was stuck on the subway below Ground Zero. The attack left him and his wife and three children homeless for three months. His children were rescued by firemen from the schools they attended just before the towers collapsed.

As a human being, an artist, and a Christian, how would Fujimura respond to the events of 9/11 and the continued experience of its devastating aftermath? The tragedy raised profound questions for Fujimura about the meaning of his life and the meaning of art. He asked, "Is New York City like Babylon or Jerusalem? How do I remain faithful here, even among the rubble?"[1]

He wrote to friends, "Create we must, and respond to this dark hour. The world needs artists who dedicate themselves to communicate the images of Shalom. Jesus is the Shalom." How does an artist who is a Christian convey the Shalom-Peace in the midst of war? Among the response to the tragedy was Fujimura's exhibit of abstract paintings called "Water Flames." Fujimura

discovered that the way to Peace in a fallen world is through the fire; he found the theme for his work in the works of the poets Dante and T. S. Eliot.

A rarity in contemporary culture, Fujimura is both a Christian and one of America's preeminent visual artists. He has brought into modern abstract art the ancient Japanese technique *nihonga,* which he spent six years studying in Japan. He has also brought themes of beauty and truth, redemption and healing. The founder of the faith-based International Arts Movement and an elder at a Presbyterian church in Greenwich Village, Fujimura acknowledges that some critics "don't know what shelf to categorize my works on. They do see the obvious religious dimension, but, even if they like it, it is out of their semantics as contemporary critics." Yet his work is highly respected in the art world and resonates with both secular and Christian audiences.

Greg Wolfe, editor of the literary and arts journal *Image,* says that Fujimura demonstrates to the mainstream culture that "art which grapples with the reality of traditional experience in a biblical context can be as good as anything anyone is doing in visual arts" while also challenging Christians "to be more discerning as we are called by the Apostle Paul to learn the signs of the times."

Fujimura's International Arts Movement is dedicated to encouraging thoughtful art in the midst of modern society. His leadership in the arts has been recognized by a presidential appointment to the National Council of the Arts. In December of 2005, *World* magazine awarded Makoto Fujimura its cover as "Daniel of the Year" for restoring "art's good name among Christians" and giving "Christians a good name in the arts."

In an interview with the MacLaurin Institute, Fujimura was asked how being an artist has contributed to his understanding of God's character. He said, "God is the ultimate Creator, and we are the 'little creators.' The Bible, from Genesis to Revelation, makes it very clear that God's character is defined by his love for the world and by grace working through broken people. Being an artist makes one realize how God's love is imbedded in creation and in our creativity." Fujimura sees, in addition to the church often neglecting aesthetics, that "there's also a deep theological issue at work that does not allow the whole of our humanity to be integrated in our life and worship." Our hope for "recover[ing] the arts and creativity in the church," he tells us, comes from "rediscover[ing] the holistic gospel."[1]

You can learn more about Fujimura's fascinating story and art in Mindy Belz's *World* cover article "Art Aflame."[2]

ECONOMIC ACTIVITY

We have endeavored throughout this book to develop a biblical Christian view of work, which is, of course, essentially linked to economic activity. Much has already been said about economics, but I do want to mention some other key ideas about this domain and its emphasis and importance throughout Christian history.

As we have learned, man was made for enterprise, for personal economic activity. This is why I have referred to man as *homo oikonomia*—"economic man." Human beings, made in the image of God, were made for business. Dennis Peacocke writes in *Doing Business God's Way*, "The way God runs His Creation qualifies Him as the most prominent and productive businessman of all."[62] In other words, humankind was made to join God in the enterprise of building the kingdom.

Unfortunately, rather than joining in God's enterprise, our work and economic activity in the modern world are often marked by people and corporations rushing greedily to make more and more money while wasting nature's known resources. From this unethical attitude, we can see just how far our societies have fallen from a biblical understanding about the frugality and thrift that should surround economic activity. It is a confirmation of the New Testament's teaching that "the love of money is the root of all evil," and therefore people have "pierced themselves through with many sorrows" (1 Tim. 6:10 KJV).

James, too, has harsh words for the rich whose love is money, not God:

> Now listen, you rich people, weep and wail because of the misery that is coming upon you. Your wealth has rotted, and moths have eaten your clothes. Your gold and silver are corroded. Their corrosion will testify against you and eat your flesh like fire. You have hoarded wealth in the last days. Look! The wages you failed to pay the workmen who mowed your fields are crying out against you. The cries of the harvesters have reached the ears of the Lord Almighty. You have lived on earth in luxury and self-indulgence. (James 5:1–5a)

Please note that James is not rebuking people just because they are rich. After all, God does call some people to be very rich indeed, and they can be good stewards of that wealth. Rather, James is rebuking those who practice what we today would call unfair and unjust employment policies, especially through withholding just wages. They have gained their wealth through such unjust means (see v. 4).

History is rife with such examples. Think of what many major oil companies have done in developing countries. They have signed contracts with corrupt governments allowing the oil companies to extract a valuable national resource with very little return going to the people working in the oil fields and the nation itself. Think of the so-called sweatshops in the developing world, where the smallest of wages are paid to people working virtually as slave laborers to supply the richer world, including many of us, with various kinds of (often inessential) products. Today, the Western world is guilty of much injustice and unethical behavior and policies in the economic domain. As we move to a post-Christian world, we see an increasing void of moral standards. The collapse of Enron in 2001 and the bankruptcy of Global Crossing in 2002 are a testimony to this increased greed and corruption at the highest levels of corporate life. The housing crash in 2007 and 2008 is a reflection of unsound lending and borrowing practices based on maximizing profits without moral constraints.

Since man is economic man, a goal of the Christian must be to redeem the economic domain through the application of biblical principles of economics. The Scriptures are filled with proverbs, parables, and prophetic utterances related to economic activity. In addition to specific passages, the Bible reflects a Hebrew metaphysic in which the physical world is honored as God's creation, affirming the value of our work in this time and place. In keeping with Scripture, throughout history Christians have contributed in significant ways to the economic domain.

THE STORY OF THE MANTHEI GROUP

Business owner Jim Manthei writes,

The Manthei Group consists of six brothers and cousins who grew up together in northern Michigan. We were raised in two families who shared business partnerships and a strong Christian faith. It was in the late 1960s that the six of us decided to invest and work as a group. We thought that if we worked as a team, understanding one another's giftings, we could accomplish more than if we worked as individuals. We now have businesses that include veneer manufacturing, mobile home/recreational vehicle parks, land development, redi-mix plants, road building, and internationally marketed landscape products. We are all believers in Christ and share a common goal of spreading the gospel.

As believers, the members of the Manthei Group have individually served on various international mission boards, and we are very involved with foreign missions. Making money and giving it away on the foreign mission field is the way we were brought up, and this has come naturally for us. A lot of Christians have giving hearts and are faithful supporters of missions. For us, the greater challenge has been learning how to integrate our faith into our daily lives at work through understanding that the "secular" aspect of work is actually part of the sacred calling that God has placed in our lives.

I think what has helped us grow along this path more than anything has been dealing with personal struggles we have encountered with relationships within our group.

Jesus himself labored in this domain. We don't know what kind of money Jesus made when he worked as a carpenter or what he did with that money. But we can assume that just as he fulfilled obedience to God's laws[63] in every other domain, he did so in his economic life as well. Using his carpenter's tools—his chisels, saws, planes, and hammers—Jesus dignified labor, even with his dirty fingernails and callused hands. And when he came into his ministry at age thirty, he used numerous lessons, stories, and parables about economic life to illustrate eternal truths about the kingdom.

The apostle Paul, too, understood the necessity of frugal and thrifty economic activity. He clearly understood God's view of the economic domain. We know that during many periods of his public ministry, which lasted for decades, Paul did not think it beneath himself to take time out for manual labor. In fact, the Epistles make the point a number of times about Paul's day-to-day labor through which he helped to support his own calling financially. Acts 18:3 reveals that Paul worked as a tentmaker, a trade he probably learned in his early years at Tarsus, his hometown. Since tents were usually made from leather, this meant that Paul had to be trained as a leatherworker.

The six of us started to meet on a biweekly basis with a local pastor and several of our children who are involved in our companies. We went through a course called *Gospel Transformations,* which helped us to understand how bad we really are and how good God is. After this, we spent several months going through a video teaching series called *On Earth as It Is in Heaven,* taught by Darrow Miller and Bob Moffitt. Through this study we have grown in understanding God's call in our lives to model Christ in our local community. Following this, we also studied a book by Gregory Boyd, *Repenting of Religion: Turning from Judgment to the Love of God.*

As a result of these growing times, the Manthei Group decided to start a clinic in our community to minister to our employees and their families. We have a full-time nurse and a couple of doctors who work part time.

We provide free health care, teach nutrition, and offer financial and family counseling. At first, many employees were very skeptical, thinking we were trying to invade their personal lives. But the clinic has grown, and we have served many people and have helped several turn their lives around. This has been a way of honoring our employees and showing them that we care for them and God cares for them. We are now starting to have more intentional involvement in our local community, giving and serving and helping reach community goals. We want to build bridges into our community, being sensitive to the Holy Spirit's leading. Our goal is now to use our lives and businesses to serve God by serving others.

And it appears that Paul worked in this capacity on a regular basis. "We work hard with our own hands," Paul writes (1 Cor. 4:12). And in 2 Thessalonians 3:7–10 we read,

> For you yourselves know how you ought to follow our example. We were not idle when we were with you, nor did we eat anyone's food without paying for it. On the contrary, we worked night and day, laboring and toiling so that we would not be a burden to any of you. We did this, not because we do not have the right to such help, but in order to make ourselves a model for you to follow. For even when we were with you, we gave you this rule: "If a man will not work, he shall not eat."

Moving forward in church history, the Franciscan monk Fra Luca Pacioli, a theologian and mathematician, published a book in 1494 about the science and theology of mathematics. In it he wrote a chapter that established double-entry bookkeeping, a method in which a transaction is entered as a debit to one account and a credit to another so that the totals of debits and credits are equal. This father of modern accounting wrote that people should enter economic transactions "in the name of God."[64] Of this humble follower of Christ, Kennedy writes, "The methodology he developed changed the future of business forever and led to the development of spread sheets. His ingenious accounting equation of 'Assets = Liabilities + Owner's Equity' is used worldwide today."[65]

The economic world we know today was also greatly shaped by Protestant Reformer John Calvin. Kennedy writes about Calvin's contribution to economic change: "Calvin freed money from the bondage in which it had been held for centuries, and he unleashed the powers that capitalism has produced."[66]

Calvin's ideas were part of a much larger economic movement that swept the nations influenced by the Protestant Reformation. In fact, it was the biblical worldview recovered by the Reformers that economic historians have recognized as a major factor in the development of "middle-class" society. Prior to the Reformation in Europe, the vast majority of people in the world were poor. Most all the peoples and nations were, to use modern language, underdeveloped. There were but a few wealthy people, including royal families, tribal chiefs, certain political operatives, some private landowners, successful merchants, and mercantilists, who controlled commerce. But essentially everyone else was poor; some were indentured servants, serfs, or slaves.

After the Reformation, in those countries of Northern Europe that were touched by the Reformers, many were lifted out of poverty. For the first time in human history, there was a middle class of significant enough numbers to have become an important sector of society. These were people neither poor nor truly wealthy but participating fully enough in the nation's economy to both enjoy broader opportunities and have a significant influence on the life of the nation.

What is it about the Bible's teachings that brought whole nations out of poverty?

In his book *The Wealth and Poverty of Nations*, economic historian David S. Landes raises the question, "Why are some nations so rich and some so poor?" Landes shows the powerful influence of Chinese and Islamic cultures and asks why they did not produce the dynamic rising of whole nations out of poverty the way that the economic experiment of Europe did. He attributes it to Judeo-Christian "religious values," or worldview. Landes writes,

> Different scholars have suggested a variety of reasons, typically related to religious values:
> 1. The Judeo-Christian respect for manual labor....
> 2. The Judeo-Christian subordination of nature to man. This is a sharp departure from widespread animistic beliefs and practices that saw something of the divine in every tree and stream (hence naiads and

dryads). Ecologists today might think these animistic beliefs prefer-able to what replaced them, but no one was listening to pagan nature worship in Christian Europe.

3. The Judeo-Christian sense of linear time. Other societies thought of time as cyclical, returning to earlier stages and starting over again, meaning no human progress in history and no meaning of work for man. Linear time is progressive or regressive, moving on to better things or declining from some earlier, happier state. For Europeans since the medieval era to our own day, the progressive view prevailed.

4. In the last analysis, however, I would stress the market. *Enterprise was free* in Europe. Innovation worked and paid, and rulers and vested interests were limited in their ability to prevent or discourage inno-vation. Success bred imitation and emulation; also a sense of power that would in the long run *raise men almost to the level of gods* [italics added].[67]

So, the difference, according to Landes, was religious worldview: the dignity of labor, humankind having dominion over creation, history that is going somewhere, and a free market. Landes got the first three right but, in my opinion, got the fourth point backward. The high view of man was not a result of enterprise; it was the biblical con-cept of a high view of man—the image of God—which led to enterprise. Man is the secondary creator, innovator, inventor, and artist. It is these worldview elements and others that raised nations out of poverty.

Two other social and political economists from two different centuries have artic-ulated the thesis that economic development is more about mindset and values than about natural resources: Max Weber (1864–1920) of Germany and Michael Novak (1933–present) of the U.S. First, let's look at Weber.

Max Weber lived in Germany during the same century as Karl Marx (1818–1883). The world knows the name of Karl Marx because of Marxism and his now-discredited social and economic movement known as communism. Fewer people outside of the field of sociology know of Max Weber. However, both had an interest in social and economic philosophy.

Marx, as a thorough-going materialist, believed in a closed system, zero-sum eco-nomic model,[68] where man is a consumer and resources are limited. If some people have more resources than others, it is because they have stolen from the others in one way or another. Marx's socioeconomic system was meant to address this discrepancy, but by the end of the twentieth century, the world witnessed the collapse of the communist order. The system collapsed because the ideas it was founded on were not valid.

Max Weber had the same interest as Marx but was working from a different economic set of assumptions. Weber understood that the system was open and held to a positive-sum economic model. He understood that ideas have consequences. He made the observation that there was an ethic in Protestantism that gave dignity to man's labor. This Protestant ethic was taught from the pulpits of the Reformation. As the ethical principles were applied by the masses, culture was transformed, and new political and economic systems were developed to reflect those principles.

The Reformation not only brought a change to the church; it also brought a change in European culture that in turn transformed nation after nation—a process which five hundred years later has flourished into the global economy. Today a shift in the worldview of countries that are enslaved in poverty can most assuredly have an impact on the development and economic climate of those nations

Similarly, it can be argued that free enterprise has a revolutionary power to impact nations mired in oppression and injustice and that by its own nature and for its own survival, businesses must work to that end. Writer and economic philosopher Michael Novak argues that business needs not only to work from a moral framework but also to contribute to a moral *climate* in the culture—to cultivate virtue and soulcraft.[69] Novak writes that moral ecology in the soul of business is just as important as the natural ecology with which the world (properly) concerns itself. Though some argue that "realism" means to recognize that business can't afford to overly concern itself with moral concerns, in fact the very DNA of enterprise—its genetic code, if you will—demands free and just societies. To be fully successful, businesses must support the rule of law and unleash the potential of free men and women to act responsibly toward the weakest members of the community. For a corporation to act contrary to what Novak calls "moral ecology" through vice, corruption, or an attack on the godly principles revealed to us in Scripture is to undermine the society and ultimately bring about its own death.

Novak sounds a warning to business in a free society:

> In sum, business has many responsibilities to the moral ecology of our nation, and especially to the culture of virtue. It has been wrong—devastatingly wrong—for advertisers in the name of business to promote assaults on traditional virtues. These are the muscles, ligaments, sinews of the free society. Cut them, and you have paralyzed liberty.[70]

Clearly, the economic domain has enormous potential for good. All human beings are "economic man." It is up to Christians today to discover callings in the economic arena, to seek to expand free enterprise, to provide jobs, to help the poor out of poverty, and to produce economic bounty.

TED CORWIN'S STORY

Ted Corwin is a man who, like so many of us, knows what it is like to be rejected by one's boss or organizational culture. We pick up his story when he is "politically" forced out of a job that he loves. The rejection was devastating. As part of his time of healing and regrouping, he took some time to seek the Lord. During this time of reflection, Ted sensed the Lord saying to him, "Build a Christian organization. Share your faith. Help others grow. Be an example of a house built on a solid foundation. Be humble. Care. Go into business."

This was quite a message for someone who thought, "[I don't] have it in me to start a business. I'm too conservative and I don't want to fail." Nonetheless, Corwin was convinced that it was the Lord who was calling him into something that he was not equipped for; he knew that if it was God's call on his life, the Lord would help him succeed. Ted contacted a couple of friends for advice. One was an older friend who knew the ins and outs of furniture manufacturing. The second was a friend who consulted with businesspeople on how to connect faith and work or how to connect one's business to mission.

Out of much counsel, prayer, and obedience, Designmaster Furniture was incorporated in March 1989 to specialize in the manufacture of quality dining room furniture. Jesus' admonition to Peter in John 21:17—"Feed my sheep"—has set the purpose of Designmaster. Corwin writes that the purpose of Designmaster can be viewed from several perspectives.

- We feed the employees and sales representatives of Designmaster physically with work, so that they can provide for their families.
- We feed the stakeholders of Designmaster spiritually by praying with them and for them and by sharing with them how God is at work in our lives.
- We tithe from the profits of Designmaster, using product and cash to help fund Christian charities and ministries.

Further, because of their personal relationships with Jesus Christ, Designmaster's leadership have chosen to value the following:

- Obedience through prayer
- Godly relationships
- Truth
- Quality work
- Freedom and accountability

Ted Corwin and his team are consciously seeking to integrate their faith in Christ with their work in the marketplace.

Our Callings Today

- Reestablish a biblical theology and ethics of economic activity that stands against economic corruption.
- Focus on economic activity that stewards the earth and human development.
- Develop a mission and vision statement that directly links your business to the advancement of the kingdom of God.
- Personally work hard.
- Pay a fair and family wage so that the breadwinner in the family can support the family and allow the nurturer to remain home and nurture the next generation of citizens.
- Engage in the political process to develop policies that support entrepreneurship and free enterprise.
- Support laws that preserve property rights and economic freedom.
- Encourage the creation of business in poor communities.
- Teach the biblical virtues of thrift, hard work, excellence of work, and calling in communities of the poor.
- Reward hard work and excellent work in the marketplace. Extend rewards based on merit and not on nepotism and tenure.
- Establish microsavings and microlending programs for poor communities.
- Establish the use of accurate measures and good accounting practices.
- Think in terms of producing and creating wealth rather than taking and receiving wealth.
- Tithe a part of your business profits to increase the health and wholesomeness of the larger community.

SCIENCE

It has been said that science is man's thinking God's thoughts after him. Science involves the human quest to understand the universe through empirical study. Historically, the word *science* has not been limited to the way in which we understand it today, as the methodological development and application of natural laws. Until the nineteenth century, *science* meant the study of any field of knowledge, and those who studied these fields formally were known as natural philosophers. It is important to note that during the Middle Ages, when there was no metaphysical separation between the spiritual and physical realms, theology, being the integration point of all university education, was called the *queen of the sciences.*

The domain of science, in which we may include technology, is very complex and has meant quite different things throughout history. Two historical streams in particular stand out, the early deductive method and the more modern inductive method. Let's look at each of these important streams.

As far as we know, the first significant stream was developed by the early Greeks, who engaged in systematic thinking about natural phenomena. Nature was seen by them to be controlled by "impersonal" natural laws, which could be discovered and understood. In such a model, it is necessary to start someplace, with a first step that is so obvious that it cannot be disagreed with. Examples would be fire is hot, ice is cold, clay left in the sun hardens, water boils when heated, and so on. Kenneth McLeish writes,

> All such ideas depend on observation of Nature—and indeed it is possible to live one's life comfortably and securely simply by accepting them, without bothering about explanations.... There is a continuum of common sense "knowledge" about the natural world which is enough for most people.[71]

This method of studying nature is called deduction, and it is almost entirely an intellectual exercise.

In ancient times, and even up through the medieval period, the deductive method was regarded as one of the highest achievements of human thought. And it was. The great weakness of this model, however, is that it depends on thought alone. It lacks the kind of rigorous observation and experimentation with nature that is necessary for testing to see whether the first steps are flawed. From about the fifteenth century onward, more and more deductive "scientific" theories were overturned, and "modern science," with its methods of induction, was born.

The method of induction is the other significant scientific stream in history, and it is a 180-degree change from deduction in how people investigate the world of nature. With deductive reasoning one starts with a *particular statement* and proceeds intellectually by logical steps until a *general conclusion* is reached (e.g., the earth is the center of the universe, so the planets orbit the earth). With the inductive scientific method, one starts with a large set of *general observations* and arrives at a *particular conclusion* (e.g., the sun has risen every day in human experience so far, and the sun will rise tomorrow). It is from this kind of rigorous investigation of nature that what we today call "scientific laws" have been discovered and applied.

Although some ancient Greek scientists[72] and later, during the medieval period, some Arab and Muslim scientists made notable discoveries in astronomy, mathematics, and medicine, it was Christianity during the fourteenth through nineteenth centuries that really created the metaphysical framework for the rapid rise of science. All this occurred within the spread of Christianity, with its understanding of the cultural mandate. Christians knew that God had created a world that functioned by universal, physical laws that could be discovered, understood, and applied to the glory of God. And many Christians made science their *life*work.

It is believed that in the thirteenth century, Robert Grosseteste (c. 1175–1253), a Franciscan bishop and the first chancellor of Oxford University, was the first to seriously propose using, and experiment according to, the inductive method of science.[73] Also in the thirteenth century, another notable Franciscan monk, Roger Bacon (c. 1214–1294), contended that "all things must be verified by experience."[74] Bacon studied at Oxford and Paris, and he is most known for his clear anticipation of the methods of modern science. He believed that the end of all true philosophy is to arrive at a knowledge of the Creator through knowledge of the external world.

In the sixteenth century, the leaders of the Protestant Reformation taught that God had revealed himself in two "books." Francis Bacon (1561–1626), another follower of Jesus and one of the early promoters of the inductive method, wrote, "There are two books laid before us to study, to prevent our falling into error; first, the volume of the Scriptures, which reveal the will of God; then the volume of the Creatures, which express his power."[75] In other words, there are God-ordained natural laws that can be known by methodically investigating God's created order. Bacon almost single-handedly turned Europe's thoughts toward this by developing and promoting his method of induction. Bacon also taught that the works produced using the laws of nature ought to be motivated by Christian charity. Knowledge gained, Bacon said, ought to be used to serve others by alleviating human suffering and increasing human well-being. His method, which is second nature to scientists today, involves examining multitudes of particular experiences and developing general laws of nature from that. In this way, we are studying and understanding what God has actually wrought in the creation.[76]

Several other noteworthy Christians who were "founders of modern science" include Johannes Kepler (1571–1630), a German astronomer who coined the phrase that as we discover the laws of nature, we are "thinking God's thoughts after him."[77] Kepler wrote, "Since we astronomers are priests of the highest God in regard to the book of nature, it befits us to be thoughtful, not of the glory of our minds, but rather, above all else, of the glory of God.[78]

Isaac Newton (1642–1727), an English philosopher and mathematician, wrote, "I have a foundational belief in the Bible as the Word of God, written by men who were inspired. I study the Bible daily."[79] Recognized as one of the greatest scientists, Newton made considerable contributions to the study of light and also invented a reflecting telescope. But he is best known for his formulations of the laws of gravity and motion.

The appeal and benefits of science and technology today are so powerful across the world that even animistic societies are aggressively pursuing them. Perhaps because of all of the many legitimate benefits of scientific discovery, the world seems to be in a mad rush just to discover new things. In this sense we have moved far beyond obedience to God in fulfilling the cultural mandate. Indeed, medical science in particular is moving so fast that it is extremely difficult to say what kind of ethical restraints ought to be placed on it. One only has to think of advancing DNA research and the mapping of the human genome to wonder about the serious ramifications down the road. Ought a particular kind of science or technology be developed just because it can be? How can the benefits of scientific and technological advances be extended to the poor? What new discoveries are yet to be made that will help push back the effects of the Fall?

Some Christians have a calling into the sciences. Let them apply the fruits of scientific discovery to push back the curse as far as it is found.

FRANCIS COLLINS'S STORY

It may surprise some contemporary believers that the former director of the Human Genome Project is an evangelical Christian. This renowned scientist, Francis Collins, looks at his study of human DNA with a different worldview than one might expect. "The elegance and complexity of the human genome is a source of profound wonder," he says. "That wonder only strengthens my faith, as it provides glimpses of aspects of humanity, which God has known all along, but which we are just now beginning to discover."[1]

Like other scientists through the ages, Collins recognizes that faith and science are not at odds. As he explains, "Science explores the natural world. Faith explores the supernatural world....Does that make them separate and impossible to integrate into one person, one experience, one thought?...No, from my perspective these two world views coexist in me, and in many of you, right now. We are not torn apart by that; we are not forced into contradictions.

Rather, I believe that we are enriched and blessed. We have an opportunity to practice science as a form of worship. We have a chance to see God as the greatest scientist. As we discover things about the world, we can appreciate the wonders of God's creation. What a gift it is to be a scientist and be able to do that."[2]

For the Human Genome Project, Collins and his team worked for thirteen years to complete the mapping of the three billion letter pairs that capture the human DNA sequence. This DNA sequence directs all the biological properties of our bodies, determining whether we have blue eyes or brown, whether we are at high risk for heart disease or a particular type of cancer. The project was completed in 2003, creating a new body of knowledge that will aid scientific and medical advances but also bring potential for significant abuse.

Knowledge of the human DNA map offers great opportunities to improve the effectiveness of treatments for disease. Just as past advances in medicine have spared millions of people from polio and smallpox, genetic mapping allows further possibilities for alleviating disease. However, along with great possibilities come real dangers, including genetic discrimination and unequal access for the poor.

Perhaps the danger of most concern is the potential manipulation of DNA to affect the makeup of future generations, something Collins is well aware of. He recognizes that there must be a firm line between using DNA knowledge to treat diseases in the current generation and using it to produce "designer babies" in the future. To show this distinction, he explains the term *germ line*. "The germ line is the part of the DNA that does get passed to the next generation. Most of our DNA is not germ line....If I had cystic fibrosis and I wanted that cured in my lungs and you could change the genes in my lungs that have that glitch, I'd want you to do that. But that would not affect my offspring. I think that's a critical distinction. And all of the promise that I see for genetic therapies for diabetes, or heart disease, or cancer does not require you to go into the germ line to make those changes."[3]

The relative newness of this knowledge means that Christians like Collins have a great opportunity to help shape the ethics around its use. The church as a body and the church scattered in science and government can be influential in determining whether society ethically or unethically uses the discoveries God has allowed us to make.

Ultimately, as Francis Collins recognizes, God is the *only* scientist who will ever know all of the secrets of his creation. We are privileged to join in the work of the "greatest scientist."

Our Callings Today

- Encourage the reintegration in science of the study of the twin revelations of God's world and his Word. This challenges the metaphysical assumptions of materialistic or naturalistic science.
- Encourage students with a proclivity for science to study science and to pursue advanced degrees so that they may teach and do research in the sciences.
- Work in the developing world to educate people in the orderliness of the universe, the inductive principles of discovery and problem solving, and basic science and technology; and help them build up their societies in this vital area.
- Pursue research to develop technology that fights "natural evil," such as flooding; earthquakes; plant, animal, and human diseases; and other devastating events.
- Pursue research into the prevention and treatment of disease, birth defects, injuries, and other health issues.

- Bring moral criteria and ethics back into the scientific arena. It is not enough to do science and technology simply because "now we can do this or that." We must ask, "Ought we do it?"
- Cross-pollinate wisdom in health, agricultural, animal, and aquacultural sciences from one nation to another. Create a free exchange of ideas in science and technology.
- Introduce the use of appropriate technologies to help the poor take significant intermediate steps between stone-age agriculture and modern agriculture.
- Support policies that encourage greater productivity and stewardship of the land.

We have a great cloud of witnesses who have lived their lives as Christians in the gates of the city, bringing biblical principles, vision, and life to all the domains. Will we do the same in the twenty-first century?

GEORGE WASHINGTON CARVER'S STORY

A renowned African American scientist and inventor in the early twentieth century, George Washington Carver (c. 1861–1943) lived in dedication to the service of the Great Creator and in passionate pursuit of his dreams. Whereas most scientists at the time (and many today) felt that faith and science could not be juxtaposed, Carver considered them inseparable; his study and discovery of the natural world were simply ways that he came to know God in a deeper way. As Carver himself put it, "Nature and its varied forms are little windows through which God permits me to commune with Him and to see much of His glory, majesty, and power by simply lifting the curtain and looking in."[1]

From a young age, George was so interested in plants and had such a natural talent for keeping them alive that he was nick-named "The Plant Doctor." Neighbors from miles around brought him plants to revive. As he grew older, Carver's questions about the natural world only mounted, and realizing that those around him could not answer them, he set off alone to pursue his quest for knowledge. Speaking of his childhood, Carver said, "I wanted to know the name of every stone and flower and insect and bird and beast. I wanted to know where it got its color, where it got its life—but there was no one to tell me."[2]

George faced many obstacles in the pursuit of his dream: he was born a slave during the Civil War and was orphaned as a baby, he was barred from admission at schools because of his race, he witnessed and endured racially motivated beatings and attacks, and he dealt constantly with perpetual distrust and hatred, all difficulties that might have pushed him to give up his passion and settle into a path that required less from him. Instead, George treated each defeat as a learning experience. His tenacity and creativity in pushing past barriers, combined with the support of a few key mentors, kept him on the path toward that which he knew he was made to do.

Eventually, George went to work as a professor at the Tuskegee Institute in Alabama, the all-black school established by Booker T. Washington to educate former slaves. As Carver's fame grew, he was offered positions at other organizations that would have dramatically increased his salary, but he chose to stay at Tuskegee for all of his teaching years, recognizing the important influence he had there.

Carver's influence stretched far beyond the campus boundaries, however. In addition to mentoring students both spiritually and academically, Carver was deeply committed to using his ever-increasing expertise to help struggling Southern farmers. Southern agriculture was in deep trouble. The industry was completely dependent on the success of its cotton crops, and now, after growing the same crop for so many years, farmers were finding that it no longer grew well. In addition, the boll weevil, an insect feared for its ability to destroy cotton plants, had made its way up from Mexico. George saw this as a perfect opportunity to introduce and encourage the planting of different crops. These new crops weren't susceptible to the boll weevil, would restore the missing nutrients to the soil, and would even provide a way for farmers to feed their own families off the land.

George spent much time in his lab, working to find as many practical uses for the new crops as possible. To share this knowledge, George published "three-fold bulletins" about the products he was encouraging farmers to grow, in an effort to help them get the most out of every crop. These popular bulletins included planting advice for farmers, recipes and many other practical uses of the crop for their wives, and scientific information about the plant for the hundreds of Tuskegee agricultural graduates scattered around the area as teachers and farmers. In addition to the bulletins, George made Tuskegee Institute a resource center for farmers in the area. To get the word out even further, he helped establish a wagon that traveled throughout the South providing agricultural information.

Through Carver's quiet and persistent influence, farming methods in the South began to change, and organizations around the country came to call on his methods and wisdom. Eventually, Carver's work and influence extended to the highest levels of science and government and reached across the world. Among other honors, Carver was called upon to testify before Congress, hosted President Theodore Roosevelt at Tuskegee, and advised officials from Africa and the Soviet Union on farming methods.

For George, however, each of these opportunities was simply an occasion to share his love of God and of science. He particularly desired that those influenced by him would use whatever nature was around them as a means of coming to know their Creator in a deeper way, as he did. "To those who have as yet not learned the secret of true happiness, which is the joy of coming into the closest relationship with the Maker and Preserver of all things: begin now to study the little things in your own door yard, going from the known to the nearest related unknown for indeed each new truth brings one nearer to God."[3]

George Washington Carver is credited as one of the first advocates of sustainable agriculture and organic fertilizing techniques and for making known hundreds of practical uses for products derived from the peanut, sweet potato, pecan, and clay. Though popularly remembered for inventing hundreds of peanut-based products, Carver accomplished much, much more. Through his life of study and service, Carver surely lived out that which he was fond of saying: "No individual has any right to come into the world and go out of it without leaving behind him distinct and legitimate reasons for having passed through it."[4]

CHAPTER 20

THE GREAT
COMMANDMENT

It has been said that a world without Christ is a world without love and compassion. This is strikingly true today in a world where conditions in cities, for example, breed alienation, distrust, and cruelty. Without true love and compassion, social life spreads the seeds of discontent, bitterness, and violence. Stemming from our sinful depravity, people's inhumanity to one another causes much of the social unrest and violence in the world. Contrary to the secular belief that man is basically good, human beings are born with a propensity to sin. Both Scripture and history reveal that human beings are self-centered, self-serving, and often barbaric. They need to be "civilized" into obeying the rule of law, being compassionate to strangers, putting the needs of others before self, loving one another and one's enemies, and even practicing what people of old called "refinement of manners." Sociologist Rodney Stark argues that Christianity overwhelmed pagan Greco-Roman society by manifesting a superior set of ideas in its midst:

> Something distinctive did come into the world with the development of Judeo-Christian thought: the linking of a highly social ethical code with religion. There was nothing new in the idea that the supernatural makes behavioral demands on humans—the gods have always wanted sacrifices and worship. Nor was there anything new in the notion that the supernatural will respond to offerings—that the gods can be induced to exchange services for sacrifices. What was new was the notion that more than self-interested exchange

relations were possible between humans and the supernatural. The Christian teaching that God loves those who love him was alien to pagan beliefs.... Equally alien to paganism was the notion that because God loves humanity, Christians cannot please God unless they love one another. Indeed, as God demonstrates his love through sacrifice, humans must demonstrate their love through sacrifice on behalf of one another. Moreover, such responsibilities were to be extended beyond the bonds of family and tribe, indeed to "all those who in every place call on the name of our Lord Jesus Christ" (1 Cor. 1:2). These were revolutionary ideas.[1]

For a society to become civil, individuals must become loving and moral. Brutish individuals create brutish societies. Brutish societies breed poverty. In the misery of the Greco-Roman society, the early Christians brought not only hope but also social transformation. Stark writes,

Christianity served as a revitalization movement that arose in response to the misery, chaos, fear, and brutality of life in the urban Greco-Roman world.... [It provided] new norms and new kinds of social relationships able to cope with many urgent urban problems. To cities filled with the homeless and impoverished, Christianity offered charity as well as hope. To cities filled with newcomers and strangers, Christianity offered an immediate basis for attachments. To cities filled with orphans and widows, Christianity provided a new and expanded sense of family. To cities torn by violent ethnic strife, Christianity offered a new basis for social solidarity.... And to cities faced with epidemics, fires and earthquakes, Christianity offered effective nursing services.... For what they brought was not simply an urban movement, but a new culture capable of making life in Greco-Roman cities more tolerable.[2]

What Christ and his followers have done, as Stark notes closing his book, is nothing less than the humanizing of man.[3]

THE HUMANIZING OF MAN AND THE GREAT COMMANDMENT

It is no accident that these observations are made about the effect of the Christianity that has followed Jesus. Jesus said that it is by our love for one another that we will be known as his followers.[4] And Jesus summed up all the Law and the Prophets this way: love God and love your neighbor as yourself.[5] In fact, this is what Jesus said when he was asked, "Of all the commandments, which is the most important?"

"The most important one...is this: 'Hear, O Israel, the Lord our God, the Lord is one. Love the Lord your God with all your heart and with all your soul and with all your mind and with all your strength.' The second is this: 'Love your neighbor as yourself.' There is no commandment greater than these." (Mark 12:29–31)

Whatever domain we are called to, in whatever specific way we are called upon to occupy the gates of our city, this Great Commandment is the basis for our work. Whatever our vocation, if we follow Jesus, we will manifest in our work God's love for *all* people, young and old, men and women, slave and free, whatever color and whatever creed. In this aspect, we will reclaim what it means to be truly human, made in the image of God.

Christians down through history, working in a multitude of domains, have modeled for us how to see and treat people as God does, a true marker of the culture of the kingdom. Let's look at four areas of life that followers of Jesus have helped to bring into line with God's intentions: the sanctity of human life; the emancipation of slaves and racial reconciliation; dignity and respect for women, wives, and marriage; and mercy and compassion for the poor.[6] These four areas remain places where we are called to live out the Great Commandment today.

THE SANCTITY OF HUMAN LIFE

The Greco-Roman world Christ entered was one of great, commonplace cruelty, violence, and barbarity. Think of the gladiators. As people today attend a soccer match or a baseball game, the ancient Romans filled coliseums to see human beings killed as a kind of sports event. Historian William Stearns Davis writes that the gladiatorial games "illustrate completely the pitiless spirit and carelessness of human life lurking behind the pomp, glitter, and cultural pretensions of the great imperial age."[7] In addition, as a form of entertainment for himself and for the Roman elite, the emperor Nero (r. AD 54–68) would throw Christians to the lions in the arenas, have them crucified, or burn them at the stake to provide light for roadways and garden parties.[8]

Suicide was another common act of violence, so common that to "take one's own life was [considered] an act of self-glory."[9] In fact, suicide was so "normal" that a saying arose about it. When it came time to take one's own life, people often responded with the refrain "open your veins."[10] Many Roman leaders, such as Pontius Pilate, Senators Brutus and Cassius, Anthony, and Emperor Hadrian committed suicide.[11]

Infanticide and child abandonment were two other common acts of barbarity. Infanticide had been justified by philosophers such as Seneca, Plato, and Aristotle[12] and was canonized in law. "The Twelve Tables"—the earliest known Roman legal code, written about 450 BC—permitted a father to expose any female infant and any deformed or weak male infant.[13] Because of the Roman concept of paterfamilias (that fathers held absolute power in families), the Roman father had absolute life-or-death power over his children. George Grant writes that because of paterfamilias,

> the birth of a Roman was not a biological fact. Infants were received into the world only as the family willed. A Roman did not have a child; he took a child. Immediately after birthing, if the family decided not to raise the child—literally, lifting him above the earth—he was simply abandoned. There were special high places or walls where the newborn was taken and exposed to die.[14]

This "natural" disregard for young children in those days is exhibited in the story that we find so abhorrent theses days of Herod's murder of all the baby boys two years old and younger recorded in Matthew 2:16.

Abortion was also common. Because of paterfamilias, a Roman husband could order his wife to have an abortion at his own whim.[15] In Rome, some women aborted for economic reasons, some to cover their adultery, and some, by being childless, to have more "influence."[16]

The modern Western world, despite extensive Christian foundations, is now faring little better. During the twentieth century, Western nations experienced a turning point, moving socially from the biblical view of "the sanctity of human life" to the modern secular-pagan value system of "the quality of life." The modern West is returning to paganism through the practices of abortion, infanticide, euthanasia, and stem cell research using human embryos.

Yet even from the time of the early church, all human life, including that of the unborn, was seen as sacred by Christians. And as the church grew in the early centuries, the influence of the Christians' high view of life ended many pagan practices. For instance, by the fourth century, "Under the reign of the Christian emperor Theodosius I (378–395), gladiatorial contests were terminated in the East, and his son Honorius ended them in 404 in the West."[17]

The Christian high view of all human life gradually changed people's view of suicide, infanticide, child abandonment, and abortion. Because they understood "thou shall not kill" to include "self killing," the early church fathers stood against suicide. And as the followers of Christ increased in number, infanticide and child abandonment diminished in the Greco-Roman world. D. James Kennedy writes, "The cry went out to bring the children to church. Foundling homes, orphanages, and nursery homes started to house the children."[18] In fact, an influential early church document called the Didache (written between 85 and 110 and often referred to as the Teaching of the Apostles) states in its second paragraph, "Thou shalt not murder a child by abortion, nor kill them when born." The medieval church continued this tradition, issuing over four thousand canons between the fourth and twelfth centuries that recognized the sacredness of life. The Reformation church, similar to its Roman Catholic counterpart, also reaffirmed the sanctity of human life. [19]

The modern church has had a mixed response. Catholicism has largely been a bulwark for the sanctity of human life, as has much of evangelical Christendom. But many "mainline" Protestant denominations are more aligned with secular thought on issues of abortion and euthanasia. Nevertheless, in America, for instance, Christians of all sorts have established thousands of crisis pregnancy centers, where women can receive advice and support to save the lives of their unborn babies. This is a great calling in a nation where, shockingly, approximately 1.5 million babies each year are sacrificed before birth through abortion, with (until recently) approximately 13,000 killed each year at the moment of birth by "partial-birth abortion."

It is incumbent upon all Christians to fight for the sanctity of all human life, both the young and the old, those who are healthy and those who are infirm or disabled. Today Christians are leading the fight to protect human life through starting and volunteering in crisis pregnancy centers for mothers and babies and in hospices serving those at the end of life.

Our Callings Today

- Establish pro-life policies and procedures in hospitals.
- Work to bring in national pro-life legislation.
- Care for babies who have been left to die under doctor's orders, and call people's attention to this "medical practice" through the media.
- Support the enforcement or the enactment of laws that protect all human life.
- Work in support of healthy families through nonprofit or government social services.
- Work within government to improve the lives of children under the care of the state.
- Provide foster care for children.
- Adopt orphans and abandoned children.
- Work with homeless and other at-risk youth.
- Care for the elderly, sick, and disabled in one's own family and extend the provision of that care to others.
- Commit to serving the elderly and the sick in your church community, including those unable to be present at worship.
- Learn about, pray for, and be a voice for those devalued in your own or other communities or countries, including the disabled, the sick, the poor, ethnic and religious minorities, and girls and women.

JILL STANEK'S STORY

Jill Stanek is a registered nurse who came to understand what it means to live as a Christian in the midst of a broken world. She writes,

I had been working for a year at Christ Hospital in Oak Lawn, Illinois, as a registered nurse in the Labor and Delivery Department, when I heard in report that we were aborting a second-trimester baby with Down's syndrome. I was completely shocked. In fact, I had specifically chosen to work at Christ Hospital because it was a Christian hospital and not involved, so I thought, in abortion. It hurt so much that the very place these abortions were being committed was at a hospital named after my Lord and Savior Jesus Christ. I was further grieved to learn that the hospital's religious affiliates, the Evangelical Lutheran Church of America and the United Church of Christ, were pro-abortion. I had no idea that any Christian denomination could be pro-abortion!

But what was most distressing was to learn of the method Christ Hospital uses to abort, called induced labor abortion, now also known as "live birth abortion." In this particular abortion procedure, doctors do not attempt to kill the baby in the uterus. The goal is simply to prematurely deliver a baby who dies during the birth process or soon afterward....

It is not uncommon for a live aborted baby to linger for an hour or two or even longer. At Christ Hospital one of these babies lived for almost an entire eight-hour shift....

In the event that an aborted baby is born alive, she or he receives "comfort care," defined as keeping the baby warm in a blanket until she or he dies. Parents may hold the baby if they wish. If the parents do not want to hold their dying aborted baby, a staff member cares for the baby until she or he dies. If staff does not have the time or desire to hold the baby, the baby is taken to Christ Hospital's new Comfort Room, which is complete with a First Foto machine, if parents want professional pictures of their aborted baby; baptismal supplies, gowns, and certificates; foot printing equipment; baby bracelets for mementos; and a rocking chair. Before the Comfort Room was established, babies were taken to the Soiled Utility Room to die.

One night, a nursing coworker was taking a Down's syndrome baby who was aborted alive to our Soiled Utility Room because his parents did not want to hold him and she did not have time to hold him. I could not bear the thought of this suffering child dying alone in a Soiled Utility Room, so I cradled and rocked him for the 45 minutes that he lived. He was between 21 and 22 weeks old, weighed about 1/2 pound, and was about 10 inches long. He was too weak to move very much, expending any energy he had trying to breathe. Toward the end he was so quiet that I could not tell if he was still alive. I held him up to the light to see through his chest wall whether his heart was still beating. After he was pronounced dead, we folded his little arms across his chest, wrapped him in a tiny shroud, and carried him to the hospital morgue where all of our dead patients are taken.

After I held that baby, the weight of what I knew became too much for me to bear. I had two choices. One choice was to leave the hospital and go work at a hospital that didn't commit abortions. The other was to attempt to change Christ Hospital's abortion practice. Then, I read a Scripture that spoke directly to me and my situation. Proverbs 24:11–12 says, "Rescue those who are unjustly sentenced to death; don't stand back and let them die. Don't try to disclaim responsibility by saying you didn't know about it. For God, who knows all hearts, knows yours, and he knows you knew! And

he will reward everyone according to his deeds." I decided that to quit at that point would be irresponsible and disobedient to God. Sure, I might be more comfortable if I left the hospital, but babies would continue to die.[1]

What would you do in this situation, separate your faith from your work or connect your work to the kingdom of God? Jill made her choice. She stood against the policies of the hospital. She went public with her charges and ended up testifying four times before National and Illinois Congressional Subcommittees. On October 31, 2001, after a two-and-a-half-year battle, Jill Stanek was fired from her job. What was her "crime"? She spoke truth to power and defended the right of a child to life. Would we do the same?

THE EMANCIPATION OF SLAVES AND RACIAL RECONCILIATION

In the world that Jesus entered, half of the population of the Roman Empire and 75 percent of the Athenians were slaves.[20] This number included both menial laborers and skilled craftsmen. Schmidt writes,

> Slaves performed virtually all of the physical or manual work. Thus, the Appian Way, the Seven Wonders of the World, and even the beautiful sculptures from that period were the work of slaves. Every time present-day tourists are impressed by the magnificent ancient buildings and statues...in the countries of the Middle East or in Europe, they are looking at the products of slave labor.[21]

The Greek philosopher Aristotle (384–322 BC) was representative of the era when he described slavery as "natural, expedient, and just."[22] Elsewhere he wrote that "a slave is a living tool, just as a tool is an inanimate slave. Therefore there can be no friendship with a slave as slave."[23]

During the Middle Ages, slavery was common among Arabs and Mongols as well as among Vikings and other Europeans. Saint Patrick was captured and taken as a slave to Ireland. Many American Indian tribes practiced slavery as well.[24] Black-on-black slavery could be found in Africa, and it was largely black Africans who later sold their fellow Africans to the European traders. Even after abandoning slavery in their own nations, many European states still permitted slavery in their colonies, and the practice continued legally in the newly independent United States until 1865 and in Brazil until 1888. In the twentieth century, slaves were owned legally in Ethiopia until 1941, in Saudi Arabia until 1962, in Peru until 1964, and in India until 1976.[25]

Today, slavery remains a tragic international problem. All over the world, in Europe, Southeast Asia, India, the Americas, Africa, and the Middle East, the modern-day slave trade flourishes. Boys are usually enslaved as laborers or child soldiers; women and girls are most often sold into the commercial sex trade, some as young as age five. Even in the U.S., women, often imported under false pretenses, are illegally held captive in the sex business. Immigrants have been found working in sweatshops with little or no compensation, some supposedly "paying back" those who brought them here—a form of slavery or at least indentured labor. Across the world, trafficking in humans is a huge money maker, usually tied to organized crime. Hundreds of thousands of people are trafficked across national borders each year, and millions more are sold and used within their own countries. In India millions more are virtually slaves through the caste system.

Jesus Christ died to break down the barriers between race, class, and caste prejudice that are at the root of slavery. We see this by extension of some seminal principles that Paul introduces in his epistles. Ephesians 2:11–22 reveals that through the blood of Christ and the cross, "circumcised" Jews and the "uncircumcised" Gentiles become "one new man." On the most basic level our common humanity means that divisions based on race, class, ethnic group, and caste are to be abolished. The dividing walls are to be torn down. In Christ, this rises to the highest compulsion, because Christ's precious blood was shed to make one new man. Galatians 3:28 teaches that "in Christ" there is neither "slave nor free . . . for you are all one in Christ Jesus" (see also Col. 3:11).

The early church, although it did not change the existing social structure of slavery, nevertheless sought where possible to change attitudes toward slavery. A striking example is the account of Paul sending a runaway slave, Onesimus, back to his master, Philemon, who was a well-to-do Christian in Colossae. Apparently Onesimus had stolen from Philemon, or done some other sort of considerable damage to his master, and then had run away. Somehow Onesimus ended up in Rome, where Paul gave him refuge and he became a Christian. Seeking to transform just a small area of the existing slavery construct, Paul eventually sent Onesimus back to Philemon with a letter saying that he should receive Onesimus back as a brother in the Lord. Evidently it was unthinkable to Paul that one Christian should "own" another Christian. (See the book of Philemon for the whole story.)

Later the Christian attitude toward slavery spread politically. In AD 315 Constantine "imposed the death penalty on those who stole children to bring them up as slaves."[26] St. Augustine (AD 354–430) declared that slavery was the product of sin and was contrary to God's divine plan.[27] In 1102 a London church council outlawed slavery in England.[28] By "the twelfth century slaves in Europe were rare, and by the fourteenth century slavery was almost unknown on the Continent."[29]

The sixteenth century, however, brought a revival of the slave trade in the colonies of European nations. Approximately ten million slaves were sent to the Americas.

The Christian response to slavery in modern times was led in large part, as we have already seen, by William Wilberforce, a follower of Christ and member of the British Parliament, and by the Clapham Sect who fought for decades to end slavery in the British Empire. The Abolition Act of 1833 emancipated 700,000 British-held slaves. In America a great religious revival in the late eighteenth and early nineteenth centuries helped to ignite the abolitionist movement. The great revivalist and evangelist Charles G. Finney founded Oberlin College to train evangelists and to spearhead the fight against slavery. It is said that Finney hid fugitive slaves in his own attic.[30] In 1835, in America, two-thirds of the members of the abolition movement were clergy.[31] And many other leaders of this movement, such as Charles Torrey, Harriet Beecher Stowe, and William Lloyd Garrison, were followers of Christ. They lived out their callings in a very heated national environment. It was a harsh struggle, with intense feelings on both sides of an issue that split most national denominations and political parties. People were killed for their views, and slavery was a chief ingredient in America's bloody and costly Civil War (1861–1865). The Thirteenth Amendment to the U.S. Constitution, which was proposed and ratified in 1865, abolished slavery.

In our modern context, in the USA, it was largely Christians who led the civil rights movement. John M. Perkins grew up in the South as a sharecropper. He became a civil rights activist and founded the John M. Perkins Foundation for Reconciliation and Development. Perkins worked to apply biblical principles in the realm of racial reconciliation and economic development for those born into poverty. Perhaps the most famous of the modern leaders of the civil rights movement was Dr. Martin Luther King Jr., a Baptist pastor who began the Southern Christian Leadership Conference in 1957, whose purpose was to use the moral authority of Scripture and the organizing power of black churches to lead a nonviolent movement to bring about civil rights. On August 28, 1963, from the steps of the Lincoln Memorial during the March on Washington

DOLPHUS WEARY'S STORY

"I ain't comin' back!" was Dolphus Weary's vow after finally leaving behind the crippling poverty, racism, and injustice of Mendenhall, Mississippi, in the 1960s. As a black man in the Deep South during the beginnings of the Civil Rights movement, not only were opportunities few, Dolphus and other African Americans dealt with the daily reality of indiscriminate harassment and violence.

When Dolphus had the opportunity to attend Los Angeles Baptist College (LABC) in California as one of its first black students, his experience there was life changing. Unlike in Mississippi, Dolphus was able to receive an education equal to that which was offered to white students. Opportunities began to open up in front of him, and he was excited to have escaped the demoralizing life in which so many people were still trapped in Mississippi.

Despite Dolphus's promising future, he still dealt with more subtle racism and suspicion at LABC. After witnessing the delight of some white students upon hearing the news of Martin Luther King Jr.'s assassination, Dolphus realized that he could no longer just seek to fit in and make himself comfortable but must find the courage to speak out. Though hurt by the behavior of his classmates, Dolphus knew that he could be used by God to open doors of understanding in students who had been taught bigotry by their families and communities and that the purpose of his time at LABC

went beyond earning a degree; it was also an opportunity to educate and challenge those around him in their attitudes toward other racial groups.

Later, nearing the completion of a second degree, a master's in Christian education, Dolphus began to think more seriously about his future direction, now, together with his wife, Rosie. Dolphus had first come to California on a basketball scholarship and had an opportunity to tour East Asia with a basketball team. While on tour, he was amazed that he, as a black man from Mississippi, was treated with such respect and admiration and began to consider returning with Rosie to minister in the Asian countries where he had been so well received.

It wasn't long, however, before the urgings of one of Dolphus's mentors, a man named John Perkins, and God's gentle call began to beckon him back to Mississippi. At first, Dolphus resisted, reminded of his vow to never return to the place that had so oppressed him. But over time, his heart changed. "I realized that no matter how far I ran, whether to California or even to Taiwan, I could never run away from the Mendenhall inside of me, the one in my head and in my heart. Until I overcame that, I'd always be enslaved to a sense of hopelessness. And yet I knew that in myself I couldn't overcome it— only God could....Going back to Mississippi seemed to involve service and a sacrifice of my own desires on behalf of others who needed hope. I felt that God was urging me, 'Dolphus, I have something for you to do in Mississippi.'"[1]

When Dolphus and Rosie returned to live in Mendenhall, the black community was crippled in a cycle of poverty and it was clear that much of the racism and hopelessness with which they had grown up was still present. As they reacquainted themselves with their neighbors and the community, the needs for basic health care, quality education, legal aid, pastoral training, and more became clear. In the more than thirty years since then, Mendenhall Ministries has grown to address these needs by founding and operating institutions that had never been present in the community before: a sliding scale health clinic; a quality, affordable private school and a tutoring program; a thrift store that provides jobs and reasonably priced merchandise; a community center that gives youth opportunities for fellowship and recreation; and more. All of these ministries are centered around Mendenhall Bible Church.

In the beginning, Dolphus and his staff struggled with how to integrate the gospel with ministries that met people's physical needs. They recognized that often people couldn't even begin to take in the words of the gospel because of their pressing physical needs. And yet, without transformation from the inside, few of the physical needs that the ministry might be able to meet would have much lasting effect. At times it seemed that they were operating two separate ministries: people would come to the clinic or school for health or education needs but be sent to the church for any spiritual questions. Over time, that has changed. In Dolphus's own words, "What we want is for every worker to do his work out of a spirit of Christlike service. And we want every one of them to know how to lead someone to Jesus Christ and to actually see that as part of his job."[2]

Now the president of Mission Mississippi, for the past ten years Dolphus has focused on racial reconciliation. The Jackson, Mississippi, ministry sponsors and coordinates opportunities for people of different denominations and races to meet, get to know each other, and serve the Lord together. Working to heal the racial and denominational divisions among Christian churches, Dolphus speaks extensively to both black and white congregations around the United States, challenging believers with the question, "How should the redeemed live?" from powerful texts such as Ephesians 2.[3] He doesn't ask people to change their denomination but their attitude of separation. "Mission Mississippi, which many see as a voice of hope, helps close that old historical racial gap," Dolphus says. "We're now doing things that we couldn't have done five to ten years ago."[4]

From Mendenhall and Jackson to communities around the nation, anyone who has crossed paths with Dolphus Weary has experienced the transforming result of one man being faithful to God's call.

for Jobs and Freedom, Dr. King gave a speech entitled "I Have a Dream." That speech both electrified those who heard it and called the nation to the principles of her founding, that "all men are created equal." It was a defining moment in the American Civil Rights Movement.

It was figures like Perkins and King who called America and the world to their God-given responsibility to recognize in law and practice the dignity of all human beings. Today many believers are following Christ's call to free those who are enslaved and to bring reconciliation. One group, the International Justice Mission, is employing Christian lawyers and activists to challenge child sex slavery internationally. It is the call of Christians today to work against racism, casteism, and tribalism wherever they are prevalent in the world today.

Our Callings Today

- Demonstrate the power of the blood of Christ to break down barriers between caste, race, and class by modeling in our churches "one new man" (see Ephesians 2).
- Build relationships at work or in your communities with people who are from different ethnic and racial backgrounds.
- Put pressure on our governments to condemn Sudan for its modern slave practices, as well as other nations for participation or complicity with human trafficking and the commercial sex industry.
- Work in civil rights and human rights arenas.
- Stand with the church in India and call her to oppose in word and practice the functional equivalent of slavery in the Hindu caste system.
- Form an *artists for justice* or *mothers for justice* group in your country or state.
- Study international law or civil rights law and become a lawyer activist.

DIGNITY AND RESPECT FOR WOMEN, WIVES, AND MARRIAGE

The Greco-Roman world that Christ entered was not unlike the "sexist" world today. Women during that time often had the social status of a slave. Aristotle said, "Silence gives grace to woman."[32] According to Athenian law, a woman of any age was always considered a child "and therefore was the legal property of some man at all stages in her life."[33] In Greek life, it was usual that a woman could leave her home only in the company of a male escort, usually a slave. Girls were not permitted to go to school, and a woman could not speak in public.[34]

While a Roman woman had more freedom than her Greek sister, when compared with men she had virtually no rights and privileges. The Roman law of *manus* established the husbands' "ownership" and absolute control over their wives' lives.[35] There was, in fact, so little respect for women that female prisoners were often jailed in the same cells with men, creating terribly abusive conditions. And regarding the unmarried, Philip Schaff writes, "The virtue of chastity, in our Christian sense, was almost unknown among the heathens. Woman was essentially a slave of man's lower passions."[36] Regarding marriage, Schmidt notes the second century historian Tacitus stating that "sexual immorality was so pronounced that a chaste wife was seen as a rarity."[37]

Further, infanticide in the Greco-Roman world was partly aimed at eliminating the "inferior" child—the female. Newborn baby girls were routinely killed through exposure or drowning. A letter from a Roman soldier named Hilarion, stationed in North Africa, to his pregnant wife, Alis, shows this typical attitude:

> Know that I am still in Alexandria. And do not worry if they all come back and I remain in Alexandria. I ask and beg you to take good care of our baby son, and as soon as I receive payment I shall send it to you. If you are delivered of a child [before I come home], if it is a boy keep it, if a girl discard it. You have sent me word, "Don't forget me." How can I forget you. I beg you not to worry.[38]

Later societies have also had attitudes and laws regarding women that make the modern Christian world cringe. In the Hindu world of India, women are believed to have been, in a previous life, men who had bad karma. By this understanding, being a woman is punishment for the "sin" of a past life. Child bride marriages and *suttee*— widow burning—have been among the cultural practices stemming from this Hindu view of women. Although modern India has legislated against *suttee* and this practice is now relatively rare, today other problems persist. Wives are still being killed, often by burning, either because they are judged unsatisfactory or, all too often, because the husband's family would like to receive another dowry. (The giving of dowries is illegal but still common.) Though these wife killings are as illegal as any other murder, they continue and are a sad reality that speaks of persistently evil cultural beliefs, as well as corruption in India's justice system.

Also resistant to change is the practice of the child bride, which continues in India and in many other nations. In Ethiopia, where 57 percent of Ethiopian women are married before the age of eighteen, it's not uncommon for girls as young as nine years old to be married against their will. Early marriage tragically denies girls an education and exposes them to much greater risk of domestic violence, HIV/AIDS, and death or disablement in childbirth.

Sadly, millions of the world's girls are victims of abortion and infanticide. Some researchers estimate that due to prenatal sex determination and selective abortions, as many as ten million girls have not been born in India alone during the past twenty years.[39] A law passed in India over a decade ago making gender-based abortions illegal has not changed the cultural perceptions that drive the demand.

All over the world, a false belief in male superiority leads to great injustice and a corruption of God's intentions for men and women, both made in his image. In China, Japan, and Korea, Confucianism teaches a hierarchical relationship between men and women. The husband-wife relationship is one of "the superior husband" dominating "the inferior wife," which, of course, leads to and perpetuates valuing male children over female children. Islam instructs, through the Koran (Sura 4:34), that "men stand superior to women.... But those whose perverseness ye fear, admonish them and remove them into bedchambers and beat them; but if they submit to you then do not seek a way against them."[40] In Latin America and South America, *machismo* is the word for a popular ideal of masculinity, which includes the notion of male superiority. In animistic Africa, women are seen as the property of men. "Real men," as one Rwandan told me, "beat their wives." Even when that is not the attitude, in many animistic cultures the man is still the tyrannical head of the family and a wife is required to submit. In some situations, women must kneel when greeting men. There may also be contexts, such as in a group of men and women, in which the women cannot have joint conversations with the men.

While in many cases in these cultures the men protect their women well and in some cultures men work hard farming or herding to feed and provide for the family, it is an undeniable fact that the unbiblical belief in male superiority has devastating consequences for everyone. In fact, in the realm of sexual mores, it is a common cultural mindset in parts of Africa that girls and women have no right to say no and may even be raped without consequences to the perpetrator. This is one of the factors making the fight against HIV/AIDS so difficult. The HIV/AIDS epidemic is also exacerbated in some cultures by the tradition of wife inheritance and the fact that women cannot own property. In these cultures, at the death of her husband, a woman who resists being "inherited" by his family is thrown out of her home by her husband's relatives. In order to provide for her children and have a place to live, she may be forced to accept a risky sexual arrangement with a relative or someone outside the family.

A world away in the experience of its women and girls, the West has its own challenges. While popular culture still promotes a view of women and even girls as sexual objects, and while some women still suffer domestic violence, most women have much more opportunity to fulfill their God-given potential and dreams than women in underdeveloped countries. Protected by law that is not only in place but enforced, undergirded by a broad cultural belief in the value of all people, women have the freedom to marry or not marry, to obtain an education, and to follow their callings. However, in a sad twist, because worth is found in the marketplace in Western culture, women who choose to make homes and care for families are often undervalued because they do not earn money, the coin of value. Secular culture often promotes the idea that for a woman to have real dignity, she must have a paying job because her dignity and basic worth are determined by her income. In fact, in recent decades many men have shifted from hoping to be able to support their families fully to looking at prospective wives as economic assets, someone to bring more wealth into the household. Furthermore, we have now constructed an economy that demands that women be part of the public workforce so that there will be enough workers to keep the wheels of affluence turning. Now we must have two people working in order to obtain the lifestyle we have learned to consider necessary. Therefore, while Western culture promotes the equality and worth of women from a marketplace point of view, a woman's intrinsic worth as the image of God and her work as a nurturer of children has little to no value.

This pursuit of materialistic wealth and values means that we sacrifice the things that matter most, our marriages and our children. We have reached an epidemic proportion of divorce or lifestyles that do not call for marriage in the first place. At the same time, children are put in daycare within a few weeks or months of birth so their mothers can return to work in the marketplace. Children are too often being raised by underpaid daycare workers who are strangers to the family.

The biblical picture is far different. From Genesis to Revelation, women are instilled with dignity. From creation, they are made in the image of God and have equal worth and responsibility as men. From the first wedding in Genesis to the marriage of Christ and the church in Revelation, marriage and family is established as a sacred institution. Christ himself was a revolutionary in his generation in the way he challenged cultural norms and in his treatment and view of women.

It is a common misunderstanding in modern culture that men like Jesus and Paul held a low view of women. That is far from the facts. Women flocked to Jesus because he publicly taught and demonstrated the freedom, dignity, and equality that they had from God since the beginning of creation. The accounts of Jesus' conversations with the woman at the well[41] and the woman caught in adultery[42] bear this out. In both instances, Jesus was violating prohibitions of traditional rabbinic law. Jesus appeared first to women after his resurrection, even calling them to publicly announce the resurrection.[43] It is as if the resurrection marks the beginning of a new era of "emancipation" for women in the world. Clearly, Jesus was breaking a very old mold of Jewish cultural life.

Jesus was also a reformer when it came to marriage. He taught about the equality that the wife and husband have had since the beginning.[44] In fact, he raised the bar considerably higher for marriages by saying that if a man lusts for another woman, he has committed adultery with her in his heart. In other words, it doesn't take the physical act to have adultery.[45] Even a husband's thought life toward his wife is therefore crucial.

KIM ALLEN'S STORY

Kim Allen was a "career woman" who came to see the power of being a mother who home-schools her children. She is investing her time, talent, and the best hours of her day in building a strong family and, through her children, investing in the future of her community and nation by raising her children to be nation builders.

One evening after graduating from college, while teaching in Japan, I posed the question to my students, "What do you want to do after you finish school?"

"Become mothers and wives," they enthusiastically replied.

"Is that all?" I blurted out, surprised by their low aspirations.

Well, almost twenty years later, despite myself and by God's abundant mercy, I am now a wife of fifteen years and mother of five. God has graciously opened my eyes to his beautiful plan, not just to become all I could be, but to embrace my role as helpmeet to my terrific husband. Although I was raised to be independent, God is teaching me what it means to submit to my husband out of rev-

erence for Christ. As I began the journey of marriage, I had to make a mental shift from "me" to "we." God has made us both unique with certain individual gifts that we could choose to use separately or together to further his kingdom. I can see that we are truly more effective as we combine these complementary gifts and work as a team.

My sphere of influence and center of operations is home, but from this base it is possible by God's grace to invest in the lives of my husband and children as well as reach out to others. From here I can love and serve my husband by keeping the household running, by encouraging him in his vision, by praying for him daily, and by respecting him as the spiritual leader of our family.

Today I realize that part of God's intention for marriage is to raise godly children (Mal. 2:15). I've learned that I can't raise even one child and guarantee that he or she will grow up to follow God, but I can teach them to know God and his Word. My job is to be faithful to train them up in the way they should go. God is responsible for the outcome.

The early church adopted Christ's God-centered view of women and marital relationships. Women were gladly accepted into the faith and initiated into the church by baptism, and they participated in the Lord's Supper and worship. Again, it was Paul who wrote that in Christ there is neither male nor female.[46] And, like Jesus, Paul had many women actively engaged in his "ministry teams."[47] The early church condemned "divorce, incest, marital infidelity, and polygamy."[48] In 374 Emperor Valentinian I moved to repeal the one-thousand-year-old Roman provision of *patria potestas,* the absolute (life or death) power of a man over his wife and children.[49]

God has given my husband and me a vision for our children. We want to see them growing in their love for the Lord, living a life of active faith, as well as loving others. We are working to cultivate in them a heart to serve, particularly the lost and hurting. We also long to impart a love for the truth. We want them to be self-governing and have a love for beauty and God's creation, a passion for learning and discovery, and a love for other cultures and nations. A lofty vision— and one that seems impossible on days when the breakfast devotion is on patience, and two hours later I lose it when the kids are fighting and I have a migraine! Thank God that he is able to work even through weak vessels to accomplish his purposes.

When I was growing up, education was focused around grades and my activities, such as swim team. Today I see education not just as a subject to be conquered, or the pursuit of good grades. It is now more exciting because each subject reveals part of God's character. In science we explore God's creativity. In math, we see his order. In history, we see the unfolding of his redemptive story. In addition to these more academic topics, part of education is learning to love our neighbor, practicing hospitality, and serving church and community. We can do simple things like prepare meals for the sick, visit next-door neighbors, develop friendships with refugee families, or take a mission trip to Mexico.

Motherhood is the greatest challenge and blessing I've known. Whether I'm changing diapers, making peanut butter sandwiches, explaining fractions, or reading about ancient Greece, I'm occupying until he comes! Instead of a second-rate calling, I see it as the highest privilege to spend my days at home serving my husband and raising my children.

My experience is not unique. I've known dozens of women who have walked similar paths. After earning degrees and being established in a career, they have turned their hearts toward home. They have found fulfillment and peace in responding to God's calling for them to "love their husbands and children, to be self-controlled and pure, to be busy at home, to be kind, and to be subject to their husbands, so that no one will malign the word of God" (Titus 2:4–5).

A new culture of respect arose as a result of Christian values regarding women. The writer of Hebrews reflects God's heart for marriage: "Marriage should be honored by all, and the marriage bed kept pure, for God will judge the adulterer and all the sexually immoral" (Heb.13:4). In AD 125 an Athenian philosopher and Christian named Aristides wrote to Emperor Hadrian about the attitude and behavior of the followers of Christ toward sex and marriage:

They do not commit adultery or immorality.... Their wives, O king, are as pure as virgins, and their daughters are modest. Their men abstain from all unlawful sexual contact and from impurity, in the hopes of recompense that is to come in another world.[50]

The cultural norms that inform our lives today and seem obvious have their roots in early Christian virtues. British historian Edward Gibbon (1737–1794) reminds us that after years of Roman disrespect for women and marriage, "the dignity of marriage was restored by the Christians."[51] Constantius II (r. 337–361), Emperor Constantine's son, ordered the separation of men and women prisoners[52] for the protection of women.

Although Christ entered a polygamous world, he taught monogamy.[53] Where Christianity has spread, polygamous relationships have largely been abandoned. In the modern era, William Carey and other followers of Christ worked in their callings to bring an end to *suttee* and to childhood marriages in India. Christians in China worked to bring women freedom from the painful and demeaning foot binding they suffered. And it is Christians who are challenging clitoridectomy (female genital mutilation) in Africa and the female sex trade in parts of Asia and around the world.

Amy Carmichael's life is a striking example of the Christian calling to liberate girls and women. When Carmichael, an Irish missionary, traveled to India, she discovered that girls as young as five years old were being sold into temple prostitution. She took a stand against this practice, which also meant at times standing against the British and Indian authorities and even some fellow missionaries! She fought hard for the dignity and honor of these little girls. She established a home and school, called Donhavur Fellowship, for those girls whom she could save from sexual internment and abuse. Her life was literally poured out in this calling.

L. F. Cervantes writes in New Catholic Encyclopedia (1967) that "the birth of Jesus was the turning point in the history of woman."[54] This is hardly an overstatement. That Jewish carpenter was nothing less than a revolutionary. Today many Christians are discovering callings in which they can advance the march of the freedom and dignity of women that Christ unleashed.[55]

Our Callings Today

- Fight against the trade in girls and women as sexual objects, whether in "the flesh markets" in the Western world, the machismo of Latin cultures, or sexual enslavement in the commercial sex trade.
- Treat all women with respect and dignity because they are made in the image of God.
- Resist pressures in Western society that have made the marketplace determine human worth. This trend forces women into the marketplace to seek their identity, which often leads to the breakdown of the family.

YWAM PUERTO RICO'S STORY

A few years ago I was contacted by Yarley Niño, one of the leaders of the Youth With A Mission (YWAM) center in Puerto Rico. She told of how my first book, *Discipling Nations: The Power of Truth to Transform Cultures,* had so impacted her and some of the leaders at the ministry and training center that her team had begun to see the importance of abandoning the dualistic worldview of the church for the powerful, integrated, and wholistic worldview of the Bible. As a result, they began to see both their individual and corporate lives from a very new perspective.

In the summer of 2003 we met at a Global Arts Workshop where I presented a series of lectures I called "Worldview and the Arts: The Call for Balladeers." The arts are perhaps the most powerful tool for shaping culture. Musicians, filmmakers, poets, and writers are at the cutting edge of cultural formation. In this series, I acknowledged how Christians have used art in worship and evangelism. YWAM has in fact been known for its schools of worship, and for years, I have been challenging YWAM to start a school that would prepare Christians who are gifted in the arts to speak prophetically into their cultures. Again in these lectures I called for Christian artists to begin to think from biblical principle and paradigm and then to consciously speak truth, goodness, and beauty—the trilogy of kingdom culture—to their nations. The young men and

women from Puerto Rico heard the call, and some of them formed a group called DNA (Disciple Nations through the Arts).

In 2005 I had the privilege of facilitating a Worldview and Development Workshop at their ministry center in Puerto Rico. One evening I was asked to speak on the maternal heart of God.[1] In the middle of the session, the Spirit of God broke into our midst and brought a spirit of brokenness and repentance concerning how the machismo culture of Puerto Rico had crushed women. Little did I know what this evening would mean in the lives of these young artists.

When I returned to the center in the summer of 2006 to present a weeklong series of lectures entitled "Raising Up Esther," the artists greeted me eagerly with the creative work they had done since we were last together. A number of the team members showed me their journals of poetry dealing with the dignity of women. Another member, Miguel Rodriguez, introduced me to a forty-five minute movie the team had made to tell a story of the sanctity of life and the dignity of women. Then he showed me an album of eleven original songs and musical scores that members of DNA have written, performed, and recorded. This group of young artists are under compulsion to speak to their nation, through the arts, in order to move the culture from one that denigrates women to one that honors women. May their tribe increase.

- Create friendly environments where women are encouraged to develop their leadership potential.
- Value motherhood, raising children, and making a home.
- In word and deed exhibit the sanctity of marriage.
- Build faithful, beautiful marriages that honor Christ.
- Start or join programs for developing chastity among teens.
- Fight against female genital mutilation.
- Minister to those who are trapped in prostitution for economic reasons.
- Work with women trapped in or escaping from domestic violence.
- Work for the education of girls where they have less access to schooling than boys.

MERCY AND COMPASSION FOR THE POOR

In the world that Christ entered, compassion and mercy were considered signs of weakness, often even seen as vices. Plautus (c. 254–184 BC), a Roman philosopher, summarizes the Roman attitude: "You do a beggar bad service by giving him food and drink; you lose what you give and prolong his life for more misery."[56] The Romans practiced *liberalitas:* giving to please a recipient who would later return the favor.[57] In fact, according to Kennedy's findings, "antiquity has left no trace of any organized charitable effort."[58] The poor and the needy fared no better in other societies that did not have the gospel. Citing Edward Ryan, Schmidt notes that the "bonzas, or Japanese priests, by maintaining that the sick and needy were odious to the gods, prevented the rich from relieving them."[59] And even today in the rich Western world, helping the poor is, for the most part, not seen as an individual responsibility.

In great contrast, Jesus Christ's whole life could be defined as one of giving to the poor. Open any page of the New Testament and you see the evidence. The parable of the good Samaritan[60] and Jesus' teaching on "the sheep and the goats" (Matt. 25:31–46) are poignant examples, calling Christians to serve the poor, the needy, and the disenfranchised. Indeed, it is this calling that is, or should be, the trademark of the Christian.

In contrast to the surrounding Greco-Roman world, which practiced *liberalitas,* the early church practiced *caritas,* giving to meet physical and economic needs without expecting anything in return.[61] In this manner the early Christians modeled their understanding of *agape,* that great New Testament Greek word used to express the love of God for man. True agape always gives but expects nothing in return; it always places the value on the receiver. Therefore the early Christians were simply loving the poor and the needy the way God loved them. It was the reasonable thing to do. One of the early church fathers, Tertullian (c. 155–230), wrote, "It is our care of the helpless, our practice of loving kindness, that brands us in the eyes of many of our opponents. 'Only look,' they say, 'look how they love one another!'"[62] He also reported Christians who had created a voluntary fund to support "widows, the physically disabled, needy orphans, the sick, prisoners incarcerated for their Christian faith, and teachers requiring help; it provided burials for poor people and sometimes funds for the release of slaves."[63] The pagan Roman emperor Julian (r. 361–363) wrote, "I think that when the poor happen to be neglected and overlooked by the priests, the impious Galileans [he is referring to Christians as "impious" because they refused to bow the knee and worship the emperor] observed this and devoted themselves to benevolence."[64] And in a different communication, he said, "The impious Galileans support not only their poor, but ours as well, everyone can see that our people lack aid from us."[65]

The Christian church since then has had an amazing record of caring for the poor and the needy around the world. Countless are the almshouses, orphanages, hospitals, soup kitchens, housing for refugees, schools, and other charitable works and societies begun by Christian religious orders, churches, and service organizations. Examples from the past two hundred years abound. George Müller's orphanage movement in England was caring for and educating more than eight thousand children at the time of his death in 1898.[66] Also in England, Charles Spurgeon's Metropolitan Tabernacle Church demonstrated God's love to the poor and disenfranchised through over sixty different ministries. In the U.S., Charles Loring Brace founded the Children's Aid Society to provide homes for abandoned children. In 1887, a number of Christian leaders from Denver, Colorado, founded the Charity Organization Society, now known as United Way.

In the developing world there are vital contemporary examples of the church at work to help the poor and needy. One shining example is Kampala Pentecostal Church in Kampala, Uganda. Under the leadership of Pastor Gary Skinner, this group of believers, at the time of this writing, has provided homes for more than two thousand AIDS orphans. The vision of this one church, with a current membership of fifteen thousand people in fifteen hundred cells, is to provide homes for ten thousand AIDS orphans and to birth a church-based response to the AIDS pandemic throughout Africa. Each cell has been challenged to "adopt" one person who is dying of AIDS and to care for that person and his or her family.

Another example is Abba Love, a large cell church in Jakarta, Indonesia, which is ministering to poor Muslims in slums near the church by providing health care, schools for children, and care for widows and orphans.

The Christian relief and development organization Food for the Hungry International works to save lives during war and famine. In Mozambique during the 1990s, it fed half a million people a month for two years and then provided seeds and tools for people to grow their own food when the famine ended.

My Ghanaian friend Chris Ampadu has said that in most African societies where there is communal life, each family is usually capable of caring for its own sick and poor. Families use the resources available to them to treat their needy with respect and compassion. However, one of the devastating effects of the HIV/AIDS epidemic in Africa is the breakdown of such networks caused by the death of many members of the same families and communities, leaving too few or even no one to care for the sick or, most sadly, to properly raise surviving children.

Today, in the West, organizations like Food for the Hungry and Youth With A Mission are providing opportunities for tens of thousands of men and women to live and work incarnationally among people who are poor and needy. After Hurricane Katrina struck the Gulf Coast of the USA, it was local churches from all over America that proved to be the first responders. Born out of a love for the poor in the United States, Kit Danley founded Neighborhood Ministries in Phoenix, Arizona, and Amy Sherman established Charlottesville Abundant Life Ministries in Charlotteville, Virginia. The time is now, for all Christians to engage in either a small or large way in ministering compassion to the poor.

Our Callings Today

- Care for those with AIDS.
- Provide home and shelter for AIDS orphans.
- Help the poor and hungry to begin caring for themselves.
- Build homes for poor Muslims (as some churches are doing in the Philippines).
- Tutor poor children who are struggling in school.
- Visit those who are in prison.
- Assist at a local soup kitchen.
- Work among refugees.
- Start or support an Angel Tree program, which gives presents at Christmastime to poor children from their imprisoned parents.
- Entrepreneurs, businesspeople, and corporate executives: establish businesses in blighted neighborhoods.
- Lawyers and politicians: work for the establishment of laws that support free enterprise and reward human initiative.
- Bankers: establish microsavings programs in poor communities as part of your community service.
- Building contractors: help to build low-income housing in both middle-class and blighted communities.

DAVID BUSSAU'S STORY

Starting with a rented hot dog stand at age fifteen, Australian entrepreneur David Bussau showed his gift for business early. Fifteen businesses later, at age thirty-five, he retired from a multimillion-dollar construction business, having reached what he calls the "economics of enough."

After doing aid work in a remote village in Indonesia after an earthquake and finding that building infrastructure like a school, bridges, and roads wasn't breaking the cycle of poverty in the community, Bussau turned his gifting into an organization that tackles poverty at the grassroots. He cofounded Opportunity International, an organization that provides small loans to entrepreneurs in twenty-seven developing countries.

Today, the microenterprise loans Bussau pioneered are an exciting means through which God is working to help the poor in a way that acknowledges their identity. Many Christian relief agencies now offer programs that enable people in developing countries to take out small loans to start or expand a business. Microloans are repaid on time over 95 percent of the time and have been used to grow a wide variety of businesses, developing thousands of villages in the process.

A Christian, Bussau set as his goal stewarding resources to benefit others. He sees wealth creation as a critical aspect of stewardship. With microenterprise development, he and others are challenging the conventional wealth redistribution model of development and are instead *creating* wealth responsibly. Bussau says, "Each of us has the capacity to be incredibly productive, and those who realise this are the ones who make the difference in the world. For me the challenge is to find ways to release that incredible potential in human beings, to enable that creative force and drive to be expressed."[1]

THE FULL GOSPEL

In conclusion, the gospel of Christ is the "full gospel." Christ taught us to pray, "your kingdom come, your will be done on earth as it is in heaven." As his followers heeded this call throughout history, they brought progressive transformation into cultures and nations. Christians are called to be history makers. We are not meant to stand on the sidelines and watch history go by. We are to live *coram Deo*, contributing now as firstfruits examples of the full expression of the kingdom that is yet to come to all domains. Anything less than this is not living according to the gospel of God.

Many readers of this book may be living in societies, such as in the developing world, where the social topics discussed in this chapter will become much-needed focuses of their callings. Others will be living in societies where those changes are already present to varying degrees. If so, their callings today include asking what further injustices need addressing and what other exciting discoveries and possibilities await us as we learn from the Bible to see our world by the light of the gospel. There is not a society on earth that doesn't need more of God's wisdom and kingdom influence. As Christians, we are called to lead the way through our callings *in the world.*

Christ has called his followers to take the whole gospel to every person, in every nation, and to every sector of society. As we have witnessed, the Great Commission is comprehensive. It is a call to go to the ends of the earth (*geographic*—Acts 1:8), to go to all creation (*ktisisographic*—Mark 16:15), and to penetrate the culture (*demographic*—Matthew 28:18–20). And what are we to bring? We begin with the good news of Jesus Christ. And we end with bringing the culture of the kingdom of God: truth, goodness, and beauty. As we infuse kingdom culture into the Great Commission, the fruit is "your kingdom come, your will be done on earth as it is in heaven."

KINGDOM CULTURE AND THE GREAT COMMISSION

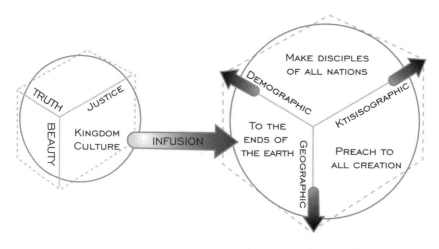

It is my hope and prayer that this survey of the gates and domains, and the application of the Great Commandment (manifesting God's love for *all* people) to our work in the domains, has helped us grasp more firmly the powerful, full gospel of the kingdom of God. It is a gospel that brings women and men to a saving knowledge of Christ. But it does not end there. It calls for Christians to enter the gates of the city and the domains of life with the only true hope for a lost and confused world.

In part 7, Churches without Walls, we'll seek to make this entrance of hope a reality. Let's move out of our buildings into the world. Let's follow the banner of Christ and his kingdom to the gates of the city.

PART 7 : CHURCHES WITHOUT WALLS

CHAPTER 21

SERVING AS GATEKEEPERS

By now we have seen that it is imperative that each of us increasingly connects our vocation to the kingdom of God. As Dallas Willard reminds us, to do our work "as Jesus would... is the very heart of discipleship, and we cannot effectively be an apprentice of Jesus without integrating our job into The Kingdom Among Us."[1]

The Christian who is occupying the gates of the city can be said to be a "king-domizer"[2]—one who is seeking to make one's place of work a place where the kingdom can break through into reality. Such a believer consciously seeks to bring truth, beauty, and goodness into the marketplace and public square, gathering with the church community for worship and equipping and scattering for service and discipling nations. Kingdomizers do their work for Christ and his kingdom, not primarily for money.[3]

A kingdomizer is

- a doctor, not for money but for Jesus and for health in the community;
- a lawyer, not for money but for Jesus and for justice in society;
- an engineer, not for money but for Jesus and for the fight against the ravages of natural evil;
- an artist, not for money but for Jesus and the advancement of truth and beauty in the world;
- a businessperson, not for self-aggrandizement but for Jesus and for economic sufficiency for the society.

"KINGDOMIZERS"

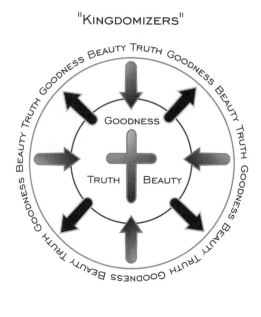

When we pray, "your kingdom come, your will be done on earth as it is in heaven," we are praying to make earth more like heaven. When we cease to pray and so act, earth becomes more like hell. In our work, we have the potential to make the world more hellish and the opportunity to make the world more heavenly, more like God intended in creation.

How can you begin today, in principle and in practice, to occupy the gates of the city?

OCCUPYING THE GATES IN PRINCIPLE

First, each of us can begin *right now* to occupy the gates of the city in principle by attacking the stronghold of the mind. We need to begin to think like Christians in all of life, including our work. We need to confess that we have gone along with the spirit of the age. Romans 12:2 calls for the Christian to cease being conformed to the world's systems. This bondage is broken through the renewal of the mind. Paul reminds us in 2 Corinthians 10:4–6 that the battle we are faced with is a battle of ideas and ideals. It is a battle for the minds of people and cultures. There are strongholds in our minds that need to be broken by bringing every thought captive to Christ.

Second, each of us can seek to understand and manifest that Christ is to be pre-eminent in all things.[4] As we have seen, we are to bring kingdom principles to bear in all domains of society: in law (to bring justice), in business (to bring honesty and integrity), in science (to bring objectivity), in communication (to bring truth), and in art (to bring beauty).

Third, we each can restore the concept and content of virtue to the gates by seeking in some small way to practice what is true, good, and beautiful. This is to be done in all areas of our lives.

Fourth, we can begin to occupy the gates by seeing the church as a people, not a building. As we'll explore in the next chapter, our concept of church should free the people to be in the world, at the city gates, in the marketplace, in the public square, and in the universities as small incarnational communities.

OCCUPYING THE GATES IN PRACTICE

What are some practical things that you can begin to do immediately to have greater influence in the gate that you are to occupy?

First, if you have not done so, you should seek to identify the domain(s) you are called to serve in.[5]

Second, you can pray the Lord's Prayer as it relates to your domain. Pray, "Your kingdom come, your will be done in *this domain* as it is in heaven." Begin to ask, If Christ worked in this arena, how would he change things? As you answer this question, you can begin to see your agenda.

Third, work to discover how God has equipped you to provide leadership for that domain.

Fourth, study the Scriptures in relationship to your vocation. Develop a biblical theology of vocation specific to your calling so that you can begin to have the mind of Christ as it relates to your work.

Fifth, develop a series of Bible studies that can be used to teach others biblical principles that relate to your domain.[6]

Sixth, band together in a church-based or work-based cell group that focuses on being a community of the redeemed in that domain. Examples include a medical cell for the local hospital, an engineering cell for the company, and a cell of students and professors for the university.

Seventh, get further formal or informal equipping, as needed, to increase excellence, professionalism, and credentialing in your vocational area. This could include reading conceptual books that relate to a biblical theology for your domain or pursuing further academic or technical training.

Eighth, create equipping materials to prepare other Christians for the marketplace. Write pamphlets and books that help to kingdomize the workplace. Lead workshops in your local church or workplace to help Christians begin to connect their work to the kingdom. When they have completed the workshop, they can be commissioned for the workplace.

TO WHAT END?

To what end are we to be keepers of the gates, to be kingdomizers? To the end that cultures are transformed and nations—not merely individuals in each nation—are discipled. Jesus has raised up the church to disciple the nations.[7] He is the King of heaven and earth now.[8] His kingdom is to be advancing in this world.[9] When we pray the Lord's Prayer, "your kingdom come," we are praying for the advancement of Christ's reign on earth as it is in heaven. Dallas Willard writes,

> So when Jesus directs us to pray, "Thy kingdom come," he does not mean we should pray for it to come into existence. Rather, we pray for it to take over at all points in the personal, social, and political order where it is now excluded: "on earth as it is in heaven." With this prayer we are invoking it, as in faith we are acting it, into the real world of our daily existence.[10]

Nations are discipled as they are taught to obey "all that I have commanded" (Matt. 28: 20). What would a discipled nation look like? Dr. Jun Vencer of DAWN Ministries has provided a helpful summary of the goal. A discipled nation, he says, would be characterized by the following:

- Economic sufficiency
- Social peace
- Public justice
- National righteousness
- And where all aspects of life are centered around the Lordship of Jesus Christ[11]

Similarly, Lawrence Harrison, scholar and longtime USAID worker in the Caribbean, writes of the longings of people all over the world that

> Life is better than death.
> Health is better than sickness.
> Liberty is better than slavery.
> Prosperity is better than poverty.
> Education is better than ignorance.
> Justice is better than injustice.[12]

We live in the world that God has made, and people are longing for the life for which they were made. Each Christian has a role to play in satisfying the longings of his or her neighbors and coworkers. Health professionals can provide personal care, health education, and new technologies to promote better health. Businesspeople and entrepreneurs can create businesses that don't just make a profit but do so by creating a humane work environment and by contributing to the long-term health and wholesomeness of the larger community. Teachers can bring not only academic knowledge but also truth, wisdom, and character development to the schools and universities where they work. Lawyers, judges, and politicians can establish and adjudicate laws that are just and equitable. Each Christian has an occupation in the gates of the city.

EXAMPLE OF A GATEKEEPER: WILLIAM CAREY

Most of us called to occupy the gates of the city will remain unknown to the wider world. Yet each of us has a calling that can find inspiration in the transforming *life*work of William Carey, a man whose work continues to influence multiple domains many generations after his death. Known as the father of modern missions, William Carey was no ordinary missionary in his day, and he remains exceptional in ours. In the remarkable little book by Vishal and Ruth Mangalwadi, *The Legacy of William Carey*, we see how God used a humble English shoemaker to influence the people of India. Carey brought the biblical mind to his strategy and methodology of missions, understanding that the gospel was to impact every area of society.

In the opening chapter of the book, the Mangalwadis expose us to Carey through the eyes of a number of Indian university students who are taking part in a nationwide History of India competition. One of the questions was "Who is William Carey?" These are some of their answers:

> "William Carey was a Christian missionary," answers a science student. "And he was also the botanist after whom *Careya herbacea* is named. It is one of the three varieties of eucalyptus found only in India.
>
> "Carey brought the English daisy to India and introduced the Linnaean system to gardening. He also published the first books on science and natural history in India, such as William Roxburgh's *Flora Indica*, because he believed the biblical view that, 'All Thy works praise Thee, O Lord.' Carey believed that nature is declared 'good' by its Creator; it is not *maya* (illusion), to be shunned, but a subject worthy of human study. He frequently lectured on science and tried to show that even lowly insects are not souls in bondage, but creatures worthy of our attention."[13]

"William Carey introduced the study of astronomy into the Subcontinent," declares a student of mathematics. "He was deeply concerned about the destructive cultural ramifications of astrology: fatalism, superstitious fear, and an inability to organize and manage time.

"Carey wanted to introduce India to the scientific culture of astronomy. He did not believe that the heavenly bodies were 'deities that governed our lives.' He knew that human beings are created to govern nature, and that the sun, moon, and planets are created to assist us in our task of governing. Carey thought that the heavenly bodies ought to be carefully studied, since the Creator had made them to be signs or markers. They help divide the monotony of space into directions—East, West, North, and South; and of time into days, years, and seasons. They make it possible for us to devise calendars; to study geography and history; to plan our lives, our work, and our social order. The culture of astronomy sets us free to be rulers, whereas the culture of astrology makes us subjects, our lives determined by our stars."[14]

"William Carey," says a feminist social science scholar, "was the first man to stand against both the ruthless murders and the widespread oppression of women—virtually synonymous with Hinduism in the eighteenth and nine-teenth centuries. The male in India was crushing the female through polygamy, female infanticide, child marriage, widow-burning, euthanasia, and forced female illiteracy—all sanctioned by religion. The British government timidly accepted these social evils as being an irreversible and intrinsic part of India's religious mores. Carey began to conduct systematic sociological and scriptural research on these issues. He published his reports in order to raise public opinion and protest both in Bengal and in England. He influenced a whole generation of civil servants—his students at Fort William College—to resist these evils. Carey opened schools for girls. When widows converted to Christianity, he arranged marriages for them. It was Carey's persistent, twenty-five-year battle against *sati*, widow-burning, which finally led to Lord Bentinck's famous Edict in 1829, banning one of the most abominable of all religious practices."[15]

Through these students' descriptions of the mind-changing, world-changing influence wrought in their country by the biblical worldview of William Carey, we can see the potential for transforming work in these and other domains today.

It is clear that each Christian is called to serve as a gatekeeper; each Christian is called to a *life*work that connects the whole of his or her life and work to the kingdom of God. It is also clear that we are called, not in isolation but as part of Christ's church. To see Christians living out their callings in the gates of their cities and to see the fulfillment of people's longing for the kingdom for which they were made will require a renewed understanding of "church." In the last two chapters of this book, we'll consider what it means to be Christ's body in the world.

CHAPTER 22

THE BODY OF CHRIST:

CHURCHES WITHOUT WALLS

Jesus declared, "Upon this rock I will build my church; and the gates of hell shall not prevail against it" (Matt. 16:18 KJV). These words reveal that Christ's church is on the move in enemy territory. The gates of hell shall not withstand the attack of the church. "I will build" marks the advancement of Christ's kingdom and agenda. It will occur because the Lord of the universe has said it.

In this picture, who is on the offense? The church. Christ conquered the fear of death at the cross and death itself at the resurrection. He now is King of heaven and earth. Satan is on the defense. He lost the major battle of the war for the universe. He is in retreat. Christ is leading his forces in the mopping-up operations. We are to follow Christ and his banner to the very gates of hell.

The war continues between God and Satan, between truth and falsehood, between good and evil, between light and darkness, between life and death. The forces of evil are no match for the onslaught of the kingdom. The kingdom of God will prevail in the end.

This war manifests itself here on earth in very concrete ways that have consequences for both individuals and cultures. There are battles that need to be fought on many fronts. There is a battle for truth and against lies, for the culture of life and against the culture of death; another for justice and against corruption; another for beauty and against the mundane and hideous; another for plenty and against hunger; another for economic sufficiency and against poverty; another for wisdom and against ignorance; and another for health and against disease. Servants of the King are to occupy themselves—using their natural gifts, talents, and abilities—to fight these battles. They are to make a unique contribution, in their life and vocation, to occupy enemy territory for Christ.

As part of God's army, we do not fight with swords, guns, or bombs but with truth, beauty, and justice. We do not advance by ship or in tanks but on our knees and in humble service. As each Christian takes his place of deployment, he is to plant the banner of Christ.

THE UNIQUE CONTRIBUTION

The war in which we are summoned to serve today has ebbed and waned throughout history, sometimes the kingdom of God advancing, sometimes the forces of darkness advancing. At this moment in history there has been unparalleled advancement in evangelism and church planting. There have never been more Christians or churches in the world than there are today. But the impact of the church on Western culture is diminishing dramatically. The kingdom of darkness is deeply impacting nations even as the church is growing numerically. The church has virtually lost the West to secularism, and secularism is collapsing under the weight of greed and corruption on its insufficient foundation. Postmodernism or neo-paganism is currently making strides for the hearts and minds of nations, especially in post-Christian Europe and the major cities of North America. In much of the developing world, the mindset and value system of spiritism continue to hold sway, diminishing the impact of the numerical growth of the church.

So what is the problem? The church, in our generation, has a mindset that Satan is on the offensive and the church is on the defensive. This mentality is exactly opposite from the teaching of the Scripture and is creating a defeatist mentality in the church.

We need to be reminded of who won the battle of the cross and who won the battle over death. Christ and his kingdom will continue to advance until his triumph is completed. He is the coming King of Israel written about in Isaiah 9:6–7:

> For to us a child is born,
>   to us a son is given,
>   and the government will be on his shoulders.

And he will be called
  Wonderful Counselor, Mighty God,
  Everlasting Father, Prince of Peace.
Of the increase of his government and peace
  there will be no end.
He will reign on David's throne
  and over his kingdom,
establishing and upholding it
  with justice and righteousness
  from that time on and forever.
The zeal of the LORD Almighty
  will accomplish this.

God will accomplish his work of redemption completely. The gates of hell will not prevail.

If this is true, the church must have the mindset of pushing forward against the kingdom of darkness. She is to be proactive, attacking the very gates of hell, not disengaged or remote. Neither is she to be reactive—on the defensive, responding to the attacks of the kingdom of darkness.

The false mindset of the sacred-secular dichotomy is one that would see the gates of the city—the domains of government or media or science—as "the gates of hell" themselves. By their resulting separatist or antagonistic stance toward the world, evangelical Gnostics have sometimes shown that they (mistakenly) equate working in "the gates of the city" or "in the world" with working in the very gates of hell. Obviously this is not the case. The spheres of human society are ordained by God or grow out of our God-given mandate to steward all of creation. The harmony found in creation before the Fall is the goal of the end of time where there will be a harmony between man's creation—the city—and God's creation—nature.[1]

Clearly the gates of the city, the domains of society, are not the gates of hell that the church is to the move against; they are not the object of the church's attack. As Paul writes, "Our struggle is not against flesh and blood, but against the rulers, against the authorities, against the powers of this dark world and against the spiritual forces of evil in the heavenly realms" (Eph. 6:12). Like the broader cultures of which they are a part, the domains of society that we are called to occupy and influence have differing degrees of kingdom culture, counterfeit culture, and natural culture. We attack the gates of hell not by lashing out in frustration by ineffective action, nor by closeting ourselves away, but by manifesting more of the culture of the kingdom in the city gates. On the strength of Jesus' word, his church is to take the initiative. It is to take the offense. Because Jesus has said so, truth *will* challenge the lie, good *will* overcome evil, love *will* overcome hate, and light *will* overcome darkness.

AN INCARNATIONAL COMMUNITY

What is the church? At her core, she is an incarnational community. At her core, she is not a building. She is not defined by her ecclesiastical structure and polity. No, she is a community of believers who are to incarnate the Word in a broken world.

First, the church is community. The church is described as the body of Christ,[2] the bride of Christ,[3] and a holy nation and royal priesthood.[4] These are all living, organic descriptions. The church is not static. What marks a church is her people and their life together, not the place or building where they gather, worship, and are equipped for battle and service.

A building may be the place where believers come together for worship and equipping, but the building is not the church. Rather, the church is a *community* of believers, a community of the redeemed through which God works. In identifying the church as the body of Christ, Paul reveals that this community is a unity of the diversity of many unique members[5] with a variety of gifts, service, and ministries.[6] This is a community that reflects God's own nature and purposes.

Second, the church is incarnational. Calling the church "the body of Christ" reminds her that she is an *incarnational* community. Just as Christ was "the Word [that] became flesh and made his dwelling among us" (John 1:14), so now the Word (Jesus) is to be incarnate today through his church. As we have come to Christ, we have entered his kingdom. As the church, we are to live as he would live in the midst of the world.[7]

DUAL CITIZENSHIP

In *The City of God,* St. Augustine said that we are citizens of "two cities." Christ is the King of both heaven and earth, now and in the future.[8] Because his laws are eternal and immutable, biblical principles apply in both heaven and earth. The Christian is, in each moment, a citizen of both heaven[9] and this world[10] and is subject to Christ's laws in both realms.

God's kingdom is now and not yet. The Christian is to live in the reality of the future return of the King while manifesting the presence of the kingdom in the world today. God's kingdom is fully established in heaven, and it is to be substantially advancing on earth now. This means that the Kingdom of Light will be challenging Satan's kingdom of darkness. The future aspects of the kingdom will achieve full harvest when Christ returns. His kingdom will be consummated under one rule. Shalom peace will reign! Until then, Christians will be citizens of two kingdoms, with a foot in each one.

THE CHURCH AND THE WORLD

The church is to be at the same time both separate from the world (sanctified—set apart) and actively engaged (occupying for Christ) in the world. Jesus makes this clear when he prays for his disciples in the High Priestly Prayer at the Last Supper (John 17:15–19):

> "My prayer is not that you take them out of the world but that you protect them from the evil one. They are not of the world, even as I am not of it. Sanctify them by the truth; your word is truth. As you sent me into the world, I have sent them into the world. For them I sanctify myself, that they too may be truly sanctified."

Directly before the journey to the cross, Christ prays for himself, his disciples, and all believers.[11] He prays for his disciples to be in the world but not of the world. What does this mean? There are two mentalities that many church bodies function by that oppose the correct concept of "being in the world but not of the world." The first is what I call the fortress church.

The Fortress Church

The fortress church seeks to physically separate from the world. To use the expression of Christ's prayer in reverse, the church is "out of the world and into the building." The church, in an attempt to keep herself from the world and the devil, separates herself from the neighborhood by the walls of the church building. She leaves the world behind and disengages from culture. In this view, all that God wants is the church to be hidden behind the protective walls of an independent, isolated culture. Too often this has been the stance of many fundamentalist and evangelical churches.

THE FORTRESS CHURCH
Disengaged
In the church and out of the world

To Death   To Heaven

The Syncretic Church

The second mentality I call the syncretic church. In syncretism the church shares the same basic moral and metaphysical framework of the larger society. She is conformed to the world instead of being conformed to Christ. To warp the expression of Christ's prayer, the church is "in the world and of the world." In seeking to be relevant or attractive to society, she becomes like the society, indistinguishable from the culture. Rather than transforming culture for Christ, the church is transformed by the world until it is no longer distinguishable from it. Too often the so-called liberal denominations and many of today's "seeker friendly" churches have succumbed to this trend.

THE SYNCRETIC CHURCH
CONFORMED
INDISTINGUISHABLE FROM THE WORLD

TO DEATH

The Kingdom Church

In the radical middle is the kingdom church. This church is engaged in society and at the same time is morally and metaphysically consecrated. To use the accurate expression of Christ's prayer, the church is "in the world but not of the world." The church is always reforming herself and seeking to transform society. She is always countercultural. She seeks to build kingdom communities and kingdom cultures that engage the world with truth, beauty, and justice.

The Greek word for church is *ekklesia,* which means "to call out." To be called out means to be called from something and to something. As the church, we are called out from the world's mindset, ethos, and aesthetic but not from the world itself. We are called to be set apart by Christ, to Christ, and for Christ.

We are called out of the world into the kingdom. But because we are to be in the world relating to it but not of the world, the calling out is a separation from the world's system, its mindset, ethos, and aesthetic, into the kingdom worldview and culture.

The church's calling is to be an incarnational community that reflects and exhibits the character of God. This calling out is to overwhelm the community and nation at large with God's fidelity, holiness, and beauty. It is to be a people with a different way of thinking (truth), a different way of living (virtue), and a different way of expression (loveliness, splendor).

The notion of being the "called-out ones" is true for both the universal and the local expressions of the body of Christ. The church is to be set apart morally and metaphysically but not physically. She is to be a holy and particular people[12] living in the marketplace and public square[13] as incarnational communities. Individual Christians, the church scattered, are to be socially and physically engaged in the community and nation, bringing the kingdom into the world, in all the domains of society, while wholly consecrated, with a biblical mind, a biblical aesthetic, and a biblical ethic. The kingdom community is like salt and light,[14] like leaven in the loaf:[15] informing, explaining, enlightening, demonstrating, influencing, and affecting the community. It is not controlling, commanding, dictating, or manipulating. It is not disengaged, detached, isolated, or inaccessible. She is to be a lighthouse in the world, not a fortress against the world. She is to bring flavor, preservation, and cleansing, bringing life to the community.

THE KINGDOM CHURCH
REFORMING: IMPACTING THE WORLD
IN THE WORLD BUT NOT OF THE WORLD

To Life

GETTING IT BACKWARD

Much of the modern evangelical church in the West has it absolutely backward today. It is both out of the world and conformed to the world. It is physically separate and metaphysically and ideologically conformed. Today the Western church is for the most part worldly—we act religious when gathered, and we act like the world when we are scattered. Too often, we act like Christians when it is "convenient," when there is no cost.

Dietrich Bonhoeffer, who was martyred by the Nazi Third Reich for resisting its claim to absolute power, decried the syncretism in the German church of his day, which is so similar to the church in our own time. He writes of the concept of cheap grace that is the staple of both liberal and evangelical churches today:

> If grace is the data for my Christian life, it means that I set out to live the Christian life *in the world with all my sins justified beforehand.* I can go and sin as much as I like, and rely on this grace to forgive me, for after all the world is justified in principle by grace. I can therefore cling to my bourgeois secular existence, and *remain as I was before,* but with the added assurance that the grace of God will cover me. It is under the influence of this kind of "grace" that the world has been made "Christian," but at the cost of *secularizing the Christian religion as never before.... The Christian life comes to mean nothing more than living in the world and as the world,* in being no different from the world, in fact, in being prohibited from being different from the world for the sake of grace [italics added].[16]

During the Third Reich, 90 percent of all Germans were professing Christians. But most of the church had totally submitted itself to the state. This sad condition permeates much of the Christian world today. In the Western church, Christianity is largely syncretized with secular materialism.

In observing our world today, it is clear that the true "success" of a church is determined not by the materialist criterion of its size and wealth but by the organic criteria of its godliness and its positive impact on the surrounding culture. There have never been more Christians in the world than there are today. There have never been more churches than there are today. There have never been as many large churches as there are today. Yet nations are still broken, impoverished, and enslaved. Individuals are shadows of the human beings that God intended. There is little substantial healing taking place.

Usually we get only what we set out to do. For the past fifty years, the mantra has been "church growth." The church worldwide is achieving this goal. But to what end? Is the church alive, is the Word being made flesh in the lives of the believers, is the larger community and nation being transformed by the local church? Unfortunately there are too few places where communities and nations are being impacted, let alone transformed.

PROGRAM-ORIENTED CHURCHES

One reason for the failure of the church to impact culture is a misunderstanding of the church as a building or a set of programs. A program-oriented church (POC) is a church that defines itself by its programs. Its goal is to get people out of the world (the secular place), into the church (the sacred place). The POC often sees the church as a building or as a people who are the church when they are in a "church meeting" or "doing church work." These churches are defined by the weekly calendar of meetings and activities. Often the number of meetings attended marks a person's spirituality. Often the success of the church is defined by the number of meetings and the number of people attending those meetings. The more meetings there are, the more "successful" the church.

Author and theologian Elton Trueblood describes the error of this phenomenon: "It is a gross error to suppose that the Christian cause goes forward solely or chiefly on weekends. What happens on the regular weekdays may be far more important, so far as the Christian faith is concerned, than what happens on Sundays."[17] To this could be added that what happens outside the walls of the church building may have more to do with the advancement of the kingdom than what happens inside the walls. A university professor from Korea once lamented to me that the pressure of responsibility for the "jobs" and meetings he had at his church kept him from effectively functioning and ministering to his students at the university.

EVERY CHRISTIAN A MINISTER

In contrast to the concept of the church as a building or a set of programs, we are to realize that the church is an incarnational community.

The church gathers and scatters. It gathers for worship and equipping and scatters for ministry. In the program-oriented church the pastoral staff are seen as the ministers. The laypeople exist to support the pastoral staff in "their" ministries. In a kingdom-oriented church, the people are the ministers. The pastors' and teachers' function is to equip the saints for ministry, not to do the ministry themselves. We need to restore the ministers to the gates of the city.

THE CHURCH: GATHERED AND SCATTERED

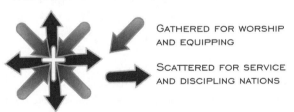

GATHERED FOR WORSHIP AND EQUIPPING

SCATTERED FOR SERVICE AND DISCIPLING NATIONS

The apostle Peter reminds us, "But you are a chosen people, a royal priesthood, a holy nation, a people belonging to God, that you may declare the praises of him who called you out of darkness into his wonderful light" (1 Pet. 2:9) The Scripture announces clearly that every Christian is a minister, every member a priest. This has been called the priesthood of believers! I remember as a young man seeing the placard at the front of a church that captured this truth. It read:

The Pastor—the equipper;
The Congregation—the ministers!

Hendricks calls the layman "The New Clergy."[18] This captures the imagination. But it is not a new concept; rather, it is a biblical concept that has been lost and needs to be restored.

The Great Commission releases all Christians into the marketplace. When Christ says, "Therefore go" (Matt. 28:19), the phrase literally means "as you go" or "are going." It assumes that the Christian is engaged in the gates of the city, doing business, carrying on relationships, hearing announcements, etc. The church gathers for equipping and worship and then scatters to the gates of the city to bring kingdom culture to the people.

GATES OF THE CITY

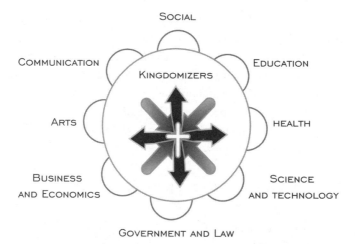

Because evangelical Gnosticism has blinded the church in relationship to the Great Commission, it is worth addressing two issues that relate to "going": the issue of deployment and the issue of vocation.

In terms of deployment, the evangelical Gnostic assumes that this passage addresses professional missionaries who are going to work overseas. However, a biblical worldview assumes that this passage is for all Christians wherever they are assigned. The second issue is that of vocation. Evangelical Gnostics assume that the passage is for professional religious workers. Biblical theism assumes that all Christians are called into discipling nations, and it is further assumed that this may take place in any moral vocation. The priesthood of believers understands that all Christians are priests and that they have an assigned deployment or domain where they are to serve.

EQUIPPING THE MINISTERS

The church has a vital role to play in preparing Christians for their deployment in the marketplace and public square. George Grant summarizes the work of the church in raising up those leaders in his book *Changing of the Guard*:

> The Church is to *train* God's people for the work of ministry. If our nation is to have thoroughly equipped pastors, then the Church must train young men for the ministry of the Gospel (Romans 10:14–15). If our nation is to have thoroughly equipped teachers, then the Church must train young mothers and fathers for the ministry of education (Titus 2:1–15). If our nation is to have thoroughly equipped craftsmen, artists, musicians, philosophers, doctors, laborers, lawyer, scientists, and merchants, then the Church must train them for the ministry of acculturation (2 Timothy 3:16–17). And, of course, if our nation is to have thoroughly equipped magistrates, then the Church must train them for the ministry of political action.[19]

What does it take to equip the ministers for the gates of the city?

First, it takes pastors and teachers being willing to equip the saints. The model of the pastor as superstar, doing the entire ministry, must be abandoned. So must the business model of pastor as administrator or business manager of the megachurch. Paul reveals the major role of the pastor and teacher in Ephesians 4:11–12:

> It was he who gave some to be apostles, some to be prophets, some to be evangelists, and some to be pastors and teachers, to prepare God's people for works of service, so that the body of Christ may be built up.

Note the progression in this passage. The task given to the apostles, prophets, evangelists, pastors, and teachers is to equip the saints. For what purpose? For works of service. To what end? That the body of Christ might be built up.

The word *prepare* in Ephesians 4:12 is the Greek word *katartismos* which means "complete furnishing," or "equipping"[20] As we have seen, the people—the saints—are the ministers. They need to be equipped for works of service. So, how are the ministers equipped for service? By those who have gifts in leading and in teaching the Word. The role of equipping the saints is not higher than that of the ministers; it is merely different. It is not the role of pastor-teachers to do all the work of ministry, but it is their role to equip the saints for their assignments.[21]

Second, equipping the ministers for the gates of the city will take a consistent teaching from the pulpit on the theology of vocation. I have been a Christian since 1957. In all the years since then I have heard only two sermons devoted to the subject of work. The first was by Francis Schaeffer at L'Abri Fellowship in Switzerland. The second was by a pastor in the U.S. who wrongly proclaimed that work was part of the curse. In reality, the cause of Christ can advance more during six days of the week than on Sunday, more in the marketplace than in the walls of the church building. Because of this, we need to spend more time teaching on subjects of the kingdom and vocation than on the solely "spiritual" focus found in so many churches.

Third, it will take discipleship classes to prepare people to work wholistically in the marketplace. In addition to speaking from the pulpit on vocational themes, there need to be cell groups, or kingdomizer classes, in the church to disciple Christians for the marketplace. We spend most of our time in Sunday school, Bible study, and even cell meetings to prepare people to function spiritually. We need to train businesspeople to be godly in their business practice and to bring kingdom principles into the marketplace. We need to prepare Christian lawyers and judges to seek justice in society and to drive issues to the supreme court of the land if necessary, not to simply make a living or give corrupt judgments, as happens in too many countries.

Fourth, it will take public acknowledgement to commission and send equipped businesspeople to minister in the marketplace; lawyers into the judicial system; public servants into government, the police force, and the fire department; stewards onto the farms, orchards, and vineyards; homemakers into the home. Each Christian is to be ordained for his or her ministry, to be set apart for the assignment given by Christ. The church is to release each person into his or her destiny.

Fifth, it will take cell groups of Christians, from individual domains in society, in a city or a country to apply biblical truth and principles in their own sectors. As an example, a church that has a medical worker can send him or her to a cell group of Christian medical personnel, not to simply have fellowship together but to develop a strategy for penetrating the hospital with the kingdom. On a state or national level Christian sectoral professionals can band together to seek to impact public policy and legislation for righteousness. This pattern may be applied for any sphere of society.

SENDING LEADERS TO THE GATES OF THE CITY

Restoring the ministers to the gates of the city is critical. Our communities and nations desperately need kingdom leadership. Pastor E. W. Lutzer, of the famous Moody Church in Chicago, described the choice before today's church when he decried how the church in Germany failed to critique its own culture and was instead largely complacent with the rise of Hitler and even, for the sake of being good Germans, supported the Third Reich. Their choice is our choice: "The church had to choose between a Christ who was Lord over a shrinking 'spiritual sphere' and a Christ who was 'Lord over all.'"[22] In his book *Hitler's Cross*, Lutzer shows that patterns exist today in the USA which are very similar to those that existed in Germany at the rise of Hitler's power. He challenges the church in the USA and, by implication, the church in the rest of the world:

> If the cross of Christ is the greatest expression of God's love to the world, then those of us who follow him must show our love to the world as well.
>
> It is time that Christians become leaders in art, education, politics, and law. Let's not make the mistake of the German church and isolate the spiritual sphere from the political, social, and cultural.
>
> Since we share this planet with all of humanity, we must reestablish leadership in all of those areas where Christians often led the way. Education, politics, and law—here is where we must gain credibility so that the world will listen to our message. The Cross should be seen wherever Christians are found.[23]

Leadership experts Warren Bennis and Burt Nanus contribute a similar theme:

> If there was ever a moment in history when a comprehensive strategic view of leadership was needed, not just by a few leaders in high office but by large numbers of leaders in every job...it is now.[24]

The domains of society are in need of kingdom leadership that manifests the true nature and purposes of God and his creation. The work of the church is twenty-four hours a day, seven days a week, not just Sundays. It is in the world, not in a building. The work of the church is to bring the kingdom mind and value system into the world, not the world's mind and value system into the church. When a critical mass of members of Christ's body embrace their callings as his ministers and are equipped to live and work in the world as incarnational communities, truth, goodness, and beauty will flow with liveliness from the church into the community and nation. Through Christ's body, God will make himself known.

CHAPTER 23

OCCUPY TILL I COME

In the journey that we have taken together, we have seen that the church and we as individual Christians have largely withdrawn from our cultures and privatized our faith. We have seen that our strategies for evangelism and church planting have largely worked. There have never been more Christians and more churches and more large churches in the world than there are today. And yet our communities and nations are too often hopelessly broken.

We have seen that the reason for this brokenness is that we have abandoned the powerful and integrative biblical worldview and exchanged it for an anemic, dualistic worldview of evangelical Gnosticism. This worldview has reduced our vision to simply going to church and going to heaven. We have lost the powerful vision to which Christ has called us.

In this book we have sought to lay the foundation for a return to the powerful biblical worldview and the role of the church to be externally focused, into the world and into the marketplace. We have called the church to be the church on Monday, taking her place in the gates of the city. This means that each Christian is to live *coram Deo*.

DWELLING IN THE PRESENCE

As members of Christ's body, we are called to work with him to the end that "the earth will be filled with the knowledge of the glory of the LORD, as the waters cover the sea"

(Hab. 2:14). We are to be agents for the coming kingdom of God. Paul writes that in Christ Jesus we "are being built together to become a dwelling in which God lives by his Spirit" (Eph. 2:22). We are "members of God's household, built on the foundation of the apostles and prophets, with Christ Jesus himself as the chief cornerstone. In him the whole building is joined together and rises to become a holy temple in the Lord" (Eph. 2:19–21). Just as God's presence dwelt among his people Israel in the temple, his presence dwells in this new temple, a temple without walls.

In the motif of the kingdom coming, we are reminded that man is increasingly dwelling in the presence of God. God will be our God and we will be his people. Genesis 3:8, Exodus 25:8, and John 1:14 are the clarion reminders that God dwells among men. And if God dwells among men, then men dwell in the presence of the living God. We are called and privileged to live all of our lives before the face of God.

The stories of the building of the tabernacle and the temple in the Old Testament create for us pictures of people dwelling in the presence of God to use their gifts and skills to make a dwelling place for God among men. God called artisans and craftsmen to take inert things and shape them for the glory of God. In creating earth, God made a place for man to dwell. Man, in creating the tabernacle and temple, made places for God to dwell.

God has created a myriad of godly occupations to fill the earth with the knowledge of the Lord. As we have mentioned previously, this is illustrated in the giftings that it took to build the tabernacle:

> Then the LORD said to Moses, "See, I have chosen Bezalel son of Uri, the son of Hur, of the tribe of Judah, and I have filled him with the Spirit of God, with skill, ability and knowledge in all kinds of crafts—to make artistic designs for work in gold, silver and bronze, to cut and set stones, to work in wood, and to engage in all kinds of craftsmanship. Moreover, I have appointed Oholiab son of Ahisamach, of the tribe of Dan, to help him. Also I have given skill to all the craftsmen to make everything I have commanded you."
>
> ...Then Moses said to the Israelites, "See, the LORD has chosen Bezalel son of Uri, the son of Hur....And he has given both him and Oholiab son of Ahisamach, of the tribe of Dan, the ability to teach others. He has filled them with skill to do all kinds of work as craftsmen, designers, embroiderers in blue, purple and scarlet yarn and fine linen, and weavers—all of them master craftsmen and designers. So Bezalel, Oholiab and every skilled person to whom the LORD has given skill and ability to know how to carry out all the work of constructing the sanctuary are to do the work just as the LORD has commanded."

Then Moses summoned Bezalel and Oholiab and every skilled person to whom the LORD had given ability and who was willing to come and do the work." (Exod. 31:1–6; 35:30–36:2)

What an incredible picture! God has built a house for man, and now God's people are to build a house for God. God had a detailed plan for the tabernacle. He called for the people of Israel to make provision for his house.[1] The people brought free will offerings that exceeded the need for the tabernacle.[2] Then the Lord called Bezalel son of Uri, a master artisan, to lead the project. Bezalel was filled with the Spirit of God and equipped for the task. God also provided skilled craftsmen who had the ability to teach others to work under Bezalel's leadership. God had a plan. He called people to complete that plan. He equipped and empowered them, as Francis Schaeffer would say, to "do the Lord's work in the Lord's way."

D. B. Hegeman, writing in *Plowing in Hope*, reminds us of the glory of the diversity of gifting and skills use in the tabernacle:

The variety of *occupations* used in the building of the tabernacle and temple is astounding: lumbermen, carpenters, spinners, dyers, weavers, embroiderers, seamstresses, foundry workers and metallurgists, goldsmiths, engravers, jewelers, tanners, perfumers, quarry workers, and stone masons. Then there were those who provided direct logistical support: tool makers, keepers of draft animals, seafarers, and laborers. ... There were those who were involved in the worship activities after the sanctuaries were completed: priests and attendants, musicians, singers, musical instrument makers, and psalmists. The gracious circumstances of O.T. redemption are a resounding celebration of vocational diversity and human skill. The tabernacle and temple were both emblematic—on a small scale—of the grand diversity which was to mark the global culturative endeavor given to man in the Garden of Eden. And they point forward to the wondrous culturative potentialities which will be released after the consummation, when a glorified, sinless humanity fulfills with perfection the culturative development of the New Earth [italics added].[3]

As we build, we are to build with the end in mind. That end is the coming of the kingdom of God. The questions for us are, How do we live before the face of God? How might we use our gifts, talents, and abilities to advance his kingdom? How can our lives and work contribute to the future place, the City of God, where God will dwell with us forever? Just as the men and women of Moses' day were gifted for building the tabernacle—God's dwelling place—so we have been equipped in our generation to contribute to the fullness of the coming kingdom of God.

LIVING IN BETWEEN

We are living before the second coming but *after* the first coming of Christ. Christ came among us and died to restore our primary relationship with God and create the foundation for substantial healing of all of our secondary relationships. We must not "wait" for Christ's return, we must work for Christ's return. We live in a time of expectancy. During the days granted for our lives, we are to be about Christ's business. We are to do business; we are to heed his command to "occupy till I come!" The place of my occupation is to be the place that I claim for Christ and his kingdom.

I remember, as a child, watching a movie about the invasion of Europe during World War II. A scene in the movie showed a large map of Nazi-controlled Europe, the British Isles, and the English Channel. On the map was a large arrow in the middle of the English Channel that marked the invading Allied armada. Then there were arrows that were a little smaller representing invasion points along the beaches of Normandy. Well inside Nazi-controlled France, key crossroads, bridges, fuel depots, and train yards were all identified with smaller arrows showing where paratroopers or airborne army troops would land. This was the battle map for D-Day. In this plan, every person had a role to play; each soldier, sailor, and airman had a critical part in the liberation of Europe. Each soldier was to fight to liberate land, to establish a beachhead of freedom in France. They were to fight for and occupy territory for the displacement of tyranny and the freedom of Europe. Soldiers had been drafted, trained (discipled), equipped, and made part of the overall battle plan.

D-DAY: THE REOCCUPATION

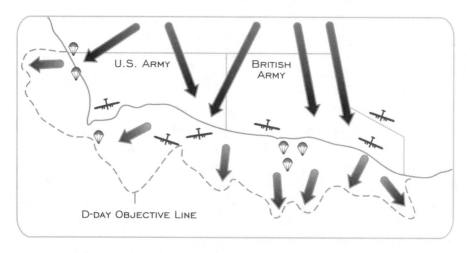

D-DAY OBJECTIVE LINE

This has created a vivid picture in my own mind. The business of the Christian is to occupy territory for Christ. We are to oppose the tyranny of the world, the flesh, and the devil in any of the places, structures, and institutions where we are engaged in our *life*work. Our great opportunity is to fight for freedom, for the reign of justice, for the coming of compassion, for economic sufficiency for all, for social peace, and for greater wholesomeness in our communities. As each Allied solder had an assignment, so does each Christian. Christ has captured a beachhead in each of our lives with plans to advance further.

Perhaps we can understand the words of Christ, "Occupy till I come!" by looking at another World War II drama. General Douglas MacArthur, commander of the Allied forces in the Pacific during World War II, was driven out of the Philippines by the invading Japanese forces. After he was flown to the Northern Territory in Australia to plan for the relief of the Philippines as a part of the larger offensive against Japan, MacArthur sent word back to the Philippine resistance: "I came out of Bataan and *I shall return.*"[4] General MacArthur wanted the world to know that he had escaped the Japanese plan to capture him and that he wanted the Philippine resistance to continue to fight because he would be coming back to the Philippines. Two years and seven months after his message was sent to the world, he returned to the Philippines to restore its freedom.

This is essentially what Christ has called his people to do. He conquered death at the resurrection; he has gone to the Father to get the kingdom and to return. In the meantime, he tells his people, "Fight on, for I shall return!" We are not to surrender to the enemy forces. We are to not to wait passively for Christ's return. We are to occupy till he comes.

We are living between the first and second comings of Christ. We live in the time between the *now* and the *not yet* of the kingdom of God. We are not to be spectators in the midst of the battle for the heart and soul of nations and cultures. Each Christian is given a life and a work. Our *life*work is to occupy for Christ. The Reformers in Europe and the Puritans in America had a strong sense of understanding of the role that vocation played in the kingdom enterprise. The Puritan pastor Richard Steele wrote, "He that hath lent you talents hath also said, 'Occupy till I come!' How is it that you stand all day idle? . . . Your trade is your proper province."[5] Luther understood both the nature and timelessness of the task when he reputedly said, "If I knew that Christ would return tomorrow, I would plant a tree today."

We are not to wait! We are to work to hasten the day of his coming!

HASTEN THE DAY OF HIS COMING!

In this time between Christ's first and second comings, we live in both the earthly and heavenly kingdoms, serving as ambassadors for the latter. Through the apostle Peter, the Lord reveals more about the believer's stance in this in-between time. In 2 Peter 3:10 Peter reflects on the future return of Christ and the believer's role prior to his second coming: "But the day of the Lord will come like a thief, in which the heavens will pass away with a roar and the elements will be destroyed with intense heat, and the earth and its works will be burned up" (NASB). In light of these coming events, how are we to live our lives? This is the question raised and answered in 2 Peter 3:11–12. Three things are expected: (1) we are to live holy and godly lives, (2) we are to look forward to the day of his coming, and (3) we are to hasten the day of his coming. Incredible! Somehow the activity of the believer and the believing church influences the return of Christ.

Our lives should be lived on the historical fact of Christ's first coming. Our strategies and statements should be made on the certainty of his second coming.

We are to be rebels in our world. We are to stand against the forces of evil. We are to move against the tide of our culture. We are to live in the reality of the existence of God and of his work in history. We are to shape history by the things that we say and the choices we make, in a way that gives evidence and honor to the living God.

We are to be lawyers seeking justice and truth; students becoming educated for the wonder of knowledge; parents recognizing the sacred trust of their children; writers creating worlds that reflect God's creation; farmers bringing forth bounty on their land; citizens casting ballots and joining school boards; business leaders raising questions of ethics in the marketplace; people establishing trust with their neighbors; and churches developing ministries to the poor, the widow, and the orphan.

FINDING WORK ONLY A KNIGHT CAN DO!

In the classic story *St. George and the Dragon,* a knight's Christian virtues of truth, justice, and courage war against the dragon, representing the pagan virtues of sin and evil. When St. George has extended the peace of the kingdom to one place, he looks for a new work "which only a knight can do!" This story reminds us of the call of the kingdom of God. As the story goes,

> One day St. George rode throughout the country. Everywhere he saw the men busy at their work in the fields, the women singing at work in their homes, and the little children shouting at their play.
>
> "These people are all safe and happy. They need me no more," said St. George.
>
> "But somewhere perhaps there is trouble and fear. There may be someplace where little children cannot play in safety, some woman may have been

carried away from her home—perhaps there are even dragons left to be slain. Tomorrow I shall ride away and never stop *until I find work which only a knight can do.*"[6]

Much like St. George, we should be looking for work that only a Christian can do. Fortunately, the Lord has given us an awe-inspiring charge to disciple the nations, beginning where we are *right now*. Pope John Paul II captures the imagination of all of God's children, young and old, when he writes,

> I wish, finally, to address you, dear young people, and to repeat these words to you with affection: be generous in giving your life to the Lord. Do not be afraid! You have nothing to fear, because God is the Lord of history and of the universe. Let grow in you the desire for great and noble projects. Nourish a sense of solidarity: these are the sign of the divine action in your heart. Place at the use of your communities the talents which Providence has lavished on you. The more ready you are to give yourself to God and others, the more you will discover the authentic meaning of life. God expects much of you![7]

The command has been given: "Occupy till I come!"

INTRODUCTION

1. John Fuellenbach, *The Kingdom of God: The Message of Jesus Today* (Maryknoll, N.Y.: Orbis Books, 1995), 9.
2. E. Stanley Jones, *The Unshakable Kingdom and the Unchanging Person* (Nashville: Abingdon Press, 1971), 19.
3. Ibid.
4. Fuellenbach, *The Kingdom of God,* 15.
5. Ibid., 6.
6. 1 Cor. 12:27.
7. I first heard the term *kingdomizer* used by Paul Jeong of Natural Church Development Korea at the Disciple Nations Alliance Forum, Phoenix, Arizona, April 16, 2002. We are to be agents of the King and his kingdom in our life and in our work. We are to *kingdomize* our work.
8. The author worked for Food for the Hungry International (www.fhi.net) for twenty-six years and now works for the Disciple Nations Alliance (www.disciplenations.org).
9. The two major understandings of the universe that I want to distinguish here are an open universe and a closed universe. The Bible reveals that before the universe existed, God existed. God created the universe, and thus the universe is "open" to his intervention as well as to the intrusion of angels and human beings. God, angels and demons, and man can all impact this world by their decisions and actions. In an open system, resources are created and discovered and thus wealth can grow. The concept that resources can grow is referred to as a *positive-sum* economic model. This is in contrast to a "closed" system, the view of Darwinism, secularism, or naturalism. In this view of reality, there is no God, there are no demons and angels, and man is a product of evolutionary forces. The universe is a large machine, with man a part of that machine. In a closed system there are no beings free to act, and resources are physical things in the ground and are thus finite; wealth is limited. This concept of a "fixed" amount of resources is referred to as a *zero-sum* economic model.

CHAPTER 1: WORLDVIEWS AT WORK

1. For more about worldviews see my book *Discipling Nations: The Power of Truth to Transform Cultures* (Seattle: YWAM Publishing, 1998) or James W. Sire's *The Universe Next Door: A Basic Worldview Catalog* (Downers Grove, Ill.: InterVarsity Press, 1997).

2. See 1 Cor. 2:16; 2 Cor. 10:5; Rom. 12:2.
3. Os Guinness, *The Call: Finding and Fulfilling the Central Purpose of Your Life* (Nashville: Word Publishing, 1998), 141.
4. Related to me at a Vision Conference in Rostov, Russia, June 2002. For information on Vision Conferences, see the Disciple Nations Alliance website, www.disciplenations.org/vc.
5. Bobby Boyd, Dewayne Mize, Dennis Robbins, and Warren Haynes, "Finally Friday," Trevcor Music Corporation (Title Code: 360247010).

CHAPTER 2: HOW DID WE GET HERE?

1. I use the words *wholistic* and *wholism* as used by my friend and colaborer Dr. Bob Moffitt, President of the Harvest Foundation. Wholism speaks of the whole of God's Word to the whole man in the whole world. We recognize that *wholism* is a coined word. But we prefer it to the word more commonly used, *holism*, which has been co-opted by the New Age movement and reflects a unity without diversity.
2. John 1:1–4, 14.
3. Eusebius, *Demonstration of the Gospel (Demonstratio Evangelica)*, quoted in W. R. Forrester, *Christian Vocation* (New York: Charles Scribner's Sons, 1953), 42, quoted in Leland Ryken, *Redeeming the Time* (Grand Rapids: Baker Books, 1995), 74.
4. Donald K. McKim, ed., *Westminster Dictionary of Theological Terms* (Louisville, Ky.: John Knox Press, 1996), 62.
5. Alister E. McGrath, *Reformation Thought: An Introduction* (Malden, Mass: Blackwell Publishers, 2001), 266–67.
6. Dietrich Bonhoeffer, *The Cost of Discipleship* (New York: MacMillan Publishing Co., 1977), 51–52.
7. *LovetoKnow Classic Encyclopedia,* s.v. "Pietism," http://www.1911encyclopedia.org/Pietism (accessed May 27, 2009).
8. The founders of modern—theistic—science were God-fearing, Bible-believing men like Francis Bacon (1561–1626), Johannes Kepler (1571–1630), Blaise Pascal (1623–1662), and Isaac Newton (1642–1727). For these men there was no separation between faith and reason, between the natural realm and the spiritual realm.
9. Ralph D. Winter, "The Future of Evangelicals in Mission," *Mission Frontiers,* September–October 2007.
10. Vishal and Ruth Mangalwadi, *The Legacy of William Carey: A Model for the Transformation of a Culture* (Wheaton, Ill.: Crossway Books, 1999). The Mangalwadis' book is worth its weight in gold. I highly recommend it to anyone interested in transforming culture.
11. Woodrow Kroll, *Taking Back the Good Book: How America Forgot the Bible and Why It Matters to You* (Wheaton, Ill.: Good News/Crossway, 2007), 41.
12. Kenneth Woodward and David Gates, "How the Bible Made America," *Newsweek,* December 27, 1982.

CHAPTER 3: THE SACRED-SECULAR DICHOTOMY

1. Rev. 21:1, 5–6.
2. For more on this see chapter 13 of my book *Discipling Nations: The Power of Truth to Transform Cultures* (Seattle: YWAM Publishing, 1998).
3. Isa. 30:28; Heb. 12:27–28; Rev. 16:18–19.

4. 1 Cor. 3:10–15; 2 Pet. 3:10.
5. Matt. 22:37; Mark 12:30.
6. Col. 1:20.

Babette's Feast

Babette's Feast, DVD, directed by Gabriel Axel (1987; Los Angeles: MGM Studios, 2001).

Michael Baer's Story

Michael R. Baer, *Business as Mission: The Power of Business in the Kingdom of God* (Seattle: YWAM Publishing, 2006), 10–12. Excerpted with permission.

CHAPTER 4: ONE LORD, ONE REALM

1. Scott D. Allen, Darrow L. Miller, and Bob Moffitt, "God's Unshakable Kingdom," *Kingdom Lifestyle Bible Studies* (Seattle: YWAM Publishing, 2005), 15.
2. Luke 18:31–33.
3. Matt. 26:11.
4. A term for resources that are available to be used to produce more wealth.

CHAPTER 5: CORAM DEO

1. Eph. 1:7–10.
2. William Whitaker, *WORDS*, s.v. "coram," http://www.archives.nd.edu/cgi-bin/wordz .pl?keyword=coram (accessed May 27, 2009).
3. Cotton Mather, "A Christian at His Calling," quoted in Ralph Barton Perry, *Puritanism and Democracy* (New York: Vanguard, 1944), 127, quoted in Leland Ryken, *Redeeming the Time* (Grand Rapids: Baker Books, 1995), 106.
4. John Milton quoted in Leland Ryken, *Worldly Saints: The Puritans As They Really Were* (Grand Rapids: Zondervan, 1990), 28.
5. Ryken, *Worldly Saints*, 28.
6. Robert Young, *Young's Literal Translation* (Oak Harbor, Wash.: Logos Research Systems, 1997), S. Jn 1:14.
7. *Enhanced Strong's Lexicon*, s.v. "skenoo."
8. 1 John 2:1.
9. Thomas Carlyle, *Past and Present* (1843; Project Gutenberg, 1996), www.gutenberg.org/ files/13534/13534.txt (accessed May 27, 2009).
10. Martin Luther, *The Babylonian Captivity of the Church* (1520; Project Wittenberg Online Electronic Study Edition, 2002), www.ctsfw.edu/etext/luther/babylonian/babylonian .htm (accessed May 27, 2009).
11. Exod. 33:20.
12. Phil. 2:1–11.
13. Os Guinness, *The Call: Finding and Fulfilling the Central Purpose of Your Life* (Nashville: Word Publishing, 1998), 200.
14. Kathryn Spink and Mother Teresa, *Life in the Spirit: Reflections, Meditations, Prayers, Mother Teresa of Calcutta* (New York: HarperCollins, 1983), 74.
15. Abraham Kuyper, *Lectures on Calvinism* (Grand Rapids: William B. Eerdmans, 1943), 52.

16. *1828 American Dictionary of the English Language,* s.v. "consecrated."
17. Ryken, *Redeeming the Time,* 104.
18. E. Stanley Jones, *The Unshakable Kingdom and the Unchanging Person* (Nashville: Abingdon Press, 1972), 159.

Ana Santos's Story

Ana Santos, in testimony written for the author, August 13, 2007.

John Beckett's Story

John D. Beckett, *Loving Monday: Succeeding in Business Without Selling Your Soul* (Downers Grove, Ill.: InterVarsity Press, 2001). See also "About John Beckett," www.lovingmonday.com /about (accessed January 26, 2008).

CHAPTER 6: THE NEED FOR A BIBLICAL THEOLOGY OF VOCATION

1. Dorothy L. Sayers, "Why Work?" in *Creed or Chaos?* (New York: Harcourt, Brace and Company, 1949), 56.
2. Pope John Paul II, *Message of the Holy Father for the XXXV World Day of Prayer for Vocations,* May 3, 1998, http://www.vatican.va/holy_father/john_paul_ii/messages/vocations/ documents/hf_jp-ii_mes_24091997_xxxv-voc-1998_en.html (accessed May 27, 2009).
3. Dallas Willard, *The Spirit of the Disciplines* (New York: HarperCollins, 1998), 14.

CHAPTER 7: THE ESSENTIAL METANARRATIVE

1. Gen. 1:4, 10, 12, 18, 21, 25.
2. Gen 1:7, 9, 11, 15, 24, 30.
3. Col. 1:20.
4. "For we are God's workmanship, created in Christ Jesus to do good works, which God prepared in advance for us to do." The word *workmanship* here is the Greek word *poiema,* the root of the word *poem.*
5. Os Guinness, *The Call: Finding and Fulfilling the Central Purpose of Your Life* (Nashville: Word Publishing, 1998), 178.

CHAPTER 8: CULTURE

1. Jemimah Wright, "Girl Survived Tribe's Custom of Live Burial," *Telegraph,* June 22, 2007, http://www.telegraph.co.uk/news/worldnews/1555339/Girl-survived-tribe's-custom-of -live-baby-burial.html (accessed May 27, 2009).
2. J. R. R. Tolkien, *Tree and Leaf* (London: Unwin Books, 1964), 61.
3. Vishal Mangalwadi, untitled lecture (Mercy Ship's Foundation in Community Development School, Tyler, Texas, May 1995).
4. Henry Van Til, quoted in David Bruce Hegeman, *Plowing in Hope: Toward a Biblical Theology of Culture* (Moscow, Idaho: Canon Press, 1999), 15.
5. *The Compact Edition of the Oxford English Dictionary* (Oxford: Oxford University Press, 1971), s.v. "cult."

6. Hegeman, *Plowing in Hope,* 13–14.
7. George Grant, *The Micah Mandate: Balancing the Christian Life* (Nashville: Cumberland House, 1999), 243.
8. The basic idea for this came from Colin Harbinson of YWAM, *The Arts and Cultural Restoration,* www.colinharbinson.com/order/cultrestbook.html (accessed May 27, 2009).
9. Douglas Jones and Douglas Wilson, *Angels in the Architecture: A Protestant Vision for Middle Earth* (Moscow, Idaho: Canon Press, 1998), 18.
10. Matt. 6:9–13.
11. C. S. Lewis, *The Last Battle* (1956; repr., New York: The MacMillan Company, 1967), 149.

Kathleen Norris's Story

1. Steven Barclay Agency, "Kathleen Norris," www.barclayagency.com/norris.html (accessed January 31, 2008).
2. Ibid.
3. "Homiletics Interview: Kathleen Norris: Flowers in the Desert," *Homiletics Online,* http://homileticsonline.com/subscriber/interviews/norris.asp (accessed January 26, 2008). Reprinted with permission of HomileticsOnline, www.HomileticsOnline.com.

CHAPTER 9: ELEMENTS OF THE CULTURAL MANDATE

1. *The American Heritage Dictionary of the English Language,* s.v. "cultivate."
2. *The Compact Edition of the Oxford English Dictionary,* s.v. "culture."
3. *The American Heritage Dictionary of the English Language,* s.v. "culture."
4. Gen. 2:15.
5. Gen. 2:19.
6. See Gen. 1:26–28.
7. *Enhanced Strong's Lexicon,* s.v. "abad."
8. Ibid., s.v. "shamar."
9. John Calvin, *Commentaries on the First Book of Moses called Genesis,* trans. Rev. John King (Grand Rapids: Baker Book House, 1979), 125.
10. For more on this please see my book *Discipling Nations: The Power of Truth to Transform Cultures* (Seattle: YWAM Publishing, 1998), chapters 7 and 11.
11. Isa. 11:9; Hab. 2:14.
12. Gen. 1–2.
13. Rev. 21–22.
14. Rev. 22:1–5.
15. David Bruce Hegeman, *Plowing in Hope: Toward a Biblical Theology of Culture* (Moscow, Idaho: Canon Press, 1999), 33–34.

CHAPTER 10: THE FALL, THE CROSS, AND CULTURE

1. Rom. 8:18–23.
2. Col. 1:20.
3. Dallas Willard, *The Divine Conspiracy* (San Francisco: HarperSanFrancisco, 1998), 27.
4. C. S. Lewis, *Out of the Silent Planet* (New York: Scribner, 2003).
5. Gen. 3:17–18.

6. Pope John Paul II, *Laborem Exercens* (On Human Work) (Washington, D.C.: United States Catholic Conference, 1981), 1, quoted in Chuck Colson and Jack Eckerd, *Why America Doesn't Work* (Nashville: W Publishing Group, 1991), 31.

7. See Gen. 3:14–15.

8. Rom. 8:18–23.

9. Col. 2:15.

10. David Bruce Hegeman, *Plowing in Hope: Toward a Biblical Theology of Culture* (Moscow, Idaho: Canon Press, 1999), 71.

11. Gen. 12:1–3.

12. Rev. 19:6–9.

13. Rev. 21:2.

14. Matt. 2:11.

15. Hegeman, *Plowing in Hope*, 86.

16. Isa. 60:1–3; Rev. 21:24.

17. Isa. 60:18; Rev. 21:4.

18. Isa. 60:11; Rev. 21:25.

19. Isa. 60:6–7, 9, 13, 17; Rev. 21:24, 26.

20. Anthony Hoekema, *The Bible and the Future* (Grand Rapids: William B. Eerdmans Publishing Co., 1979), 285, quoted in Hegeman, *Plowing in Hope*, 87–88.

21. Hegeman, *Plowing in Hope*, 88.

22. G. B. Caird, *The Revelation of Saint John* (San Francisco: HarperSanFrancisco, 1966) quoted in Hegeman, *Plowing in Hope*, 93.

23. C. S. Lewis, *The Last Battle* (New York: MacMillan Publishing, 1956).

24. Ibid., 162.

25. Ibid.

26. Herman Bavinck quoted in Charles Colson and Nancy Pearcey, *How Now Shall We Live?* (Wheaton, Ill.: Tyndale House Publishers, Inc., 1999), 293.

CHAPTER 11: THE CALL

1. Os Guinness, *The Call: Finding and Fulfilling the Central Purpose of Your Life* (Nashville: Word Publishing, 1998), 42.

2. *1828 American Dictionary of the English Language*, s.v. "vocation."

3. John Fuellenbach, *The Kingdom of God: The Message of Jesus Today* (Maryknoll, N.Y.: Orbis Books, 1995), 9.

4. Guinness, *The Call*, 34.

5. The Greek word *keleo* is translated *call* 125 times and *bid* 16 times. A second Greek word, *klesis* is translated *calling* 10 times and *vocation* one time. The Old Testament word *qara* is translated *call* 528 times and *cried* 98 times.

6. *1828 American Dictionary of the English Language*, s.v. "call."

7. Robert Laird Harris, Gleason Leonard Archer, and Bruce K. Waltke, eds., *Theological Wordbook of the Old Testament*, vol. 1 (Chicago: Moody Press, 1980), s.v. "barak," 132.

8. Exod. 35:4–5, 10.

9. Matt. 28:18–20.

10. Matt. 25:14–17; Luke 19:12–13.

11. *Enhanced Strong's Lexicon*, s.v. "katartismos."

12. Ibid., s.v. "katartizo."

13. Michael Novak, *Business as a Calling: Work and the Examined Life* (New York: The Free Press, 1996), 40.
14. Guinness, *The Call,* 13.
15. Gen. 11:31; 12:1, 4.
16. Heb. 11:10.
17. Heb. 11:12–16.
18. Guinness, *The Call,* 151.
19. Rev. 5:9–10.

CHAPTER 12: THE GENERAL CALL

1. Gen. 1:4, 10, 12, 18, 21, 25.
2. Gen. 1:7, 9, 11, 15, 30.
3. F. Foulkes, "Peace," *The New Bible Dictionary* (Wheaton, Ill.: Tyndale House Publishers, 1962), in Logos Library System 2.1, Logos Research Systems, Oak Harbor, Wash.
4. Ibid.
5. Ibid.
6. *Substantial healing* is a term used by Francis Schaeffer. It reflects that some healing must take place in the secondary relationship as a manifestation of the restoration of the primary relationship of the individual to God. While this will be real healing, it will not be complete in any one area until Christ returns.
7. *Enhanced Strong's Lexicon,* s.v., "sozo."
8. Matt. 16:24.
9. Rom. 1:17.
10. Rom. 12:2; 1 Cor. 2:16.
11. Rom. 8:19–22.
12. Luke 19:12–13.
13. Isa. 11:6–9; 60:1–13; Rev. 22:1–5.
14. Matt. 28:18.
15. Rev. 19:11–16.
16. Luke 11:20; 17:21.
17. Luke 19:12, 15.

CHAPTER 13: THE PARTICULAR CALL

1. *Enhanced Strong's Lexicon,* s.v "poiema."
2. For example, the word *ergon* speaks of the work (deeds) of Christ in Matt. 11:2 and Luke 24:19; the work of the gospel in John 6:27–29 and Phil. 2:30; the good work of service to those in need in Matt. 5:16, Col. 1:9–10; and the work of "employment" or "occupation" in Mark 13:34; John 4:34; 17:4; Acts 13:2; and 1 Thess. 5:12–13.
3. Colin Brown, ed., *The New International Dictionary of New Testament Theology,* vol. 3 (Grand Rapids: Zondervan, 1979), 1147–1151. For example, see Gen. 2:15; Exod. 20:9; Deut. 5:13.
4. See Matt. 25:34–40; Luke 10:25–37; Eph. 4:12.
5. Pope John Paul II, *Message of the Holy Father for the XXXV World Day of Prayer for Vocations,* May 3, 1998, http://www.vatican.va/holy_father/john_paul_ii/messages/vocations/documents/hf_jp-ii_mes_24091997_xxxv-voc-1998_en.html (accessed May 27, 2009).

6. Michael Novak, *Business as a Calling: Work and the Examined Life* (New York: The Free Press, 1996), 34.

7. Rom. 12:4–5; Eph. 1:22–23; 4:12–13.

8. Pope John Paul II, *Message of the Holy Father for the XXXV World Day of Prayer for Vocations.*

9. Dallas Willard, *The Divine Conspiracy: Rediscovering Our Hidden Life in God* (San Francisco: HarperSanFrancisco, 1998), 14.

10. Frederic W. Farrar, *The Fall of Man and Other Sermons* (London: Macmillan and Co., 1878), 210–211, http://books.google.com/books?id=A3Q3AAAAMAAJ.

11. This transcription of Don Matheny's sermon "I Qualify!," which I heard preached at a conference for cell church pastors in May 2003 in Cape Town, South Africa, was given to me by Matheny. Matheny is the pastor of Nairobi Lighthouse Church in Nairobi, Kenya.

12. George Grant, *The Micah Mandate: Balancing the Christian Life,* 2nd ed. (Nashville: Cumberland House Publishing, 1999), 25.

13. Philip Yancey, "Living with Furious Opposites," *Christianity Today,* September 4, 2000, www.christianitytoday.com/ct/2000/september4/4.70.html.

14. H. Lyndon Kilmer, *Helen Keller* (New York: Skillen and Fortas, 1964), 194, quoted in Grant, *The Micah Mandate,* 250.

15. Elizabeth R. Skoglund, *Amma: The Life and Words of Amy Carmichael* (Grand Rapids: Baker Books, 1994), 110–112.

16. Gen. 2:9; Exod. 15:26; Gen. 1:6–9; Deut. 25:13–16; Luke 19:12–13, 15.

17. Paul S. Minear, "Work and Vocation in Scripture," in *Work and Vocation: A Christian Discussion,* ed. John Oliver Nelson (New York: Harper, 1954), 32–83.

18. Willard, *The Divine Conspiracy,* 14.

19. Ibid., 283.

20. Exod. 25:8.

21. John 1:14.

22. Matt. 28:19–20; John 17:15–18; Eph. 2:22.

23. Brother Lawrence [Nicholas Herman], *The Practice of the Presence of God* (Springdale, Pa.: Whitaker House, 1982), 20.

Lisa Etter's and Hayden Smith's Stories

Lisa Etter and Hayden Smith, interview by Cynthia Kniffin for the author, September 25, 2007.

Jemimah Wright's Story

Jemimah Wright, in testimony written for the author, February 11, 2008.

CHAPTER 14: CHARACTERISTICS OF OUR *Life*WORK

1. Prov. 30:8–9.

2. Mark 10:35–45.

3. Matt. 6:33.

4. Eph. 2:8–9.

5. Martin Luther, "Exposition on Deuteronomy 8:17–18," in *What Luther Says: An Anthology,* ed. Ewald M. Plass (St. Louis: Concordia, 1959), 1495, quoted in Leland Ryken, *Redeeming the Time* (Grand Rapids: Baker Books, 1995), 99.

6. John Calvin, *Commentary of Psalm 127:2,* in Leland Ryken, *Worldly Saints: The Puritans As They Really Were* (Grand Rapids: Zondervan, 1990), 32.

7. Cotton Mather, *Sober Sentiments,* quoted in Ralph Barton Perry, *Puritanism and Democracy* (New York: Vanguard, 1944), 312, quoted in Ryken, *Redeeming the Time,* 99.

8. Leland Ryken, *Worldly Saints: The Puritans As They Really Were* (Grand Rapids: Zondervan, 1990), 33.

9. Luke 19:13.

10. Gen. 1:14–19.

11. John Wesley, "The Use of Money" (Sermon 50, text from the 1872 edition), http://gbgm -umc.org/umw/wesley/serm-050.stm (accessed May 27, 2009).

12. Mark 13:32–33.

13. Os Guinness, *The Call: Finding and Fulfilling the Central Purpose of Your Life* (Nashville: Word Publishing, 1998), 132, 133.

14. Heb. 11:10.

15. Exod. 31:1–6; 35:30–36:1.

16. 2 Chron. 2–3.

17. Exod. 25:8; 40:33–34, 38.

18. Matt. 6:9–10, 33; 28:19–20; Luke 19:10–13.

19. Guinness, *The Call,* 198–199.

20. Wesley, "The Use of Money."

21. Related by Cleiton and Eli Oliveira after a Vision Conference in Belém, Brazil, in May 2002.

22. George Swinnock, *The Christian Man's Calling* in Richard B. Schlatter, *The Social Ideas of Religious Leaders:1660–1688* (1940; repr., New York: Octagon Books, 1971), 189, quoted in Ryken, *Worldly Saints,* 15.

23. John Politan (sermon, Food for the Hungry Chapel, Phoenix, Ariz., February 9, 2000, taken from Scott Allen's notes).

24. Charles Colson, "What's So Important About Faith and Work?" *BreakPoint Commentary* #020201, February 1, 2002.

25. Glimpses of Christian History, "July 26, 1833: Dying Wilberforce Learned Slaves Were Finally Liberated," http://www.christianhistorytimeline.com/DAILYF/2001/07/daily -07-26-2001.shtml (accessed May 27, 2009).

26. Charles Colson, "Can Adversity Be a Blessing?" *BreakPoint Commentary* #020503, May 3, 2002.

CHAPTER 15: STEWARDSHIP

1. Gen. 1:26–28.

2. Luke 16:1–15.

3. Luke 19:11–26.

4. Luke 16:8.

5. Luke 19:16–17.

6. Luke 19:18–19.

7. Luke 19:20–26.

8. Virtue is the practice of what is true and good. In his 1828 dictionary, Noah Webster said, "Virtue is nothing but voluntary obedience to truth." He called it "a particular moral excellence." Virtues differ from the modern word *values* in that values are subjective, representing personal and social standards; values do not demand practice. Virtues, on the other hand, are founded in a framework of moral absolutes and obedience.

9. John Wesley, "The Use of Money" (Sermon 50, text from the 1872 edition), http://gbgm-umc.org/umw/wesley/serm-050.stm (accessed May 27, 2009).

10. Martin Luther, "Exposition on Exodus 13:18," in *What Luther Says: An Anthology,* ed. Ewald M. Plass (St. Louis: Concordia, 1959), 1496, quoted in Leland Ryken, *Redeeming the Time* (Grand Rapids: Baker Books, 1995), 102.

11. Robert Bolton, *General Directions for a Comfortable Walking with God* (Ligonier, Pa.: Soli Deo Gloria, 1991), 77, quoted in Ryken, *Redeeming the Time,* 102.

12. *Enhanced Strong's Lexicon,* s.v. "melakah."

13. As we saw in chapter 13, *abad* is also used in the Decalogue.

14. Exod. 20:8–11.

15. Gen. 1:28.

16. John Milton, *Paradise Lost,* bk. 4, lines 618–20, quoted in Leland Ryken, *Worldly Saints: The Puritans As They Really Were* (Grand Rapids: Zondervan, 1990), 35.

17. Wesley, "The Use of Money."

18. Col. 1:17; Heb. 1:3.

19. *Merriam-Webster's Online Dictionary,* s.v. "husbandry."

20. Rom. 8:19–21.

21. Rev. 11:18.

22. Ryken, *Worldly Saints,* 99.

23. Samuel Willard, *A Complete Body of Divinity,* quoted in Stephen Foster, *Their Solitary Way: The Puritan Social Ethic in the First Century of Settlement in New England* (New Haven: Yale University Press, 1971), 128, quoted in Ryken, *Worldly Saints,* 100.

24. Matt. 6:33.

25. Doug Sherman and William Hendricks, *Your Work Matters to God* (Colorado Springs: NavPress, 1988), 185.

26. Wesley, "The Use of Money."

27. Ibid.

28. *1828 American Dictionary of the English Language,* s.v. "selfishness."

29. John 3:16; 1 John 4:9–10, 16.

30. Ps. 23; Mark 10:45; John 13:2–17.

31. John 3:16; Phil. 2:6–8.

32. Phil. 2:4.

33. Wesley, "The Use of Money."

CHAPTER 16: THE ECONOMICS OF GIVING

1. Col. 1:20.

2. Matt. 28:18–20.

3. Richard Baxter, *A Christian Directory,* in *Protestantism and Capitalism: The Weber Thesis and Its Critics,* ed. Robert W. Green (Boston: D. C. Heath, 1959), 72, quoted in Leland Ryken, *Worldly Saints: The Puritans As They Really Were* (Grand Rapids: Zondervan, 1990), 31.

4. Phil. 2:4–8.

5. Matt. 25:31–46.

6. William Perkins, *Vocations or Callings of Men,* in *Works,* 1:757, in Leland Ryken, *Redeeming the Time* (Grand Rapids: Baker Books, 1995), 106.

7. Charles Spurgeon, *Metropolitan Tabernacle Pulpit*, vol. 23 (London, U.K.: Morgan & Chase, 1930), 19, quoted in George Grant, *Bringing in the Sheaves: Transforming Poverty into Productivity* (Brentwood, Tenn.: Wolgemuth & Hyatt, 1988), 54.

8. See my book *Discipling Nations: The Power of Truth to Transform Cultures* (Seattle: YWAM Publishing,1998), chapter 6.

9. See Scott Allen and Darrow Miller, *The Forest in the Seed* (Phoenix: Disciple Nations Alliance, 2007).

10. See my book *Discipling Nations,* chapters 7 and 11.

11. *Zero-sum* is an economic term derived from a naturalistic view of reality. It assumes that resources are physical things "in the ground." By nature they are finite or limited. If one person or nation gains more, it is at the loss of another person or nation.

12. Marvin Olasky, *The Tragedy of American Compassion* (Washington, D.C.: Regnery Gateway, 1992).

13. Daniel A. Bazikian, "Book Review: The Tragedy of American Compassion by Marvin Olasky," http://www.thefreemanonline.org/columns/book-review-the-tragedy-of-american -compassion-by-marvin-olasky/ (accessed May 27, 2009).

14. E. E. Ryden, *The Story of Christian Hymnody* (Philadelphia: Fortress Press, 1959), 139.

15. See verses 29 and 36.

16. Stephen Neill, *A History of Christian Missions* (New York: Penguin Books, 1966), 42.

17. Olasky, *The Tragedy of American Compassion,* 19.

18. Ibid., 225.

19. Lev. 19:9–10; 23:22; Deut. 24: 19–21.

CHAPTER 17: THE KINGDOM ADVANCES FROM THE INSIDE OUT

1. Gen. 6:5–6; Rom. 3:23.

2. Grover Gunn, "Making Waves," *TableTalk* (January 2001): 12.

3. 2 Cor. 5:17.

4. Matt. 25:35–40.

5. Luke 10:25–37.

6. For more on this, see my book *Nurturing the Nations: Reclaiming the Dignity of Women in Building Healthy Cultures* (Colorado Springs: Paternoster Publishing, 2008).

7. Col. 1:20.

8. Mark 16:15.

9. Col. 1:20.

10. Rom. 8:19–21.

11. Gunn, "Making Waves," 12.

12. Dallas Willard, *The Divine Conspiracy: Rediscovering Our Hidden Life in God* (San Francisco: HarperSanFrancisco, 1998), 14.

CHAPTER 18: THE GATES OF THE CITY

1. Exod. 32:26 KJV.

2. Neh. 2:8 KJV.

3. 1 Kings 6:34–35.

4. Gen. 19:1; Judg. 16:3; Jer. 37:13.

5. Gen. 22:17–18.
6. Gen. 23:17–18; 2 Kings 7:1; Neh. 3:1, 3, 28.
7. Neh. 8.
8. Deut. 16:18–21 (KJV); 21:18–20; Josh. 20:4; Ruth 4:1–2, 11; 2 Kings 23:8; Prov. 22:22 (KJV); Amos 5:15 (KJV) .
9. 2 Sam. 19:8; 1 Kings 22:10; Prov. 31:23; Dan. 2:48–49 (KJV).
10. 2 Kings 7:1; 2 Chron. 32:6–8; Prov. 31:31; Jer. 7:2; 17:19–27; 36:10.
11. Gen. 19:1; Ruth 4:11; Ps. 69:12; Amos 5:12 (KJV).
12. Neh. 3:14.
13. Roy Moore and John Perry, *So Help Me God: The Ten Commandments, Judicial Tyranny, and the Battle for Religious Freedom* (Nashville: B&H Publishing Group, 2005), front flap.
14. Rom. 13:1–6.
15. Jer. 7:2; 17:19–20.
16. See also Prov. 8:1–4.
17. Rom. 1:18–23.

Sherron Watkins's Story

Sherron Watkins's story is told in numerous media accounts, from the *Wall Street Journal* to *Time* to *Today's Christian Woman*. For example, see Bob Jones, "Reluctant Hero," *World*, vol. 17, no. 4 (February 2, 2002) and Franklin Pellegrini, "Person of the Week: 'Enron Whistleblower' Sherron Watkins," *Time*, January 18, 2002.

Marvin Olasky's Story

1. Marvin Olasky, *The Tragedy of American Compassion* (Washington, D.C.: Regnery Gateway, 1992).

CHAPTER 19: THE DOMAINS

1. Rodney Stark, *The Rise of Christianity: A Sociologist Reconsiders History* (Princeton: Princeton University Press, 1996), 211.
2. Thomas Cahill, *Desire of the Everlasting Hills: The World Before and After Jesus* (New York: Doubleday, 1999), 310–311.
3. Paul L. Maier in Alvin J. Schmidt, *Under the Influence: How Christianity Transformed Civilization* (Grand Rapids: Zondervan, 2001), 8.
4. Gen. 2:24.
5. Matt. 16:18.
6. Gen. 9:6.
7. J. I. Packard, *Concise Theology: A Guide to Historic Christian Beliefs* (Wheaton, Ill.: Tyndale House Publishers, 1993), in Logos Library System 2.1, Logos Research Systems, Oak Harbor, Wash.
8. R. J. Slater, *Teaching and Learning America's Christian History* (San Francisco: Foundation for American Christian Education, 1960), 199, quoted in Elizabeth Youmans, *The Christian Principle of Self-Government* (unpublished, 2005), 1.
9. Youmans, *The Christian Principle of Self-Government*, 1. To learn more about Chrysalis International, see http://www.chrysalisinternational.org/default.asp.

10. H. Dolson, *William Penn: Quaker Hero* (New York: Random House, 1961), 155, quoted in Youmans, *The Christian Principle of Self-Government*, 1.
11. Rom. 1:18–20.
12. Schmidt, *Under the Influence*, 253.
13. See Ps. 147:19–20.
14. Schmidt, *Under the Influence*, 249–250.
15. D. James Kennedy and Jerry Newcombe, *What If Jesus Had Never Been Born?* (Nashville: Thomas Nelson, 1994), 81.
16. Schmidt, *Under the Influence*, 251.
17. Matt. 22:21.
18. Rom. 1:18–20; 2:14–15.
19. Schmidt, *Under the Influence*, 256.
20. Rom. 1:25.
21. Schmidt, *Under the Influence*, 171.
22. Ibid.
23. Ibid., 173.
24. Charles H. Haskins, *The Rise of Universities* (New York: Henry Holt, 1923), 3, quoted in Schmidt, *Under the Influence*, 186.
25. Ellwood P. Cubberly, *The History of Education* (Boston: Houghton Mifflin, 1948), 218, quoted in Schmidt, *Under the Influence*, 187.
26. Paul Lee Tan, *Encyclopedia of 7700 Illustrations: Signs of the Times* (Rockville, Md.: Assurance Publishers, 1984), 157, quoted in Schmidt, *Under the Influence*, 190.
27. Kennedy and Newcombe, *What If Jesus Had Never Been Born?*, 52.
28. Ibid., 43.
29. William Boyd, *The History of Western Education* (New York: Barnes and Noble, 1955), 189, quoted in Schmidt, *Under the Influence*, 177.
30. John Jefferson Davis, *Your Wealth in God's World: Does the Bible Support the Free Market?* (Phillipsburg, N.J.: Presbyterian and Reformed Publishing Co., 1984), 65, quoted in Kennedy and Newcombe, *What If Jesus Had Never Been Born?*, 144.
31. Matt. 25:36.
32. Cyprian, *Mortality* 15–20, 1958 ed., quoted in Rodney Stark, *The Rise of Christianity*, 81.
33. Kennedy and Newcombe, *What If Jesus Had Never Been Born?*, 145.
34. David Riesman, *The Story of Medicine in the Middle Ages* (New York: Harper and Brothers, 1936), 356, quoted in Schmidt, *Under the Influence*, 157.
35. Kennedy and Newcombe, *What If Jesus Had Never Been Born?*, 151.
36. Schmidt, *Under the Influence*, 166.
37. Kennedy and Newcombe, *What If Jesus Had Never Been Born?*, 152.
38. Schmidt, *Under the Influence*, 160.
39. Ibid., 162–163.
40. Ibid., 165.
41. Gen. 2:19.
42. Exod. 31:1–6; 35:30–36:1.
43. J. R. R. Tolkien, *Tree and Leaf* (London: Unwin Books, 1964), 44.
44. Edith Schaeffer, *Hidden Art* (London: The Norfolk Press, 1971), 24.
45. See chapter 8 for a discussion of culture as worship and the three major cultural grids of kingdom culture, counterfeit culture, and natural culture.

46. Exod. 20:4, 23.

47. Exod. 25; 1 Kings 7:2–37.

48. Mindy Belz, "Art Aflame," *World*, December 17, 2005, http://www.worldmag.com/articles/11356 (accessed May 27, 2009).

49. Exod. 31:1–11; 35:4–39:43.

50. Exod. 40:34–38.

51. Cynthia Pearl Maus, *Christ and the Fine Arts: An Anthology of Pictures, Poetry, Music, and Stories Centering in the Life of Christ*, rev. and enlarged ed. (New York: Harper and Row Publishers, 1938, 1959), 2, quoted in Kennedy and Newcombe, *What If Jesus Had Never Been Born?*, 174.

52. Kennedy and Newcombe, *What If Jesus Had Never Been Born?*, 182.

53. Paul Griffiths, "Opera," in *The Oxford Companion to Music*, ed. Denis Arnold (New York: Oxford University Press, 1983), 3:1291, quoted in Schmidt, *Under the Influence*, 316–317.

54. Kennedy and Newcombe, *What If Jesus Had Never Been Born?*, 182.

55. Ibid.

56. Kennedy and Newcombe, *What If Jesus Had Never Been Born?*, 185.

57. Plato, *The Republic*, quoted in Schmidt, *Under the Influence*, 342.

58. The word *balladeer* was used during medieval times to refer to people who sang ballads—stories put to song—in public places. I am using the word for those Christians who are artists (not just songwriters and singers) who are called to be a prophetic voice to their culture or the nations. Their call is to consciously bring kingdom culture—truth, goodness, and beauty—into the marketplace and public square.

59. Flannery O'Connor, *Mystery and Manners: Occasional Prose* (New York: Farrar, Straus and Giroux, 1969), 172–173.

60. Dorothy L. Sayers, "Why Work?" in *Creed or Chaos?* (New York: Harcourt, Brace and Company, 1949), 57.

61. O'Connor, *Mystery and Manners*, 74.

62. Dennis Peacocke, *Almighty & Sons: Doing Business God's Way* (Santa Rosa, Calif.: Rebuild, 1995), ix.

63. Matt. 5:17.

64. Kennedy and Newcombe, *What If Jesus Had Never Been Born?*, 111.

65. Ibid.

66. Ibid., 114.

67. David S. Landes, *The Wealth and Poverty of Nations: Why Some Are So Rich and Some So Poor* (New York: W. W. Norton & Company, 1998), 58–59.

68. For a full explanation of closed and open systems, please see chapter 16.

69. Michael Novak, *Business as a Calling: Work and the Examined Life* (New York: The Free Press, 1996), 112.

70. Ibid.,159.

71. Kenneth McLeish, *Key Ideas in Human Thought* (Prima Publishing, 1995), 658–659.

72. Men such as Pythagoras, Hippocrates, and Euclid.

73. Thomas Goldstein, *Dawn of Modern Science: From the Arabs to Leonardo da Vinci* (Boston: Houghton Mifflin, 1980), 171, quoted in Schmidt, *Under the Influence*, 219.

74. Roger Bacon, *Opus Majus*, trans. Robert Belle Burke (New York: Russell and Russell, 1962), 584, quoted in Schmidt, *Under the Influence*, 219.

75. Henry Morris, *Men of Science Men of God* (San Diego: Master Books, 1984), 35, quoted in Kennedy and Newcombe, *What If Jesus Had Never Been Born?*, 97.

76. John Peck and Charles Strohmer, *Uncommon Sense: God's Wisdom for Our Complex and Changing World* (London: SPCK Publishing, 2001), 155.
77. Kennedy and Newcombe, *What If Jesus Had Never Been Born?*, 99.
78. Morris, *Men of Science Men of God*, 34–35, quoted in Kennedy and Newcombe, *What If Jesus Had Never Been Born?*, 99.
79. *Heroes of History*, vol. 4 (West Frankford, Ill.: Caleb Publishers, 1992), 36, quoted in Kennedy and Newcombe, *What If Jesus Had Never Been Born?*, 100.

John W. Whitehead's Story

1. "History of The Rutherford Institute," The Rutherford Institute, http://www.rutherford .org/About/History.asp (accessed May 27, 2009).
2. "About Us," The Rutherford Institute, http://www.rutherford.org/About/AboutUs.asp (accessed May 27, 2009).
3. "Rutherford Attorneys Weigh In On 'Nuremberg Files' Case, Ask U.S. Supreme Court To Affirm Right Of Pro-Life Activists To Engage In Non-Violent Speech," *The Rutherford Institute News*, April 6, 2006, http://rutherford.org/articles_db/press_release .asp?article_id=610 (accessed May 27, 2009).
4. "U.S. Supreme Court Ruling Calls For Emergency Exception While Affirming Parents' Right To Be Notified If Minor Child Opts To Have An Abortion," *The Rutherford Institute News*, January 19, 2006, http://rutherford.org/articles_db/press_release.asp?article _id=597 (accessed May 27, 2009).
5. "Rutherford Institute President Commends U.S. Supreme Court Decision To Limit President's Power To Detain 'Enemy Combatants,'" *The Rutherford Institute News*, June 28, 2004, http:// rutherford.org/articles_db/press_release.asp?article_id=497 (accessed May 27, 2009).
6. "John W. Whitehead Testifies To U.S. Senate Constitution Subcommittee On Steps The Next President Must Take To Restore Rule Of Law In America," *The Rutherford Institute News*, September 16, 2008, http://www.rutherford.org/articles_db/press_release.asp?article _id=726 (accessed May 27, 2009).

Elizabeth Youmans's Story

1. Elizabeth L. Youmans, Ed.D., *Education of Children, a Biblical Perspective* (Food for the Hungry International Child Development Seminar, Lima, Peru, May 27–30, 2002).
2. Elizabeth Youmans, Ed.D., "The Christian View of Children PowerPoint," Chrysalis International, http://www.chrysalisinternational.org/assets/pdfs/Chr_View_of_Child _PPT.pdf (accessed May 27, 2009).

Mary Holmgren's Story

Written for the author by Marit Newton, daughter of Mary Holmgren, July 7, 2008.

Stefan Eicher's Story

Stefan Eicher, in testimony written for the author, August 6, 2007.

Makoto Fujimura's Story

1. The quotations in this paragraph all come from the MacLaurin Institute's interview with Makoto Fujimura, "Discovering Grace Through Art with Makoto Fujimura," *The MacLaurin Institute*, Summer 2008, 3.

2. The substance for this story and all quotations not otherwise attributed come from Mindy Belz, "Art Aflame," *World,* December 17, 2005, http://www.worldmag.com/articles/11356 (accessed January 30, 2008).

The Story of the Manthei Group

Jim Manthei, in testimony written for the author, July 31, 2007.

Ted Corwin's Story

The substance for this story comes from the author's correspondence with Ted Corwin and from Corwin's account in "On My Own?" *Guideposts,* March 1999, reprinted at http://www .designmasterfurniture.com/History.aspx (accessed September 20, 2008).

Francis Collins's Story

Francis Collins's story was adapted from the *2009 Personal Prayer Diary and Daily Planner* (Seattle: YWAM Publishing, 2008), 43. Used by permission.

1. Francis Collins, *Faith and the Human Genome* (address given to American Scientific Affiliation, Malibu, Calif., August 4, 2002), http://www.asa3.org/ASA/PSCF/2003/PSCF9 -03Collins.pdf (accessed May 27, 2009).
2. Ibid.
3. Francis Collins, interview by Bob Abernathy, *Religion and Ethics Newsweekly,* PBS, June 16, 2000, http://www.pbs.org/wnet/religionandethics/transcripts/collins.html (accessed May 27, 2009).

George Washington Carver's Story

1. George Washington Carver and Gary R. Kremer, *George Washington Carver: In His Own Words* (Columbia: University of Missouri Press, 1991), 143.
2. Linda McMurry Edwards, *George Washington Carver: The Life of the Great American Agriculturist* (New York: Rosen Publishing, 2004), 18.
3. Carver and Kremer, *George Washington Carver: In His Own Words,* 143.
4. Ibid., 1.

CHAPTER 20: THE GREAT COMMANDMENT

1. Rodney Stark, *The Rise of Christianity: A Sociologist Reconsiders History* (Princeton: Princeton University Press, 1996), 86.
2. Ibid., 161–162.
3. Ibid., 215.
4. John 13:34–35.
5. Matt. 22:36–40.
6. In discussing these areas of Christian influence, I will be relying heavily on Alvin Schmidt's book *Under the Influence: How Christianity Transformed Society,* Rodney Stark's book *The Rise of Christianity: A Sociologist Reconsiders History,* and the book by D. James Kennedy and Jerry Newcombe, *What If Jesus Had Never Been Born?*
7. William Stearns Davis, *A Day in Old Rome* (Boston: Allyn & Bacon, 1925), 389, quoted in Alvin J. Schmidt, *Under the Influence: How Christianity Transformed Society* (Grand Rapids: Zondervan, 2001), 61.

8. D. James Kennedy and Jerry Newcombe, *What If Jesus Had Never Been Born?* (Nashville: Thomas Nelson, 1994), 22.

9. Schmidt, *Under the Influence*, 67.

10. Ibid., 68.

11. Kennedy and Newcombe, *What If Jesus Had Never Been Born?*, 25.

12. Stark, *The Rise of Christianity*, 118.

13. Michael J. Gorman, *Abortion and the Early Church* (Downers Grove, Ill: InterVarsity Press, 1980), 25, quoted in Stark, *The Rise of Christianity*, 118.

14. George Grant, *Third Time Around: A History of the Pro-Life Movement from the First Century to the* Present (Franklin, Tenn.: Legacy, 1991), 20, quoted in Kennedy and Newcombe, *What If Jesus Had Never Been Born?*, 11.

15. Stark, *The Rise of Christianity*, 120.

16. Schmidt, *Under the Influence*, 55.

17. Ibid., 63.

18. Kennedy and Newcombe, *What If Jesus Had Never Been Born?*, 12.

19. Schmidt, *Under the Influence*, 59.

20. Kennedy and Newcombe, *What If Jesus Had Never Been Born?*, 18.

21. Schmidt, *Under the Influence*, 272–273.

22. Aristotle, *Politics* 1.1255, quoted in Schmidt, *Under the Influence*, 272.

23. Aristotle, *Nichomachen Ethics* 8.11, quoted in Schmidt, *Under the Influence*, 274.

24. David R. James, "Slavery and Involuntary Servitude," in *Encyclopedia of Sociology*, ed. Edgar F. Borgatta and Marie L. Borgatta (New York: Macmillan, 1992), 4:1792, quoted in Schmidt, *Under the Influence*, 272.

25. Schmidt, *Under the Influence*, 273.

26. Charles Schmidt, *The Social Results of Early Christianity*, trans. Mrs. Thorpe (London, U.K.: Wm. Isbister Ltd., 1889), 430, quoted in Alvin Schmidt, *Under the Influence*, 274.

27. St. Augustine, *The City of God*, trans. Marcus Dods (New York: Random House, 2000), 693.

28. Kenneth Scott Latourette, *A History of Christianity* (New York: Harper and Brothers, 1953), 558, quoted in Schmidt, *Under the Influence*, 276.

29. W. E. H. Lecky, *History of European Morals: From Augustus to Charlemagne* (New York: D. Appleton, 1927), 2:71; quoted in Schmidt, *Under the Influence*, 275.

30. Sherwood Eliot Wirt, *The Social Conscience of the Evangelical* (New York: Harper and Row, 1968), 39, quoted in Kennedy and Newcombe, *What If Jesus Had Never Been Born?*, 22.

31. *Liberty* (September/October 1984), quoted in Kennedy and Newcombe, *What If Jesus Had Never Been Born?*, 22.

32. Aristotle, *Politics* 1.1260a, quoted in Schmidt, *Under the Influence*, 99.

33. Stark, *The Rise of Christianity*, 102.

34. Schmidt, *Under the Influence*, 98–99.

35. J. P. V. D. Balsdon, *Roman Women: Their History and Habits* (New York: John Day, 1963), 272, quoted in Schmidt, *Under the Influence*, 100.

36. Philip Schaff, *The Person of Christ: The Miracle of History* (Boston: American Tract Society, 1865), 210, quoted in Schmidt, *Under the Influence*, 101.

37. Schmidt, *Under the Influence*, 82.

38. Tacitus *Annals* 3.34, quoted in Schmidt, *Under the Influence*, 82.

39. Christine Toomey, "Gender Genocide," *The Sunday Times*, August 26, 2007, http://www.timesonline.co.uk/tol/news/world/asia/article2307893.ece (accessed May 27, 2009).

40. Koran, *Sura* 4.34, quoted in Schmidt, *Under the Influence,* 97.

41. John 4:4–29.

42. John 8:1–11.

43. Matt. 28:1–10.

44. Matt. 19:4–6.

45. Matt. 5:28.

46. Gal. 3: 28.

47. Rom. 16:1–2, 6; 1 Cor. 16:19; Phil. 4:2–3; Col. 4:15.

48. Stark, *The Rise of Christianity,* 104.

49. William C. Morey, *Outlines of Roman Law* (New York: G. P. Putnam's Sons, 1884), 150, quoted in Schmidt, *Under the Influence,* 111.

50. Wirt, *The Social Conscience of the Evangelical,* 29, quoted in Kennedy and Newcombe, *What If Jesus Had Never Been Born?,* 131.

51. Edward Gibbon, *The History of the Decline and Fall of the Roman Empire* (1789; repr., London: Penguin Books, 1994), 813, quoted in Schmidt, *Under the Influence,* 84.

52. C. Schmidt, *The Social Results of Early Christianity,* 441–42, quoted in A. Schmidt, *Under the Influence,* 65.

53. Matt. 19:4–6.

54. L. F. Cervantes, "Women," *New Catholic Encyclopedia* (New York: McGraw-Hill, 1967), 14:991, quoted in Schmidt, *Under the Influence,* 98.

55. For more on this issue of women, see my book *Nurturing the Nations: Reclaiming the Dignity of Women in Building Healthy Cultures* (Colorado Springs: Paternoster Publishing, 2008).

56. Plautus *Trinummus* 2.338–39, quoted in Schmidt, *Under the Influence,* 129.

57. Schmidt, *Under the Influence,* 126.

58. Kennedy and Newcombe, *What If Jesus Had Never Been Born?,* 29.

59. Edward Ryan, *The History of the Effects of Religion on Mankind: In Countries Ancient and Modern, Barbarous and Civilized* (Dublin: T. M. Bates, 1802), 268, quoted in Schmidt, *Under the Influence,* 131.

60. Luke 10:25–37.

61. Schmidt, *Under the Influence,* 126.

62. Tertullian, "Apology," *The Ante-Nicene Fathers,* ed. Alexander Roberts and James Donaldson (Grand Rapids: Eerdmans, 1989), 39, in Stark, *The Rise of Christianity,* 87.

63. Adolf Harnack, *The Mission and Expansion of Early Christianity in the First Three Centuries,* trans. James Moffat (New York: G. P. Putnam's Sons, 1908), 1:153, quoted in Schmidt, *Under the Influence,* 125–26.

64. Stark, *The Rise of Christianity,* 84.

65. Ibid.

66. Cyril J. Davey, "George Müller," in *Great Leaders of the Christian Church,* ed. John Woodbridge (Chicago: Moody Press, 1988), 320, quoted in Schmidt, *Under the Influence,* 133.

Jill Stanek's Story

1. Jill Stanek, "Live Birth Abortions: Testimony of Jill Stanek," Priests for Life, http://www.priestsforlife.org/testimony/jillstanektestimony.htm (accessed September 8, 2008). Used by permission of Priests for Life.

Dolphus Weary's Story

1. Dolphus Weary and William Hendricks, *I Ain't Comin' Back* (Wheaton, Ill.: Tyndale, 1990), 88.
2. Ibid., 125.
3. For example, see the Rev. Dolphus Weary, "How Should the Redeemed Live?" sermon preached at Bethany Presbyterian Church, Seattle, Washington, September 16, 2007, http://www.bethanypc.org/sermons/2007/index.htm.
4. Daniel Townsend, "Dolphus Weary," *Jackson Free Press,* April 20, 2005, http://www.jacksonfreepress.com/index.php/site/comments/dolphus_weary.

Kim Allen's Story

Kim Allen, in testimony written for the author, February 3, 2008.

YWAM Puerto Rico's Story

1. For more on the maternal heart of God, see my book *Nurturing the Nations: Reclaiming the Dignity of Women in Building Healthy Cultures* (Colorado Springs: Paternoster Publishing, 2008).

David Bussau's Story

David Bussau's story was adapted from the *2009 Personal Prayer Diary and Daily Planner* (Seattle: YWAM Publishing, 2008), 55. Used by permission.

1. David Bussau, MyImpact, http://www.myimpact.ch/Our%20Work/Our%20work_book%20MyImpact/Interviewees/Australia/Our%20work_book%20MyImpact_Interviewee_DavidBussau_OpportunitiesInternational_main.htm (accessed May 27, 2009).

CHAPTER 21: SERVING AS GATEKEEPERS

1. Dallas Willard, *The Divine Conspiracy: Rediscovering our Hidden Life in God* (San Francisco: HarperSanFrancisco, 1998), 287.
2. The term *kingdomizer* was used by Paul Jeong of Natural Church Development Korea at the Disciple Nations Alliance Forum, Phoenix, Arizona, April 16, 2002.
3. It is not that money is bad. It is not. It is the love of money that is a root of all sorts of evil (1 Tim. 6:10). The kingdom is of first importance (Matt. 6:33). Money is secondary.
4. Col. 1:18.
5. A tool for this, "Discovering Your Call," can be found on the Monday Church website, www.MondayChurch.org.
6. A tool for this, "Biblical Theology of Vocation," can be found on the Monday Church website, www.MondayChurch.org.
7. Matt. 28:19.
8. Matt. 28:18.
9. Matt. 6:10.
10. Willard, *The Divine Conspiracy,* 26.
11. Related by Jun Vencer's fellow worker Roy Wingerd at the Disciple Nations Alliance Forum in Phoenix, Arizona, April 16, 2002.

12. Lawrence E. Harrison, "Why Culture Matters," in *Culture Matters: How Values Shape Human Progress,* eds. Lawrence E. Harrison and Samuel P. Huntington (New York: Basic Books, 2000), xxvi-xxvii.
13. Vishal and Ruth Mangalwadi, *The Legacy of William Carey: A Model for the Transformation of a Culture* (Wheaton, Ill.: Crossway Books, 1999), 17.
14. Ibid., 21.
15. Ibid., 22–23.

CHAPTER 22: THE BODY OF CHRIST

1. See Rev. 21–22.
2. Eph. 1:22–23.
3. Rev. 19:7.
4. 1 Pet. 2:9.
5. 1 Cor. 12:12.
6. 1 Cor. 12:4–6.
7. A great resource is a book by Disciple Nations Alliance cofounder Dr. Bob Moffitt, *If Jesus Were Mayor.* This book can be purchased at the Disciple Nations Alliance Bookstore, www.disciplenations.org/store.
8. Matt. 28:18.
9. Phil. 3:20.
10. Romans 13:1–7.
11. John 17.
12. John 17:17, 19; 1 Pet. 2:9.
13. John 17:15, 18.
14. Matt. 5:13–16.
15. Matt. 13:33.
16. Dietrich Bonhoeffer, *The Cost of Discipleship* (New York: Macmillan, 1977), 54.
17. Elton Trueblood, *Your Other Vocation* (New York: Harper and Brothers, 1952), 57, quoted in Doug Sherman and William Hendricks, *Your Work Matters to God* (Colorado Springs: NavPress, 1988), 217.
18. Sherman and Hendricks, *Your Work Matters to God,* 215.
19. George Grant, *The Changing of the Guard: Biblical Principles for Political Action* (Ft. Worth: Dominion Press, 1987), 130.
20. *Enhanced Strong's Lexicon,* s.v. "katartismos."
21. To find great resources for pastors to equip their people for the work of ministry in the world, go to the website of Harvest Foundation, a partner in the Disciple Nations Alliance, www.harvestfoundation.org.
22. Erwin W. Lutzer, *Hitler's Cross: The Revealing Story of How the Cross of Christ Was Used as a Symbol of the Nazi Agenda* (Chicago: Moody Press, 1995), 133.
23. Ibid., 204.
24. Warren Bennis and Burt Nanus, *Leaders: Strategies for Taking Charge* (New York: Harper and Row, 1985), 20, quoted in David J. Vaughan, *The Pillars of Leadership* (Nashville: Cumberland House Publishing, 2000), 13.

CHAPTER 23: OCCUPY TILL I COME

1. Exod. 35:4–9.
2. Exod. 36:3–7.
3. David Bruce Hegeman, *Plowing In Hope: Toward a Biblical Theology of Culture* (Moscow, Idaho: Canon Press, 1999), 52–53.
4. Australia's War 1939–1945, "The Old War Horse: The Battle of Surigao Strait, 25 October 1944," http://www.ww2australia.gov.au/waratsea/story_warhorse.html (accessed September 11, 2008).
5. Richard Steele, *The Tradesman's Calling*, in R. H. Tawney, *Religion and the Rise of Capitalism* (New York: Harcourt, Brace, 1926), 240, 321, quoted in Leland Ryken, *Worldly Saints: The Puritans As They Really Were* (Grand Rapids: Zondervan, 1990), 27.
6. William J. Bennett, ed., *The Book of Virtues: A Treasury of Great Moral Stories* (New York: Simon & Schuster, 1993), 192–195.
7. Pope John Paul II, *Message of His Holiness Pope John Paul II for the XXXIII World Day of Prayer for Vocations,* August 15, 1995, http://www.va/holy_father/john_paul_ii/messages/vocations/documents/hf_jp-ii_mes_15081995_world-day-for-vocations_en.html (accessed May 27, 2009).

We hope this book has challenged and inspired you with a vision for advancing God's kingdom through your unique vocation.

To help you go deeper and apply the principles presented in this book, we invite you to visit www.MondayChurch.org. Here you will find a host of resources, including the following:

- A chapter-by-chapter study guide with questions for reflection, discussion, and application
- A free, downloadable companion Bible study designed for individual and small group application
- A personal inventory to help you discover your unique design and calling
- Information on hosting a conference on how vocation relates to the advancement of the kingdom of God
- Helpful suggestions for how pastors and church leaders can envision and equip their congregations to advance God's kingdom through their vocations
- And much more!

www.MondayChurch.org

Founded by:
Harvest and Food for
the Hungry International

Equipping the Church to Transform the World

The Disciple Nations Alliance (DNA) is part of a global movement of individuals, churches, and organizations with a common vision: to see the global Church rise to her full potential as God's instrument for the healing, blessing, and transformation of the nations.

DNA was founded in 1997 through a partnership between Food for the Hungry (www.fh.org) and Harvest (www.harvestfoundation.org). Our mission is to influence the *paradigm* and *practice* of local churches around the world, helping them recognize and abandon false beliefs, and embrace a robust biblical worldview—bringing truth, justice, and beauty into every sphere of society, and to demonstrate Christ's love in practical ways, addressing the brokenness in their communities and nations beginning with their own resources.

For further information about the Disciple Nations Alliance as well as access to a host of resources, curricula, books, study materials, and application tools, please visit our website.

www.DiscipleNations.org

E-mail: info@disciplenations.org

Darrow L. Miller is cofounder of the Disciple Nations Alliance and a featured author and teacher. For over twenty-five years Darrow has been a popular conference speaker on topics that include Christianity and culture, apologetics, worldview, poverty, and the dignity of women. From 1981 to 2007 Darrow worked with Food for the Hungry (FH), serving as vice president from 1994 on. Before joining FH, Darrow spent three years on staff at L'Abri Fellowship in Switzerland, where he was discipled by Francis Schaeffer. He also served as a student pastor at Northern Arizona University and as a pastor of Sherman Street Fellowship in urban Denver, Colorado. In addition to earning his master's degree in adult education from Arizona State University, Darrow pursued graduate studies in philosophy, theology, Christian apologetics, biblical studies, and missions in the United States, Israel, and Switzerland. Darrow has authored numerous studies, articles, Bible studies, and books, including *Discipling Nations: The Power of Truth to Transform Cultures* (YWAM Publishing, 1998) and *Nurturing the Nations: Reclaiming the Dignity of Women for Building Healthy Cultures* (Authentic/Paternoster, 2008).